Principles of Economics
MACRO

IRWIN PUBLICATIONS IN ECONOMICS

Advisory Editor   Martin S. Feldstein   Harvard University

Principles of Economics
MACRO

Willis L. Peterson
University of Minnesota

Sixth Edition 1986

IRWIN

Homewood, Illinois 60430

© RICHARD D. IRWIN, INC., 1971, 1974, 1977, 1980, 1983, and 1986

ISBN 0-256-03346-3

Library of Congress Catalog Card No. 85-80349

Printed in the United States of America

1 2 3 4 5 6 7 8 9 0 D 3 2 1 0 9 8 7 6

PREFACE

This book is designed to be used as the core text in a one-quarter or one-semester principles course in macroeconomics. It is intended for students who have either had no previous training in economics or have taken only the micro principles course. The introductory material on demand and supply in Chapter 2 should provide sufficient background in this area for those students just beginning their study of economics. This material may be omitted for those students who have had a micro principles course.

Although the material in this book is somewhat more advanced than has been traditionally presented in principles texts, the general reaction received from the thousands of students I have taught using the previous five editions is that the material is challenging but not more difficult to grasp than their other basic science courses, such as biology, chemistry, mathematics, or physics. Because concepts and analysis of problems are emphasized as opposed to descriptive material, the text tends to be relatively compact. It is easy, therefore, to underestimate the amount of material presented.

Probably the most noticeable change in this Sixth Edition over the Fifth is the addition of a new chapter entitled "The Aggregate Demand–Aggregate Supply Model." This model is used primarily to draw out the differences between the major macro theories presented before it. Also the chapter on "Fiscal Policy and Problems" has been repositioned just before the chapter on

"Monetary Policy and Problems." The material in the book is now divided into six major divisions. Hopefully, this reorganization and repackaging will help the reader gain a clearer picture of the subject matter. Also in the interest of clarity and to keep the book in the forefront of developments in theory and current events, numerous paragraphs have been rewritten. Of course, the tables have been updated using the most recent data available.

Willis L. Peterson

CONTENTS

Inflation Record. The Economic Effects of Inflation. The Money Rate versus the Real Rate of Interest.

PART IV

MONEY AND BANKING 185

10 MONEY AND THE NEW QUANTITY THEORY 187

Characteristics of Money. Functions of Money. What Gives Money Purchasing Power? Gresham's Law. A Cashless Society. Definitions of Money. Money and Prices. Velocity of Money. The Quantity Equation of Exchange. Benefits of Holding Money. Cost of Holding Money. The Proportion of Income Held as Money. Factors Affecting the Proportion of Income Held as Money. How Money Affects the Economy in the Context of the New Quantity Theory.

11 COMMERCIAL BANKING AND THE FEDERAL RESERVE SYSTEM 207

The Balance Sheet. Evolution of Banking. Commercial Banks. The Federal Reserve System. Commercial Bank Transaction. Money Creation. Multiple Expansion. Bond Purchases. Summary of Commercial Bank Transactions. An Implication of Fractional Reserve Banking. Federal Reserve Transactions.

PART V

POLICIES AND PROBLEMS 227

12 FISCAL POLICY AND PROBLEMS 229

Evolution of Fiscal Policy in the United States. Built-In Stabilizers. Fiscal Policy in the Context of the Simple Keynesian Model: *Government Spending Multiplier. Tax Multiplier. Balanced-Budget Multiplier.* Problems with the Keynesian Models. Fiscal Policy in the Context of Rational Expectations. Fiscal Policy in the Context of Supply Side Economics. Financing Problems. Timing Problems. Adjustment Problems. Political Problems. Fiscal Instability. The National Debt. Who Pays the Economic Cost of Wars?

13 MONETARY POLICY AND PROBLEMS 253

Money versus the Interest Rate. Primary Tools of Monetary Policy. Secondary Tools of Monetary Policy. Monetary Policy in the Context of the Simple Keynesian Model. Problems with the Keynesian Models. Monetarists versus the Keynesians. Monetary Policy in the Context of the New Quantity Theory. Problems with the Quantity Theory. Adjustment Problems. Monetary Policy in the Context of Rational Expectations. Timing Problems. Lags in the Effect of Monetary Policy. Rules versus Discretion: The Friedman Proposal. Monetary Instability. How Federal Deficits can Cause Inflation and Unemployment. Price and Wage Controls.

PART VI

THE INTERNATIONAL ECONOMY   301

PART I

MACRO FOUNDATIONS

CHAPTER 1

INTRODUCTION TO MACROECONOMICS

"MICRO" VERSUS "MACRO" ECONOMICS

During its approximately 200-year history, economics has evolved into two major subdisciplines: microeconomics and macroeconomics. As its name implies, microeconomics is concerned mainly with small segments of the total economy—individual consumers and producers or groups of consumers and producers that are known as markets or industries. The subject matter of microeconomics deals in part with allocating resources to their most valuable uses so as to maximize the total output of the economy. Considerable emphasis also is placed on wage and price determination, which affects the distribution of the total output.

Macroeconomics, the topic of this book, is concerned mainly with economic aggregates, or the economy as a whole. The subject matter of macroeconomics deals to a large extent with the problems of unemployment and inflation. In large part, these problems also influence the total output of society and the distribution of this output.

The existence of unemployment implies that the total output of society is smaller than it need otherwise be. Unemployment also has an effect on the distribution of society's output in that the unemployed suffer a reduction in income, which in turn means that they cannot place as large a claim on society's goods and services. In regard to inflation, it is acknowledged that this phenomenon causes increased uncertainty in the economy. If, as a result, investment is curtailed, future output is diminished from what it would otherwise be. Investment funds may also be diminished during inflation because of the disincentive that inflation places on saving, particularly if interest rates are held at artificially low levels by usury laws. Also, as will be pointed out in later chapters, attempts to reduce inflation invariably lead to increased unemployment, which reduces total output and alters its distribution. Inflation has other undesirable distributional effects as well. Those whose wages rise less rapidly than the price level lose relative to those who are able to maintain the purchasing power of their earnings. Perhaps the main distributional effect of inflation is that it reduces the real wealth of those who hold the major portion of their assets in the form of money while increasing the wealth of those who own assets, such as real estate, that rise in value during inflation. (The economic effects of inflation will be discussed in more detail in Chapter 3.)

One can say, therefore, that both micro- and macroeconomics deal with the size of society's output of goods and services and the distribution of this output. After completing the study of the micro and macro areas, however, one will see that the methods of analysis used in each differ to a considerable degree.

It should also be said that macroeconomics can itself be divided into two major subdivisions. One is sometimes referred to as a study of income and employment theory; the other, as the study of monetary theory. The first deals to a large extent with the effects of government spending and taxation on the level of economic activity. The second is concerned mainly with the effect of the quantity of money and interest rates on the economy. As you might expect, then, the actions of government are very important in the study of macroeconomics.

POLITICS AND ECONOMICS—POLITICAL ECONOMY

In view of the importance of government in the study of macroeconomics, we should not be surprised to learn that politics and economics are closely related. Indeed, economics has been called the study of political economy. This was especially true during the 19th century. With the passage of time, political science and economics gradually emerged as separate, although closely related, disciplines.

We would expect, too, that much of the disagreement and controversy inherent in politics would carry over into economics, particularly in the macro area. This cannot be denied. People of a more conservative political outlook tend to prefer a society with a minimum of government intervention. Although it is unwise to generalize too much here, it seems reasonably safe to say that economists of a more conservative political philosophy also prefer a minimum of government intervention, particularly in the economic activities of society.

Virtually all economists probably would agree on the need for a certain amount of federal government intervention. For example, there is little question about the need for government regulation of the money supply or the provision for certain public goods such as national defense or roads. Moving toward the liberal pole (and we should recognize various degrees of liberalism or conservatism rather than an all-or-none situation), we find people who are willing to delegate more decision-making authority to government. Again, the more liberal economists tend to fall within this category. Although most economists make a sincere attempt at being objective or "scientific" in their profession, it is important to recognize that their political philosophies may, to some degree, carry over into their economic analyses.

There are, of course, exceptions in each group. We find some economists, probably a growing number, who would be labeled as fairly conservative because of their objection to increased government intervention in the marketplace. But these same economists might at the same time appear quite liberal on other issues such as their support of a more equalitarian distribution of income. Thus, it is often misleading to label someone, particularly an economist, conservative or liberal solely on the basis of one or two criteria.

POSITIVE VERSUS NORMATIVE ECONOMICS

Economists, recognizing that they do have different political philosophies and that these divergent points of view may influence policy recommendations, have attempted to sort out as much as possible the *positive* from the *normative*. We can think of positive economics as "what is" and normative economics as "what should be." Positive economic statements commonly contain the words "*if*" and "then." *If* a certain action is taken, *then* such and such will occur. For example, an economist may determine that *if* there is a tax increase, *then* X billions of dollars will be removed from the private sector of the economy. This is a positive statement. To say that an X-billion dollar tax increase should be enacted is a normative statement. Normative statements frequently call for some sort of action, whereas positive statements generally cite the consequences of a proposal or action.

One should not conclude, however, that all positive statements are true. For example, it has been argued that if government spending is increased, unemployment will decrease. This is a positive statement, but recent experience has led some economists to argue that this is not necessarily true. In all sciences, there are ideas that at one time were regarded as true or correct but were subsequently rejected in light of new evidence or ideas. It is not necessarily true either that all positive statements are objective and devoid of value judgments. Deciding what is important does involve some value judgment. Moreover, in conducting a study the researcher must decide what data to collect, how to organize and analyze the data, and other procedures. Beware of the statement, "Let the facts speak for themselves." What the facts say depends a great deal on which facts are used and how they are presented.[1]

THE INDIVIDUAL VERSUS SOCIETY

Most of us are accustomed to looking at the world from the perspective of the individual. However, we find in our study of macroeconomics that what is true for the individual person need not hold true for society, or even for groups of people. Standing up to watch a touchdown run at a football game provides a

---

[1] For an entertaining little book on the use of statistics, see Darrell Huff, *How to Lie with Statistics* (New York: W. W. Norton, 1954).

good noneconomic example. If just one person stands up, that person can gain a much better view, but if everyone in the stadium stands up, no one is much better off.

The distinction between the individual and society is especially important in monetary policy. Any individual would be considered better off if the amount of money earned were doubled, for this would mean the person now has access to twice the amount of goods and services. But if the total quantity of money in the entire economy were doubled, the total quantity of real goods and services available to the people would not necessarily change. As we go along we will encounter other situations where circumstances are much different for the individual than for society.

CAUSE AND EFFECT

If two events happen in proximity to each other, there is a temptation to conclude that the second event was caused by the first. Whenever we observe two events such as these, we should always inquire whether there might have been a third event that caused both to occur. A good example is the stock market crash of 1929 and the ensuing Great Depression of the early 1930s. This order of events has prompted some people to argue that the stock market crash caused the Great Depression. But as we shall see later, a third independent event probably offers a better explanation for the Great Depression than does the stock market crash, although the crash probably contributed to the depressed state of the economy once unemployment began to increase.

The possibility of one event causing two other events to occur is illustrated by the diagram below. In this example, event *A* occurs first, and then events *C* and *B* occur as a consequence of *A*. If event *C* happens to take place after event *B,* one might be led to believe that *B* caused *C,* especially if event *A* is not evident or well publicized. Before concluding that one event has caused a later, second event, one should always ask, was there a third, less noticeable event that caused both to occur? Even if the answer turns out to be no, it is still a good idea to ask the question.

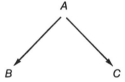

UNLEARNING PRECONCEPTIONS

One of the characteristics of studying economics, particularly macroeconomics, is that most people bring with them at the start at least some preconceived ideas of how the economy functions. In fact it is almost impossible not to form economic opinions in view of the vast amount of reporting of economics by the news media. This is both good and bad. It is good because people are becoming more aware of the importance of government economic policy in their lives. But it is bad to the extent that people form erroneous ideas of how the economy operates and the effect of government policy. Unfortunately many myths, half-truths, and misconceptions about the economy appear in the news media just about every day.

One of the major reasons for this problem is that there are many influential people both in government and in the news who are carrying out economic analysis without the benefit of economics training. Few, if any, professional occupations can make this claim (or excuse). To practice law or medicine one must have the appropriate degree from an accredited college. Indeed, to be a plumber or electrician a person must complete a number of years of apprenticeship training. Not so in economics. Economics is practiced by everyone, and the importance of one's practice increases with his or her influence over the nation's affairs. Nations have paid a dear price for having leaders who have had little or no understanding of economics.

Throughout this book it is more than likely that you will come across ideas quite different from those you had previously learned and accepted. Understandably it is difficult to unlearn old ideas, but economics training will be of much greater value if you approach it with an open mind, allowing the new ideas you encounter to at least compete with your old preconceptions.

ECONOMIC THEORIES—A FRAMEWORK FOR THINKING

Needless to say, the economy is very complex. Each day millions of economic decisions are made by millions of people. Some of these decisions, especially those made by the government, have far-reaching and long-lasting consequences. To study each decision, however, even the major ones, would be a hopelessly complicated task. We would soon be bogged down in a maze of dull and uninteresting detail. Thus, economists have found it useful to construct theories of the economy. A *theory* is a statement (verbal, graphical, or mathematical) which contains the important information bearing on a decision or problem. As such, economic theories provide a framework for thinking. They help us to identify and separate the important information for making economic decisions from the trivial or unimportant.

In a sense, economic theories or models are similar to movies or stage plays in that they present only the important and necessary information. While watching a movie we seldom see details or incidents that do not bear directly on the plot. For example, one never sees the leading character searching for a parking place, standing in line to check in baggage at an air terminal, going through customs, or sitting for extended periods in the plane. These details would be just boring and uninteresting, adding nothing to the entertainment. Instead we generally observe the plane taking off or landing, which in a few seconds can convey the idea of a several-thousand-mile journey. In other words, only the important and necessary information is presented. The same is true of an economic theory. For example, if we are interested in why the price of beef is increasing, we do not consider the price of golf balls or umbrellas, because these prices have little, if any, bearing on the price of beef. Theories highlight the necessary and important information bearing on a decision or problem.

Theories are mainly used to explain past events and predict future events. If we can understand why an event happened at some point in the past, then, if the same causal factors should reappear, we should be able to predict the reoccurrence of the event.

We should point out, too, that just about everyone utilizes theory of one kind or another from the time he or she is old enough to think. To take a very simple example, we know that if we touch a hot stove we will burn a finger. Essentially this is a theory. In essence, the "hot stove theory" both explains and predicts. It explains why you might have a sore finger, and it predicts that should you touch another hot stove you will again burn a finger.

In the main, theories are developed by observing events and then generalizing from these events. Most of us formed the "hot stove theory" by touching a stove and observing (and feeling) what happened. From one or two observations we were able to generalize that touching all hot stoves results in burned fingers. Economic theories are developed in a similar manner. By identifying the prime causal factors of economic events, economists attempt to explain these events and thus predict future events.

It is common to hear people say that something is "all right in theory but not in practice." A little reflection will reveal, however, that such a statement is illogical. If a theory is correct, that is, if it can explain or predict events, then whatever the theory predicts will happen. Something cannot be correct and incorrect at the same time. If a theory does not predict or explain an event, then it is either incomplete or incorrect. Such theories need to be reformulated, perhaps by adding new, pertinent information so that they are consistent with reality. Theories are continually being tested as they are used. Those that stand the test of time and use generally are correct. Sometimes, however, a theory may appear to be incorrect if it is applied to a set of circumstances for which it was not intended.

In the use of economic theory, it is common to see the phrases *other things equal* and *other things constant*. In order to simplify reality, it is useful to consider the impact of one factor at a time, in effect holding everything else constant, conceptually at least. This practice allows us to focus our attention on a specific point of interest, pushing into the background other factors or bits of information, even though they may also be important and be a part of the theory. It is recognized that in the real world there may be a number of important factors operating simultaneously. But if we tried to incorporate all of them at once into the analysis, it soon would become too complex to be of much use. Thus the *other things equal* phrase is not an attempt to distort the real world but rather an attempt to better understand and predict the world's events by making the theory more manageable and at the same time more powerful.

Unfortunately the word *theory* has suffered from a bad press for a long time. To students, the word often brings to mind abstract material devoid of any practical application. The feeling is probably justified if theory is learned purely for the sake of learning theory. But economic theory is not developed for its own sake; it is developed because it can be useful to explain and predict events. As we proceed, you will find that an attempt is made to apply the theories to real-world situations. Thus, if you do not find the world dull, you should not find theory dull.

Economic theories also are known as *principles, models, or hypotheses.* Essentially all three words mean the same thing. The word *principles* in the title of the book reflects the idea that it is basically a book on economic theories. Chapter 2 presents the theories of demand and supply; Chapter 6 and its appendix present the Keynesian models; Chapter 7 is on the rational expectations hypothesis; Chapter 9 covers the aggregate-demand–aggregate-supply model; Chapter 10 focuses on the quantity theory of money; and Chapter 14 presents the theory of international trade. These economic theories are intended to help explain and predict economic phenomena, principally unemployment and inflation. If the theories can do this, then they should be useful in helping the country avoid or at least minimize these two problems.

THE PRODUCTION POSSIBILITIES CURVE

In studying the problems of unemployment and inflation, it is useful to have some understanding of how a market economy operates. In the remainder of this chapter and in the chapter that follows, we will present some of the basic facts of economic life. A more thorough coverage of this material is found within the subject matter of microeconomics.[2] If you have already studied microeconomics, these sections should provide a brief review and refresh your memory. If this is your first exposure to economics, these sections should give you ample background information to understand the material that is presented in the remainder of the book.

One of the more important economic facts of life to always bear in mind is that resources are scarce or limited, and therefore the output of goods and services is limited. This holds true for the individual, the state or region and the nation. It also holds true regardless of the economic system—capitalism, communism, or any mixture.

Of course, the limited nature of output in itself need not be a problem. The rub comes because for all practical purposes human wants are unlimited, or at least are substantially greater than the goods and services that can be produced to satisfy these wants. Thus persons and nations must "make do" with fewer goods and services than they would really like to have. The phenomenon of unlimited human wants pressing against a limited output of goods and services gives rise to the necessity of making economic decisions. We cannot have everything we would like; so we have to choose the items that give us the most satisfaction for our effort or money.

Because resources are limited it follows that when we choose more of one good or service, such as a more expensive automobile, we have to give up something else, such as a vacation trip or a new color television set. Similarly, at the national level, if a country wishes to increase its supply of military armaments, it must give up other goods and services such as housing, medical care, and education. Economists refer to what has to be given up in order to produce more of something else as *opportunity cost*. For example, the opportunity cost of a trip to Europe might be a new car, a larger house, or a U.S. vacation trip, depending on what the family would have bought instead of the trip to Europe. At the national level the opportunity cost of more arms might be better housing or medical care, again depending on what the people would have produced with the resources that were not used on the arms. Of course, if the nation decides to produce the medical care or housing, the opportunity cost of these items may be a reduction in arms or national defense. Everything has an opportunity cost; nothing is absolutely free.[3]

---

[2] See Willis L. Peterson, *Principles of Economics: Micro*, 6th ed. (Homewood, Ill.: Richard D. Irwin, 1986), chaps. 1–8. Copyright © 1986 by Richard D. Irwin, Inc.

[3] It is assumed here that all available resources are employed in the most efficient manner possible. We will consider shortly the outcome when resource efficiency or employment can be increased.

A useful device for illustrating opportunity cost is the production possibilities curve. This curve is a line showing various possible combinations of two goods that can be produced with a given or fixed level of resources. The production possibilities curve shown in Figure 1–1 illustrates the various com-

---

FIGURE 1–1   A production possibilities curve

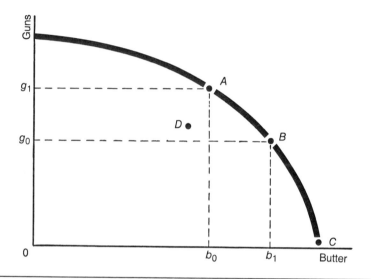

---

binations of "guns" (military goods and services) and "butter" (all other goods and services) that a nation can produce with its limited resources. It is important to recognize that the production possibilities curve traces out the *maximum* possible output of these two goods that the nation can produce. For example, if the nation is at point A on the curve, it is producing g_1 quantity of guns and b_0 quantity of butter. The nation may want to have more of both guns and butter but it cannot; the curve traces out the possible maximum amounts that can be produced during a given year or time period.

It is possible, of course, for the nation to produce more butter if it is willing to decrease its output of guns; that is, it could move from point A to point B on the production possibilities curve. Now it would be producing g_0 of guns, a smaller amount, and b_1 of butter, a larger amount. (Keep in mind that points more distant from the origin represent larger quantities.) Point C represents the extreme case of zero guns and all butter. Here the nation is devoting all its resources to the production of nonmilitary goods.

Although we can be sure that a nation cannot be anywhere outside the production possibilities frontier (by definition this is impossible), there is nothing that guarantees that a nation will be on the surface of the curve. For example, a nation could be at point D. This means that it is not receiving the maximum possible output from its available resources. There are two reasons why this might occur: (1) the nation is not utilizing its resources in the most efficient manner or (2) some of its resources are not employed. The subject matter of microeconomics deals in large part with achieving an efficient use of resources; in this book much of our discussion will be concerned with attaining a full employment of resources.

It is interesting to note that, if a nation is able to move from a submaximum point, such as point *D,* it may be able to increase its output of both goods simultaneously. By moving to point *A,* for example, it could increase its output of both guns and butter.

It should be understood that the production possibilities curve represents a country's output potential at a point in time. For example, it may represent output possibilities for a country during 1986. But there is nothing that requires the curve to remain fixed over a span of time. Indeed the production possibilities curve for most nations has been moving or shifting to the right over time, as illustrated by Figure 1–2. Economists call this phenomenon *economic growth.*

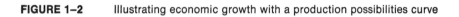

FIGURE 1–2   Illustrating economic growth with a production possibilities curve

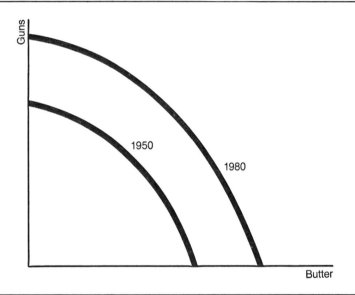

Economic growth has been pursued by most, if not all, nations because it provides the people with a larger total output of goods and services. Since just about everyone in the world today, especially the poor, would like to consume more goods and services than he or she currently does, economic growth remains a desirable goal. We might mention here that, among the goods and services we desire more of, we might well include a cleaner environment.

The causes of economic growth are still not well understood. Some nations, such as the United States, Canada, Japan, and the western and northern European countries, have been quite successful in achieving growth; others, namely the so-called less developed countries, have been less successful. We will consider the topic of economic growth in more detail in Chapter 16. For now we might just say that economic growth appears to be highly dependent on the growth of capital (machines, tools, buildings, etc.) and on the growth of new knowledge or technology. Increases in the two categories of resources are likely to be related. The production of new forms of capital, such as the computer, first requires the knowledge to be able to build such a machine and to operate it. Knowledge is an important resource. At any rate, growth in capital and knowledge increases the total resources of a country, allowing it to produce more goods and services with the same population. Expansion of a nation's total resources is illustrated by an outward shift of the production possibilities curve.

One additional aspect of the production possibilities curve may have caught your attention, namely the slight curvature that has been drawn into the line. Again, this is a topic that is covered more thoroughly in Chapter 1 of the micro book. To satisfy your curiosity for the moment (or refresh your memory), we might mention that the curvature of the line implies that resources are not equally productive in all uses. In the context of the above example, it means that some resources are not as productive in the production of guns as they are in the production of butter. Agricultural land might be an example.

The curvature of the line reflects this idea because, as we move away from butter toward guns, it is necessary to give up progressively larger amounts of butter to obtain each additional gun. In a way this makes sense, because some resources that are well suited to the production of butter will have to be pressed into service in the production of guns. As mentioned, agricultural land is not particularly well suited for the production of military goods. Of course, the same phenomenon holds true when we move away from guns toward butter.

In order to more fully grasp this idea, it would be helpful to draw a production possibility curve of your own. Measure off equal increments of guns along the vertical axis. Then move from zero guns and all butter to zero butter and all guns. Notice that as you move up the gun axis and to the left along the butter axis, you give up progressively more butter to obtain each additional unit of guns.

THE ALLOCATION OF RESOURCES

Perhaps the major point to be drawn from our discussion of the production possibilities curve is that total output during any production period is limited, and an increase in one good can be obtained only by a decrease in the other if we are on the surface of the curve. Because of the two-dimensional nature of the diagram, it is limited to presenting two goods, or two broad categories of goods, at a time. In addition to guns and butter, we could have depicted any number of different pairs of goods or services, such as consumption versus investment goods, public versus private goods, or agricultural versus nonagricultural goods.[4] Which pair is chosen depends on the question to be answered, or the point to be made. Regardless of the pair of goods we choose to represent on the production possibilities curve, there is one thing the curve itself cannot tell us, and that is the particular mix of the two goods or categories of goods that will in fact be produced. In other words, the production possibilities curve

---

[4] The first pair denotes the distinction between goods meant to be consumed at the present and goods that increase the output of consumption goods in the future. The second pair reflects the distinction between goods distributed by the government and paid for by tax money or special fees, and goods purchased by the individual.

reflects only the possible range of choices; it does not determine the exact choice that will be made. Nor does it explain fully why the choice may change over time. A brief introduction of how these choices are made in both the private and public sectors of the economy is presented in Chapter 2.

MAIN POINTS OF CHAPTER 1

1. **Economics** has evolved into two major subdisciplines: micro- and macroeconomics. **Macroeconomics,** the topic of this book, is concerned mainly with economic aggregates, or the economy as a whole. The problems of unemployment and inflation constitute the major part of the subject matter of macroeconomics.

2. Because macroeconomics deals to a large degree with the actions of government, political considerations become important, which helps explain why economics is sometimes called the study of political economy.

3. Although **positive** statements involve "what is" and **normative** statements involve "what should be," it is not valid to conclude that all positive statements are correct or free of value judgment.

4. When studying economics, especially macroeconomics, it is important to recognize that what might be true for the individual need not be true for groups of people or for society as a whole.

5. The fact that two events may occur in proximity to each other does not necessarily mean that one is the cause of the other. Both might be caused by some third event.

6. People undertaking the study of economics often bring with them preconceived ideas of how the economy functions. Unfortunately some of these ideas are erroneous or only partly true and therefore should be discarded, or "unlearned."

7. **Economic models** or theories provide a framework for thinking and as such they are useful to explain past events and to help predict future events. The words *models, theories, principles, and hypotheses* all have about the same meaning.

8. In every society human wants far outstrip the goods and services that can be produced to satisfy these wants.

9. **Opportunity cost** is defined as what has to be given up to produce more of something else.

10. A **production possibilities curve** is a line showing various possible combinations of two goods that can be purchased with a given or fixed amount of resources.

11. The production possibilities curve reflects the idea that the output of a nation is limited and an increase in the output of one good or service must result in a decrease in another good or service, provided the economy is operating on the surface of the curve.

12. If all resources are not fully employed or utilized in the most efficient manner, the output of a nation will be smaller than it need be. This is illustrated by a point below the surface of the production possibilities curve.

13. The outward shift of the production possibilities curve reflects **economic growth,** which is made possible by an increase in capital and new technology.

14. The curvature of the production possibilities curve reflects the idea that resources are not equally productive in all uses.

QUESTIONS FOR THOUGHT AND DISCUSSION

1. How do liberals and conservatives differ on the following issues?
   a. Power of the federal government.
   b. Taxes.

c. Government regulation of business.

d. Military spending.

2. Indicate whether the following statements are normative or positive.

a. If inflation is decreased, then unemployment will increase.

b. The deficit should be reduced.

c. If interest rates decline, then people will spend more on houses and cars.

3. During the early 1970s the United States experienced higher rates of inflation after OPEC raised oil prices. Can we conclude therefore that OPEC was the cause of our inflation?

4. a. What is theory and why is it useful?

b. In what way is a theory like a movie or stage play?

5. a. What is opportunity cost?

b. What is the opportunity cost of this course for you?

6. a. What is a production possibilities curve?

b. What important economic "facts of life" are demonstrated by the production possibilities curve?

7. Using a production possibilities curve, illustrate the following.

a. Public goods increase at the expense of private goods.

b. A nation goes to war.

c. A drought reduces food production.

d. The economy grows.

e. Unemployment exists.

CHAPTER 2

INTRODUCTION TO DEMAND AND SUPPLY

In nations characterized by reasonably free markets, such as the United States and other noncommunist countries, the economy can be divided into two major sectors: private and public. The private sector consists of the thousands of business firms ranging from small, family-owned and operated enterprises to the giant corporations. The public sector is made up of all units of federal, state, and local governments. In this chapter the major emphasis is on how decisions are made regarding the mix of goods and services produced in the private sector. Here we will see that the mix of these goods and services is determined in large part by their relative prices and that relative prices are determined mainly by demand and supply. The topics of demand and supply and the price-making process constitute a major part of microeconomics. Indeed, microeconomics is frequently referred to as "price theory." The end of this chapter contains a brief discussion of the decision-making process in the public sector.

DEMAND DEFINED

Let us begin with demand. We can define *demand* as a relationship between price and quantity. For most goods and services, we can observe an inverse relationship between price and quantity; that is, when price is relatively high, the quantity of an item that people buy per week, per month, or per year will tend to be relatively low. Conversely, if price is relatively low, the amount that people buy tends to be somewhat greater.

The idea that people buy less of an item when its price is high and more when its price is low has a certain intuitive appeal. There are two reasons for this behavior. First, a relatively high price prompts people to look for lower-priced substitutes. For example, when the price of beef is high, people tend to cut back on beef consumption and eat more pork, chicken, fish, cheese, and other substitutes. On the other hand, when the price of beef is low, it becomes a substitute for other, relatively more expensive protein sources. A second reason people buy less of an item when its price increases is because their incomes do not go as far. In a sense, a higher price forces people to make do with a little less of the item. Conversely, if an item's price declines, people may use some of their increased purchasing power to buy more of the item.

Economists often illustrate this relationship with a diagram. Price is placed on the vertical axis and quantity on the horizontal axis. By choosing various possible prices and observing the amounts people will buy at these prices, we can trace out a downward sloping line, as illustrated by Figure 2–1. For exam-

FIGURE 2–1   A demand curve

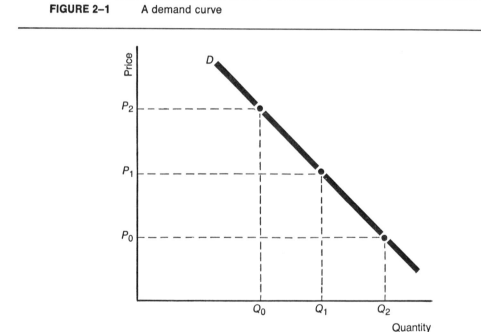

ple, if price is high, say at P_2, quantity will be low at Q_0. As price declines to P_1 and P_0, quantity increases to Q_1 and Q_2, respectively. If we assume that the same relationship holds between these points as on the points, we can connect them and obtain a downward-sloping line. Economists call this a *demand curve,* even though it is often drawn as a straight, downward-sloping line.

SUPPLY DEFINED

Let us turn next to the concept of supply. We also can define *supply* as a relationship between price and quantity. For most goods and services, a positive relationship can be observed between price and quantity; that is, when price is relatively high, the quantity of an item that producers or sellers will place on the market tends to be relatively large. Conversely, when price is relatively low, the quantity supplied also will be low.

The idea that producers will place more on the market when price is high and less when price is low also is intuitively appealing. In this case, a high price provides an incentive for producers to increase output because their profits will be greater than when price is low, other things being equal. And the prospect of relatively high profits tends to result in producers' cutting back on less profitable activities and increasing the output of the high-priced item. For example, if shoes are high priced, shoe manufacturers may build more manufacturing capacity for shoes and cut back on the production of other items. Also there will be a tendency for producers of other, less profitable items to switch over to shoes in an effort to "get a piece of the action." The opposite occurs if shoe prices are low relative to prices of other goods and services. Some shoe manufacturers may get out of the shoe-manufacturing business entirely, while others may cut back shoe production in an attempt to expand output of other, more profitable things. After all, producers are consumers too. We would expect them to also try to get the most for their effort and money.

FIGURE 2–2   A supply curve

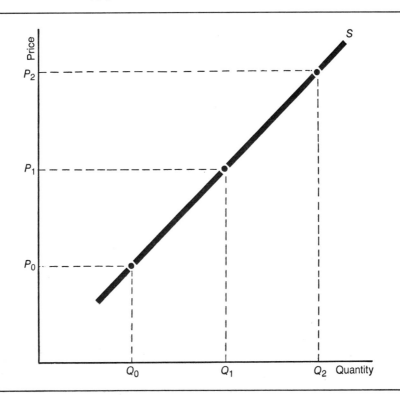

As in the case of demand, economists often illustrate the supply relationship with a diagram, again placing price on the vertical axis and quantity on the horizontal axis. With a positive relationship between price and quantity, the observed points trace out an upward-sloping line, as illustrated by Figure 2–2. For example, if price is relatively high, say at P_2, quantity supplied also will be high, as indicated by Q_2. As price declines to P_1 and P_0, quantity supplied also declines to Q_1 and Q_0, respectively. Economists call the line that is traced out by this price-quantity relationship a *supply curve*, even though it is often drawn as a straight, upward-sloping line.

EQUILIBRIUM PRICE AND QUANTITY

It is important to recognize at this point that demand alone, or supply alone, cannot tell us which price and quantity will actually exist. They only tell us the various possible prices and quantities that might prevail. But when we combine the two concepts, the exact market price and quantity can readily be determined. The demand and supply curves are something like two blades of a scissors; both are necessary to do the job.

The process of price and quantity determination can best be understood by superimposing the demand and supply curves on the same diagram, as shown by Figure 2–3. This is possible because both have price on the vertical axis and quantity on the horizontal axis.

FIGURE 2–3   Determination of equilibrium price and quantity

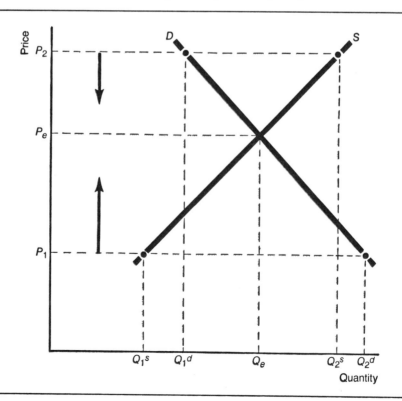

Perhaps the easiest way to see which price will prevail is to begin with a price that would not be likely to prevail, at least for long, say the high price P_2. At this price, consumers buy a relatively small amount, $Q_1{}^d$, but producers supply a relatively large amount, $Q_2{}^s$. As you can see, the outcome of this situation would be a buildup of unsold goods or services. As a result, there would be a downward pressure on price. Some buyers, seeing the glut in the market, may press sellers to lower the price. And some sellers, seeing the buildup of inventories, may initiate some price reductions in an effort to entice buyers to take a larger amount of their output.

Alternatively, let's see what happens if price is relatively low, say at P_1. In this case quantity demanded, as shown by $Q_2{}^d$, is larger than quantity supplied, $Q_1{}^s$. Now there will be a shortage of the item as demanders indicate a willingness to buy more than suppliers wish to sell. At this low price, some buyers are not able to obtain all they would like to buy, while some sellers are experiencing empty shelves or are drawing down their inventories. As a consequence, some buyers will be likely to offer sellers a higher price in order to obtain some of the scarce good. Also we can be quite sure that at least some sellers will ask for a higher price as long as they can be sure of selling their entire stock.

So far, we have seen that neither the high price P_2 nor the low price P_1 could long prevail in the market. Forces are present to drive P_2 down or P_1 up. By now it is probably evident that there is only one price, P_e, that can prevail without the presence of downward or upward pressure, for at price P_e buyers are willing to take off the market exactly the same quantity that sellers are willing to offer. In other words, the market is in equilibrium. For this reason, P_e and Q_e often are referred to as equilibrium price and quantity, respectively.

In summary, we can say that the demand for and supply of a good or service determine the price and quantity of that good or service. In the context of the production possibilities curve, we can say that demand and supply determine where on the curve a nation will be. If the demand for and the supply of the good on the vertical axis are large relative to those of the good on the horizontal axis, the economy will be at some point on the upper portion of the curve.

One might conclude at this point that once a market gets into equilibrium, price and quantity should remain unchanged for all time to come. Right? Wrong! What happens in virtually all markets is that the demand and supply curves themselves are continually shifting or changing positions. Once they are in a new position, equilibrium price, quantity, or both are likely to be different. Once this occurs, the equilibrating process must start over again.

SHIFTS IN DEMAND

The two possible shifts in demand are illustrated in Figure 2–4. The shift to the right from D_1 to D_2 represents an *increase* in demand. This means that buyers are willing to take a larger quantity off the market at any given price. On the other hand, a shift to the left from D_1 to D_0 is referred to as a *decrease* in demand. In this situation buyers decrease the quantity they will take off the market at any given price. The reasons demand may increase or decrease are discussed briefly in the section on demand shifters.

Notice the effects of shifts in demand on the equilibrium price and quantity. When demand increases, both price and quantity increase. Intuitively this

---

FIGURE 2–4   Shifts in demand

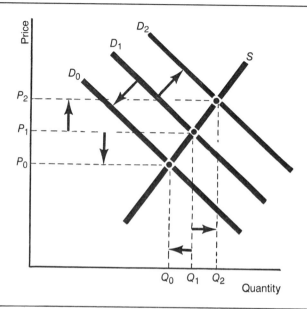

makes sense. When people want to buy more of something they will generally bid up the price of the item, and producers are likely to respond by increasing its production as it becomes more profitable. Conversely, when demand decreases, the equilibrium price and quantity both decrease. In this case the decrease in the desire of buyers to purchase the product causes a decrease in its price, and producers respond by decreasing the output of this item because it now has become less profitable.

SHIFTS IN SUPPLY

Figure 2–5 is intended to illustrate the two possible shifts in supply. The shift to the right from S_1 to S_2 represents an *increase* in supply. This means that sellers become willing to place a larger quantity on the market at any given price. On the other hand, a shift to the left from S_1 to S_0 is a *decrease* in supply. In this situation, sellers decrease the quantity they will place on the market at any given price. The reasons supply may increase or decrease are discussed briefly in the section on supply shifters.

Notice the effects of the shifts in supply on the equilibrium price and quantity. When supply increases, quantity increases but price decreases. As sellers place a greater quantity of the item on the market, it becomes more plentiful, and its price declines. As price declines, buyers now find this item a better buy, and as a result they become willing to take more off the market. Conversely, a decrease in supply causes an increase in price because the good in question becomes less plentiful. The higher price discourages people from buying it, so quantity decreases.

Before turning to the factors that cause demand and supply to shift, a distinction should be drawn between a change (shift) in demand or supply and a

FIGURE 2–5   Shifts in supply

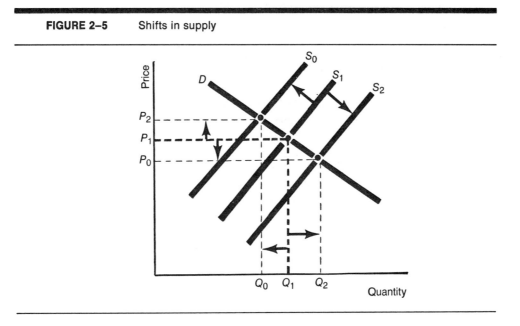

change in the quantity demanded or supplied. For example, an *increase in demand* refers to a shift to the right by the demand curve, whereas an *increase in quantity demanded* refers to a movement downward along a given demand curve. The latter would be caused by an increase in supply. The same distinctions should be made between a *decrease in demand* and a *decrease in quantity demanded*. The latter would be caused by a decrease in supply.

The same terminology should be applied to the supply side. For example, an *increase in supply* refers to a shift to the right by the supply curve, whereas an *increase in quantity supplied* refers to a movement upward along the supply curve. This movement would be caused by an increase in demand. The same is true for a *decrease in supply* and a *decrease in quantity supplied*.

Keep in mind that a change in price does not cause a change (shift) in demand or supply. Because price is shown on the vertical axis of the demand-supply diagram, a change in price just causes a movement up or down along the same demand and supply curves. Let us now briefly consider the main factors that cause shifts in the demand and supply curves. There are five demand shifters and five supply shifters that apply to most goods and services.

DEMAND SHIFTERS

1. Changes in prices of related goods or services. The demand for a good, say pork, will increase if the price of a substitute good, such as beef, increases. Consumers, in an attempt to avoid buying as much of the higher-priced beef, increase their purchases of pork, thereby increasing the demand for pork, i.e., shifting the demand for pork to the right. The opposite would, of course, hold true if the price of a substitute good declined.

2. Changes in money incomes of consumers. The demand for most goods and services tends to increase or shift to the right as the money income of consumers increase.[1] Again this is reasonable to expect; when we have more money to spend, we are able to increase our purchases of certain items. By the same token, a decrease in consumer incomes, say because of an increase in unemployment, tends to decrease the demand for many items, that is, shift it to the left.

3. Changes in expectations of consumers regarding future prices and incomes. If consumers expect the price of an item to increase in the future, they are likely to attempt to increase their rates of purchase of the item in order to stock up before the price rise. Similarly, if people expect their future incomes to be larger than their present incomes, we can expect them to buy more at the present then if they expected "hard times" ahead. The opposite would be true, of course, for expected lower prices or incomes in the future.

4. Changes in tastes and preferences. Sometimes people will step up their purchases of an item if they suddenly take a liking to it. For example, the demands for motorcycles and blue jeans have increased in recent years. On the other hand, yo-yos and bobby sox no longer are "in."

5. Changes in number of consumers. The total market demand for an item will be greater as the number of consumers in the market increases. Nationwide, the demand for most goods and services has been shifting to the right because of population growth. Of course, in places where population has declined, such as in rural areas and small towns during the 1950s and 1960s, the demand for many goods and services has declined.

These five demand shifters include those that apply to most goods and services. There may be other demand shifters that occur because of special circumstances. For example, if the purchase of a good or service is illegal and subject to a stiff penalty, people may decide the risk is not worth taking and therefore refrain from buying it. The markets for illegal goods and services are discussed in greater detail in Chapter 8 of the companion micro text.

SUPPLY SHIFTERS

1. Changes in the prices of resources. A decrease in the price of resources (hence a decrease in production costs) has the effect of increasing the supply of the item produced, i.e., shifting its supply to the right. As costs decline, producers can sell an item for a lower price and still retain their previous profit margins. (Bear in mind that an increase in supply also means that producers are willing to supply a given quantity for a lower price.) Of course, an increase in resource prices has the opposite effect, namely, to decrease supply, or shift it to the left.

2. Changes in prices of alternative items that may be produced. If there is a decrease in the prices of other goods or services that require about the same kinds of resources to produce, then we can expect the

---
[1] Some exceptions include cold-water flats, old-fashioned washboards, and starchy foods.

supply of the item in question to increase. For example, a firm that is producing both footballs and basketballs will be likely to increase its supply of footballs if the market price of basketballs decreases. On the other hand, an increase in the price of an item can be expected to decrease the supply of alternative goods or services.

3. Changes in expectations of producers regarding future prices. If producers expect the prices of their products to decrease in the future, they may sell off part of their inventories, thereby increasing the present supply, in order to take advantage of favorable prices at the present. Accordingly, if producers expect higher prices in the future, they may decrease their present supplies in order to have more to sell when price is expected to be higher.

4. Changes in technology. A change in technology always has the effect of increasing the supply of the item being produced because it has the effect of lowering production costs. If the new technology did not lower production costs, producers would have no incentive to adopt it.

5. Changes in number of producers. The total market supply of an item will increase if the number of producers increases, assuming the average size of the producers remains constant. Finally, the supply of a good or service will decline or shift to the left with a decrease in the number of producers, again assuming no change in the average size of producers.

These five supply shifters include those that apply to most goods and services. There may be other supply shifters that occur because of special circumstances. For example, in the production of agricultural products, changes in weather or growing conditions represent an important supply shifter. Unusually good weather should bring forth an increase in the supply of these products, while unfavorable conditions such as drought likely will decrease supply, that is, shift the supply curve to the left.

THE PUBLIC SECTOR

To summarize the preceding discussion on demand and supply, it can be said that prices are determined by demand and supply, and the output mix of goods and services is in turn determined by prices. It is important to remember that the allocation of resources by prices applies mainly to the private sector of the economy where the production and consumption decisions are made by private firms and individuals. Yet we know that a large and growing share of the nation's goods and services is distributed by the federal, state, and local units of government. As shown in Table 2–1, government spending for goods and services amounted to 36.9 percent of the U.S. gross national product (GNP) in 1984, up from 12.3 percent in 1930. Some of the major items that fall in this category are military goods and services, police and fire protection, highway and street systems, postal service, public schools, public parks, and various welfare programs.

The task faced by society in deciding on the amount and mix of these so-called public goods and services is exceedingly complex and difficult. As op-

TABLE 2–1   Government spending as a percent of U.S. GNP, selected years, 1930–84

Year	Federal government	State and local governments	Total government
1930	3.7%	8.6%	12.3%
1940	9.6	8.8	18.4
1950	15.1	6.2	21.3
1960	18.3	8.7	27.0
1970	19.9	13.5	33.4
1980	22.9	13.5	36.4
1984	24.0	12.9	36.9

Source: *Economic Report of the President,* 1985, p. 320.

posed to the impersonal and more or less "automatic" allocation of resources by demand and supply in the private sector, the allocation of resources in the public sector has to be done "by hand," so to speak. That is, elected or appointed officials of the government must make the day-to-day decisions regarding what public goods and how much of each are to be provided. Of course, in a democracy these officials serve at the discretion of the voters, so in this sense the ultimate, long-run decisions rest in the hands of the general public.

As a general rule we can say that the mix of public and private goods should be that which maximizes the welfare of society. The problem is that no one really knows what this particular mix is. Moreover, the optimum mix is likely to be different for different people. For example, the more politically conservative members of society tend to prefer a smaller proportion of total output devoted to public goods than do their more liberal counterparts. Hence the actual mix of public and private goods turns out to be a compromise between the wishes of different groups in society.

Given the public's political persuasion, it is reasonable to believe also that the price or cost of a public good will influence their choices. Even though some public goods and services (such as the services of the military and public schools) do not carry "price tags," they nevertheless have to be paid for by somebody, namely taxpayers. If taxpayers feel the cost of a public good is low in relation to its benefits, people will probably voice a desire for more of it. On the other hand, if taxpayers feel that a certain public good is not a "good buy" in relation to other public and private goods available, public officials will probably feel pressure to reduce the output of such a good. In this sense, there is a demand for public goods and services just as there is for private goods and services. In other words, we would expect people to want to buy more of a public good when its price (or cost) is relatively low than when it is high priced.

Last, it should be acknowledged that in the United States most public goods are produced by the private sector under contract to the government. For example, military and space hardware, police cars, and fire engines all are produced by private firms. In contrast, most public services are provided by people directly employed by the government, such as postal service employees, public school teachers, and military personnel.

MAIN POINTS OF CHAPTER 2

1. Demand is defined as an inverse relationship between price and quantity; people buy more of an item when its price is low, and vice versa.

2. Supply is defined as a positive relationship between price and quantity; producers supply more of an item when its price is high, and vice versa.

3. Equilibrium price occurs at the point where buyers are willing to buy the exact amount that sellers are willing to sell. This corresponds to the intersection of the demand and supply curves.

4. If the price is higher than the equilibrium, the quantity supplied will be greater than the quantity demanded, resulting in a surplus and downward pressure on price. If price is lower than the equilibrium, the quantity supplied will be less than the quantity demanded, resulting in a shortage and upward pressure on price.

5. An **increase in demand** means that buyers become willing to take a larger quantity off the market at any given price. This is illustrated by a shift to the right in the demand curve. The opposite is true for a decrease in demand.

6. When demand increases (shifts to the right), both equilibrium price and quantity increase. When demand decreases, both price and quantity decrease.

7. An **increase in supply** means that sellers become willing to place a larger quantity on the market at any given price. This is illustrated by a shift to the right in the supply curve. The opposite is true for a decrease in supply.

8. When supply increases (shifts to the right), the equilibrium price decreases but quantity increases. When supply decreases, price increases and quantity decreases.

9. A shift in the demand for a good or service can occur as the result of changes in: (*a*) prices of related goods, (*b*) consumer incomes, (*c*) expectations of future prices and incomes, (*d*) tastes and preferences, and (*e*) number of consumers.

10. A shift in the supply of a good or service can occur as the result of changes in: (*a*) prices of resources, (*b*) prices of alternative goods or services that could be produced, (*c*) producer expectations of future prices, (*d*) technology, and (*e*) number of producers.

11. In contrast to the impersonal and largely "automatic" allocation of resources by demand and supply in the private sector, the allocation of resources in the public sector has to be carried out by government officials, who in a democracy serve at the discretion of the people.

QUESTIONS FOR THOUGHT AND DISCUSSION

1. *a.* What is demand?
  b. Why do people tend to buy less of a good when its price increases and more when its price decreases? Illustrate this relationship with a demand curve.

2. *a.* What is supply?
  b. Why do producers tend to produce more when price increases and less when price decreases? Illustrate this relationship with a supply curve.

3. Under what conditions will there be a surplus of a product? A shortage?

4. *a.* According to the theory of demand, is it possible for consumers to want to buy more of a product at a given price? Explain.
  b. According to the theory of supply, is it possible for a producer to want to sell more of a product at a given price? Explain.

5. Explain how each of the following circumstances would affect the demand for U.S. automobiles. Also indicate what would happen to the equilibrium price and quantity of this product, assuming no change in supply.

  a. The price of foreign cars increases.
  b. The money incomes of consumers increase.
  c. Consumers expect higher prices next year.
  d. Consumers change their preference toward European styling.
  e. Population increases.

6. Explain how each of the following circumstances would affect the supply of wheat. Also indicate what would happen to the equilibrium price and quantity of this product, assuming no change in demand.
  a. The price of labor increases.
  b. There is an increase in the price of beef, an alternative product that can be produced.
  c. Producers expect higher prices next month.
  d. New, higher-yielding varieties become available.
  e. There is an increase in the number of farms of a given size.

PART II

THE MACRO ECONOMY

CHAPTER 3

UNEMPLOYMENT AND INFLATION

FULL EMPLOYMENT DEFINED

Perhaps the best way to begin the discussion of unemployment is to define the meaning of full employment. *Full employment* exists when everyone who is willing and able to work at the prevailing wage rate can find a job in the line of work for which he or she is qualified.

There are several points worth noting in this definition. First, full employment, or unemployment, as used in the context of macroeconomics generally refers to people rather than capital, that is, buildings, machines, land, and other supplies. As a rule society has not been as concerned with the unemployment of nonhuman inputs as with the unemployment of human beings. It is not difficult to understand why. Machines or buildings do not become hungry or cold if their income stops, nor do they suffer from the psychological ills of being idle. Yet we should not dismiss the problem of unemployed capital entirely. For one thing, the employment of human beings is often tied to the employment of capital. This is illustrated by the increase in unemployment brought on by the closing of a factory or mine, especially in a small community. We should also bear in mind that all capital is owned by human beings. Hence a reduction in the earnings of capital means a reduction in the earnings of the owners of capital.

Third, we should not lose sight of the fact that capital as well as labor contributes to the total output of society. Thus, if some capital is unemployed, the total output that is available to society will be less than maximum.

A second point to note about the definition of full employment is that at full employment not every adult need be gainfully employed. For example, full-time college students, homemakers who choose not to work outside the home, and retired people would not be considered employed. Of course, this is not to say that these people are idle or "nonproductive"; it is just that they are not considered part of the labor force. Also, there are a few people who have decided that work is too distasteful and have removed themselves from the labor force.

A third subtle but fairly important point in the definition of full employment relates to the willingness of people to take jobs that are available. For example, consider the case of a $400-per-week construction worker who is laid off. If no other construction jobs are available in the area, that worker files for unemployment insurance and is considered unemployed. The fact that this person is unemployed, however, does not mean he or she is unemployable. There may be other, comparable jobs available that the construction worker would be qualified for, such as janitor or factory worker, but chooses not to accept. Rather than work in a different occupation, this person chooses to be unemployed.

This is not intended to be a criticism of the construction worker or anyone who decides on this line of action. For the individual it can be the most rational thing to do. If a person expects to be back at work again in a few weeks, it may not pay to seek another job. Certainly if a person's unemployment compensation approaches the take-home pay of another, lower-paying job, there is not much incentive to take such a job. Of course, if a person is unemployed for a prolonged period of time so that unemployment payments run out, then the unemployed person might be more willing to accept a comparable or even less desirable job. The main point is that a certain amount of unemployment may refer to unemployment from a specific job or line of work rather than not being able to find any job at all.

We should also be aware that some unemployed people probably would be willing to work at their previous jobs for a lower wage rather than be out of work altogether. For example, the construction worker may be willing to work for $300 per week rather than being forced to accept, say, $125 per week in unemployment compensation or even $250 per week at an alternative job.

Unfortunately for the unemployed, wage rates tend to be rather inflexible on the down side. If a choice is to be made between an across-the-board wage cut and a layoff of the most recently hired people, both employers and labor unions tend to favor the latter alternative. A reduction in wages affects all employees of a firm or industry and, needles to say, does not make them very happy. And both employers and labor unions are reluctant to antagonize the rank and file of the labor force. No firm with disgruntled employees can prosper, and a labor union cannot be a very effective bargaining agent if its members have the feeling of being "sold out." The other alternative, laying off the youngest and least skilled workers, affects only a small part of the labor force. Once they have left, they are no longer disgruntled employees who can cause disruptions in production. Nor do these people have much power within labor unions; many are not even members.

The main point to remember here is that there is something of a built-in incentive for both employers and labor unions to choose unemployment over lower wages. At least some unemployed people would probably choose to work at their old jobs at less than the prevailing wage rather than be unemployed, but they seldom have the opportunity to make this choice. Of course, when unemployment in a firm or industry becomes so long-term and severe that a company's survival comes into question, wage reductions do occur. During the Great Depression of the 1930s, virtually all money wages declined. Wage reductions also occurred in the early 1980s when unemployment again became abnormally high, especially in the auto industry. It is nice to have a job at high wages, but when it comes to the choice of having no job versus one at lower wages, workers and their unions generally prefer the latter, particularly when unemployment compensation runs out.

THE UNEMPLOYMENT RATE

Figures on the number of unemployed people in the United States are gathered each month by the Bureau of Labor Statistics from a sample of about 60,000 households. Actually, living quarters rather than people are selected for the survey. About 15,000 groups of addresses, each including about four dwellings that are relatively close together, are selected to be representative of the entire country. The occupants of a selected dwelling are visited by an interviewer for eight months—four consecutive months in the current year and the same four months in the following year.

In order to determine the unemployment rate, figures must be gathered on both employed and unemployed individuals. *Employed* people include those 16 years of age or older who:

1. Did any work at all during the survey week as paid employees.
2. Worked in their own businesses or professions.
3. Worked 15 hours per week or more as an "unpaid" member of a family farm or business.
4. Were temporarily absent from their jobs for reasons such as illness, vacation, strike, or bad weather.

To be counted among the *unemployed,* an individual 16 years or older must have:

1. Not worked during the survey week.
2. Made specific efforts to find work within the past four weeks of the survey.
3. Been available for work during the survey week.

The labor force is defined as the sum of the employed plus unemployed:

$$\text{Labor force} = \text{Employed} + \text{Unemployed}$$

The *unemployment rate* is computed by dividing the number of unemployed people by the number in the labor force and multiplying by 100 to convert to a percent:

$$\text{Unemployment rate} = \frac{\text{Unemployed}}{\text{Labor force}} \times 100$$

The figures in Table 3–1 provide an indication of the relative size of each of these groups in the United States in 1984. At that time the labor force (employed plus unemployed) made up about 63 percent of the total noninstitutional population over the age of 16. This number is referred to as the "labor force participation rate."

TABLE 3–1   U.S. population and labor force statistics, 1984

Noninstitutional population, 16 and over	176.4 million
Labor force*	115.2 million
Employed	106.7 million
Unemployed	8.5 million
Unemployed rate	7.4 percent

* Includes armed forces.
Source: *Economic Report of the President*, 1985, p. 266.

THE NATURAL RATE OF UNEMPLOYMENT

From the discussion thus far it might appear that any unemployment at all is undesirable and that we should not be satisfied until we attain a goal of zero unemployment. Would such a goal be reasonable or even desirable? Probably not. We should bear in mind that the economy is continually changing and adapting to new opportunities. Very few business activities continue to remain unchanged month after month, much less year after year. As a result we may observe a temporary loss of work for certain employees because of short-term fluctuations in business activity, changes in employment opportunities, or a voluntary termination of work because of a desire to change jobs. Unemployment resulting from the above circumstances is frequently called the *natural rate of unemployment*. In years past it was called frictional unemployment, reflecting the idea that changes in the economy require adjustments that do not occur immediately or without some cost in terms of unemployment.

We know that many occupations experience busy and slack seasons during the year. Construction work, for example, typically has experienced a seasonal decline during the winter. People who work in this industry expect temporary layoffs, and their salaries during the busy season generally compensate them for this. Another example occurs in the auto industry, where a company may lay off part of its labor force for a week or two in order to bring its inventory back to a desired level.

It is a common occurrence as well in a dynamic, growing economy for employment opportunities to change. Because of changes in consumer demand, some firms or industries tend to decline and fade away, only to be replaced by others. Workers who find themselves in declining industries or firms must relocate to other, growing industries. Even though there may be other, comparable jobs available, most people prefer to take some time to search out the best.

Related to this is the unemployment brought about by employees who quit their jobs in order to search out more desirable ones. In many cases people cannot take time off to interview and search while holding down a full-time job. Anyone who has gone through a job search knows that it can be very time-consuming. Sometimes a new job requires traveling, buying and selling a house, or finding a different apartment. Probably most people who quit a job for one reason or another are reasonably certain of finding another. And in most cases they succeed within a few weeks. Their earnings may have been temporarily interrupted, but in the long run they are able to make up the loss in their new and better jobs.

The natural rate of unemployment appears to have increased during the 1960s and 1970s. In the early 1960s the most frequently quoted figures tended to be in the range of a 3 to 4 percent unemployment rate. In more recent years, figures in the 5 to 6 percent range are commonly quoted. There are a number of reasons for the increase in the natural rate of unemployment. One is the increase in the labor force participation rate of high school and college students and married women. Because these people tend to enter and leave the labor force more frequently than married men, a greater proportion of the labor force will be looking for jobs at any given time, and a higher unemployment rate will result. In addition, an increase in unemployment compensation and welfare benefits is likely to increase the natural unemployment rate because people can be more selective in taking new jobs after they have been laid off, which also increases the overall average level of unemployment. Indeed, some welfare programs require people to be unemployed to collect benefits; by meeting the requirements of the program, the beneficiaries increase the unemployment rate. In a sense, the supply of unemployment benefits creates a demand for these benefits. Also, it has been argued that an increase in the power of labor unions to raise wages will lead to an increasing level of unemployment. The auto and steel industries during the 1970s can be used as examples of this phenomenon.

One might expect the state of the economy itself also to influence the natural rate of unemployment. If the economy is sluggish and jobs are hard to find, we would expect the time it takes a person to relocate in a new job after being laid off from a declining business or voluntarily leaving a former job to be longer than when the economy is booming and the labor market is tight. For example, during World War II, the total U.S. unemployment rate dipped to between 1 and 2 percent.

The main point to be drawn from this section is that some fraction of the labor force, normally between 5 and 6 percent, can be expected to be temporarily out of work because of adjustments in the economy and movement between jobs. For purposes of economic policy, the economy can be considered at or near full employment if the rate of unemployment is at this order of magnitude. Our main interest in the discussion relating to unemployment will be with situations where the total economy experiences a slowdown in economic activity and the overall unemployment rate rises above the 5 to 6 percent range.

U.S. UNEMPLOYMENT RECORD

Looking back over the past half-century, we observe substantial variations in the U.S. unemployment rate. As shown in Table 3–2, with an unemployment rate of 3.2 percent, 1929 was a year of relatively full employment. Then came the crash. Four years later, in 1933, the United States, in the depth of the Great Depression, suffered from an astronomical unemployment rate of 24.9 percent. We will have more to say about the Great Depression in later chapters.

TABLE 3–2	U.S. unemployment rates, selected years, 1929–84

Year	Unemployment rate	Year	Unemployment rate
1929	3.2%	1975	8.5%
1934	21.7	1976	7.7
1939	17.2	1977	7.0
1944	1.2	1978	6.0
1949	5.9	1979	5.8
1954	5.5	1980	7.1
1959	5.5	1981	7.5
1964	5.2	1982	9.5
1969	3.5	1983	9.5
1974	5.6	1984	7.4

Source: *Economic Report of the President,* 1985, p. 266.

The Great Depression was no overnight sensation, however; it lasted all the way through the 1930s. In 1939, just before the U.S. entry into World War II, unemployment still was as high as 17.2 percent. Then at the height of World War II, 1944, unemployment fell to an almost unbelievable low of 1.2 percent. The drain of manpower into the military and the strong demand for labor undoubtedly contributed to this low figure.

The return to a peacetime economy was accompanied by a rise in unemployment, reaching 5.9 percent in 1949. During the Korean conflict the unemployment rate again declined, reaching a low of 2.9 percent in 1953. Toward the end of the 1950s, the country found itself in the "1958 recession" with an unemployment rate of 6.8 percent.[1] Unemployment tended to drift downward during the 1960s, particularly during the Vietnam buildup toward the latter part of the decade. However, coinciding with the U.S. troop withdrawals from Vietnam and attempts to reduce inflation, the U.S. unemployment rate exhibited a sharp upswing during the early 1970s, rising to 8.5 percent in 1975. After a slight dip during the late 1970s, the unemployment rate exhibited another increase in the early 1980s coinciding with the Reagan administration's attempt to reduce inflation and the size of the federal government.

It is fairly evident from these figures that war and low rates of unemployment tend to be positively correlated. During the periods when the United States was involved in World War II, Korea, and Vietnam, the onset of hostilities was followed by a decrease in unemployment, while the return to peacetime was accompanied by a rise in unemployment.

Is war therefore a necessary condition for full employment? We will be better able to answer this question in later chapters. For now, it is sufficient to say that large increases in military personnel and spending no doubt contribute to reducing unemployment and increasing inflation. After each war, the release of military personnel and reduction in military spending along with government

---

[1] The question is sometimes asked: What is the difference between a recession and a depression? It has been said that it is a recession when your neighbor is out of work and a depression when you yourself are out of work; that is, a depression is worse than a recession.

efforts to control inflation are likely to increase unemployment. One might argue, therefore, that war causes both inflation and unemployment but at different times.

DURATION OF UNEMPLOYMENT

So far we have been concerned mainly with the total amount of unemployment in the economy. But we should also consider how long the unemployed are out of work. It is one thing to be out of work for two or three weeks but quite another to lose one's main income for several months. The first case might result in a strained budget, but the second could mean the loss of home or car or even hunger for the family. Thus, we should be as concerned about the duration of unemployment as about the unemployment rate.

Figures showing the average number of weeks the unemployed were out of work in 1984 are presented in Table 3–3. It is somewhat encouraging to see that

TABLE 3–3   Duration of unemployment, 1984

Duration of unemployment	Percent of unemployment
Less than 5 weeks	39%
5–14 weeks	29
15–26 weeks	13
27 weeks or more	19
	100%

Source: *Economic Report of the President*, 1985, p. 269.

39 percent of those who were laid off in 1984 were unemployed for less than five weeks—a relatively short time. Although such an interruption in earnings may put a cramp in a family's budget, it is not likely to deprive the family of essentials such as food and housing, particularly when unemployment compensation makes up part of the loss.

As might be expected, when the overall level of unemployment increases, the duration of unemployment also increases. For example, in 1983 (not shown in Table 3–3), when the unemployment rate was 9.5 percent, 24 percent of the unemployed were out of work for 27 weeks or more, while only 33 percent were jobless for less than five weeks.

We should bear in mind, too, that even at fairly low levels of unemployment, some people will be out of work for long periods of time. These might include people from depressed areas or those who have few skills to offer in the job market. Unfortunately, it is not likely that government policies or programs to stimulate the entire economy can do much for these people. Instead, programs are needed to improve employment opportunities in specific geographic areas or to help people relocate to areas where jobs are available. Many of the long-term unemployed lack the skills demanded in the job market. Job training programs to increase marketable skills may be of some help to these people.

DISGUISED UNEMPLOYMENT

We should also be aware that employment figures may disguise a certain amount of unemployment. Consider the case of an aeronautical engineer who is laid off and accepts employment as a parking lot attendant, which may be the best alternative at least for the immediate time. Although he is no longer unemployed, his income and his contribution to society's output are considerably less than they might otherwise be. When people have no choice but to work in jobs that do not fully utilize their capabilities, they are in part unemployed, or *underemployed,* as economists might say. Thus a reduction in unemployment accomplished by the taking of less desirable jobs may in fact overstate the true reduction that takes place.

The manner in which unemployment statistics are collected also may result in a downward bias to the true unemployment figure. Recall that for a person to be unemployed, that individual must have made specific efforts to find employment in the past four weeks. For a person who has been out of work for months and has been turned down repeatedly in the quest for work, there will likely come a time when he or she gives up looking, at least until some concrete opportunity presents itself. A person who has given up trying to find a job would, according to the unemployment survey, not be included in the labor force and hence would not be considered unemployed. However, that person still would not be working. This phenomenon is known as the *discouraged worker effect.* Both the underemployment phenomenon and the discouraged worker effect contribute to *disguised unemployment.* And disguised unemployment causes the official unemployment statistics to understate the extent of the unemployment problem.

WHO ARE THE UNEMPLOYED?

Although average unemployment figures such as 5 or 6 percent are useful in providing an indication of the seriousness of the unemployment problems, they do not tell us anything about the differences in employment among individuals or groups in society. As you might expect, not all employees face an equal chance of being laid off or finding a new job.

As shown in Table 3–4, unemployment is more prevalent among the young and the least skilled. Note that in 1984, when the overall unemployment rate in the United States averaged 7.4 percent of the labor force, young males between the ages of 16 and 19 experienced an unemployment rate of 19.6 percent. Part

TABLE 3–4 Unemployment rates by groups, 1984

All workers	7.4
Males, 16 to 19 years	19.6
Females, 16 to 19 years	18.0
Males, 20 years and over	6.6
Females, 20 years and over	6.8
Married men	4.6

Source: *Economic Report of the President,* 1985, p. 271.

of this group came from high school and college dropouts and part from 1984 high school graduates who were not able to find a job immediately after graduation. Females in this age group experienced a slightly lower unemployment rate, 18 percent, although this figure is still over twice the national average rate.

There probably are a number of reasons for the exceptionally high unemployment rate among teenagers. Recent high school graduates or dropouts require some time to find their first fulltime jobs. Because of lack of experience and skills, jobs for these people probably are the most difficult to find. Also, studies have shown that minimum wage laws are at least partly to blame for this problem. If the hourly wages of new, inexperienced workers are fixed higher than their contribution to output, employers will lose money by hiring them; hence, they will not do so.[2]

In general, the more skills a person has, the less chance he or she has of being laid off. We would expect employers to be reluctant to lay off a person who cannot be replaced easily. The employer who lays off a skilled person runs the risk of not getting that person back when business conditions improve. If the individual does not come back, then the firm must bear the expense of finding a suitable replacement and retraining or "breaking the new employee in." For this reason a firm may actually choose to lose money on a skilled person for a few months rather than lay that person off. The unskilled person, however, is more easily replaced; so there is a greater tendency on the part of an employer to let such an individual go as soon as the person is not producing the value of his or her wage.

It is interesting to observe the relatively low level of unemployment among married men as opposed to other groups. Part of the explanation, no doubt, is the longer seniority on the job, since married men as a group are older than single men. In addition, married men with families to support are likely to look harder for another job when laid off and also to be more willing to accept other, less desirable employment on a temporary basis.

COSTS OF UNEMPLOYMENT

From the standpoint of the individual, the economic cost of unemployment is, of course, the loss or reduction in income from being out of work. Granted, a large share of U.S. workers now are eligible for unemployment compensation, which eases the problem somewhat. However, during 1984 the average weekly unemployment check was about $123. For a family accustomed to a $400- or $450-per week check, this reduction in income comes as a severe shock to the family budget.

We must leave to the psychologists and sociologists the identification and measure of the mental and social problems that result from unemployment. In spite of how much we dislike trudging off to work or school on Monday mornings, most people find a life of idleness even more distasteful, especially when they have little or no income to buy recreation. Living off the "dole" may keep one alive, but it does not lead to a very enjoyable or interesting life.

It is necessary as well to look at the economic costs of unemployment from the standpoint of the total economy or society. Unemployment means that the

---

[2] Further discussion of this problem is presented in Chapter 11 (The Labor Market) of the companion micro text.

economy is producing a smaller amount of real output of goods and services than it could otherwise enjoy. For this reason, nearly everyone loses from unemployment because there is a smaller output to be distributed among the members of society. Payment of unemployment compensation to the unemployed does not reduce the loss in total output. However, it is a method of redistributing the claims to society's output. Essentially, by introducing unemployment compensation society is saying that employed people are willing to give up a part of their claims on the output of the economy and share it with their less fortunate neighbors who are out of work.

THE EMPLOYMENT RATE

The discussion so far in this chapter has focused largely on the negative state of the economy, that is, the extent of unemployment. An alternative view of the economy can be obtained by looking at the *employment rate,* which can be defined as the percent of the adult population aged 16–64 that is employed:

$$\text{Employment rate} = \frac{\text{Employed}}{\text{Population, 16–64}} \times 100$$

Figures on the U.S. employment rate for selected years from 1929 to 1984 are presented in Table 3–5. Perhaps the most interesting aspect of this table is the

TABLE 3–5   U.S. employment rates, selected years, 1929–84

Year	Employment rate	Year	Employment rate
1929	62%	1975	64%
1934	50	1976	65
1939	53	1977	66
1944	60	1978	68
1949	60	1979	70
1954	60	1980	69
1959	62	1981	70
1964	62	1982	68
1969	65	1983	69
1974	65	1984	71

Note: From 1929 to 1944 the employment figures consist of all persons 14 years of age and older in civilian occupations, whereas the 1949–84 figures are for people 16 years and older in these occupations.
Source: *Economic Report of the President,* 1985, pp. 265–66.

pronounced upward trend in the employment rate over the period. In 1944, a year with an exceptionally low unemployment rate (1.2 percent), the employment rate was only 60 percent. In contrast, during 1983, when the unemployment rate averaged 9.5 percent, the employment rate was up to 69 percent. The employment rate is continuing to increase; in 1984 it reached a record 71 percent. Much of the increase in the employment rate is due to the increased participation of women in the labor force.

There are several reasons why the employment rate may be a better measure of the state of the economy than the more commonly used unemployment rate. First, the unemployment rate may increase, not because of a slowdown in the economy, but rather because of an increase in the number of people who desire to become members of the labor force. For example, during the 1970s the unemployment rate was higher than it was during the 1960s. Yet the employment rate also increased during the 1970s. Thus the economy probably was not quite so sluggish during the 1970s as the unemployment rate might lead us to believe. As mentioned, much of the increase in the employment rate during the 1970s was the result of the increased participation of women in the labor force. In 1969, 43 percent of women 20 years old and over held jobs outside the home; by 1984, this figure had increased to 54 percent.

A second advantage of the employment rate is that it is not biased by changes in the desirability of being in the labor force. It has been argued that in recent years the unemployment rate is biased upward because, in order to qualify for benefits under certain welfare programs, some people have to declare themselves unemployed. In other words, these people have an incentive to be declared unemployed. This phenomenon would not affect the employment rate because the total number of employed people would not change.

A third advantage of the employment rate is that it is not biased by the "discouraged worker effect." People who quit looking for work and go off the unemployment rolls reduce the measured rate of unemployment when in fact nothing has changed. Such action does not change the employment rate.

THE CONSUMER PRICE INDEX

We now turn to the second major problem area of macroeconomics: inflation. *Inflation* is defined as a sustained increase in the general price level. The most commonly used measured of the general price level in the United States is the *consumer price index* (CPI). The CPI is constructed by the U.S. Department of Labor, Bureau of Labor Statistics. As its name implies, the CPI is intended to reflect the prices of goods and services purchased by consumers. Basically, the CPI measures the cost of a "bundle" or "market basket" of selected goods and services in a given year as compared to the cost of the same bundle in a base year. The bundle includes several thousand items sold by about 23,000 establishments in 85 cities. The list of items included in the CPI was expanded and revised substantially in 1978. Added were such things as electronic calculators and microwave ovens, whereas items that have declined in use, such as recapped tires, were dropped. The mix of goods in the bundle reflects the buying habits of all metropolitan area residents during the years 1972 and 1973.

In calculating the cost of the bundle, the price of each good or service is multiplied by its quantity purchased during the specified period. As a result, the items that make up a large share of an average family's budget weigh more heavily in computing the cost of the bundle than items purchased in small amounts. For example, the quantity of safety pins purchased by an average family during a year is likely to be small compared to food or housing. Even if the price of safety pins should double, the overall price level as measured by the CPI would show only a small increase because safety pins make up such a small part of the budget. On the other hand, doubling the price of transportation or housing would cause a greater increase in the CPI because these items loom large in the family budget.

In order to obtain a better understanding of how the CPI is constructed, it will be useful to construct one from a simple example. Consider just three items: a loaf of bread, a jug of wine, and a theater ticket—items that might be used to represent the cost of eating, drinking, and being merry.

What we want to do is construct a number that will tell us how much, if at all, the prices of these items have changed over a period of time. Essentially we will represent three prices by just one number. The official CPI, of course, represents the prices of several thousand items with just one number, but the technique of construction is the same. Assume that the time period we are interested in is from 1967 to 1985. Let 1967 be the so-called base year—the year we use for comparison. The average prices of the three items for 1967 and 1985 are shown below:

Item	1967 price	1967 quantity	1985 price
Loaf of bread	$0.25	50	$0.65
Jug of wine	1.75	10	5.00
Theater ticket	1.85	20	6.00

The next thing we must determine is the quantity of each item that is consumed. If we just add raw prices, then the theater ticket, for example, carries ten times more weight than the loaf of bread in 1985. This could be misleading if the person did not go to the theater very often. Therefore, in constructing a price index, we have to assign a quantity to each item so that the budget reflects its importance.

The Department of Labor CPI uses base-year quantities; let us do the same. Some plausible quantities of these items that might have been consumed by an average person during 1967 are shown in the middle column of the above table.

The next step is to multiply price times quantity of each item for each year. The results are shown below.

Item	1967: $P \times Q$	1985: $P \times Q$
Bread	$12.50	$ 32.50
Wine	17.50	50.00
Tickets	37.00	120.00
Total	$67.00	$202.50

These figures tell us that the same bundle of goods and services that cost $67.00 in 1972 sold for $202.50 in 1985. We can represent this change as an index by dividing the 1985 cost by the 1967 cost and multiplying by 100. We obtain:

$$\text{1985 index} = \frac{202.50}{67.00} \times 100 = 302$$

The 1985 index of 302 tells us that the price of this bundle of goods and services increased 202 percent from 1967 to 1985.[3] Recall that a percent change is computed by finding the change in the number between the base year and the

---

[3] This figure is only an example and is not intended to reflect the actual price change of the items listed.

current year and then dividing by the base-year figure. In the CPI, the base year is always equal to 100. To convert to a percent, the answer is then multiplied by 100. In this example the percent change is equal to

$$\frac{302 - 100}{100} \times 100 = 202$$

The CPI allows us to combine the movement of many prices into a single number.

The general formula for constructing this index is as follows:

$$I_p = \frac{\Sigma_i Q_{0i} P_{1i}}{\Sigma_i Q_{0i} P_{0i}}$$

where Q_{0i} and P_{0i} represent the base-year quantity and price of the ith good or service, and P_{1i} represents the current-year price of the ith good or service. The Σ_i instructs us to sum all the $P \times Q$'s as we did above. This formula is essentially the one used by the Department of Labor to construct the CPI for each year. The formula is sometimes known as the Laspeyres formula, after the man who popularized it.

When using the CPI to measure the change in the general level of prices, we should be aware of some possible biases that tend to creep in. Perhaps most important is the bias caused by improvements in the quality of goods and services over time. In constructing the CPI, the Department of Labor attempts to hold quality as constant as possible. For example, in comparing automobile prices, it chooses prices of comparably equipped cars. It would not be meaningful to take the price of a car without air conditioning in 1952 and compare it with the price of one with air conditioning in 1985, for example.

However, there are certain quality changes that are difficult to hold constant. The engine in a 1985 car may run 100,000 miles, while a 1952 engine may stand up for only 75,000 miles before a major overhaul. This type of quality change cannot easily be taken into account. Because most durable goods have undergone some quality improvements over the years, many of which are difficult to measure, the CPI probably overstates the true rise in prices that can be attributed purely to inflation. In other words, part of any price rise might be attributed to better quality and part to pure inflation.

An even more difficult problem of measuring quality change relates to the environment. Because of environmental regulations, business firms have had to spend billions of dollars on installing pollution control devices and filing reports to federal and state governments. Some of the pollution control devices are included in the products, such as catalytic converters on cars, while others, such as "scrubbers" in smokestacks, become part of the manufacturing establishments. In either case the cost of these devices along with the cost of preparing reports must be borne by consumers through higher prices for the goods they buy. If prices of the affected goods did not go up, resources would leave these industries and go where they could earn more. The main point is that the higher prices are picked up by the CPI and imply inflation. Yet, if pollution control devices do improve the quality of the environment, then people are buying higher-quality products, because they are buying cleaner air and water along with the conventional goods. One might argue that the improvement in the environment is offset to some degree by the decrease in performance (quality) of automobiles because of pollution control devices. At any rate, if the improvement in the quality of the environment is greater than the deterioration in the performance of products, the CPI will overstate the true increase in the price level.

Another bias can stem from a change in the relative prices of items purchased. Notice in the above example that the price of theater tickets increased relatively more than the price of bread or wine. When the price of a good or service rises more than other prices, there is a tendency on the part of consumers to economize on the higher-priced items by substituting more of the cheaper items for it. In our example, the consumer may substitute drinking wine in place of attending the theater.

But in the construction of the 1985 price index, we assumed that the consumer bought the same relative amounts of the items in 1985 as in 1967. If in fact the consumer bought fewer theater tickets and more wine, because of the relative increase in the price of tickets, then the 1985 cost, $202.50 in our example, overstates the true cost of the bundle of goods that the consumer actually bought. This second bias, often called the "old-index-number problem" by statisticians and economists, also tends to make the CPI overstate the "true" rise in prices.

In times of increased unemployment such as occurred during 1982 and 1983, prices of many consumer items tend to sell at a discount. For example, automobile dealers and manufacturers marked down car prices or gave rebates in an attempt to increase sales during those years. Because the CPI measures list prices rather than actual discounted prices, it is likely to overstate the rise in the price level during periods of depressed business activity.

A second commonly used index to measure the change in the general price level is the producer price index, formerly known as wholesale price index (WPI). This index, also constructed by the Department of Labor, is the same type of index as the CPI except that it reflects prices at the wholesale level of both consumer goods and industrial products. The producer price index excludes prices of personal services, however.

U.S. INFLATION RECORD

Although most people are aware that prices have been rising in recent years, it will be useful to briefly review the U.S. inflation record over the past half-century (starting with the Great Depression) in order to see more clearly the periods in which inflation has been most prevalent. The U.S. CPI from 1929 to 1984 is presented in Table 3–6. In this table 1984 is used as the base year, that is, the year the CPI = 100.

In comparing the size of the CPI in 1934 with the 1984 figure, which is over seven times larger, it becomes evident that the general price level has increased more than sevenfold in the United States over the four decades falling within the 1934–84 period. In other words, it took $7.69 in 1984 to buy what $1 bought in 1934.

Of course, the CPI did not increase at a steady rate. Indeed, as shown in Table 3–6, the price level actually declined between 1929 and 1939. Moving into World War II, prices exhibited some increase, but the largest jump came during the 1944–49 period. After 1954 the price level increased at a rather modest rate (at least by present standards) until the mid 1960s. Then from 1964 to 1984 the CPI more than tripled.

TABLE 3–6   U.S. Consumer Price Index, selected years, 1929–84 (1984 = 100)

Year	CPI	Year	CPI
1929	17	1975	52
1934	13	1976	55
1939	13	1977	58
1944	17	1978	63
1949	23	1979	70
1954	26	1980	79
1959	28	1981	88
1964	30	1982	93
1969	35	1983	96
1974	47	1984	100

Source: *Economic Report
of the President,* 1985, p. 294.

Although the observed changes in the CPI provide an indication of the inflationary tendency of the economy, a somewhat more direct method of measuring inflation is by determining the annual percent change in the price level. This measure is called the *rate of inflation* or, simply, the *inflation rate.* The most accurate measure of the rate of inflation during a given year is obtained by finding the change in the CPI from the end of the preceding year to the end of the year in question (December to December), dividing by its initial value, and multiplying by 100 to convert to percent. For example, the 4.0 percent inflation rate for 1984 is computed as follows (the CPI figures are based on 1967 = 100):

$$\frac{315.5 - 303.5}{303.5} \times 100 = 4.0 \text{ percent}$$

A somewhat rougher measure of the inflation rate can be obtained by computing the year-to-year percent changes in the CPI from figures such as those in Table 3–6. The figures presented in Table 3–7 are five-year averages of the year-to-year percent changes in the CPI for the years within each period. (The negative number for the 1930–34 period means that prices declined on the average during this period.) Note that the highest rates of inflation occurred in

TABLE 3–7   U.S. annual inflation rates, five-year averages, 1930–84

Period	Average inflation rate	Period	Average inflation rate
1930–34	−4.7%	1955–59	1.6%
1935–39	0.8	1960–64	1.2
1940–44	4.9	1965–69	3.4
1945–49	6.4	1970–74	6.1
1950–54	2.5	1975–79	8.2
		1980–84	6.6

Source: *Economic Report of the President,* 1970,
p. 229, and 1985, p. 295.

the years immediately following World War II and during the 1970s and early 1980s. The explanation of why the inflation rate was relatively high during these years constitutes a major part of the chapters to follow.

THE ECONOMIC EFFECTS OF INFLATION

During years of relatively high inflation, the attention of wage earners is usually drawn to the race between wages and prices. If prices rise faster than wages, it is obvious that wage earners are harmed by inflation. Yet it may come as a surprise to learn that during the 1947–84 period, in only 8 of those 38 years did prices rise faster than average hourly earnings of all private nonagricultural workers in the United States.[4] Those years were 1951, 1973–75, 1979–81, and 1984. During these years, real wages declined about 10 cents per hour per year on the average. Granted, these overall average figures no doubt cover up instances where specific individuals or groups have suffered losses in other years. Nevertheless, it does not appear that wage earners have suffered large-scale reductions in their real wages on account of inflation.

One reason why people may think that inflation diminishes their standard of living is that they see how much less each dollar they earn will buy. But one should also bear in mind that part of the increase in wages that people have obtained was to keep pace with inflation. It is not correct to assume that wages would have increased as much as they did if the price level had remained stable. Although each dollar does not go as far during inflation, people can still be as well or even better off if they have more dollars.

The preceding discussion is not intended to play down the effects of inflation, but rather to turn our attention away from earnings toward assets, where inflation tends to have a much greater effect on the average person. People own assets of various forms, including cash and checking account money, money in savings accounts, stocks and bonds, and real or physical assets such as land, buildings, automobiles, appliances, clothing, and jewelry. The form in which a person holds his or her assets in large part determines how inflation affects the individual.

The asset that suffers the most from inflation is cash and checking account money. Because a dollar is always a dollar regardless of what happens to the price level, an increase in prices reduces the purchasing power of money. For example, a person who held $1,000 during 1981, when the price level increased 8.9 percent, suffered an $89 loss in the purchasing power of this money. At the end of the year the $1,000 would buy $911 worth of goods and services in the price level that prevailed at the beginning of the year.

One might ask, if inflation is a tax on money, why don't people exchange their money for assets that go up in value with the price level, such as real estate? Some people, if they expect inflation, will make an effort to do so, which is the main reason real estate prices increased so much during the 1970s. But it is important to recognize that every dollar that exists always has to be held by someone. So if one person draws down his or her money holdings, someone else must end up holding more. Hence the inflation tax always takes its toll.

---

[4] *Economic Report of the President,* 1985, p. 276.

Because the exact rate of inflation rarely, if ever, can be predicted with certainty, inflation also tends to redistribute income and wealth. For example, if a union contract is written with the expectation that prices will increase by 6 percent over the year, and then prices actually increase by 11 percent, this wage increase will not be enough to stay abreast of inflation, as occurred in 1979. In this case there is some redistribution of income away from employees to employers. Of course, the opposite is likely to occur if inflation is less than is expected. Real wages may go up more than was intended by both employers and employees, and as a result employees, at least those who keep their jobs, gain at the expense of employers.

Gains and losses also may occur in pension plans. Workers who contribute money to a pension plan that does not pay out at higher rates in the event of inflation tend to lose, to the benefit of the organizations that administer the plans, mainly firms and labor unions. Much of the money that is paid into pension plans is invested in assets that increase with the price level. When the assets are sold and the pensioners are paid off in so-called cheap dollars, the organization may end up with a considerable amount left over. In this case, the pensioners end up receiving considerably less than they expected to receive in terms of real purchasing power. This has not been true of the social security program, however, where payments have more than kept pace with inflation.[5] Still, the depreciation in the value of money has hit retired people relatively hard because many kept a large part of their savings in savings accounts where the rate of interest has not been high enough to offset the adverse effect of inflation.

Bonds and life insurance policies have redistributive effects similar to pension plans that do not adjust their payments for inflation. In this case people purchase bonds and insurance policies with relatively valuable dollars but are paid back in dollars with less purchasing power. This occurs because bonds and insurance policies tend to have a fixed face value, regardless of the price level that exists when they mature. Again, if the funds received from the sale of bonds and insurance policies are invested in real assets, such as real estate, that go up with the price level, the organizations issuing the bonds and insurance policies gain at the expense of those who buy them. Traditionally stocks have been considered a better hedge against inflation because their market value can increase with the price level. Of course, in short-run situations stock prices may decline during inflationary times, as occurred during 1975 and early 1981. Consequently, stocks are best used as a long-run inflation hedge.

In view of the decrease in the value of money along with the losses suffered through retirement plans, bonds, and insurance policies, one might ask how an average person can protect himself or herself against inflation. The answer is that it is very hard. For the average household, the family dwelling (if owned) is probably the surest hedge against inflation, since real estate prices are highly responsive to price-level changes. During the late 1970s, the higher interest paid by the money market funds began to provide some protection against the loss in the purchasing power of money. However, income taxes reduced this rate, particularly for middle- and high-income people. For a young person, investment in education is a fairly good inflation hedge because the extra earn-

---

[5] Between 1950 and 1984 the average real monthly social security payment to retired persons more than doubled.

ings that education makes possible increase with the price level. If a person borrows to buy a house or obtain more education, inflation may bring about some additional gains that are discussed in the following section.

Not only does an unexpected increase in the rate of inflation redistribute income and wealth, but an unexpected slowing down or decrease in the rate of inflation has similar effects. After inflation has been experienced for a number of years, and people come to expect it in the future, the prices of real assets such as real estate and precious metals (gold and silver) are bid up as wealthholders attempt to get out of money and into real assets. Also, nominal or money rates of interest tend to be high during such a period. If the rate of inflation begins to decline and people come to expect a return to more stable prices, the demand for real assets also will decrease, causing a decline in their prices. In turn, people who purchase these assets with the expectation that inflation will continue, suffer losses. The losses are compounded if the assets were purchased with borrowed funds carrying a relatively high rate of interest. The above situation describes what happened to many young farmers and land speculators during the late 1970s. Some were unable to make even the interest payments on their land in the early to mid-1980s, and were forced to sell at a loss. Bringing inflation under control, particularly if the decrease is unexpected, can adversely affect people as much as an unexpected increase in inflation. Clearly, it is better that the inflation would have not occurred in the first place.

THE MONEY RATE VERSUS THE REAL RATE OF INTEREST

The existence of inflation also has an important impact on the borrowing and lending of money. A simple example will illustrate the point. Suppose you borrow $1,000 for one year at an interest charge of 10 percent. Also suppose that the rate of inflation that occurs during the year is also 10 percent. When you repay the loan at the end of the year, you pay back the original $1,000 plus $100 in interest for the use of the money. But notice also that at the end of the year it takes $1,100 to buy the same goods that $1,000 could have bought at the beginning. In other words, the loan is paid back in cheap dollars. The lender had no more real purchasing power at the end of the year than at the beginning. This in turn means that, if you had used the money to purchase real property or education which increased in value with the price level, you would have borrowed the money "free of charge." The $1,100 that you paid back at the end of the year was worth the same in real purchasing power as the $1,000 at the beginning. By the same token, the lender made the loan "free of charge" because that person did not have any more in real purchasing power at the end of the year than at the beginning.

The only way that lenders can protect themselves during inflation is to charge higher rates of interest. Of course, borrowers are likely to be willing to pay higher rates because they know that loans will be paid back with dollars of less purchasing power. During times of inflation both lenders and borrowers should be as interested in the real rate of interest as in the money rate. The money rate of interest is simply the rate that is quoted on a loan or savings account. The real rate of interest reflects the "real" returns from a loan or savings account after inflation has been deducted. It is calculated as follows:

$$r = i - \% \Delta P$$

where r is the real rate of interest, i is the money rate, and $\% \Delta P$ is the percent change in the price level, that is, the rate of inflation. For example, if the money rate is 8 percent and the rate of inflation is 8 percent, the real rate is zero. Because the exact rate of inflation cannot be predicted with certainty, the real rate may turn out to be negative. For example, the real rate would be -4 percent if inflation were 12 percent and the money rate 8 percent.

It is possible, of course, that even if most people correctly anticipate the rate of inflation, the money rate may not be able to increase enough to fully offset the effects of inflation. This may occur because of usury laws that place a ceiling on how high the money rate can go. For example, in many states during 1981, usury laws prohibited the money rate of interest on savings accounts to exceed the 8.9 percent inflation rate. As a result, the real rate of interest paid on savings accounts during 1981 turned out to be negative, meaning that savers had less real purchasing power in the bank at the end of the year than at the beginning. To make matters worse, the purchasing power of savings is reduced even more because of the income tax on interest earnings. One might ask, If the real rate is negative, why do people bother to put money in savings accounts? The answer is that even though people lose some purchasing power by placing money in a savings account and earning a negative real rate of interest, they lose less than if they held the money as cash or left it in their checking accounts.

Because of the difficulty of predicting when inflation will occur, together with usury laws that place limits on how high money rates of interest can go, there has been a tendency for real rates to be low when inflation was increasing and vice versa. As shown in Table 3–8, during the early 1930s, when the nation was sliding into the Great Depression and the price level was declining, the real rate of interest was higher (7.0 percent) than it was during the next 50 years. Conversely, during and immediately after World War II, when the nation experienced relatively high rates of inflation, the real rate of interest was negative. In years of relatively stable prices, such as the 1950s and early 1960s, the real rate of interest became positive once again in the neighborhood of 1 to 2

TABLE 3–8   Real rates of interest in the United States, five-year averages, 1930–84

Period	Real rate of interest	Period	Real rate of interest
1930–34	+7.0	1955–59	+1.6
1935–39	0.0	1960–64	+2.3
1940–44	−4.3	1965–69	+2.4
1945–49	−5.3	1970–74	+1.0
1950–54	−0.5	1975–79	−1.3
		1980–84	+5.0

Note: Rates are computed by subtracting the average inflation (or deflation) rate during each period from the average interest rate paid on four- to six-month prime commercial paper during the corresponding period.
Source: *Economic Report of the President*, 1985, p. 310.

percent. Then as inflation speeded up in the 1970s, the real rate declined, turning negative in the 1975–79 period. The unusually high money rates of interest of the 1980–84 period caused the real rate to turn positive again during those years.

MAIN POINTS OF CHAPTER 3

1. **Full employment** is defined as a situation where everyone who is willing and able to work at the prevailing wage rate can find a job in the line of work for which he or she is qualified.

2. Many people who are unemployed choose to remain so rather than accept a less desirable or lower-paying job. In reality, these people are unemployed but not necessarily unemployable.

3. Both employees and labor unions tend to have a built-in incentive to prefer the alternative of laying off employees to an across-the-board wage cut. Layoffs tend to affect only a small proportion of all employees, particularly the young, those with little seniority, and the unskilled.

4. Employed people include everyone aged 16 or older who worked at all as paid employees, worked in their own businesses or professions, worked 15 hours per week or more as unpaid family labor, or were temporarily away from their jobs because of illness, vacation, or other reasons.

5. To be counted among the unemployed, a person must have not worked during the survey week but made specific efforts to find a job within the past four weeks and been available for work during the survey week.

6. The **labor force** equals the employed plus the unemployed.

7. The **unemployment rate** is found by dividing the number of unemployed people by the number of workers in the labor force.

8. The **natural rate of unemployment** refers to a temporary loss of work because of seasonal fluctuations in economic activity, contraction of certain firms or industries, and the voluntary termination of a job to look for a better one.

9. Unemployment becomes a problem for macroeconomic policy when it rises above the 5 to 6 percent range, which was considered the normal amount of unemployment in the economy during the early 1980s.

10. Fortunately, in recent years the largest share of all unemployment has been of relatively short duration.

11. Unemployment is most prevalent among the young, minority groups, and people with the fewest skills.

12. The United States has experienced a large amount of variation in its overall unemployment rate, ranging from 24.9 percent in 1933 to 1.2 percent in 1944. In 1984, unemployment averaged 7.4 percent of the labor force during the year.

13. In addition to the loss of income to unemployed individuals, the cost of unemployment includes a reduction in the total amount of goods and services available to society.

14. The **employment rate** is defined as the percent of the adult population aged 16–64 who are employed. Some advantages of this measure are that it does not indicate a downturn in economic activity when there is a surge of new entrants in the labor force, and it is not distorted by people who wish to be counted among the unemployed in order to qualify for welfare benefits or by discouraged workers who withdraw from the labor force.

15. The most commonly used measure of inflation is the **consumer price index** (CPI) which measures the percent change in the cost of a "bundle" of consumer goods and services from a base year or period to another year or period.

16. Items that make up only a small share of the average family's budget do not have as much effect on changes in the CPI as relatively large items in the budget.

17. The CPI may overstate the true increase in the price level because of quality improvements in the items included in the "bundle" and because of the bias caused by the "old-index-number problem."

18. Over the five decades falling within the 1929–84 period, the rate of inflation in the United States was highest during and immediately after World War II and during the 1970s.

19. Inflation reduces the value of money because money retains the same face value regardless of the price level.

20. Inflation also redistributes income and wealth because it cannot be predicted with certainty.

21. Inflation is particularly hard on retired people who depend on pensions that are not tied to the price level. Also, inflation reduces the value of money in savings accounts, which have been quite important for retired people.

22. The slowing down of inflation and the subsequent decline in the value of real assets, such as real estate and precious metals, causes unexpected losses to those who purchased these assets with the expectation that inflation would continue.

23. When lending or borrowing, it is important to consider the real rate of interest. This is equal to the money rate minus the percent change in the price level.

24. During the past half-century, real rates of interest tended to be low or negative during inflationary times and higher during times of falling or relatively stable prices.

QUESTIONS FOR THOUGHT AND DISCUSSION

1. Which of the following people, if any, would be included in the labor force?
   a. The owner and operator of a service station.
   b. A homemaker who works 20 hours per week as a hospital volunteer.
   c. A full-time college student.
   d. A college student working 10 hours per week on a part-time job.
   e. A construction worker, laid off because of lack of work, attempting to find another job.
   f. A recent high school graduate who is looking but has not yet found a job.

2. Which of the following people, if any, would be considered unemployed?
   a. A midwestern cash-grain farmer spending the winter in Arizona because there is nothing to do on the farm.
   b. A homemaker working 20 hours per week as a sales clerk but who would like to work 40 hours as a secretary.
   c. A sales clerk who has just been fired after being caught taking items home.
   d. A new Ph.D. driving a taxi because of an inability to obtain a teaching job.
   e. A young woman who has quit her job in New York in order to move to California where she has not yet found a job.
   f. A 62-year-old man laid off a year ago who has quit looking for work because of a lack of opportunities.

3. In a free society, is it reasonable to expect zero unemployment? Explain.

4. a. In what way does the official unemployment rate understate the unemployment problem?
   b. In what way does the official unemployment rate overstate the unemployment problem?
   c. Would the use of the employment rate as a measure of unemployment reduce these biases? Explain.

5. Why do teenagers exhibit an unemployment rate that is nearly six times higher than that of married men?

6. Is it possible for both the unemployment rate and the employment rate to increase at the same time? Explain.

7. Construct a simple consumer price index from the following data. Use 1975 as the base year. (These data are for illustrative purposes only and are not based on actual figures.) What does the computed index number mean?

Item	1975 price	1975 quantity	1985 price
Dormitory room	$800.00	1	$1,860.00
Cafeteria meal	1.00	600	2.20
Books	5.00	20	12.50

8. How might the consumer price index provide a biased picture of inflation? In your answer, state the direction of the biases.

9. *a.* If money is not a good asset to hold during inflation, why doesn't everyone convert this money to nonmonetary assets such as real estate?
   b. Would you expect the price of real estate to increase more or less than the general price level during the early stages of inflation? Explain.

10. Who benefits and who is harmed by an unexpected *increase* in the rate of inflation?

11. Who benefits and who is harmed by an unexpected *decrease* in the rate of inflation?

12. *a.* Why are money rates of interest high during inflation?
    b. Is it possible for the real rate of interest to be negative? Explain.

CHAPTER 4

MEASURES OF NATIONAL OUTPUT AND INCOME

In the study of macroeconomics it is necessary to utilize some measure of the total output or income of the economy. The measure that probably is most widely known is gross national product (GNP). This chapter is intended to provide an understanding of what GNP is and how it is measured. Special emphasis is given to the biases contained in GNP when it is used as a measure of economic well-being. At the end of the chapter some additional measures of national output or income that can be derived from GNP are presented. However, before turning to the discussion of GNP, it will be useful to provide a simplified picture of what is being measured by means of an economic flow chart of the economy.

AN ECONOMIC FLOWCHART

The simplified economy depicted by Figure 4–1 contains two sectors: the household sector and the business sector. Two types of goods are produced: consumption goods and investment goods. In reality some of these goods are purchased and distributed by the government, but, conceptually at least, all goods provided by the government can be included in one or the other of these two broad categories.

FIGURE 4–1   The flow of income and output in an economy

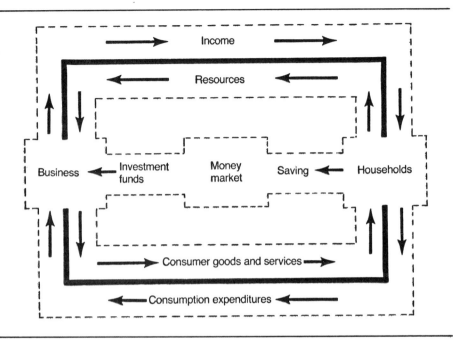

Notice in Figure 4–1 that there are two sets of circular flows. The clockwise or outer flow represents money income and expenditures. The counterclockwise or inner flow represents real resources and consumer goods and services. As shown in the upper part of the diagram, households provide resources (labor, capital, and management) and in return receive income in the form of wages, interest, rents, and profits. The lower part of the diagram illustrates the fact that households in turn spend part of their income for consumer goods and services.

Of course we know that most people do not as a rule spend all of their income; part is saved. This is illustrated in Figure 4–1 by the savings flow coming out of the household sector. The two flows coming out of the household sector represent the idea that people can do only two things with income: they can spend it, or they can save it.

The fact that people do not as a rule spend all their income on consumption goods and services (i.e., part is saved) frees part of the nation's resources for the production of investment goods—buildings, factories, machines, roads, etc. If society insisted on spending every dollar of its income on consumption goods, no resources would be available to produce investment goods. In other words, the value of the nation's resources employed in the production of goods and services is equal to the income of households (see Figure 4–1). If all income was spent on consumer goods, then by definition all resources would be used to produce consumer goods. The act of saving releases some resources from the production of consumer goods and allows them to be used in the production of investment goods, that is, capital. This is an extremely important use of resources because it adds to the total stock of capital in the economy and makes possible economic growth.

The flow of savings that comes out of the household sector is funneled into a so-called money market, where it becomes available to business firms to use for the purchase of resources to produce investment goods. It should be mentioned that business firms also provide an important source of savings in the economy by retaining part of their earnings to "plow back" into the firms, that is, reinvest. Thus savings from both households and business firms provide the wherewithal to invest.

To summarize briefly, the income generated by the production of consumption and investment goods flows into the household sector, where part is used by households for the purchase of consumption goods and part (the savings) is available to be used by business firms for the production of investment goods.

We should not be led to believe from Figure 4–1, however, that there are two separate groups in the economy—one producing and the other consuming. Certainly everyone must be a consumer to stay alive, but at the same time almost every adult is also a producer. Those who are part of the labor force produce goods and services in business places; others, such as homemakers, produce goods and services for themselves and their families at home.

The measures of national output that we will now consider represent the value of the annual flow of consumption and investment goods and services coming out of the business sector. As mentioned, some of these goods are purchased (or produced) and distributed through the government. But because of the difficulty of separating the goods and services purchased and distributed by the government into the consumption and investment categories, such goods generally are included in a separate government category (we will come back to this point later in the chapter). Therefore, the total output of the economy generally includes three broad categories of goods: (1) consumer goods, (2) investment goods, and (3) goods purchased and distributed by the government. Let us now turn to the primary measure of this national output: gross national product.

GROSS NATIONAL PRODUCT DEFINED

Gross national product (GNP) is defined as the total value of all final goods and services produced in the economy during some period of time. There are several points worth noting in this definition. First, GNP is a dollar figure. Because of the thousands of diverse goods and services that are produced in the economy, it is necessary when combining them to utilize some kind of common denominator. As we learned in the first grade, we cannot add together unlike items such as apples and oranges, or bobby pins and battleships.

However, if we assign a monetary value to each item, we are able to use the dollar, or any other kind of monetary unit, as a common denominator. The next question is: What money value should each item be assigned? Two possibilities come to mind: (1) market value and (2) cost of production. The Department of Commerce in measuring GNP has decided upon using market value whenever possible. The decision to use this criterion is not completely arbitrary, however. The market value of a good or service is an indication of how much the item adds to the well-being or satisfaction of society. If a packet of bobby pins sells for 60 cents and a new pair of shoes sells for $60, we can infer that the pair of shoes contributes about 100 times more satisfaction to society than the bobby pins, or else people would not be willing to pay 100 times more for the shoes.

One major problem of using market price as a measure of satisfaction is that not everything that is produced is bought and sold through the market. Military expenditure is one important category of nonmarket purchasing. In this case, the Department of Commerce in computing GNP is forced to use cost of production rather than market price. If a missile system costs $5 billion to produce, it is implicitly assumed in the GNP computations that the missiles contribute $5 billion worth of satisfaction to society. Of course, some people would disagree with this assumption. To some, assigning $5 billion to missiles is much like assigning $60 to a packet of bobby pins that may have cost that much to produce using a very inefficient method of production. But few women would likely receive $60 worth of satisfaction from the $60 bobby pins. As a result the product probably would go off the market and not even enter GNP. Thus, cost of production may be a misleading indicator of the satisfaction received from a product.

Another major nonmarket item included in GNP is the rental value of owner-occupied housing. Even though an owner does not pay rent, satisfaction nevertheless is obtained from the dwelling. However, it is somewhat easier to estimate the rental value of a house than that of a missile system. There is an established rental market for homes and apartments, and the Department of Commerce is able to utilize the resulting figures in estimating the dwellings' worth of society. A third major nonmarket item that is included in GNP is food produced and consumed on farms. Here again, these prices are estimated from those of comparable items sold by farmers.

The second point to note about GNP is that it is the market value of all *final* goods and services. Thus, GNP excludes the value of goods and services produced for resale or further processing. We might inquire: Why doesn't the Department of Commerce include these items? Surely the steel that goes into an automobile or the leather that goes into a pair of shoes contributes to the well-being of society. The reason for excluding these so-called intermediate goods and services is that they are already included in the market price of the final product.

A simple example will help make this clear. Consider the various stages in the manufacture of a pair of shoes. The raw material, i.e., the hide, is produced by a farmer. To simplify the example we assume the farmer is completely self-sufficient, so that the sale price of the hide on the animal is equal to the value added by the farmer. Let this be eight dollars.

In the second step, the packing plant buys the hide for $8, separates it from the animal, and sells it to the tannery for $12. But this $12 selling price must include the $8 paid to the farmer. In other words, in order to stay in business, the packing plant must be reimbursed for the original raw material it bought plus something extra for the services it carried out. The selling price at each step includes two components: (1) what was paid for the raw material (plus other resources such as fuel) and (2) the value added to the product during that stage. One can determine value added at each stage by subtracting the purchases from the value of sales, as illustrated in the following table.

Stage of production	Value of sales	Value added
Farmer	$ 8	$ 8
Packing plant	12	4
Tannery	20	8
Shoe manufacturer	40	20
Wholesaler	44	4
Retailer	60	16
	$184	$60

Notice that the value of the final product, the $60 pair of shoes sold by the retailer, is exactly equal to the sum of all the "value-added" figures in the second column. This is not just a coincidence. Each of the various steps in the production process contributed something to the finished product. Thus the selling price of the finished or final product is just an accumulation of the value added in these stages.

Gross national product, therefore, is a value-added figure. Rather than attempting to decide which products are final products and which are intermediate, the Department of Commerce estimates the value added by each industry. This is accomplished by subtracting the purchases of each industry from the value of its sales, just as we did in the example above.

A reasonable question to ask at this point is: Why make such a big thing out of the value-added figure as opposed to simply using total sales of each industry in the country? Granted GNP would be considerably larger if gross sales were used, but as long as we know why it was larger, why should it make any difference?

One reason for using value added is to avoid a bias that would occur because of merger or consolidation of business firms. Suppose, in the above example, that the packing plant and the tannery merged to become one firm. Now the $6 sale of the hide from the packing plant to the tannery would be eliminated, reducing the sum of the sales column from $184 to $172. Consequently, if GNP were measured by gross sales it could be changed simply by a change in the number of firms, even though output (or value added) remained the same. Notice that the sum of the value-added column does not change with a change in the number of steps in the production process. A second and related reason for using value added rather than sales is that goods whose production required many steps and involved many different firms would count heavily in GNP compared to goods produced by just one or two firms, even though they sold for the same retail price. Therefore, total sales figures would not provide a very meaningful measure of the total production of goods and services in the economy.

A third point to note about GNP is that it excludes "pure exchange" transactions, which include such things as the purchase and sale of securities, gifts, and secondhand sales. These transactions are omitted from GNP because nothing new is produced. If you buy a $100 stock certificate, for example, the person who sells it to you gains the $100 and you gain the certificate. From the standpoint of the total economy, nothing has changed. It must be admitted, though, that after the transaction both you and the seller should be better off than before it; if not, there would be no sense in carrying out the transaction.

About the same reasoning applies to donations and gifts. Here also, nothing new is produced or created, so they should not enter GNP computations. Of course, one could argue here as well that both the giver and receiver are better off after a gift is made than before, or else it would not be made. But it is difficult if not impossible to measure this kind of satisfaction, so it is simplest to leave it out of GNP.

A fourth and final point to note about GNP is that it is a "flow" figure as opposed to a "stock." Flows are always given per unit of time, whereas a stock has no time dimension. As a rule, GNP is given in billions of dollars per year. It is virtually impossible, though, to imagine the magnitude of a billion dollars. If you were a billionaire, for example, and invested your money in a money market fund at 10 percent, you would draw $100 million per year just in interest.

GNP AS A MEASURE OF ECONOMIC WELL–BEING

An important use of the GNP figure is to compare the standard of living or economic well-being of people within a nation over a period of time or between nations at a point in time. The presumption is that the higher the GNP (the greater the output of goods and services), the better off people are. In other words, the use of GNP to gauge economic well-being presumes that people prefer more goods to less. This presumption is not unreasonable. Given the choice between $10,000 per year of goods and services and $20,000 per year (at the same price level), it is likely that most people would choose the latter.

BIASES IN GNP

When using GNP to compare the economic well-being of a society from one year to another or to compare that of two societies, one should be aware of a number of possible biases that can cause GNP to be a distorted measure of economic well-being. Fortunately the major biases can be removed.

1. Change in the price level. Because GNP is a monetary figure, any change in the price level causes a change in GNP that is not the result of a change in real output. For example, the sixfold increase in the price level from 1929 to 1984 caused the measured growth in GNP to overstate the growth in real goods and services. In other words, if the price level had not changed over this period, the dollar value of GNP would have grown considerably less than it did.

The effect of changes in the general price level can be removed by "deflating" the GNP by the consumer price index.[1] Recall from Chapter 3 that the CPI measures the increase in the general price level. GNP is "deflated," or adjusted for changes in the general price level, by dividing the GNP figure by the CPI and multiplying by 100. For example, suppose we would like to know the value of 1984 GNP if the 1929 price level had existed in 1984. The figures in the following table provide the necessary information.

---

[1] The Department of Commerce constructs a separate price index designed specifically for deflating GNP. It is called the "implicit price deflator." Although the implicit price deflator is likely to be a more accurate deflator for GNP, we will continue to use the CPI because it is the index discussed in Chapter 3 and is most familiar.

Year	GNP current year prices ($ billions)	CPI
1929	103	100
1984	3,661	606

In this case the 1984 GNP figure ($3,661 billion) is divided by the 1984 CPI (606) and the result multiplied by 100. The answer, $604 billion, is what 1984 GNP would have been if the 1929 price level had still prevailed in 1984. Thus it is evident that the growth in real goods and services was considerably less than the raw, unadjusted GNP figures might first imply.

One might also pose the question: What would 1929 GNP have been if the 1984 price level had prevailed back then? This question also can be answered; however, in order to obtain the answer it is necessary to use 1984 as the base-year CPI. But suppose the CPI is not given to us with 1984 as the base year, i.e., 1984 = 100? This problem can be overcome by changing the base year, in this case from 1929 = 100 to 1984 = 100. To accomplish this task one need only ask: How can the 1984 CPI of 606 (when 1929 is the base year) be changed to 100? The easiest way to make the 1984 CPI equal 100 is to divide the number by itself and multiply by 100. Of course, the same thing must be done to the 1929 CPI in order for the mathematical manipulation to be "legal." Then the same deflating procedure as in the preceding paragraph can be carried out. The answer, $624 billion, tells us what 1929 GNP would have been if 1984 prices had prevailed in that year. The preceding calculations are summarized below.

a. Deflating 1984 GNP by 1984 CPI (1929 = 100):

$$\frac{3661}{606} \times 100 = \$604$$

b. Changing the base year of the CPI from 1929 to 1984:

$$1929 \text{ CPI: } \frac{100}{606} \times 100 = 16.5$$

$$1984 \text{ CPI: } \frac{606}{606} \times 100 = 100$$

c. Deflating 1929 GNP by 1929 CPI (1984 = 100):

$$\frac{\$103}{16.5} \times 100 = \$624$$

After adjusting the GNP for changes in the general price level, we obtain what is known as GNP in "constant dollars." If 1929 is used as the base year it would be "constant 1929 dollars." If 1984 is used as the base, it would be "constant 1984 dollars." Value figures that are not adjusted for changes in the price level should be labeled as "current-year dollars." When viewing a time series of value figures, it is important to know whether the figures are in current or constant dollars or prices. As illustrated above, the figures can be grossly different in the two cases. The unadjusted GNP became more than 35 times larger between 1929 and 1984, whereas GNP in constant dollars increased by a multiple of 5.9. Of course, the same deflating procedure could be carried out on all the intervening years' GNP figures to obtain the growth in real GNP over an extended period, as shown in Table 4–1. Also, the same deflating procedure could be done on any value figure, such as wages, military spending, gasoline prices, or tuition.

TABLE 4–1   United States GNP, five-year intervals, 1929–84

Year	GNP current-year prices ($ billions)	GNP constant 1984 prices ($ billions)	GNP per person 1984 prices
1929	$ 103	$ 606	$ 5,162
1934	65	500	3,957
1939	91	700	5,144
1944	210	1,235	8,844
1949	257	1,117	7,363
1954	365	1,404	8,598
1959	484	1,729	9,508
1964	632	2,107	10,913
1969	930	2,657	12,774
1974	1,413	3,006	14,048
1979	2,414	3,449	15,663
1984	3,661	3,661	15,471

Source: *Economic Report of the President*, 1985, p. 232.

Although deflating GNP by the CPI removes the major part of the bias or distortion in GNP caused by changes in the general price level, we should remember that the CPI itself can be biased. As mentioned in the previous chapter, it is difficult if not impossible to hold the quality of items constant when comparing prices over time. If, as is likely, the quality of many items has increased over time, the measured rise in the CPI is likely to overstate the "true" increase.[2] Thus when we deflate and compare current-year GNP to GNP in years past, we in effect understate current-year GNP in relation to GNP long ago. A similar bias creeps in to the extent that changes in relative prices bring about changes in the mix of goods and services purchased. As explained in Chapter 3, this "index-number problem" tends to make the measured CPI overstate the true rise in prices. Again, the effect is to bias the growth in real GNP downward.

2. Population growth. If population is growing, as is the case in most countries, including the United States, growth in total GNP even in constant dollars can overstate the true improvement in economic well-being of the individual. Thus it is desirable to compute GNP per person by dividing GNP by total population. By dividing 1929 and 1984 U.S. GNP (constant 1984 dollars) by the population in those two years, we obtain a per capita GNP of $5,162 and $15,471 for 1929 and 1984, respectively. Thus the real output per person in-

---

[2] If you doubt that quality has increased, look through a Wards or Sears catalog from the 1930s, 1940s, or 1950s.

creased about 3-fold from 1929 to 1984. The results of removing the bias caused by an increase in the price level and by the increase in population are presented in Table 4–1.

To summarize briefly, note that the nearly 36-fold growth in total current-dollar GNP is reduced to about a 6-fold growth between 1929 and 1984 when adjusted for price-level changes. After dividing through by population, we obtain a threefold increase in real GNP per capita between 1929 and 1984.

3. Nonmarket activities. A third source of bias in GNP as a measure of economic well-being can occur because GNP does not include many non-market activities in the economy. In a previous section we alluded to the fact that in measuring GNP the government attempts to estimate a value to food produced and consumed on farms and to owner-occupied housing. There are, however, other things that people value which are not in GNP.

An important nonmarket item is leisure time. Even though it is not bought and sold in the market, there can be little doubt that people place a value on it, but the value of leisure is not included in GNP. In itself the omission of the value of leisure from GNP need not bias GNP as a measure of well-being as long as the amount of leisure remains constant over time, or among countries. But if the amount of leisure time increases, measured GNP will not grow as rapidly as it would have if people were receiving larger paychecks for working the extra hours.

The amount of leisure time can be approximated by the length of the workweek. The shorter the workweek, the more leisure time is available. As shown in Table 4–2, in all manufacturing industries in the United States, the

---

TABLE 4–2 Length of workweek, U.S. manufacturing and retail trade, selected years, 1929–84

Year	Manufacturing (hours)	Retail trade (hours)	Year	Manufacturing (hours)	Retail trade (hours)
1929	44.2	—	1959	40.3	38.2
1934	34.6	—	1964	40.7	37.0
1939	37.7	43.4	1969	40.6	34.2
1944	45.2	41.0	1974	40.0	32.7
1949	39.1	40.4	1979	40.2	32.6
1954	39.6	39.2	1984	40.7	30.0

Source: *Economic Report of the President*, 1969, p. 260, and 1985, p. 276.

---

average length of the workweek declined from 44.2 hours in 1929 to 40.7 hours in 1984. However most of this decline came during the 1930s. After increasing to 45.2 hours in 1944, the workweek in manufacturing settled down to about 40 hours after World War II and has remained there ever since. In contrast, the workweek in retail trade has declined substantially from World War II to the present. However, part-time jobs have become quite common in retail trade, so the measured decline is not a true indication of the length of the workweek for full-time workers. It is probably safe to say that the leisure-time bias should not be a problem unless we are comparing current GNP with pre-1930 figures, or if we are comparing U.S. GNP with the GNP of nations with longer workweeks, mainly the less developed countries. In these cases the current U.S. GNP will understate the true current well-being.

Related to the leisure-time bias, but operating in the opposite direction, is the bias caused by the entry of women into the labor force. With the coming of laborsaving devices in the home, together with higher educational levels and increased job opportunities for women, a larger proportion of the nation's females now hold full- or part-time jobs than was true 40 or 50 years ago. For example, in 1940 about 28 percent of all women in the United States participated in the labor force, whereas in 1984 this figure increased to 54 percent. Instead of making clothes, baking bread, watching the children, washing dishes, and so forth, more women are now using part of their salaries to purchase these services in the market. The purchases of ready-to-wear clothing, convenience foods, restaurant meals, child-care services, appliances for cleaning and food preparation, and so on are included in the GNP measure. When the tasks performed by these purchases were done by hand by women in the home, they were not reflected in the GNP measure. Some offset to this bias occurs because of the decrease in employment of maids, housekeepers, and gardeners over the past 50 years. The services of these people were a part of GNP. At any rate, it appears that the movement of women from the home to factories and offices has caused our current GNP to look better than it really is in comparison to GNP 50 years ago. This is not because the goods and services produced by women are of little value to society. The bias is due to the increase in household activities that pass through the market and are therefore caught by the GNP measure.

The bias caused by leaving out nonmarket activities also becomes important when a society changes from a rural, self-sufficient economy to an urban, market-oriented economy. Years ago rural people were much more self-sufficient than either rural or urban people are today. They built and repaired their own utensils and tools, wove cloth, sewed their own clothes, built some of their own furniture, and grew their own fuel for transportation (feed for horses). Even though many of these goods and services never came through the market and hence were not caught by GNP, the people living in those days nevertheless benefited from their use.

The effect on GNP of the transformation from a self-sufficient, rural economy to a monetized, market-oriented economy is especially important for the developing nations. By catching a growing proportion of daily activities in the GNP measure, a nation can exhibit an impressive rate of economic growth that may overstate the true growth in real output.

4. Military expenditures. The inclusion in GNP of military expenditures together with police and fire-protection costs represents a potential source of bias when using GNP to measure economic well-being. During wars or times of military conflict the government increases its spending on national defense. Since military goods cannot be consumed or invested, the production of these items does not contribute to economic well-being, at least directly. Granted, if the country were defeated or destroyed by a foreign power, economic well-being as well as personal freedoms would decline drastically. Thus, most people would probably argue that some military spending is necessary. At any rate, military spending will cause a bias in GNP as a measure of changes in well-being if the percent of GNP devoted to the military changes. For example, between 1939 and 1944, the percent of GNP devoted to military spending increased from just over 1 percent to more than 40 percent (see Table 4–3).

TABLE 4–3   U.S. military spending as a percent of GNP, 1939–84

Year	Percent	Year	Percent
1939	1.3%	1964	7.9%
1944	41.6	1969	8.2
1949	5.2	1974	5.5
1954	13.0	1979	4.6
1959	9.5	1984	6.1

Source: *Economic Report of the President*, 1969, p. 227, and 1985, p. 233.

Even though GNP increased greatly over this 5-year period, economic well-being did not increase in proportion. The same phenomenon occurred during the Korean and Vietnam wars, although the bias in these cases was less pronounced than during World War II. In general, wars cause GNP to overstate the growth in economic well-being.

With the exception of the Korean and Vietnam wars, the proportion of GNP devoted to military spending has followed a long-term downward trend in the United States since World War II (see Table 4–3). This trend causes a slight downward bias in the growth of economic well-being as measured by GNP. It is a relatively easy task to remove any bias caused by military spending by subtracting this amount from GNP to arrive at nonmilitary GNP, as shown in Table 4–4. This figure provides a more accurate measure of how many goods and services are available for consumption and investment purposes. In 1984, for example, the subtraction of military spending reduced per capita GNP by $936, or about 6 percent.

TABLE 4–4   U.S. military expenditures, total and nonmilitary GNP, five-year intervals, 1939–84 (constant 1984 dollars)

Year	Military expenditures		Per capita GNP	
	Total ($ billions)	Per person ($)	Total ($)	Nonmilitary ($)
1939	$ 9	$ 731	$ 5,144	$ 5,071
1944	509	3,688	8,844	5,157
1949	60	373	7,363	6,990
1954	158	967	8,598	7,632
1959	159	900	9,508	8,608
1964	162	839	10,913	10,507
1969	212	1,050	12,774	11,725
1974	162	764	14,048	13,285
1979	159	720	15,663	14,903
1984	222	936	15,471	14,535

Source: *Economic Report of the President*, 1985, p. 233.

Whether the amount spent on the military is too large, about right, or too small is a matter of opinion. Those who argue for increased military spending believe it is cheaper in the long run to be strong militarily if doing so forestalls potential aggressor nations from stirring up trouble around the world and creating situations which may pull the country into war. The long-run downward trend in the military's share of GNP no doubt was a factor in the Reagan administration's decision to build up the military during the early 1980s. Those who favor a smaller military believe that spending billions in this area amounts to a sheer waste of resources and, if anything, increases the chances of war by creating situations where nations resort to military solutions to problems. There is no way of knowing who is right. Most everyone wants peace; the question is, What is the best way to attain it?

5. Distribution of output. Although this item is not strictly a bias, we should be mindful of the importance of the distribution of a nation's output on the economic well-being of the average person. When we computed per capita GNP, we simply divided total GNP by the number of people in the country. We obtain the same figure regardless of how GNP is distributed. But most people probably feel that society as a whole is better off if everyone is able to share in the nation's output as opposed to the case where the nation's income and wealth are concentrated in the hands of a few very rich and powerful families. The oil-rich kingdoms of the Middle East provide a good example of the latter case.

In Chapter 14 we will study in more detail some of the major problems and issues in the areas of poverty and income distribution. For now, it is sufficient that we become aware that the per capita GNP figure does not tell us anything about how the GNP is distributed. We might say, however, that this problem is less severe in the United States than in many other countries of the world. Although U.S. output is by no means shared equally, neither is it concentrated in the hands of a select few. Also, the United States has not experienced a drastic change in income distribution during its history.

The biases inherent in GNP and their effect on GNP as a measure of the growth of economic well-being in the United States from 1929 to the present are summarized below.

Bias	Effect on total GNP
Inflation	Overstates growth of well-being
Population growth	Overstates growth of well-being
Increased leisure time	Understates growth of well-being
Entry of women in labor force	Overstates growth of well-being
Decrease in maids and housekeepers	Understates growth of well-being
Less self-sufficiency	Overstates growth of well-being
Relative growth of the military	Overstates growth of well-being

EXPENDITURE COMPONENTS OF GNP

In the discussion relating to the flowchart of the economy in Figure 4–1, it was pointed out that the total output of the economy consists of consumption goods, investment goods, and goods purchased and distributed by the government. In this section we will take a somewhat more detailed look at what is included in each category. In Chapters 6 and 12 we will be particularly interested in the effect on GNP resulting from changes in the expenditures on these three categories of goods.

1. Personal consumption expenditures. As the name implies, this category includes the expenditures of individuals and households on all consumer items. It is common to further divide this category into (*a*) consumer durables such as automobiles, refrigerators, and television sets and (*b*) consumer nondurables, which include both goods (meat, bread, clothes, beverages, cosmetics, etc.) and services (medical and dental care, barber and beauty shop services, repair services, etc.).

One large item that is perhaps conspicuous by its absence is the purchase of newly constructed residential housing. The Department of Commerce includes this item in the investment category. However, the Commerce Department does compute the annual rental value of owner-occupied housing and adds this amount to consumer expenditures, along with actual rental payments on apartments and houses. Also, as mentioned, the purchases of secondhand items are not included, mainly because they represent a transfer of assets rather than a net addition to output.

2. Gross private domestic investment. Investment as used in this context refers to the expenditures on construction of physical capital or facilities, mainly buildings, machines, and tools. It does not include the purchase of stocks or bonds, or money placed in a savings account. We sometimes refer to the purchase of these items as an "investment." But this does not constitute investment as defined in the national accounts, mainly because it involves a mere transfer of assets from one party to another and not an addition to the nation's stock of physical capital or productive capacity.

The distinguishing feature of investment goods as defined in the national accounts is that they yield a stream of services or returns over a long period of time. This is in contrast to consumer goods, which tend to be used up over a shorter period. One might argue that consumer durables, such as automobiles and appliances, yield their services over a long period too. But the line between consumer durables and investment goods had to be drawn somewhere. Recall, however, that the construction of residential housing is included as an investment good.

In addition to machines, tools, and buildings, the investment component of GNP includes any change in inventories held by business firms. In order for GNP to accurately reflect the nation's output for a given year or time period, it is necessary to add any net *increase* in inventories that had taken place. In this case, the output or production of goods and services is greater than sales. Of course a large part of the nation's inventories are consumer goods, but the main thing is that they are included somewhere. By the same token, a net *decrease,* or drawing down, of inventories is subtracted from the investment figure to reflect the fact that sales of final goods and services exceeded their production.

Some explanation is in order in reference to the modifiers "gross private domestic" in the heading of this subsection. *Gross* refers to the total new investment during a given year. It does not contain any deduction for the amount of capital that has been used up or depreciated during the year. Hence gross investment will overstate the true increase in the nation's capital. Later we will discuss the measure of output when depreciation of capital has been deducted. *Private* denotes investment by the so-called private sector as opposed to government investment. Finally, *domestic* refers to investment in the United States as opposed to investment in other nations. In future discussion we will refer to only gross or net investment, with the understanding that the "private domestic" adjectives also apply.

3. Government purchases of goods and services. This category of expenditures includes the purchases of goods and services by all levels of government—federal, state, and local. Included are such items as expenditures on military hardware and personnel, police and fire protection, public school operation, roads, and public parks. However it does not include so-called transfer payments. By and large these are gifts from taxpayers to welfare and social security recipients. As such these payments do not represent a net addition to output; hence they are not counted in GNP. Of course, the expenditure of these funds by the recipients on either consumption or investment goods is reflected in GNP.

To summarize briefly, we have identified the three major components of GNP from the standpoint of expenditures on final goods and services: (1) consumption, (2) investment (gross), and (3) government spending. Traditionally, these components have been identified as C, I_g, and G, respectively. Thus an easy way to remember the makeup of GNP is to call to mind the simple formula:

$$GNP = C + I_g + G$$

Figures showing the percent of GNP accounted for by each of these three expenditure categories for selected years from 1929–1984 are presented in Table 4–5. Note in particular the declining share of GNP accounted for by private consumption expenditures and the increasing share accounted for by government expenditures.

TABLE 4–5   Percent of each of the three major expenditure categories in GNP, 1929–84

Year	Consumption	Investment	Government*
1929	75%	16%	9%
1934	79	5	16
1939	74	10	16
1944	52	3	45
1949	69	14	17
1954	65	14	21
1959	64	16	20
1964	63	15	22
1969	62	16	22
1974	63	15	22
1979	63	17	20
1984	64	17	19

* These figures are smaller than those in Table 2–1 because these do not include transfer payments and government sales.
Source: *Economic Report of the President*, 1985, p. 233.

INCOME COMPONENTS OF GNP

Although we will be interested mainly in the three expenditure components of GNP in later chapters, it should be mentioned that GNP also can be viewed from the income side. In other words, instead of measuring the expenditures on final goods and services, we can measure the income derived from the production of these goods and services. It is a bit easier to grasp the idea of this dual measure of GNP if we remember that every dollar spent on a good or service is income to somebody; that is, for every dollar of expenditure, there is a dollar of income. Thus, if we measure income we should obtain exactly the same figure as when we measure expenditures.

Traditionally, the Department of Commerce has divided the nation's income into four categories: (1) wages, (2) interest, (3) rents, and (4) profits. The first category, wages, represents the income of wage and salary workers. Interest and rents represent income earned by the owners of capital (machines, buildings, land, etc.). The fourth category, profits, is a residual representing what is left over for producers after paying wages, interest, and rents. One can view profits as payments to owners of firms for the capital they have contributed as well as a reward for taking risks in initiating and carrying on production. Of course, there is no guarantee that profits will always be positive, at least for the individual firm.

Measuring GNP in terms of income is useful in that it tells us how much of the nation's output is enjoyed by each category of resource owner. The division between wages and the other three categories is of particular interest in that it provides an indication of labor's share of national output in relation to capital's share. Of course, workers also own a substantial share of the nation's capital, particularly when we consider that pension funds, which account for over 35 percent of the stock invested in corporations, are in fact owned by workers.

Dividing income into the above four categories is generally referred to as the "functional distribution" of income. As the name implies, this distribution

TABLE 4–6   Relative shares of national income, five-year intervals, 1929–84

Year	Wages*	Interest	Rents	Profits†
1929	76%	5%	6%	12%
1934	85	8	3	3
1939	83	5	4	9
1944	83	1	3	13
1949	81	1	4	14
1954	82	1	4	13
1959	81	2	4	13
1964	81	3	3	13
1969	83	4	3	10
1974	85	6	2	7
1979	82	7	1	10
1984	79	10	3	8

* Includes compensation of employees, business and professional income, and farm income.
† Includes corporate profits before taxes with inventory evaluation adjustment.
Source: *Economic Report of the President*, 1970, p. 191, and 1985, pp. 256–57.

categorizes income by the function of its recipients—workers, owners of capital, and management. Income also can be categorized according to its "personal distribution." In this case income is divided up according to the income level of its recipients. It tells us, for example, what share of the nation's income flows to the upper 10 percent of the nation's income recipients, what share flows to the next 10 percent, etc. We will study the personal distribution of income in more detail in Chapter 14, where we discuss poverty and the distribution of income.

The relative shares of these four income categories are presented in Table 4–6. Over the 1929–84 period, wages have accounted for the major share of the nation's income, between 81 and 85 percent in most years. Although the data do not reveal any long-run trends in the share of income going to each category, there is some year-to-year variation. It is interesting to note that during the years shown when unemployment was the highest—1934, 1939, and 1974—profits were the lowest in relative terms. Thus it is in the interest of both management and labor to maintain full employment.

GOVERNMENT AS A SEPARATE SECTOR

The traditional breakdown of GNP from the standpoint of expenditures includes government purchases of goods and services as a separate item or sector. Although the three-way division of GNP into consumption, investment, and government spending turns out to be useful in future discussion, one should guard against a complete separation of government from the rest of the economy. By treating government as a separate entity, it is easy to regard the goods and services purchased by the government as neither consumption nor investment goods, and as such unavailable to the general public. But, of course, this is not true.

With the possible exception of purchases for the military and possibly police and fire protection, all goods and services purchased by the government can be classified as either consumption or investment goods. For example, expenditures on public parks and school lunches could be considered consumption goods. Government expenditures on roads and flood-control projects could be considered investment goods. The main point is that members of the public benefit from government consumption and investment expenditures as they do from private expenditures on these two kinds of goods. Even though we will follow the convention of separating government from private-sector expenditures in the remainder of this book, we should not be led to believe that government goods and services are lost or unavailable to the people. Aside from the cost of running the government bureaucracy, it does not "consume" any goods or services; the people do.

It is equally important to recognize that the government does not pay for anything either. All the money that the government spends must first come from taxpayers; and taxpayers are individual people. Even the so-called taxes on business, such as the corporation income tax, are ultimately borne by individuals through higher prices for goods and/or lower dividends received by stockholders. Strictly speaking there is no such thing as federal funds or even state funds; all government funds come from individuals. It is true that if certain goods are paid for by taxes collected by the federal government, different individuals may end up paying for the goods than if they were purchased by state or local governments, or by the people who benefit from the goods.

At the same time it should be pointed out that the necessity of levying taxes to pay for government spending could cause GNP to be smaller than it might otherwise be. The argument that an increase in government spending does not decrease the amounts of goods and services available to the people implicitly assumes that taxes do not affect the total output of the country. When taxes were relatively low, this might have been true. In recent years, however, there has been an increase in concern that higher taxes reduce GNP. The reason is that, as taxes increase, people have less incentive to work and invest. For example, welfare benefits now approach (or exceed) the take-home pay of at least some people at the low end of the wage scale. Also, people in the middle and high ranges of the income scale have less incentive to save and invest part of their incomes because they cannot keep as large a proportion of their invest-ment earnings compared to when taxes were lower. Hence, investment and GNP may be lower than they might otherwise be.

Given the size of the GNP, an increase in the government's proportion of total output also may reduce the nation's standard of living because of lower efficiency in public-sector production. Studies have shown that the costs of producing goods or services by public agencies exceed the costs of producing comparable items by private firms.[3] Higher costs reduce the quantity of real output that can be produced from a given level of resources. In this case measured GNP need not decline, but the nation's total real output and the standard of living of people could decline.

NET EXPORTS IN GNP

Although the three expenditure items, consumption, investment, and gov-ernment spending, comprise the major share of GNP, to be strictly correct we should include a fourth item—net exports. *Net exports* are defined as total exports minus total imports. For example, if the country sells $50 billion worth of goods and services to foreign countries and buys $48 billion in return, net exports are $2 billion.

It is somewhat unfortunate that foreign trade enters GNP in this manner, particularly if we wish to use GNP as a measure of economic well-being, for it implies that the more we can sell to foreign countries and the less we buy from them, the better off we are. But, again, this is not true. Goods and services we use that are produced abroad benefit us as much as things produced in this country.

The effect of subtracting imports from GNP is reduced to an absurdity if we use an extreme example. Suppose we (the United States) were able to sell everything we produced to other countries but did not buy anything in return, that is, zero imports. In this case we would not be able to enjoy any of the fruits of our labor because we would have sold them all abroad. The apparent desir-

[3] W. A. Niskanen, Jr., "Bureaucrats and Politicians," *The Journal of Law and Economics* 18 (December 1975), pp. 617–43; and W. Orzechowski, "Economic Models of Bureaucracy: Survey, Extensions and Evidence," in Thomas E. Borcharding, ed., *Budgets and Bureaucrats: The Sources of Government Growth* (Durham, N.C.: Duke University Press, 1977), pp. 229–59.

ability of exports probably stems from the extra business and employment generated by foreign sales. Yet we should keep in mind that in order for other countries to buy from us they must have dollars, which they obtain by selling goods to use in return; international trade is a two-way street. Perhaps the main point here is that both exports and imports are good if they add to the total output available to the people. We will see in Chapter 15 how international trade can result in more total goods available to people of all nations.

The reason exports are added to GNP and imports subtracted is to obtain a measure of production rather than consumption. Recall that GNP measures the output or production of final goods and services. Of course, when we refer to economic well-being we are really talking about consumption. This is another reason why GNP is not a perfect measure of economic well-being. However, in most years imports are fairly close to exports, so the two tend to cancel each other out in the actual measure of GNP. Consequently, the way foreign trade is measured usually does not result in a serious bias in GNP as a measure of economic well-being, at least for the United States. This is not to say that foreign trade is unimportant to economic well-being.

NET NATIONAL PRODUCT

In addition to gross national product, the Department of Commerce computes a number of other measures of national output or income. A second measure is net national product (NNP). Net national product differs from GNP in that the depreciation of capital (D) is subtracted. Depreciation of capital is often referred to as "capital consumption allowances." In a sense, it is the capital that is worn out or used up during the year in the production of goods and services.

$$NNP = GNP - D$$

As stated in a previous section, GNP is the total expenditure on final goods and services by consumers, investors, and government agencies. These expenditures generally are abbreviated by $C + I_g + G$, where I_g stands for gross investment.[4] Net national product, on the other hand, is denoted by $C + I_n + G$, where I_n represents net investment. Net investment equals gross investment minus depreciation.

$$GNP = C + I_g + G$$
$$NNP = C + I_n + G$$

NNP is considered to be a more accurate measure of the true output of the economy than GNP. If a nation uses up its capital to produce goods and services (as the United States did during World War II), it may have a large output temporarily, but sooner or later output will decline as the stock of capital in the country is depleted. NNP reflects how much is produced over and above that which is required to keep the nation's stock of capital intact. In Chapters 6 and 12, NNP will be used as the measure of national output or income for the country.

---

[4] Net exports are deleted to simplify the discussion.

NATIONAL INCOME

National income (NI) is equal to NNP minus indirect business taxes (T_{IB}). By and large, these are the sales, excise, and property taxes. National income is supposed to be a more accurate measure of income to labor and owners of capital because these taxes, of course, are siphoned off by the government. It should be remembered, however, that the national income measure became institutionalized before the income tax was very important or was deducted from paychecks; so years ago it was a more accurate indicator of incomes to resource owners than is the case nowadays.

PERSONAL INCOME

Personal income (PI) is defined as the income received by households before personal income taxes. It is computed by subtracting social security taxes (T_{ss}), corporate income taxes (T_{CI}), and corporate savings (S_c) from NI and adding transfer payments (T_R) to this figure. Transfer payments represent income payments from government to individuals other than for services rendered, i.e., gifts. Because personal income requires four adjustments to national income, it will be useful to summarize what we have done:

$$PI = NI - T_{ss} - T_{CI} - S_c + T_R$$

DISPOSABLE INCOME

Disposable income (DI) is equal to PI minus personal income taxes (T_{PI}). This measure represents the income that people have to spend or save. In other words, there are only two things that people can do with their disposable income; they can spend it, or they can save it. The Department of Commerce separates these two components of DI as well and publishes the annual expenditure on consumption and personal saving:

$$DI = PI - T_{PI}$$
$$DI = C + S$$

Although people no doubt value the public goods component of GNP, the figure that most people probably consider the most revealing of their own

---

TABLE 4–7   U.S. per capita disposable income, selected years, 1929–84 (constant 1984 dollars)

Year	Income	Year	Income
1929	$4,128	1959	$ 6,819
1934	3,292	1964	7,692
1939	4,037	1969	8,817
1944	6,182	1974	9,835
1949	5,531	1979	10,411
1954	5,959	1984	10,893

Source: *Economic Report of the President*, 1985, p. 261.

economic well-being is disposable income—what they have left after taxes to spend on themselves or their families, or to save. Figures giving the per capita disposable income for people in the United States from 1929 to 1984 (in constant 1984 dollars) are in Table 4–7. Notice in particular the substantial decline that occurred from 1929 to 1934, but the 2.6-fold growth of real per capita DI from 1929 to 1984.[5]

SUMMARY OF OUTPUT OR INCOME MEASURES

In this chapter five different measures of the nation's output or income have been presented. They tend to be confusing and difficult to remember, but a brief summary might be helpful.

	Gross national product
Less:	Depreciation of capital
Equals:	**Net national product**
Less:	Indirect business taxes
Equals:	**National income**
Less:	Social security taxes
	Corporate income taxes
	Corporate saving
Plus:	Transfer payments
Equals:	**Personal income**
Less:	Personal income taxes
Equals:	**Disposable income**

MAIN POINTS OF CHAPTER 4

1. An economy can be illustrated by a flowchart having a household and business sector and producing consumption and investment goods.

2. The act of saving releases resources for the production of investment goods. Investment goods have the effect of increasing the real output of society.

3. **Gross national product** (GNP) is defined as the value of all final goods and services produced in an economy over some period of time.

4. In measuring GNP the Department of Commerce uses the market value of goods that are bought and sold in the market and the cost of production for goods that are not bought and sold, such as military goods and services.

5. Gross national product is obtained by measuring the value added by each industry. This is equivalent to measuring the value of final goods and services.

6. The main advantage of measuring value added is that GNP is not changed simply by a change in the number of firms in the economy or the number of steps in the production process.

7. The use of GNP as a measure of economic well-being presumes that people prefer more goods to less.

8. Because GNP is a value figure, it is biased by a change in the general price level. This bias can be removed by deflating (or adjusting) the current-dollar GNP figures by the CPI.

---

[5] The official CPI for 1944 likely understates the true price level for that year, making the 1944 real figure higher than it should be.

9. Deflating GNP for a change in the price level is accomplished by dividing by the CPI and multiplying by 100. The resulting figure is in the price level that prevailed in the base year.

10. A more accurate picture of economic well-being is given by GNP per capita, which is obtained by dividing GNP by the population.

11. Adjusting GNP for the increase in the general price level and for the increase in population reduces GNP growth from a 35-fold increase to a 3-fold increase between 1929 and 1984.

12. Gross national product as a measure of economic well-being also can be biased because it excludes many nonmarket activities that people nevertheless value. Among these are included: (1) the value of increased leisure time, (2) the effect of increased labor force participation by women, and (3) the change from a more self-sufficient rural economy to a market-oriented urban society. The first factor causes GNP to understate the improvement in economic well-being, while the last two have the opposite effect.

13. An increase in military expenditures caused GNP to overstate the growth in economic well-being between 1929 and 1984. In 1984 per capita nonmilitary GNP was $936 less than total per capita GNP.

14. The three major expenditure components of GNP are (1) personal consumption expenditure, (2) gross private domestic investment, and (3) government spending on goods and services. Between 1929 and 1984, the proportion of GNP accounted for by private consumption expenditures decreased, while the proportion accounted for by government expenditures increased.

15. The four major income components of GNP are (1) wages, (2) interest, (3) rents, and (4) profits. Wages have accounted for the largest share of national income, averaging slightly over 80 percent since the 1930s with no apparent long-run trend.

16. The practice of separating government expenditures from private consumption and investment gives the impression that government expenditures are somehow lost or unavailable to the general public, which of course is not the case. By the same token all government expenditure is paid for by individuals through various forms of taxes and fees.

17. The increase in the relative size of government can cause GNP to decline because of the disincentive effect of higher taxes on work and investment. Also, higher costs of production in the public sector can reduce the standard of living of people from what it would otherwise be.

18. The net export component of GNP is obtained by adding exports and subtracting imports. This procedure is followed in order to obtain a measure of production rather than consumption. We should not conclude, however, that exports are good and imports are bad.

19. Other measures of national output or income include net national product, national income, personal income, and disposable income.

20. Probably the most revealing indicator of economic well-being of the average family is disposable income—what people have left to spend or save after paying their taxes.

QUESTIONS FOR THOUGHT AND DISCUSSION

1. According to the simple flowchart of the economy, income received by households must equal expenditure by households on consumer goods and services. True or false? Explain.

2. Why is it necessary to have saving in order to have investment?

3. What is GNP? How is it measured? Why is GNP measured in value-added terms rather than as total sales?

4. Is it better to value the items in GNP by their market prices or by their cost of production? Explain.

5. Which of the following would be included in GNP? Explain.
   a. Used-car sales.
   b. Stock market transactions.
   c. Rental value of owner-occupied housing.
   d. Welfare payments.
   e. Transactions in the "underground economy."
   f. Laundry done at home.
   g. Laundry done by commercial laundries.

6. State whether each of the following circumstances causes GNP to overstate or understate growth in economic well-being between 1929 and the present and explain why.
   a. An increase in the general price level.
   b. An increase in population.
   c. An increase in leisure time.
   d. An increase in barter.
   e. An increase in meals purchased in restaurants relative to meals eaten at home.
   f. An increase in the use of purchased inputs by farmers as opposed to the use of home-produced inputs.
   g. An increase in the proportion of women in the labor force.
   h. An increase in the "underground economy."
   i. An increase in military spending.
   j. An increase in expenditures for police protection because of an increase in crime.
       Answer question 7 from the following information.

Year	GNP per capita (current dollars)	Hourly wages in manufacturing (current dollars)	CPI (1967 = 100)
1930	$ 735	$ .55	50
1960	2,788	2.26	89
1984	15,471	9.17	311

7. *a.* Calculate GNP per capita and hourly wages in manufacturing in constant 1967 dollars.
   b. Calculate GNP per capita and hourly wages in manufacturing in constant 1984 dollars.

8. What are the expenditure components of GNP? What are the income components? Why must the two always be equal?

9. Money received by state and local governments from the federal government is commonly referred to as "federal funds." In what way is this not true?

10. Exports are added to GNP and imports are subtracted. It follows that the more we export and the less we import the better off we will be, because GNP will be larger. True or false? Explain.

11. Which of the measures of national income or output would most accurately reflect:
   a. The total value of output of final goods and services.
   b. How much is produced over and above that which is required to maintain the nation's stock of capital intact.
   c. How much money people have to spend or save.

12. Is DI the same thing as take-home pay? Explain.

PART III

MACRO THEORIES

CHAPTER 5

CLASSICAL ECONOMICS

Although the main emphasis of this text is on contemporary economic principles and problems, some understanding of early economic thought and how it evolved over time will be helpful in understanding the current material. Over the remainder of the text it will be interesting to observe the similarities and differences between current economic thought and that which existed in the early years of the discipline. It may come as a surprise to see that many of the ideas and issues of 200 years ago are still alive and fresh today. Understandably, it is not possible in a single chapter to present in detail a body of literature encompassing many thousands of pages. One should view this chapter as an appetizer rather than a full meal in one's economic food for thought.

The early economic writers have come to be known as classical economists—a name coined by Karl Marx. Most were from Great Britain, although there were some from France, Germany, Sweden, and Austria. Their period in history is generally regarded to extend from about 1776 to the 1870s, although some writers have placed all economic literature before the 1930s in the classical school.

GREAT BOOKS

This chapter is organized along the lines of concepts and issues rather than books or writers. But it will be helpful to have a brief introduction to the major writers of the period and their work in order to provide a frame of reference for the discussion to follow. Also, the early economists built upon each other's work, as is true of all sciences even nowadays. By virtue of the constraints of space and time, coverage of classical thought must be selective and not highly detailed. There are several excellent books summarizing and critiquing the works of the classical economists.[1]

Any discussion of classical economics must begin with Adam Smith, who is widely regarded as the founding father of economics. His best-known book, *An Inquiry into the Nature and Causes of the Wealth of Nations* (1776), is a classic, having been described as the second revolution which began that year. The book is commonly referred to by just the last four words of the full title— *The Wealth of Nations*. The major emphasis of the book was on economic growth. In general, Smith was fairly optimistic about England's chances of achieving economic growth provided changes were made in government policy which he prescribed and which will be explained in more detail in later sections.

The optimistic tone of *The Wealth of Nations* regarding future improvements in the standard of living of people became the accepted mode of economic thought over the last quarter of the 18th century. But in 1798 there appeared a book entitled *An Essay on the Principle of Population as It Affects the Future Improvements of Society,* by the Reverend Thomas Malthus. In short, Malthus argued that any gains achieved by economic growth would be wiped out by population growth, leaving mankind in a long-run state of poverty and hunger. As Malthus's bleak picture of the future became widely known in the years following the publication of his essay, Thomas Carlyle, a Scottish writer and historian, dubbed economics the "dismal science," a name that still sticks today.

As we move into the 19th century, the rate of publication of new books on economics picks up considerably; and we do something of an injustice to the many early writers for not mentioning them all. But it is necessary to limit the discussion to the books that have become best known. The next book, *Traité d'Économie Politique* (Treatise on Political Economy) (1803) by Jean-Baptiste Say, a French economist, is probably not so well known as one of the ideas contained therein. The idea has come to be known as Say's law. In simple terms Say's law can be interpreted to mean that supply creates its own demand. Say put forth this idea in response to those who argued that if a nation experienced economic growth there would eventually come a "general glut" of goods on the market that could not be sold as people reached a level of total satiation. The concern was that, when the general glut of goods appeared, not everyone who wanted to work would be able to find a job, leading to a permanent state of unemployment.

David Ricardo's *Principle of Political Economy* (1815) is often compared to Adam Smith's *Wealth of Nations*. The consensus seems to be that as an exercise in rigorous economic reasoning Ricardo's *Principles* is superior, but from the standpoint of breadth of coverage and insights into the workings of society, Smith is still the master. Ricardo is probably best known for his work on the pricing of factors of production, particularly on land rent, and for providing an

---

[1] See, for example, Thomas Sowell, *Classical Economics Reconsidered* (Princeton, N.J.: Princeton University Press, 1974); D. P. O'Brien, *The Classical Economists* (Oxford: Clarendon Press, 1975); and Mark Blaug, *Economic Theory in Retrospect* (Cambridge: Cambridge University Press, 1978). For an entertaining book on the lives and times of the classical economists, see Robert L. Heilbroner, *The Worldly Philosophers* (New York: Simon & Schuster, 1972).

economic basis for trade between two nations even when one of the countries is more productive than the other in all areas of production. The latter idea will be explained in Chapter 15 on international trade.

John Stuart Mill's two-volume work, also entitled *Principles of Political Economy* (1848), represents another milestone in early economic thought. The purpose of the book, as Mill stated in the preface, was to update *The Wealth of Nations,* "adapted to the more extended knowledge and improved ideas of the present age." Clearly Mill underestimated his accomplishment. Over 50 years later, the book was still the dominant textbook in introductory economics courses in both British and American universities. If one were to rank the books that most shaped early economic thought, Smith's *Wealth of Nations,* Ricardo's *Principles,* and Mill's *Principles* would be high on most lists.

It would not be correct to give the impression, however, that the books mentioned so far were the only things written by these famous men. Smith, for example, already had become well known before *The Wealth of Nations* for his book *The Theory of Moral Sentiments* (1759). It also should be recognized that the evolution of economic thought was made possible by the work of a large number of writers—many quite well known at least to economists. A partial list of this group would include David Hume, who is not generally considered a classical economist but whose works had a large impact on the thinking of Adam Smith; James Mill, the father of J. S. Mill; Henry Thornton, a leading figure in early monetary theory; John Cairnes, a disciple of Mill and often considered the last of the classical economists; along with the likes of Samuel Bailey; Jeremy Bentham; John Hobson; the Earl of Lauderdale; John McCulloch; Sir William Petty; Nassau Senior; Simonde de Sismondi; Sir James Stewart; Robert Torrens; and Sir Robert West.

Gradually the classical school of thought gave way during the last half of the 19th century to a new school that has come to be known as neoclassical economics. Risking the danger of oversimplifying, one might say that the primary emphasis of the classical school was on macroeconomics, including the issues of economic growth, unemployment, control of the money supply and prices, overpopulation, taxation, and international trade, along with the determination of wages and the prices of other resources, mainly land. The neoclassical school focused more on microeconomics. Neoclassical writers made significant advances in the theory of consumer behavior, the theory of the firm, and the theory of markets, with more emphasis on relative prices as opposed to the absolute level of prices. It is probably not coincidental that neoclassical writers developed the idea of the marginal or extra unit as opposed to the total or average measures. The coming of neoclassical thought is sometimes referred to as the "marginalist revolution." Stanley Jevon's *The Theory of Political Economy* (1871) marks the beginning of the new marginal analysis as well as the extensive use of mathematics. However, A. A. Cournot's *Recherches* (1838) was the first to develop the theory of the firm in mathematical terms. Walras's *Elements* (1874) also was highly mathematical in its approach.

While it would not be correct to include Karl Marx in either the classical or neoclassical school, his book *Das Kapital* (1867), which provides the basis for the Communist ideology, looms large, not only in the last half of the 19th century, but also in present-day thought, at least in the Communist nations. Later in this chapter some of the mainstreams of Marxist thought are presented.

As neoclassical theory developed, writers strove to make greater applications of economics to the everyday problems and decisions of individuals. P. H. Wicksteed's *The Common Sense of Political Economy* (1870) is a good example of these attempts. His discussion of how much train schedules could be speeded up by the shortening of family prayers, or how the value of a mother-in-law could be measured by how high a cliff one would dive off to save her, provide examples of economics in practice.

Another giant among neoclassical works is Alfred Marshall's *Principles of Economics* (1890). From the standpoint of longevity and influence, this book rivals Smith's *Wealth of Nations* and Mill's *Principles*. Indeed, Marshall may be regarded as the father of modern economics. The concepts of demand and supply presented in Chapter 2, for example, were more fully developed by him. Again, in the neoclassical tradition, Marshall's book is primarily micro in nature.

MERCANTILISM

At the time Adam Smith's *Wealth of Nations* appeared, mercantilism was the dominant mode of thinking, which in turn influenced much of government policy. *The Wealth of Nations* was written as an attack upon mercantilism. Thus, in order to understand the classical arguments, it is necessary to have some knowledge of mercantilistic thought.

One main tenet of mercantilist thought was that a nation's wealth depended primarily on the amount of gold or bullion that a nation could accumulate. Wealth was associated with gold. One method of accumulating more gold, in addition to expropriating it from the New World, was to sell more goods to other countries than were bought from them. Thus, government policies were designed to encourage exports, particularly manufactured goods, and discourage imports. Colonization policies provided expanded markets for manufactured goods as well as jobs for government administrators. The Corn Laws, which placed taxes on the imports of agricultural products, reduced imports and maintained favorable prices for large landowners. Labor unions were outlawed as conspiracies under the Combination Laws; their intended effect was to keep wages low so that British goods would have an advantage in the world market.

Whether the mercantilists really believed that their policies which facilitated the accumulation of gold were in the best interest of British society is something we cannot answer. We can be sure, however, that mercantilist policies enhanced the power and wealth of government, business interests, and large landowners at the expense of the great mass of poor people. This is not to say that the wealthy lacked social conscience, but it was somewhat warped, at least by present Western standards. The rich defended their lavish standard of living in the midst of extreme poverty by arguing that it was better for them to spend their money on luxury goods rather than give it to the poor. Giving money to the poor would just lead to idleness, which in turn would lead to all sorts of depravity. By producing luxuries for the rich, the poor would earn a little money and be kept busy.

It is interesting to note also that some of the mercantilists' ideas and policies contradicted each other. They wanted more gold and lower prices at home. But, as will be explained later, an increase in gold will lead to higher prices, which in turn will discourage exports. In fairness to the mercantilists, it should be pointed out that Britain imported a considerable amount of goods from the East Indies and the Baltic states but sold little in return to them. Hence, there was a continual concern over obtaining sufficient gold to pay for these imports. In such cases, it would have been more convincing to use this reason in their arguments rather than the one that viewed gold as good for its own sake.

THE WEALTH OF NATIONS

As mentioned, Adam Smith's *Wealth of Nations* was in part an attack on mercantilist ideas and government policies. Smith argued that it was the real output of goods and services that determined the true wealth of nations rather than the amount of money or gold that a country was able to produce or accumulate. To Adam Smith and the other classical economists, money was a "veil." If removed, it would reveal the true wealth of a country—the flow of real goods and services. This is not to say that they viewed money as unimportant. They recognized the value of money as a medium of exchange, and they also were aware of the relationship between the quantity of money in existence and the price level. But the classical argument is in sharp contrast to mercantilist thought, which viewed money as an end in itself.

Smith and the other classicists stressed the creation of new wealth rather than its transfer between people and nations. In mercantilist doctrine, there was conflict between classes and nations; what one class or nation gained, the other lost. The classicists instead emphasized the existence of harmony between social classes and nations, while at the same time recognizing areas of conflict. In matters of commerce, according to classical thought, both trading partners gained rather than having one gainer and one loser.

In *The Wealth of Nations* and later classical writings there is a genuine concern for poor people, and much emphasis is placed on bettering their lot. Smith argued that no nation can flourish if a greater part of the people is poor and impoverished. The classical economists condemned slavery on both moral and economic grounds. In the latter area they argued that slavery's inherent weakness was the lack of incentives for the workers. Ricardo worked for the repeal of the Corn Laws, which kept prices of food artificially high. These laws were especially hard on poor people. The classical economists also crusaded for the repeal of the Combination Laws, which outlawed labor unions. Some favored progressive taxation, in which the rich would pay a larger percent of their income as taxes than would the poor. The classicists also favored publicly funded education so that the children of poor families would have a better chance to break out of the cycle of poverty.

LAISSEZ-FAIRE

The term *laissez-faire* has come to be associated with the classical economists. It is defined as a policy whereby the government exercises minimum control over industry and trade. The classical economists preferred to allow competition rather than have government regulate the economy. They of course saw the necessity of a central government to enforce a system of laws, to provide for the national defense, and to supply certain public goods such as highways. While they were not pacifists, the classicists viewed wars as popularly supported adventures. They were not so naive as to believe that all wars were thrust upon the people by leaders seeking power and glory. Smith, for example, advocated a negotiated peace with America in 1776. The classical economists argued also that wars should be financed by current taxes rather than borrowing so that the people would know immediately the full economic cost of war and would therefore be less inclined to enter into armed conflict. Indeed, in all areas of government spending they favored a balanced budget, or pay-as-you-go approach.

To support the concept of laissez-faire, Adam Smith developed the idea of the "invisible hand." Here Smith argued from the powerful motive of self-interest. It is not to the benevolence of the baker that we owe our bread, he argued, but rather to the baker's self-interest. The gist of Smith's argument is that businesspeople will produce those goods that provide them with the greatest rewards. But the goods that are most profitable to produce are those goods most desired by society, else they would not be so high priced and profitable. Thus Smith argued that an economy is capable of regulating itself by this "invisible hand"; there is no need for the government to intervene. Indeed, Smith and the other classical economists maintained that government intervention promoted waste and inefficiency while supporting the vested interests of the wealthy and privileged classes.

It should also be noted that Smith and the later classical writers were as critical of private monopolies as they were of government. They interpreted monopoly very broadly as any case where a seller could influence the price of the product sold. They saw monopoly as being directed against the public good, resulting in higher prices for goods and services and distortions in the mix of goods that would be produced under a system of competition. In general, the classicists were very distrustful of both big business and big government.

It has been argued that the idea of laissez-faire grew out of a society characterized by laissez-faire. But this is not correct. The idea grew out of a society greatly influenced by both big government and private monopoly. In reality, it was an idea designed to take away their privilege and power.

While the concept of laissez-faire has been used primarily to explain how an economy is capable of allocating resources to promote the public good without the intervention of government, the idea can also be extended to the problem of unemployment. Unemployment was a problem in classical times, and the classical economists were both aware of and concerned about its existence. For the most part, the classical economists saw unemployment coming from an overproduction of specific goods rather than a general overproduction of all goods, although Ricardo thought that new technology might produce general unemployment. At any rate, the classical writers did not believe that depressions would be permanent. They argued that an economy contained mechanisms which, given time to work, would restore full employment. These mechanisms were flexible interest rates, wages, and prices.

To see the classical argument in more detail, consider a situation where there is a reduction in investment spending, which might occur because of a less optimistic attitude among businesspeople regarding future business conditions. The sudden reduction in investment would cause a surplus of funds in the so-called money market. As a result, there would be downward pressure on the interest rate, just as there is for the price of any good when a surplus exists. The decrease in the interest rate would counteract the pessimistic attitude of businesspeople by making it more profitable to invest. Also, because of the lower interest rate consumers would find it less costly to borrow funds for large purchases, which in turn would have the effect of stimulating their spending on such items. Thus the classical economists argued that the likely decrease in interest rates resulting from the decrease in investment spending would set up counteracting forces to stimulate spending and restore full employment.

The classical economists used similar reasoning with regard to wages and prices. If unemployment appeared in the labor market, there would be a tendency for wages to fall as workers competed for the available jobs. The reduction in wages would in turn serve as an incentive for employers to hire more labor and for some people to drop out of the labor market, thereby lowering unemployment. The market for goods and services would behave similarly. The resulting surplus of unsold investment and consumer goods would result in downward pressure on these prices, restoring the purchasing power of lower wages and giving investors and consumers an incentive to step up their purchases, again stimulating the economy. Thus the classical economists argued that an economy, if left alone, would return to a state of full employment in the event of temporary downturns in economic activity. One might call this the laissez-faire solution to unemployment.

SAY'S LAW

The classical economists were concerned with two kinds of unemployment: (1) that which occurs because of temporary overproduction in specific industries and (2) that resulting from a general overproduction of nearly all goods and services, commonly referred to as a general glut. The early classical writers admitted the possibility of the first type of unemployment but argued against the likelihood of the second. Actually, the first hint of what has come to be known as Say's law can be found even before *The Wealth of Nations* in the work of an early French economist, Mercier de al Rivière, a physiocrat. (The physiocrats argued that the only true net increase in wealth came from the soil; all other activities just passed the wealth around.) Rivière in his book *L'order naturel* (1767) pointed out that the value of all things sold must be equal to the value of all things bought. There are two ways of interpreting this idea. One interpretation is that it's simply a definition—the value of sales must be equal to the value of purchases. But it is clear from Rivière's book that he had something more profound in mind. The second interpretation is that the proceeds from sales provide the wherewithal to engage in purchases. Adam Smith, also writing before Say, developed the idea a little further. Smith argued that money did not have any value in and of itself but was only useful as a means of purchasing goods and services. Therefore, he argued, when people receive money from the production of goods and services, they will almost immediately turn around and spend the money on either the same things or on other goods. Thus the money earned from production (supply) provides the means to buy (demand). It is this interpretation that has given rise to the popular phrase used to describe Say's law—"Supply creates its own demand."

The crucial element of this argument is that money is valuable only as a medium of exchange. This being the case, there is no reason to hold on to money that is earned other than to make purchases. James Mill, also writing before Say, made a similar argument. Say in his book was openly contemptuous of the earlier writers who put forth essentially the same argument he expanded upon. But for some reason, perhaps because Say made the argument more widely known and precipitated much controversy, it came to be associated with him. At the time of Say's book there was much popular concern over whether a growing economy would eventually reach a state of general glut and as a consequence be unable to provide employment for a rising population.

Some of the disagreement over Say's law among the classical economists probably came from different interpretations of the law itself. Some writers appeared to give it the first of the two interpretations mentioned above, namely that the value of purchases equals the value of sales. There can be no disagreement over this interpretation, because it is always true. Later this idea came to be known as Say's Identity. It was over the second interpretation that the main disagreement arose: Will the payments made to resource owners, mainly labor in those days, enable them to buy all that is produced, thereby preventing a general glut of goods and services? Even here the classical writers had trouble defining a common ground. When they wrote about glut, some referred to the question of whether it would be general or particular, that is, in specific industries. Others posed the question of whether the glut would be permanent or temporary. Virtually all classical writers rejected the idea that a general glut could be permanent. The question that received the greatest attention was whether there could be a temporary general glut so that there would be widespread unemployment. This would be much worse than a glut in particular industries. If Say's law were valid, an economy should not experience even a temporary general glut.

The controversy and different interpretations of Say's law prevailed for over 30 years. In 1844, J.S . Mill, in his *Essays on Some Unsettled Questions of Political Economy,* put his finger on the key issue. In Mill's words, "Although he who sells, really sells only to buy, he need not buy at the same moment when he sells; and he does not therefore necessarily add to the immediate demand for one commodity when he adds to the supply of another." With these words J. S. Mill explained how it would be possible for at least a temporary general glut to occur, thereby leading to widespread unemployment. People may earn money to spend it, but if they grow apprehensive of the future, they may not spend it right away. Thus Say's law was shown to be invalid. This is not to say that the classical economists also rejected the idea of a self-correcting economy that would restore full employment after a time, as explained in the preceding section.

THE QUANTITY THEORY OF MONEY

The role of money in an economy occupied a high position in the classical economists' economic agenda. In the classical school, money in one sense is unimportant but in another sense very important. Recall that Adam Smith and the later classical writers rejected the mercantilist idea that money or gold was wealth, arguing instead that the real wealth of a nation is its output of goods and services. Money to the classicists was only a veil. In this sense it was unimportant. But they did recognize the importance of money in another sense: as a medium of exchange to facilitate trade and as a determinant of the general level of prices. Later the classicists recognized that money may be demanded as a precaution against unknown future adversity. Essentially this was J. S. Mill's argument for rejecting Say's law. People may desire to hold money for various reasons rather than spending it as soon as it is earned. Actually, Henry Thornton in his book *Paper Credit of Great Britain* (1802) pointed out much earlier that money may be hoarded during a period of alarm. As is now evident, this precautionary motive for holding money is intimately related to Say's law and the question of unemployment.

The main thread of classical monetary theory was, however, the *quantity theory of money*. The basic idea of the quantity theory is that, given the level of real output, the general level of prices moves in the same direction as the quantity of money. Contrary to what some more recent writers have asserted, the classical economists did not argue, however, that the price level is rigidly linked to the quantity of money. Classical writers, as well as neoclassical and modern economic literature dealing with the quantity theory, did not argue that a doubling of money will lead exactly to a doubling of prices. The classical writers did argue that the link between money and prices is relatively stable over the long run but that varying relationships can exist in short-run situations. For example, if prices are rising, people may attempt to reduce their preference for holding money in relation to their income. Or if unemployment threatens, they may try to increase their stock of money again in relation to their income. A more detailed explanation of the quantity theory and how prices are linked to money is presented in Chapter 10.

The interest of the classical economists in the quantity theory stemmed primarily from their concern over inflation. The classicists were particularly concerned that the use of paper money rather than gold could lead to inflation. They also pointed out the difference in outcomes of high versus increasing prices or low versus declining prices. They argued, for example, that the absolute level of prices, high or low, will not influence the rate of interest. In other words, the interest rate should be the same regardless of whether prices are high or low. But the interest rate will increase during periods of rising prices and decline during periods of falling prices. There was also a recognition that prices and wages may not be perfectly flexible. Thornton argued, for example, that in the event of a fall in prices, "probably with no correspondent fall in the rate of wages," there will be an increase in unemployment. And other writers acknowledged that monetary changes can lead to changes in output and employment, which implies less than perfect flexibility of prices.

TAXES AND THE NATIONAL DEBT

Lest with the current concern over high taxes and the national debt we think that we live in unusual times, it is instructive to see that the classical economists were also concerned over these issues. Even though the classical economists preferred a minimum of government, they recognized the necessity of government and the problems of financing it. Indeed Ricardo went so far as to say that economics is useful only when "it directs Government to right measures of taxation." This view probably stemmed from the fact that he regarded laissez-faire as the proper policy (or lack of it) elsewhere in the economy.

The classical economists were very much against deficit spending for a number of reasons. For one thing, they felt that if taxpayers did not have to pay for wars with current taxes they would be more inclined to enter into military action. If people saw their taxes rising immediately with a military buildup, they would more likely decide the cost was not worth the returns. There is evidence from classical literature that the requirement of pay-as-you-go financing of government would serve as a brake on government spending in general. It is also true that during the classical period foreigners held a substantial amount of the bonds issued by the British government. The necessity of paying off these bonds would therefore transfer wealth from Britain to other countries. A third reason for arguing against deficit financing was that the economy would suffer distortions and disincentive effects when taxes were raised to pay off the debt. This argument has resurfaced in recent years and will be discussed in more detail in Chapter 8. The classical economists in general and Ricardo in particular opposed deficit spending on something close to moral grounds, arguing that the practice "tends to make us less thrifty." Ricardo also recognized that government bonds outstanding are equivalent to taxes owed, raising the question, What is the difference if a man leaves an estate to an heir charged with a given tax or leaves a smaller fortune free of taxes? By this question, he implied that there is no difference.

While the classical economists generally favored a balanced budget, there are some hints of disagreement on this issue. The Earl of Lauderdale, for example, appears to have been the first to make the argument that internally held public debt is something the people owe to themselves. He pointed out that a transfer of money from taxpayers to bondholders does not diminish the collective wealth of the whole. He also rejected the typical classical analogies between private and public debt. Lauderdale's argument was used extensively by Keynesians in the 20th century in defense of deficit financing, and it still exists today. Lauderdale also defended the idea of a government-held sinking fund that would be used to retire the debt. Smith and Ricardo had denounced such a fund as illusory, arguing that it would just be a temptation to increase government spending. The idea of the sinking fund is that, in years when a government accumulates a surplus, this money would be invested by the government, with the interest and principal used to retire the public debt. Lauderdale argued that such a practice would be good for the country because it would increase investment and thereby contribute to the growth of the economy. Lauderdale's critics pointed out, however, that such investment would come from forced rather than voluntary saving and therefore questioned whether it was something that would benefit the people. And even Lauderdale was highly skeptical that a sinking fund would ever be established in practice.

THE MALTHUSIAN DOCTRINE

Adam Smith's *Wealth of Nations* saw the future in a rather optimistic light. Smith argued that the division of labor, which he defined very broadly as including all manner of technological improvements, would lead to increased per capita output and a growing standard of living for the people. This line of thought was in harmony with the general philosophical views of the times, which saw the eventual perfectibility of society. Malthus's ideas were in sharp contrast to the notion that the world would get better.

In essence, the Malthusian doctrine states that population growth will inevitably outrun any growth in food supplies, leaving mankind in a desperate state of poverty and hunger. Malthus went on to argue that there is either a "preventive" or a "positive" check on population at all times. By the preventive check Malthus had in mind the moral restraint of people, which may counteract the strong desire to reproduce. However, Malthus viewed mankind, especially the masses, as being rather indolent, and he felt that the desire to reproduce would outweigh the brake of moral restraint. If there were a moral restraint, he argued, it would most likely stem from a fear of starvation. Among the positive checks on population Malthus included all manner of vice, disease, and pestilence. And if these checks didn't do the trick, there was always the ultimate check of food shortages and famine.

Probing deeper into his argument, Malthus postulated that population would grow geometrically, or at a compound rate, while food production would only grow arithmetically. In other words, population growth would take the form of the progression 1 2 4 8 16 32 64 . . . , while food production increased as 1 2 3 4 5 6 7. . . . It is easy to see or, as Malthus said, even "a slight acquaintance with numbers will show," that even a small number growing at a compound rate will overwhelm a large number growing at an arithmetic rate. Given these assumed rates of growth, Malthus, of course, was right. But he offered no evidence that this is actually how population and food do grow. Surprisingly, his numbers were accepted as "gospel" (recall that he was a preacher!). No one bothered to compute, as did an American physicist at a later date, that if the human race had started with one couple living in 10,000 B.C. and had grown at a modest rate of 1 percent per year (biologically humans can increase at a maximum rate of about 5 percent per year), the earth would now be a ball of flesh several thousand light years in diameter and expanding outward faster than the speed of light. Never in history has there been a growth of any population of the magnitude feared by Malthus. Perhaps the willingness of the public to accept Malthus's numbers at that time was because of a rapid spurt in British population growth during the Industrial Revolution. However, there is little evidence that Malthus made much use of the British population census.

To strengthen his argument, Malthus brought in the now well-known "law of diminishing returns." Rigorously defined, it states that, as more and more of a variable input is added to one or more fixed inputs, beyond some point the extra output forthcoming from each additional unit of the variable input will become less and less. In Malthus's scheme, land was the main fixed input and population or labor the main variable input. Malthus did use the law rather loosely, however. He argued, for example, that man-made capital and technical improvements could not offset the limits on production set by natural resources. But it is not evident that the production of new technology is subject to the law of diminishing returns, because no one can prove that the potential stock of knowledge is finite.

Malthus went on to lay out the implications of his theory. For one thing, he argued that all deliberate attempts to improve the living conditions of the poor by government welfare programs will end in failure. Such programs just remove the positive checks to population increase, freeing people temporarily from bearing the consequences of their own improvidence, i.e., the urge to reproduce. Not only were such ideas harsh, but Malthus chose the most biting language he could muster, almost to the point of deliberately offending the sensitive reader.

Luckily for the human race, Malthus was wrong. His population theory is not taken seriously anymore, by professional demographers at least. There probably are some who argue that Malthus was right in reference to the less developed countries and that it will only be a matter of time before all countries are driven down to a level of subsistence. However, if Malthus's theory is correct, we should observe a high rate of population growth in the rich nations, due to a lack of positive restraints, and a low rate of population growth in the poor countries, because of the arithmetic nature of the growth in food production. In fact, we observe just the opposite.

The Malthusian doctrine became widely known and gained many believers during the 19th century. Indeed, economics became known as the "dismal science" because of Malthus's dire predictions. However, most present-day economists and demographers are not nearly as pessimistic about the future as were Malthus and his followers.

RICARDIAN RENT

As defined by Ricardo, "rent is that portion of the produce of the earth which is paid to the landlord for the use of the original and indestructible properties of the soil." Later it was modified to include payment, not only for the original properties, but for any permanent improvements. Ricardo and other classical writers of the time utilized the idea of differential land quality to illustrate why rent existed. The poorest land cultivated at any given time would be that whose yield just covered the cost of the labor and capital with nothing left over for rent. All land of superior quality which employed the same amount of capital and labor would by definition yield a greater output. The difference in the output of the good land over the poor land would be the rent earned by the good land.

Actually it is not necessary to have varying-quality land to have rent; all that is required is diminishing returns to capital and labor. Consider the case in which it pays the landlord to hire, say, three workers to cultivate a given portion of land. Because of diminishing returns, the extra output contributed by the first worker will exceed that of the second, and the extra output of the second will exceed that of the third. If the extra output of the third worker just covers the wage of that worker, the landlord earns zero rent on the portion of the land cultivated by that worker. But if all workers are paid the same wage, the first two workers will produce more than their wage; the difference between what they produce and what they are paid is rent to land.

In Ricardo's analysis, land is assumed to be fixed in quantity and to have no alternative use other than agriculture. This being the case, it follows that the amount of rent is determined by the price of the product. As Ricardo put it, "corn is not high because a rent is paid, but rent is paid because corn is high." Ricardo made good use of this conclusion to argue against the Corn Laws, which restricted the import of wheat and increased the domestic price of wheat. Higher prices of agricultural products result in higher rents for landlords— money that they obtain without any effort on their part. Thus Ricardo was able to show that the effect of the Corn Laws was to enrich landlords. Another policy implication of Ricardian rent is that the earnings from land can be taxed without reducing the production of agricultural products or distorting the output mix of the country.

The notion that rent is unearned income precipitated other policy recommendations as well. Henry George advocated a "single tax" on land rent to finance the government. After Ricardo's book was published, it was clearly "open season" on landlords. Also the Fabian Socialists spearheaded by George Bernard Shaw were able to enlist popular support in their efforts to establish a socialist state because of widespread moral indignation over this unearned income. In a socialist state the government owns the land and reaps the "unearned increment." Even today in Britain, so-called unearned income from land or capital is taxed at a higher rate than labor earnings, or even the winnings from lotteries.

The later work of John Stuart Mill in one sense broadened Ricardo's rent theory and in another sense narrowed it. Mill broadened the theory by recognizing that rent can accrue outside of agriculture as well, because of special advantages held by particular firms. These advantages may be patents, "superior talents for business," or other economic advantages, whether natural or acquired. Such advantages allow some firms to produce a product more cheaply than other firms, thereby earning rent on the firms' so-called fixed factors. But Mill also was the first to make it clear that a given parcel of land can have several alternative uses. (Adam Smith touched on this point but did not follow it through.) And Mill further recognized that the rent earned by this parcel of land in one use is a cost that must be paid when the land is used to produce another product. Now rent is defined as the excess of land's earnings in a given use over what it would earn in its next-best alternative use. Rent thus becomes a much smaller sum than was envisaged by Ricardo; so in this sense Mill narrowed Ricardian rent.

The existence of rent also depends on whether one is talking about firms or the industry, or whether one is talking about the short run or long run. For the firm, the use of a parcel of land or some other fixed factor to produce a specific product will have an opportunity cost, because the factor could be used to produce some other product or could be used by another firm. Hence, for the firm, at least part of the earnings of land or some other fixed factor are a cost, not rent. For the industry, however, such as all of agriculture, the earnings of land are still rent, assuming there are no good alternative uses at least for the bulk of all agricultural land. By the same token, a factor of production might not have an alternative use in the short run and thereby earn rent, but in the long run it might deteriorate, as would be true for nonland inputs, and need to be replaced. Thus what might be viewed as rent in the short run becomes a cost in the long run in order to keep the input intact, or to keep it from moving to other uses. While Ricardian rent is still a valid concept under the conditions set out by Ricardo, an input fixed in quantity with no alternative uses, it does not hold as high a position on the agenda of modern economics as in classical times, probably because of the recognition that most factors have alternative uses and because of the necessity of maintaining or replacing fixed inputs in the long run.

CLASSICAL VALUE THEORY

One of the questions that the classical economists wrestled with was, What determines the value or price of an object? Why do some things fetch a high price, while others sell for a small sum? This question occupied the attention of the classical economists during the entire classical era. Adam Smith began the analysis with an example of a primitive society where land is free and labor the only scarce, hence valuable, input. He reasoned that in such a society of hunters, if it takes twice as much labor to catch a beaver as to kill a deer, then one beaver will exchange for two deer. At first glance this example appears to depict a labor theory of value whereby the value of an object is determined by the amount of labor expended to produce it. But it would be more correct to call Smith's idea a cost-of-production theory of value. The value of an object is determined by the cost of producing it; since beaver cost twice as much to produce as deer, they sell for twice as much. He makes clear the distinction between a labor theory and a cost-of-production theory by arguing that the value of a commodity is the sum of the normal amounts paid to all resources used in making it. Some preclassical writers had suggested something close to a labor theory of value, but Smith pointed out that this theory would be valid only in the special and artificial conditions of an "early and rude state of society."

It has been pointed out by later writers that Smith's argument represents a *measure* of the cost of production rather than a *theory* of value because he did not explain how resources or inputs obtain their value. In a sense, he explained prices by prices. In fairness to Adam Smith, it should be pointed out that he was mainly interested in determining long-run values, or prices under conditions of constant costs, that is, where the supply curve is perfectly horizontal. Under these conditions, the value of an object is determined entirely by the cost of production or supply, while the quantity sold is determined by demand. Of course Smith still did not have an apparatus to determine short-run prices or prices when costs are not constant. For this we have to turn to supply and demand.

There was considerable disagreement among the classical economists regarding the importance of supply and demand in the determination of value. J. S. Mill treated cost of production and supply and demand as two separate theories, saying that supply and demand determine prices where the cost of production is inoperative. Now we know that supply is determined from the cost of production and that both supply and demand determine value. Part of the early controversy probably stemmed from different writers giving different meanings to the same words. To Ricardo and J. S. Mill, supply and demand meant quantities bought and sold. Malthus in his *Principles* book defined supply and demand as we do nowadays—as schedules or relationship between price and quantity rather than fixed amounts. He was the first to distinguish between the "extent" (quantity) of demand and the "intensity" of demand (position of the demand curve). Unfortunately, J. S. Mill's popular *Principles* text overshadowed the insights of Malthus on supply and demand for several decades. They were later developed by neoclassical writers.

MARX AND THE LABOR THEORY OF VALUE

Although Karl Marx is not generally considered to have been a classical economist, he did draw upon and modify many classical ideas. And even if one disagrees with Marxist or communist ideology, it is important to be somewhat familiar with the source of these ideas. Unlike most economic writers both before and after him, Marx in his book *Das Kapital* (1876) tried to incorporate historical, sociological, and economic forces in a single theoretical framework. Marx was highly critical of the classical economists for being too specialized, referring to them as those "vulgar economists."

In addressing the age-old question of what determines value, Marx argued that commodities are exchanged in proportion to the labor utilized in production. This is the labor theory of value. The more labor is embodied in a good, the higher its value. Recall that this is the same basic idea as that presented in Adam Smith's deer and beaver example, except that Marx deals with an economy having both labor and capital. In Marx's world, capital is indirect labor.

Marx also argued that profit is "surplus value" produced by labor. That is, laborers produce a larger value for their employers than they receive as wages. He did not argue, however, that this condition stems from the heartlessness of employers who have the power to determine wages and decide to set wages at a subsistence level. Quite the contrary, Marx asserted: Because capital has come into the hands of a relative few, labor has become a commodity traded on the market as any other, at a price determined by the labor time required to produce it. In other words, the price of labor (wage) is equal to the labor time necessary to produce the wage goods that go to maintain labor. The "reserve army of the unemployed" and competition in the labor market maintain the wage at the subsistence level. Since labor is able to produce more than the cost of its subsistence, the remainder goes to employers as surplus value. To Marx, surplus value is unpaid labor, meaning that employers receive the excess of sales over wages as unearned income. In the Marxist framework, employers pay for the exchange value of labor but receive its use value, which is greater. Notice that Marx had to have the labor theory of value in order to obtain surplus value; the two go together. But it was the latter that Marx was most interested in, as are his present-day followers.

Marx's argument, however, does not stand up under empirical scrutiny, nor is it logically sound. Marx asserted that surplus value per worker is the same in every industry. This is consistent with the labor theory of value, which states that products of equal quantities of labor will sell for equal quantities of money. But it is a known fact that capital per worker varies between industries. If profits, or surplus value per worker, are the same across industries, it follows that the rate of profit per unit of capital is smaller the larger the amount of capital per worker. In other words, the higher the degree of mechanization, the lower the rate of profit. This implies that employers have an incentive to discard machines in order to increase profits—just the opposite of what is observed in capitalist economies. Thus Marx's theory is not empirically verified.

Marx's argument also involves a basic contradiction. If competition equalizes wages between industries, it should also equalize the rate of profit on capital. But if the rate of profit on capital is the same between industries with different capital/labor ratios, there cannot be equal rates of surplus value per worker between industries, and the prices of products produced in various industries cannot correspond to the amount of labor embodied; this result contradicts the labor theory of value. This paradox came to be known as the "great contradiction." Marx saw the contradiction in his argument and attempted to correct it in the third volume of *Das Kapital,* where he argued that, although surplus value is produced in proportion to the labor employed, it is distributed in proportion to the amount of capital employed. But he still ended up arguing that all surplus value is created by labor and that all workers generate the same surplus value regardless of the capital/labor ratio.

In spite of its shortcomings, Marxists still cling to the labor theory of value whereby capitalists get a part of the total product as profits without working.

Perhaps the basic question is, Are profits really unearned income? Business people who work 50 to 60 hours per week while risking their own and other people's money to keep a business running will tell you that any theory which says they do not earn their money just does not depict reality. In chapter 6 of the companion micro text it is shown that most of what has come to be called profits is really the opportunity cost of capital and labor contributed by the owners of firms. And what profits remain, if any, are primarily the result of imperfect knowledge and the inability to forecast the future with certainty.

MAIN POINTS OF CHAPTER 5

1. The era of classical economics is generally considered to extend from about 1776 to the 1870s.

2. Adam Smith's *Wealth of Nations* is acknowledged to be the first major work in economics. Other important classical writers include Thomas Malthus, Jean-Baptiste Say, David Ricardo, John Stuart Mill, James Mill, Henry Thornton, and John Cairnes.

3. **Classical economics** evolved as a counter to mercantilist thought, which equated wealth with gold. Mercantilist policies also favored an alliance between government and large business firms.

4. To Adam Smith and later classical economists, wealth consists of the real output of goods and services. The classicists emphasized the production of new wealth—i.e., economic growth—while the mercantilists focused on its transfer between people; what one country gained, another lost. The classicists were particularly concerned about bettering the lot of poor people.

5. The classical economists generally favored a policy of **laissez-faire,** which is to minimize the influence of government in the economy.

6. In the classical view, resources were allocated to their highest-value user by the powerful motive of self-interest. Goods and services that are highly sought after will fetch high prices, which in turn will provide an incentive for producers to supply more of these items and less of other things. Resources will be allocated as though guided by some "invisible hand."

7. In the event of unemployment, market forces will cause reductions in wages, interest rates, and prices, thereby stimulating businesspeople and consumers to increase their spending, which in turn should restore full employment.

8. According to **Say's law,** supply creates its own demand. Although the classicists denied the possibility of a "general glut" of all goods over the long run, they admitted the possibility of short-term reduction in spending and temporary periods of unemployment.

9. While **Say's Identity,** which says that the value of sales must equal the value of purchases, was never open to serious question, J. S. Mill pointed out that people could at times opt not to spend all their earnings immediately, a decision leading to unsold goods and unemployment. He therefore showed how Say's law need not be valid.

10. To the classical economists, money was a "veil" and not the true determinant of wealth, but the quantity of money in existence nevertheless determined the rate of inflation and the level of prices. This idea came to be known as the **quantity theory of money.** The classical economists were more concerned about inflation than unemployment, and the quantity theory became their main tool of analysis.

11. The classical economists favored a balanced budget and sought ways to reduce the national debt, one of which they saw as the establishment of a sinking fund to retire the national debt.

12. According to Thomas Malthus, population grows geometrically while food supplies

grow arithmetically. He argued, therefore, that sooner or later famine will overtake all societies unless population growth is checked by disease or other natural disasters. While Malthus's argument has been for the most part rejected by economists, this pessimistic attitude about the future of mankind on the part of Malthus and later writers led economics to become known as the "dismal science."

13. **Rent** as defined by Ricardo is that portion of the produce of the earth which is paid to the landlord for the use of the original and indestructible properties of the soil. If land is fixed in quantity and has no alternative uses other than agriculture, the amount of rent will depend on the price of the product, not vice versa. Henry George and many later writers viewed rent as "unearned income" and advocated the confiscation of rent through taxation. John Stuart Mill pointed out, however, that from the standpoint of individual landowners land and other fixed inputs usually have several alternative uses, particularly in the long run.

14. The classical economists for many years wrestled with the problem of what determines the value or price of an object. Adam Smith thought it was determined by the cost of production. Thomas Malthus, in his *Principles,* first developed the concepts of demand and supply curves, but his ideas in this area remained dormant until they were later rediscovered by neoclassical economists.

15. Karl Marx writing in *Das Kapital* developed the **labor theory of value.** Marx argued that goods were valued in proportion to the labor time required in their production; the greater the labor time, the higher their prices. Marx argued as well that labor's price, or wage, would be equal to the time required to produce and maintain it—i.e., wages would be equal to the subsistence level of labor. Because labor was able to produce more than its subsistence, Marx argued, the excess was received by employers or capitalists as unearned income, or "surplus value."

16. Marx's labor theory of value implied that profits would be lower in capital-intensive industries, which is not the case. In the third volume of *Das Kapital,* Marx changed his view slightly and argued that surplus value is produced in proportion to the labor employed but distributed among capitalists in proportion to the amount of capital employed. For the most part, Marx's labor theory of value has been rejected by the mainstream of economic thought. Nowadays few argue that profits are unearned income.

QUESTIONS FOR THOUGHT AND DISCUSSION

1. Contrast the views of Adam Smith and the other classical economists with the earlier mercantilist traditions.

2. *a.* "It is not to the benevolence of the baker that we owe our bread, but rather to his self interest." Who said this, and what is the intended meaning?
   b. What did Adam Smith mean by the "invisible hand"?

3. According to the classical economists, a market economy should never experience unemployment. True or false? Explain.

4. *a.* What is Say's Identity, and how does it differ from Say's law?
   b. Was Say's law accepted by all classical economists? Elaborate.

5. The classical economists referred to money as a "veil." What did they mean by this word, and does it imply that to them money was not important?

6. According to the classical economists, what is the cause of inflation?

7. What did the classical economists think of deficit spending by the government?

8. How did the thinking of Thomas Malthus differ from that of Adam Smith?

9. What is Ricardian rent? Why does it exist?

10. *a.* According to David Ricardo, "Is wheat high because rent is high, or is rent high because wheat is high?" If Ricardo was correct, who were the main beneficiaries of the Corn Laws?

   b. Is there any similarity between the consequences of the Corn Laws and agricultural price supports of present times? Explain.

11. How did Adam Smith explain why some products sold for higher prices than other products? Was Smith's explanation a theory of value or a measure of value? Explain.

12. *a.* What is Karl Marx's labor theory of value?

   b. Why was the labor theory of value necessary to obtain surplus value?

CHAPTER 6

THE KEYNESIAN MODELS

INTRODUCTION TO JOHN MAYNARD KEYNES

Until the early 1930s, the classical economists' view of an automatically adjusting economy was the predominant view held by economists. But then came the Great Depression. Astronomical unemployment rates of 15 to 20 percent persisted year after year in the United States. The depression dragged on toward the mid-1930s, and the economy did not seem able to adjust to regain full employment. Granted, money rates of interest declined and prices and wages fell, but still severe unemployment persisted.

Needless to say, many economists began to voice some disenchantment with the classical theory. One English economist in particular, John Maynard Keynes, was especially influential. In 1936 Keynes came out with a book entitled *The General Theory of Employment, Interest and Money,* which presented a view of a market economy that was somewhat different from that espoused by his classical counterparts. Basically Keynes argued that there was no guarantee of full employment in a market economy. He maintained that in such an economy there is always the possibility that the "effective" demand for consumer and investment goods might not be sufficient to take off the market the entire supply that would be forthcoming from a full-employment economy.

The implication of Keynes's theory, then, is that a market economy can find itself in a sort of equilibrium in which the level of aggregate demand for consumer and investment goods is not sufficient to generate full employment of the labor force. Keynes argued, therefore, that the government may be needed to influence or augment the level of aggregate demand so as to ensure full employment.

You will note, therefore, a basic difference between the classical economists and Keynes. The classicists argued that a market economy, even though it might experience short-term unemployment, would through flexible interest rates, wages, and prices return to a state of full employment without government intervention. Keynes put less faith in market forces and argued instead for more direct government intervention. In summary, one can say that the classical economists took full employment as given and concentrated their attention on the problem of inflation. In contrast, Keynes took the price level as given and focused on unemployment. But to fully understand the Keynesian arguments and the implicit underlying assumptions, it will be useful to construct the Keynesian models. There are two: the simple Keynesian model and the more complete *IS-LM* model. The main body of this chapter deals with the simple model, while the Appendix contains the more complete *IS-LM* model.

CONSUMPTION AND SAVING

The heart of the simple Keynesian model is aggregate demand. In the context of the simple model, aggregate demand is assumed to consist of three components: (1) consumer spending, (2) investment spending, and (3) government spending. Let us look first at consumer spending.

Keynes argued that consumption is determined mainly by income. This is a fairly plausible argument. People with a $30,000-per-year income can be expected to spend more than a $20,000-per-year family, on the average. In addition, Keynes argued that, as a family's income increased, its consumption increased but not quite as much as the growth in income.

Again this is a fairly plausible argument. In order to maintain a bare minimum of food, clothing, and shelter, low-income people may have to spend their entire income and then some. College students are a good example. In fact many students probably consume more than their income, with the difference made up by gifts or borrowing. However, as incomes rise to the $20,000- to $25,000-per-year figure and beyond, families can satisfy their basic needs and in addition put something away for a "rainy day."

It will be helpful to represent this relationship between income and consumption with a diagram. In building the model, we will utilize diagrams to illustrate ideas or concepts. In a sense, a diagram is a picture of an idea. If a "picture is worth a thousand words," then a diagram is a relatively efficient and concise method of expressing a thought.

In Figure 6–1(A) we represent the two ideas or hypotheses that Keynes put forth regarding the relationship between income and consumption. First, the upward-sloping line tells us that if disposable income increases, then consumption also increases. For example, if disposable income is $8,000 per year, the consumption line tells us that consumption is about $15,000 per year. Then as we move out along the income axis, say to $32,000 per year, consumption increases to $25,000 per year.

Keyne's second hypothesis, namely, that consumption does not increase as much as income, is represented by the fact that the consumption line does

FIGURE 6–1   Relationship of income, consumption, and saving

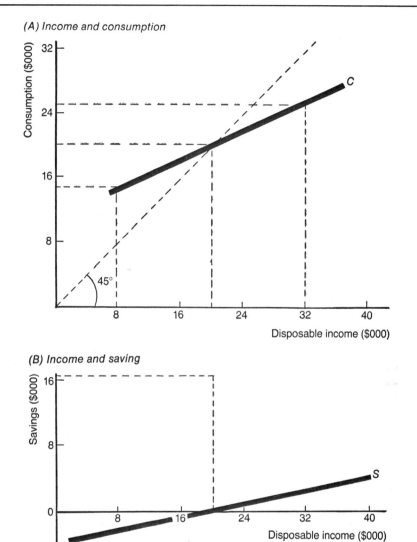

(A) Income and consumption

(B) Income and saving

not rise as rapidly as the 45-degree line. (This line is so named because it bisects the 90-degree angle made by the diagram.) Notice that anywhere on the 45-degree line, income equals consumption. Thus, if consumption increased dollar for dollar with income, the consumption line would be the same as the 45-degree line. The idea that consumption increases less rapidly than disposable income is reflected by a consumption line that is somewhat "flatter" than the 45-degree line.

The relationship between income and consumption also tells us what kind of relationship exists between income and saving. As we noted earlier, there are only two things people can do with their disposable income: spend it or save it. Hence, if we know income and consumption, we can easily derive saving. This is illustrated in Figure 6–1(B), where the distance between the consumption line and the 45-degree line represents the amount saved at the particular level of income. We can, as shown in Figure 6–1(B), represent the distance between the 45-degree line and consumption on a separate diagram. The resulting line, call it the saving line, tells us how much is saved at a given level of income.

Also notice the relationship between diagrams (A) and (B) in Figure 6–1. At the point where the consumption line intersects the 45-degree line in diagram (A), consumption is equal to income; that is, people spend all they take in. Saving, therefore, is equal to zero at this level of income, and this is shown in diagram (B) where the saving line intersects the horizontal axis. In this particular example, savings equals zero, or C equals DI, at the $20,000 income level. To the left of this intersection, consumption is greater than income, and saving is negative. And to the right of the intersection, consumption is less than income, so saving is positive.

AVERAGE PROPENSITY TO CONSUME

We can further our understanding of the relationship between consumption and income by developing the concepts of the average propensity to consume (APC) and marginal propensity to consume (MPC). The *average propensity to consume* is defined as the proportion of disposable income spent on current consumption of goods and services. It is computed as follows:

$$APC = \frac{C}{DI}$$

If we wish, we could multiply the resulting answer by 100 and express it as a percentage figure—the percent of DI that is spent on consumption goods and services.

One interesting thing to note about APC is that it becomes smaller and smaller the farther we move out along the consumption line, as shown in Figure 6–1(A). In the region to the left of the intersection of the consumption and 45-degree lines, APC is greater than one. In other words, consumption is greater than DI. At the intersection, APC equals one, and to the right, APC becomes progressively less than one.

The figures to compute APC for the United States are readily available. The results of the computations are shown in Table 6–1. With the exception of the Great Depression and World War II, two highly atypical periods, the APC in the United States has been in the range of 0.90 to 0.95; that is, people have been spending about 90 to 95 percent of their incomes and saving 5 to 10 percent. Notice also that there does not appear to be a discernible long-run trend in the size of the APC over this period.

You might reasonably ask at this point, If disposable income in the United States has been increasing over the years, is it not logical to expect that we would be moving out along the consumption line, so that APC should be

---

TABLE 6–1 Average propensity to consume in the United States, five-year intervals, 1929–84*

Year	APC	Year	APC
1929	0.93	1959	0.92
1934	0.98	1964	0.92
1939	0.95	1969	0.91
1944	0.80	1974	0.90
1949	0.93	1979	0.92
1954	0.91	1984	0.91

*Computed by dividing consumption expenditures by personal disposable income.
Source: *Economic Report of the President*, 1985, p. 261.

---

steadily declining? Yet in Table 6–1 we see that APC has remained relatively constant during a time when incomes have grown substantially.

It should be pointed out that the consumption line we are dealing with in the Keynesian model reflects *short-run* changes in consumer spending in response to short-run fluctuations in disposable income. Empirical evidence suggests, and it is reasonable to expect, that people do not change their spending habits in direct proportion to short-run changes in income. For example, if a family breadwinner is unemployed for six months and suffers, say, a 40 percent reduction in annual income, it is not likely that the family will reduce its spending by a full 40 percent during that year. The family may reduce consumer spending by 10 to 20 percent by cutting down on purchases of items they find least essential (restaurant meals, travel, entertainment, dental work, etc.) but not the full 40 percent. The deficit may come out of savings or possibly even from borrowing. The family does not cut back by the full 40 percent because it does not expect the reduction in income to be permanent. By the same token, a family that experiences a large increase in income during a given year, say because of an above-average amount of overtime or an inheritance, will probably increase its spending some during that year but not by the full amount of the extra income, because family members probably expect to be back to their former level of income the following year. Or, if the family does increase its spending, the extra purchases are likely to be consumer durables that will benefit the family over a period of several years.

Of course, if people expect the change in income to be permanent, we can expect them to change their spending habits in accordance with their change in income. When you graduate from college and obtain a full-time job, you will likely increase your rate of spending over what it is now because you expect your long-run, or permanent, income to remain at this higher level. The idea that people regulate their long-run spending habits in accordance with long-run expected income was advanced by Professor Milton Friedman at the University of Chicago.[1] It has come to be known as the permanent-income hypothesis.

---

[1] Milton Friedman, *A Theory of the Consumption Function* (Princeton, N.J.: Princeton University Press, 1957).

Friedman argued that the average propensity to consume out of so-called permanent income remains virtually constant across families of various income levels at a point in time, and over succeeding generations of people with higher and higher incomes. This could explain, then, why the average propensity to consume in the United States has remained fairly constant in spite of increasing per capita incomes.

We can reconcile the apparent contradiction between the upward-sloping consumption line that implies a decreasing APC at points farther out along the line and the long-run constancy of actual APC in the United States by viewing the consumption line as shifting up over time. The consumption line in the sample Keynesian model should be viewed as a short-run relationship between income and consumer spending. As long-run expected income increases, the consumption line shifts upward, as illustrated in Figure 6–2.

FIGURE 6–2   Upward shifts in the U.S. consumption line

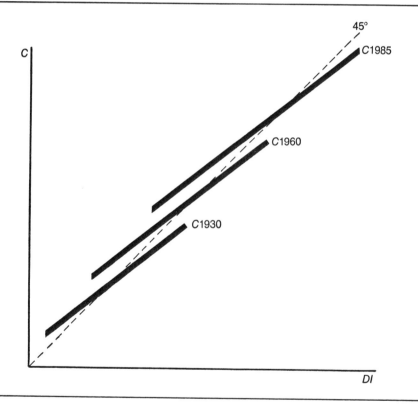

The possibility of the economy's moving out along a given consumption line was cause for concern among a number of economists during and immediately following World War II. If consumers spent a smaller and smaller share of their incomes as their incomes increased, investment spending would have to increase in order to take up the slack, so to speak, and maintain full employment. Fortunately their fears did not materialize; consumers show no long-run trend of "kicking" the spending habit regardless of their level of income.

MARGINAL PROPENSITY TO CONSUME

Marginal propensity to consume (MPC) is defined as the proportion of *extra* income spent on current consumption. For example, if your disposable income increases by a dollar and you increase your consumption by 75 cents, your MPC would be 0.75. Again, one can express this as a percentage figure by multiplying by 100. Of course, it is difficult to imagine just a one-dollar incremental increase in income. Most people enjoy something more than this when they receive a raise in pay. For this reason economists utilize a simple formula for computing MPC that provides an average MPC over a small range of increase in income. The formula is:

$$\text{MPC} = \frac{\Delta C}{\Delta DI}$$

where the Δ symbol denotes "a change in."

We should also point out that MPC is equal to the slope of the consumption line. Recall from your geometry or algebra that the slope of a line is determined by dividing the vertical change by the horizontal change for a given movement along the line. This is illustrated by the consumption line in Figure 6–3. In this

---

FIGURE 6–3   The slope of the consumption line

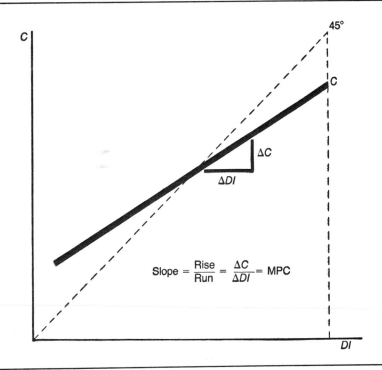

$$\text{Slope} = \frac{\text{Rise}}{\text{Run}} = \frac{\Delta C}{\Delta DI} = \text{MPC}$$

example, the vertical change is equal to ΔC and the horizontal change is ΔDI. An easy way to remember how to compute the slope of a line is by the simple formula:

$$\text{Slope} = \frac{\text{Rise}}{\text{Run}}$$

In other words, the "rise" of a line is equal to the vertical change ΔC in the consumption line, and the "run" is equal to the horizontal change, or ΔDI here. But notice that the formula for the slope of the consumption line is none other than the formula for MPC. Thus the slope of the consumption line is equal to MPC.

Unfortunately it is not nearly so easy to obtain estimates of the actual MPC for the country as it was to estimate APC. What we need is information on how people react to fairly small changes in disposable income. A number of studies, most using fairly sophisticated statistical techniques, have been done to estimate the actual MPC in the country.[2] However, the results vary considerably according to the data used and the specification of the statistical model. Most estimates of the nation's MPC appear to fall in the range of 0.60 to 0.90. Studies relating changes in consumption to changes in GNP generally provide estimates in the lower part of the range, while those using disposable income usually obtain estimates in the upper part of the range. We can expect these results because disposable income generally does not increase as much as GNP (or NNP). Part of the increase in GNP is siphoned off by increased taxes and business saving. Thus the change in the denominator of the MPC formula is larger using ΔGNP than using ΔDI. Therefore $\Delta C/\Delta DI$ is greater than $\Delta C/\Delta GNP$. For example, suppose GNP increases by \$1,000 and taxes and business saving increase by \$200. In this case DI increases by \$800. If consumption increases by \$600, MPC out of DI ($\Delta C/\Delta DI$) is equal to 0.75, while MPC out of GNP ($\Delta C/\Delta GNP$) is 0.60.

PROPENSITIES TO SAVE

Having covered the propensities to consume, it is a fairly simple matter to apply these same concepts to saving. In a parallel fashion we can talk about the average propensity to save (APS) and the marginal propensity to save (MPS). As one might expect from the preceding sections, APS is the proportion of total disposable income that is saved, and MPS is the proportion of a change in income that is saved. The formulas for computing APS and MPS are:

$$\text{APS} = \frac{S}{DI} \qquad \text{MPS} = \frac{\Delta S}{\Delta DI}$$

The fact that people can do only two things with their disposable income, spend it or save it, means that APS and MPS bear a direct relationship to APC and MPC. The proportion that is saved (APS) plus the proportion that is spent

---

[2] See, for example, H. S. Houthakker and L. D. Taylor, *Consumer Demand in the United States*, 2d ed. (Cambridge: Harvard University Press, 1970); N. Liviatan, "Estimates of Distributed Lag Consumption Functions from Cross Section Data," *Review of Economics and Statistics* 47 (February 1965), pp. 44–53; C. Y. Yang, "An International Comparison of Consumption Functions," *Review of Economics and Statistics* 46 (August 1964), pp. 279–86; and A. Zellner, "The Short Run Consumption Function," *Econometrica* 25 (1957), pp. 552–67.

(APC) must equal one. Moreover, the proportion of any change in income that is saved (MPS) plus the corresponding proportion that is spent (MPC) must also equal one. Thus we have:

$$APC + APS = 1 \quad \text{or} \quad 1 - APC = APS$$
$$MPC + MPS = 1 \quad \text{or} \quad 1 - MPC = MPS.$$

Also, the slope of the saving line, as in Figure 6–1(B), is equal to the MPS.

INVESTMENT

The second major component of the simple Keynesian model is investment. We will continue to define investment as it is defined in the national-income accounts—the physical construction of buildings (including housing), machines, tools, etc., together with any change in inventories. As we will see a bit later, inventory change will play an important role in the model.

In the interest of preserving simplicity in developing the simple Keynesian model, we will assume that investment in the economy is a set or given amount; that is, it does not change, at least over a modest range of income. The term *autonomous investment* is often used to describe this investment figure—a figure that is assumed or imposed on the model. We can represent autonomous investment by a straight horizontal line as in Figure 6–4(A). Such an investment line tells us that the level of investment remains constant over the range of income shown.

It would be a bit more realistic to assume, of course, that investment would become a larger figure, the larger the income or output of the economy. This would be represented by the upward-sloping line in Figure 6–4(B). Although

FIGURE 6–4   Investment and income

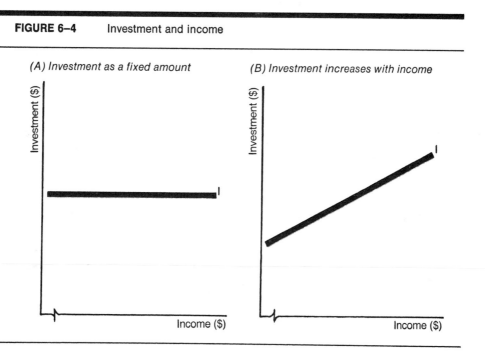

(A) Investment as a fixed amount

(B) Investment increases with income

we will develop the model under the assumption of a constant investment figure, later on we will point out how the model is affected by assuming that investment rises with income. At any rate, our major concern will be with shifts in the entire investment line and not so much with its slope. Also, to simplify the model, we will assume that saving, which provides the wherewithal to invest, is provided entirely by households.

GOVERNMENT SPENDING

The third major component of the simple Keynesian model is government spending. As pointed out in a preceding chapter, we should not think of the goods and services purchased by the government as somehow being "lost" to the private sector. With the exception of the goods and services necessary to run the government bureaucracy, everything the government purchases goes back to the people in the form of consumption goods, investment goods, or some combination of the two. Granted the higher taxes required to finance higher government expenditures may reduce actual GNP, or the higher costs of producing goods or services by the government bureaucracy may reduce the standard of living of people, but government (public) goods and services nevertheless are part of the total output of the economy and are available to the people.

Again to simplify our discussion, we will assume that government spending is a fixed or set amount; that is, it does not change over a range of income or output. We know, of course, that government purchases of goods and services tend to grow with the rest of the economy. However, for relatively small changes in income or output, which we are mainly interested in, it is not too unrealistic to assume a fixed government spending figure.

Along with a fixed level of government spending, we will assume also that total taxes are a fixed or set amount; they do not change at different levels of NNP. These often are referred to as lump-sum taxes. Again it would be more realistic to allow tax receipts to increase along with NNP, as would occur under an income tax. However, this also would make the model more complex and, as we shall see a bit later, the direction of change predicted by the model using a fixed or lump-sum tax is the same as when we use an income tax, although the magnitude of the change will be different.

In terms of a diagram we could represent government spending in exactly the same way we represented investment in Figure 6–4(A)—by a straight horizontal line. Instead of drawing a separate diagram for government spending, we can visualize it to be the same as the investment diagram, only in this case the horizontal line would be labeled G instead of I.

AGGREGATE DEMAND

We now have developed the three main components of the simple Keynesian model—consumption, investment, and government spending. The next task is to combine them to form what is called *aggregate demand*. To obtain aggregate demand, it is necessary to add these three components together. The procedure is illustrated by Figure 6–5. Let us begin with the consumption line. This line tells us the amount that consumers *desire* to spend at various levels of

FIGURE 6–5   Deriving aggregate demand

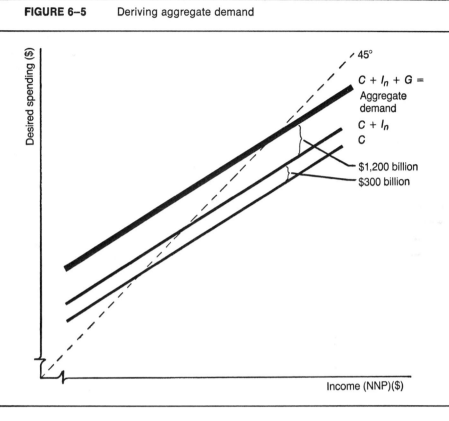

income. The desired amount of consumer spending is shown on the vertical axis and the corresponding levels of actual income on the horizontal axis.

As a measure of total income we will utilize net national product (NNP). Recall that this is similar to GNP except that depreciation of capital has been deducted. As a result NNP should be a somewhat more accurate indicator of the net output or income of the economy, although we could use GNP without any change in the model or in the analysis that follows.

Recall that the marginal propensity to consume (MPC) defines the relationship between consumption and income. In the earlier discussion we related consumption to disposable income, since this is what consumers have available to spend or to save. However, note in Figure 6–5 that NNP is represented on the horizontal axis rather than *DI*. This is all right as long as we keep in mind that for every level of NNP, there is a corresponding level of *DI* and that consumer spending depends on *DI* rather than on NNP.[3]

---

[3] If we assume that all saving is done by households (none by business) and taxes are fixed (the lump-sum variety), *DI* equals NNP minus the fixed tax. Hence changes in NNP equal changes in *DI*. Thus the slope of the consumption line (MPC) is the same regardless of whether we use ΔDI or ΔNNP in the denominator in calculating MPC in this case. In the case where some saving is done by business firms and taxes increase with NNP, which conforms more closely to the real world, *DI* does not increase as rapidly as NNP. Thus for a given ΔC, MPC will be lower using ΔNNP in the denominator than using ΔDI.

To provide some concrete figures to work with, let us assume from now on that MPC is 0.75. Thus the slope of the consumption line is assumed to be 0.75. We will not be particularly concerned with the initial level of the consumption line in our construction of the model because we will be interested mainly in studying the effects of relatively small changes or shifts in the consumption line and not in explaining its level at a point in time.

Also, to keep the example somewhat comparable to actual levels of I_n and G, we will assume that I_n equals $300 billion and G equals $1,200 billion at all levels of NNP. The addition of the $300 billion investment to the consumption line gives us a $C + I_n$ line that is $300 billion higher than the C line. Similarly the addition of the $1,200 billion government spending component provides a $C + I_n + G$ line that is $1,200 billion higher than the $C + I_n$ line shown in Figure 6–5. The resulting $C + I_n + G$ line has come to be known as *aggregate demand.* Essentially it tells how much consumers, investors, and government *desire* to spend at the various levels of income or NNP.

It is important to realize that in constructing aggregate demand simply by adding G to the $C + I_n$ line, as we have done in Figure 6–5, we have implicitly taken account of the effect of government spending on private consumption and investment. As we would expect, if the government did not provide any consumption or investment goods to the people, private purchase of consumption and investment goods would be higher than is the case with the government included. Or looking at it another way, the taxes imposed on the people to pay for government-purchased goods and services have the effect of reducing private purchases of goods and services, because taxes reduce the purchasing power of the private sector. For example, if the government takes $1,200 billion from people in the form of taxes to pay for a like amount of government spending, there will be $1,200 billion less for people to spend on private consumption and investment goods. We must keep in mind, then, that the levels of C and I_n are influenced by the level of G. In Figure 6–5, we have implicitly assumed that the downward shifts in C and I_n caused by the existence of G have already been taken into account.

AGGREGATE SUPPLY

Now that we have combined the basic components of the simple Keynesian model and derived aggregate demand, the next step is to develop the concept of aggregate supply. In the context of the simple Keynesian model, *aggregate supply* can be thought of as denoting the various possible levels of output that the business sector is willing and able to produce. With this model it is assumed that the business sector will desire to produce that value of output which it expects to be able to sell. For example, if businesspeople expect to sell $3,000 billion worth of output, they will want to produce $3,000 billion worth. If they expect to sell $3,400 billion, they will produce $3,400 billion, etc. Bear in mind too that the income figures on the horizontal axis (NNP) also represent the value of output. (Recall from Chapter 4 that income and output are just two sides of the GNP [or NNP] measure.) Thus, aggregate supply relates the figures on the horizontal axis (output in this case) with the figures on the vertical axis (spending) on a one-to-one basis. If the same scale is used on both axes, the line representing aggregate supply must exactly bisect the 90-degree angle made by the two axes. In other words, aggregate supply turns out to be the 45-degree line. This is true because of the assumption that business firms will produce exactly what they expect to be able to sell. The meaning of aggregate supply will become clearer in the next section.

EQUILIBRIUM INCOME

It is important to recognize, however, that the business sector may not be able to exactly anticipate the desired level of spending by consumers, investors, and the government as reflected by aggregate demand for any given year. For example, the business sector may expect aggregate demand to be greater than it in fact turns out to be. In this case, more goods and services might be produced than can be sold. This situation is illustrated in Figure 6–6 by the

FIGURE 6–6   Deriving equilibrium income

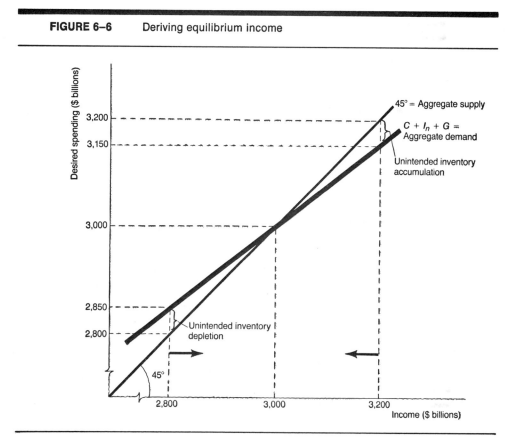

$3,200 billion level of income or output of the economy. Notice in this case that desired spending as reflected by the aggregate demand line is $3,150 billion at the $3,200 billion level of output.

The inevitable result of this situation is that $50 billion worth of goods remains unsold, which means that inventories rise by $50 billion. The business community, seeing this unintended rise in inventories, cuts back on production in the following year. And business firms will continue to reduce output, or NNP, until they reach the point where they are able to sell all they produce. This point is $3,000 billion in Figure 6–6.

Just the opposite occurs if NNP happens to be less than the point of intersection between aggregate supply and aggregate demand. Here people (including government) wish to buy more than is being produced. Inventories are drawn down unintentionally, and the business community begins to step up production, which in turn results in an increase in NNP.

By now it should be evident that there is only one point where the amount of goods and services that people wish to buy is exactly equal to the amount produced. This occurs at the intersection of the aggregate demand and aggregate supply lines. The level of NNP that corresponds to this intersection, $3,000 billion in our example, is referred to as *equilibrium income*. At this intersection there are no forces existing to either reduce or increase the level of income or output in the economy.

Once the economy moves to its equilibrium NNP, will it stay there for all time to come? No. Equilibrium NNP itself can and does change because of shifts in aggregate demand, which leads us to the next section.

SHIFTS IN AGGREGATE DEMAND

Recall that aggregate demand is made up of three components: consumption, investment, and government spending. A change in the level of any of these three components for a given level of NNP will have the effect of changing aggregate demand.

1. Consumption shifts. From the standpoint of the long-run trend in the entire economy, we can view the consumption line as gradually and continually shifting upward over time. The permanent-income hypothesis discussed in a previous section provides a possible explanation for this long-run upward trend in consumption in relation to income. Of course, since we are dealing with the entire economy, we would expect the growth in population also to push the aggregate consumption line to higher and higher levels. Although the continued long-run growth in consumption is important from the standpoint of maintaining a high level of aggregate demand, our major concern in the discussion to follow will be with short-term fluctuations or shifts in the consumption line.

One factor that can cause a shift in the short-run consumption line is a change in expectations of future economic conditions. For example, suppose people suddenly become pessimistic about the future, thinking perhaps that they might be laid off. As a result they might decide to tighten their belts and reduce their rate of consumption purchases. This is illustrated by consumption C_0 in Figure 6–7(A). Here it is shown that people wish to reduce their consumption by $10 billion at all possible income levels, which leads to a $10 billion downward shift in the aggregate demand line. The opposite might occur if people become more optimistic about the future. An increase in consumption, as illustrated by C_2 in Figure 6–7(A), would have the result of shifting aggregate demand upward.

FIGURE 6–7   The effect of changes in *C*, *I*, or *G* on aggregate demand

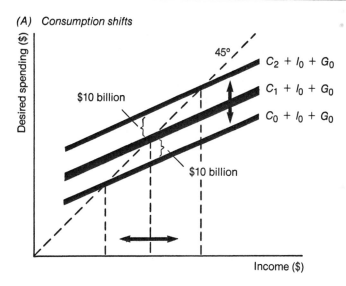

(A) *Consumption shifts*

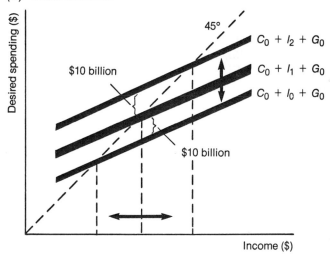

(B) *Investment shifts*

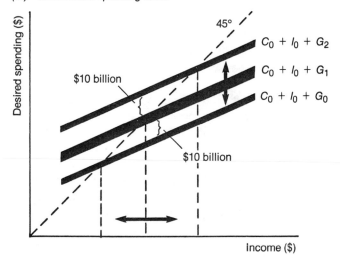

(C) *Government spending shifts*

The expectation of the availability of goods and services in the future also tends to influence consumption during a particular period. For example, if people expect war to break out in the near future and as a result expect shortages to occur, some may increase their rate of purchase in order to stock up on items that they anticipate will be in short supply or rationed. The periods preceding World War II and the Korean conflict provide examples of this behavior. This can be illustrated by an increase in consumption from C_1 to C_2 in Figure 6–7(A). Moreover an expectation of higher prices in the future, as commonly occurs during a war, tends to result in an increased rate of present consumption, also illustrated by C_2.

A third factor that is generally considered an important determinant of consumption is the availability of credit. As expected, this mainly affects the purchase of consumer durables such as appliances and automobiles. If loans become difficult to obtain, consumers tend to reduce their purchases of these items as illustrated by C_0 in Figure 6–7(A). Conversely, if credit becomes easier to obtain, we might expect consumers to respond by stepping up their purchase of items bought on time.

A factor related to the availability of credit is the size of the interest rate, particularly the real rate of interest. An increase in the rate of interest increases the overall cost of an item purchased on time. If people respond to higher prices by reducing their purchases of these items, there will be a reduction in consumption, again as illustrated by C_0 in Figure 6–7(A).

A less obvious effect of an interest rate change on present consumption is its impact on the decision to spend or to save. For example, a higher rate of interest means that a dollar of consumption given up at the present and saved will earn a higher return and will buy more in the future. In other words, the higher the rate of interest, the more a dollar saved at the present will buy in the future, for a given rate of inflation. Thus a rise in the interest rate increases the price of present consumption via-à-vis future consumption because it means giving up more in the future. As a result, an increase in the rate of interest should cause a downward shift in the consumption line for the current year or period.

Changes in the stock of goods in the hands of consumers also may affect current consumption expenditures. For example, during World War II the stock of consumer durables was depleted because of the need to devote resources to war materials production. As a result, during the immediate postwar period consumer expenditures on these items probably were substantially higher than would have been true had there been no war. Even during more normal times, there are likely to be cyclical fluctuations in the stock of durable goods that influence consumer expenditures.

2. Investment shifts. Because the ultimate aim of investment is to increase the future output of consumer goods and services, we would expect total investment also to exhibit a long-run upward trend in line with a growing economy. However, as in the case of consumption, there is also the possibility of cyclical fluctuations in investment spending by the business community.

As in the discussion of consumer spending, we would have to say that expectations by businesspeople play a key role in the determination of investment. Because investment by definition is something that pays off in the future, it is reasonable to expect that decisions to invest or not to invest depend a great deal on what investors expect the future to bring as far as business conditions are concerned. For example, if investors expect a strong future demand for consumer goods and services, i.e., a high level of employment and spending, it is more likely they will decide to step up current investment spending, as illustrated by I_2 in Figure 6–7(B). If they expect a period of depressed business activity and high unemployment, investors tend to reduce investment spending, as illustrated by I_0 in Figure 6–7(B). In this example we illustrate a $10 billion change in investment spending.

A second factor influencing the level of investment is the rate of interest. In general, the higher the rate of interest, the lower is the level of investment, and vice versa. It is fairly easy to see that when business firms borrow money to finance new investment, an increase in the rate of interest increases the overall cost of the investment by increasing the interest expense. Although we will not pursue it here, a somewhat more subtle effect of changes in the interest rate on the profitability of an investment has to do with the present value of the future returns of the investment. The higher the rate of interest, the lower is the present value of future returns. (The explanation for this phenomenon along with the procedure for calculating the present value of future income is presented in Chapter 12 of the companion micro text.) The main point to be made here is that higher rates of interest tend to reduce expected profits and therefore discourage investment. Moreover, if interest rates are high, credit may be hard to get, which would also discourage investment. Conversely, if interest rates decline and credit becomes easier to obtain, investment tends to be stimulated.

3. Government spending shifts. Since government spending is included as a separate component of aggregate demand, any decision to change the level of government spending will, of course, change the level of aggregate demand, at least in the short run. Abrupt increases in government spending have come about mainly in wartime, as illustrated by G_2 in Figure 6–7(C). Then after the end of hostilities, government spending is reduced, and G shifts downward, as shown by G_0.

In the context of the Keynesian model, the government spending component of aggregate demand takes on special significance because it can be changed by deliberate government edict to offset any changes in consumption or investment. For example, if investors become pessimistic and reduce investment by $10 billion, the government can offset this by increasing its expenditure by $10 billion, perhaps on new public works projects and the like. We will consider this topic in more detail in the upcoming chapter on fiscal policy.

THE MULTIPLIER

By now it should be clear that a shift in any one or all of the components of aggregate demand will in turn change the level of equilibrium income. An increase in C, I_n, or G, for example, increases equilibrium income, and vice versa. The next question to consider is: How much does equilibrium income change for a given change in aggregate demand? A glance at the diagrams in Figure 6–7 tells us that the change along the horizontal axis, i.e., the change in equilibrium income, is greater than the vertical shift in aggregate demand. That this must be so is purely a phenomenon of geometry. The closer the slope of the aggregate demand line is to the slope of the 45-degree line, the greater will be the change in equilibrium income for a given shift in aggregate demand. It will be easier to understand this phenomenon if you draw some aggregate demand lines of your own, with progressively steeper slopes, and observe what happens to equilibrium income when aggregate demand is shifted by a given amount.

Recall that the upward slope of aggregate demand in this simple model is due entirely to the upward-sloping characteristic of the consumption line. Thus the steeper the consumption line, the steeper is aggregate demand and the greater is the change in equilibrium income. Also, recall that we could have drawn the investment line with an upward slope as in Figure 6–4(*B*). If we had done so, this would have added to the slope of the aggregate demand line (making it steeper) and caused an even greater change in equilibrium income for a given shift in aggregate demand.

Fortunately, there is an economic rationale for the large change in equilibrium income relative to the shift in aggregate demand—it is called the *multiplier effect*. The multiplier effect occurs because spending by one group is income to another group, which in turn allows the second group to increase its spending, and so on. To illustrate the multiplier, let us take as an example a $10 billion increase in government spending. This would cause a $10 billion upward shift in aggregate demand. The extra $10 billion spent on such things as military hardware, schools, and highways becomes extra income to the people who produce and sell these items to the government. It is reasonable to believe, therefore, that these people will spend at least a part of this extra income. The part they spend is revealed by their MPC. If MPC is 0.75, they will spend 75 cents of each extra dollar of income they receive and save the remaining 25 cents. They may buy new cars, houses, vacation trips, and other goods. In turn the people who sell the $7.5 billion of goods and services receive a like amount as new incomes. We could expect this process to continue with round after round of new spending giving rise to new income, new income leading to new spending, and so on. The multiplier process is summarized in Table 6–2.

TABLE 6–2   Illustrating the multiplier process

Round	Extra spending	Extra income
1	$10.0 ———————→	$10.0
2	7.5 ⟷	7.5
3	5.6 ⟷	5.6
To infinity	$40.0	$40.0

Repeating the process round after round for an infinite number of times, the initial $10 billion increase in government spending at the maximum would give rise to a $40 billion increase in total spending in the economy (assuming MPC is 0.75). How do we know this? Surely no one would attempt to add an infinite column of numbers. Fortunately we can use a simple mathematical formula that gives the sum of an infinite convergent series. The formula is:

$$1 + X + X^2 + X^3 + \cdots + X^n = \frac{1}{1 - X}$$

where X is less than one. If we let X equal the MPC, 0.75 in this example, you will notice that each number in the extra spending and income columns in Table 6–2 is found by multiplying the initial spending increase by the numbers in the above formula. For example, the first round is 1×10, the second 0.75×10, the third $(0.75)^2 \times 10$, etc. Thus the total increase in spending (the sum of the columns) can be found by multiplying the sum of the infinite series times the original \$10 billion increase. This can be done because the \$10 billion factors out. In algebraic terms:

$$1 \times 10 + 0.75 \times 10 + (0.75)^2 \times 10 + \cdots + (0.75)^n \times 10 = \frac{1}{1 - 0.75} \times 10$$

Since $1/(1 - 0.75) = 4$, the sum of each column is \$40 billion. The 4 in this example is referred to as the government spending multiplier. It is found by the formula $1/(1 - \text{MPC})$. Hence the closer MPC is to 1, the larger is the government spending multiplier.

Although the preceding example is given in terms of a government spending increase, the same multiplier process would occur with a government spending decrease. Only now the \$10 billion decrease in government spending would cause a \$40 billion decrease in total spending (at the maximum). The same multiplier process also would occur with a change in consumption or investment spending, at any given income level. Recall that changes in the willingness of consumers or business people to spend also shifts aggregate demand, giving rise to the multiplier process. In Chapter 12 on fiscal policy, however, we will be primarily interested in the government spending multiplier.

UNEMPLOYMENT AND INFLATION

Before we leave the simple model, it will be useful to take a preliminary glimpse at how the model can be used to illustrate the cause of unemployment and inflation. Keynes and his followers argued that there is no reason why the equilibrium level of NNP necessarily had to be equal to the level of NNP that would generate full employment at stable prices. Keynes was mostly concerned about the unemployment problem. (Remember the model was first built during the early 1930s, the years of the Great Depression.) He argued, in this case, that the economy could come to rest at an equilibrium level of NNP that was less than the level necessary to generate full employment resulting in unemployment. This situation is illustrated in Figure 6–8(A). The equilibrium level of NNP, denoted by EQ, is less than the level of NNP that would correspond to full employment, denoted by FE. According to this model, there is nothing in the economy that would move it to full employment. Thus Keynes argued that the government may have to take steps to shift aggregate demand upward, thereby increasing equilibrium NNP enough to make it correspond to the full-employment level. The ways in which this can be done and some of

---

FIGURE 6-8   Illustrating unemployment and inflation by the simple model

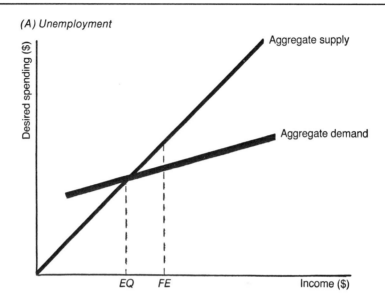

(A) Unemployment

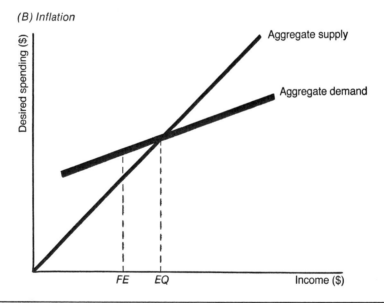

(B) Inflation

---

the problems involved constitute much of the material on fiscal policy in Chapter 12.

Although the simple model is not designed to deal with price changes, one can represent an inflationary situation as existing when equilibrium NNP is greater than the full-employment level. In this case, the economy moves past the full-employment level on its way to equilibrium [Figure 6–8(B)]. Because resources are fully employed at the full-employment level of NNP, labeled as *FE*, the increase in NNP in terms of dollars of output between *FE* and *EQ* is primarily due to the increase in prices, i.e., inflation occurs. In this case the objective of fiscal and monetary policy is to shift aggregate demand down until equilibrium NNP coincides with the full-employment level.

MAIN POINTS OF CHAPTER 6

1. In contrast to the classical economists, John Maynard Keynes argued that a market economy could experience prolonged periods of unemployment, as the United States did in the 1930s, because of insufficient demand for consumer and investment goods. Thus, he argued, there may be a need for the government to intervene in the economy to augment the demand for goods and services.

2. The heart of the simple Keynesian model is aggregate demand, which has been traditionally defined to include (1) consumption, (2) investment, and (3) government spending. Government spending encompasses both consumption and investment goods and services.

3. Keynes argued that consumption is determined mainly by income, although an increase in income does not bring forth a correspondingly large increase in consumption.

4. Average propensity to consume (APC) is defined as the proportion of disposable income that is spent on consumer goods and services, $APC = C/DI$. Marginal propensity to consume (MPC) is defined as the proportion of *extra* income that is spent on current consumption. $MPC = \Delta C/\Delta DI$. MPC is also equal to the slope of the consumption line.

5. The average propensity to consume in the United States has remained fairly constant, fluctuating in the narrow range of 0.90 to 0.95 during most of the 1929–84 period in spite of the more than doubling of per capita real disposable income. This has come about because of the upward shift of the short-run consumption line over time.

6. Statistical estimates of the actual MPC for the United States tend to fall in the range of 0.60 to 0.90.

7. The average propensity to save (APS) and the marginal propensity to save (MPS) are exactly analogous to APC and MPC except that they relate to saving rather than to consumption.

8. For the purpose of constructing the simple Keynesian model, it is assumed that investment and government spending do not change within at least a small range of income; that is, they can be represented by horizontal lines on the spending and income diagram.

9. **Aggregate demand** is constructed by adding investment and government spending to the consumption line. With this procedure it is implicitly assumed that the impact of taxation and government spending on private consumption and investment is already taken into account.

10. **Equilibrium income** occurs at the point of intersection of aggregate demand and aggregate supply. At points to the right of this intersection, aggregate supply is greater than aggregate demand, i.e., more goods and services are produced than are sold. This results in an unintended inventory accumulation, which in turn results in a reduction in output, income, and employment as the economy moves back to the equilibrium point.

11. At points to the left of this intersection, aggregate demand is greater than aggregate supply; more is sold than is produced, inventories are drawn down unintentionally, business firms step up production, and as a result the level of output, income, and employment is increased until the equilibrium is achieved.

12. Changes in equilibrium income occur because of changes or shifts in aggregate demand. And changes or shifts in aggregate demand are caused by changes or shifts in the level of consumption, investment, or government spending.

13. Changes in consumer spending (and in aggregate demand) occur primarily because of changes in the degree of optimism or pessimism on the part of consumers regarding future economic conditions, and because of changes in the interest rate and availability of credit. The same factors tend to change investment spending.

14. The fact that equilibrium income changes by a multiple of the initial change in spending is a result of the multiplier effect. The multiplier effect occurs because each additional dollar of spending by one person or group is additional income to another person or group. In each successive round of the multiplier process, part of the added income is spent and part is saved. The part that is spent represents added income to its recipients. The multiplier that applies to changes in government, consumer, or investment spending is found by the following formula: $1/(1 - MPC)$.

15. According to the simple model, unemployment will occur if equilibrium NNP is smaller than the level of NNP that will generate full employment. Inflation results from a situation where equilibrium NNP is greater than the full-employment level. Keynes was primarily concerned with the unemployment problem.

QUESTIONS FOR THOUGHT AND DISCUSSION

1. How did the thinking of Keynes and his followers differ from that of the classical economists with respect to the problems of unemployment?

2. What is the economic meaning of the upward-sloping consumption line that is less steeply sloped than the 45-degree line?

3. *a.* Differentiate marginal propensity to consume and average propensity to consume.
   b. Consider a family with a $20,000-per-year disposable income that receives a $1,000 increase in its income. If the family spends $800 of the extra $1,000, what is its MPC? What is the family's APC if it spends $20,000 of its $21,000 income?

4. *a.* What happens to MPC and APC as one moves up along a straight, upward-sloping consumption line?
   b. How can one reconcile these results with the fact that APC in the United States has remained relatively constant over the past half-century?

5. Is it possible for a family's spending to be greater than its disposable income? If so, can this situation be illustrated on a consumption line? Explain.

6. In the context of the simple Keynesian model, what is meant by aggregate demand? Aggregate supply?

7. Construct the simple Keynesian model by the following steps:
   a. Draw and label the two axes and the 45-degree line.
   b. Draw a consumption line assuming MPC = 0.75 (do not be concerned with its level).
   c. Draw a $C + I_n$ line assuming I_n = $300 billion.
   d. Draw a $C + I_n + G$ line (aggregate demand) assuming G = $1,200 billion.
   e. What crucial assumption must be made regarding the level of C and I_n in order to simply add G on the top of these?

8. *a.* Define equilibrium income (NNP).
   b. Explain what happens when actual NNP is either smaller or larger than equilibrium NNP.

9. Using the Keynesian model diagram, illustrate the following:
   a. Consumers expect increased unemployment in the future.

b. Investors become more optimistic about future business conditions.

c. Government increases its spending because of new domestic programs.

d. The interest rate increases.

10. *a.* What is the economic rationale underlying the multiplier?

b. If MPC is 0.80, how much does equilibrium NNP change if aggregate demand shifts up by $10 billion?

11. According to the simple Keynesian model, how could unemployment and inflation occur?

12. In the context of the simple Keynesian model, can an economy experience both inflation and unemployment at the same time? Explain.

THE *IS-LM* MODEL

Although the simple Keynesian model presented in Chapter 6 is a useful point of departure for studying Keynes's ideas, it is somewhat incomplete because it does not explicitly take into account the effect of money and interest rates on economic activity. The purpose of this appendix is to combine the simple Keynesian model with the demand for and supply of money and in so doing construct what has come to be known as the *IS-LM* model.

The *IS* Curve

Recall that one of the factors shifting aggregate demand in the simple model is a change in the rate of interest. As the rate of interest increases, the profitability of undertaking investment decreases. Therefore we would expect an increase in the rate of interest to decrease investment spending, other things being equal. It also is likely that consumers will decrease their spending on consumer durables such as cars and appliances as the interest rate increases because these items now become relatively expensive. Conversely, as the rate of interest declines, investment and consumer spending are likely to increase.

The effect of interest rate changes on aggregate demand is illustrated in Figure A–1. Notice that, as the interest rate decreases, aggregate demand increases. As a result the equilibrium NNP, as determined by the simple model, increases. The relationship between the rate of interest and equilibrium NNP is

---

FIGURE A–1   Relationship between the interest rate and aggregate demand

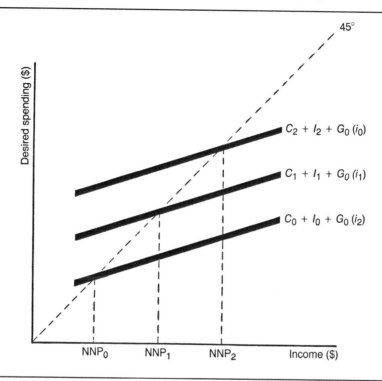

---

summarized by the *IS* curve shown in Figure A–2. The *IS* curve is derived by choosing alternative interest rates and plotting the corresponding levels of equilibrium NNP as determined by the simple model. The *IS* curve slopes downward and to the right because lower interest rates result in higher levels of equilibrium NNP. This line is called the *IS* curve because, at equilibrium NNP, the desired level of investment equals the desired level of saving; hence it became known as the "investment-equals-savings curve" or just "*IS* curve" for short.

Equilibrium in the Monetary Sector

In constructing the *IS* curve, we have shown that many equilibrium levels of NNP are possible in the so-called goods and services sector of the economy. But we have no way of determining which equilibrium level of NNP will actually prevail at a point in time. This can be done only after we have determined the equilibrium rate of interest.

To determine the equilibrium rate of interest, it is necessary to bring into the discussion the demand for and supply of money. Let us first consider the demand for money. We will define the demand for money as the amount of money people desire to hold at various possible interest rates. The interest rates referred to in this case are those earned on securities, namely stocks and bonds. These interest rates represent a cost of holding money because, by holding money as opposed to owning securities, people give up the interest

FIGURE A–2   Relationship between the interest rate and equilibrium NNP—the *IS* curve

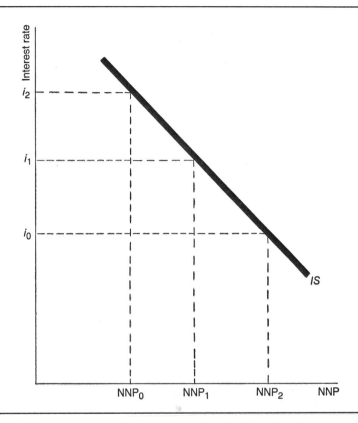

earnings from these securities. The higher the rate of interest on securities, the greater are the interest earnings given up, and the greater is the cost of holding money.

It is reasonable to believe that the higher the rate of interest on securities, that is, the higher the cost of holding money, the less money people will desire to hold, other things being equal. In other words, at relatively high rates of interest, people who hold their assets in the form of money give up a relatively large return by not owning securities. Thus we can expect people to want to hold a larger fraction of their assets in the form of securities and a smaller fraction in the form of money when the interest return on securities is comparatively high. Conversely, when the interest return on securities is low, less is given up by holding one's assets in the form of money. Thus we can expect people to desire to hold more money when the interest return on earning assets is low.

The relationship between the interest rate on securities and the amount of money people wish to hold is represented by the demand curve for money. This demand curve, when drawn as a downward-sloping line as in Figure A–3, conveys the idea that people wish to hold more money when the interest return on earning assets is low than when it is high.

In drawing the demand curve for money, just as in drawing a demand curve

FIGURE A–3 Equilibrium in the monetary sector

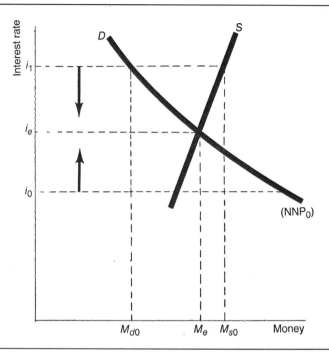

for a conventional good or service, it is necessary to hold constant all other factors that can shift the curve. In the case of the money-demand curve, a change in money income is considered to be an important demand shifter. When money incomes increase, people increase the nominal amount of money (number of dollars) they wish to hold. There are two reasons for this behavior. The first reason is that when people earn more money they spend more money; thus a larger number of dollars is required to finance the increased volume of transactions. Keynes referred to this component of the total money demand as the *transactions motive* for holding money.[1] Both households and business firms demand more money when the nominal value of income or transactions increases. The second reason is that when people have higher incomes they can afford to put more money aside as a reserve against unforeseen adversity. For example, one never knows when illness will strike or when the house, car, or appliances might require repair. Keynes called this reason for holding money the *precautionary motive*. Again, when people have more income they tend to set aside more money for this purpose.

The NNP_0 written next to the money-demand curve in Figure A–3 is intended to serve as a reminder that the curve is drawn for a given level of NNP. As NNP increases, the money-demand curve will shift to the right. We will come back to this point shortly.

In determining the equilibrium rate of interest, it is necessary to also bring in the supply of money. As will be explained in Chapters 11 and 13, the Federal

---

[1] J. M. Keynes, *The General Theory of Employment, Interest and Money* (London: Macmillan, 1936).

Reserve System in conjunction with commercial banks determines the nation's money supply. It is most realistic to represent the supply of money as an upward-sloping line as in Figure A–3. This means that when the interest rate is high, banks will be more anxious to make loans and in so doing increase the nation's money supply. (In Chapter 11, it will be explained how banks create money by making loans.) Conversely, when the interest rate is low, which generally coincides with reduced economic activity, banks find lending a more risky proposition and as a result are likely to reduce their loans outstanding and in so doing decrease the nation's money supply.

The equilibrium rate of interest is determined by the demand for and supply of money in the same way as the equilibrium price for a good is determined by the demand for and supply of that good (Chapter 2). Perhaps the easiest way to see how the equilibrium interest rate is determined is to begin by choosing a rate that does not represent equilibrium and then see what happens. Suppose by accident the interest rate happens to be i_1. At this relatively high rate the public wishes to hold only M_{d0} as money, whereas the Federal Reserve and the banking system are supplying M_{s0}. Keep in mind now that someone must be holding at all times all of the money that is supplied, M_{s0} in Figure A–3. So at interest rate i_1 people are actually holding more money than they wish to hold.

In order to explain what happens in this case, it is first necessary to explain the relationship between bond prices and their interest return. When a bond is issued the annual interest return is specified on the face of the bond. For example, a $100 bond might specify an 8 percent annual return, meaning that the bond holder receives $8 annually as interest. Regardless of how much a person pays for the bond, the $8 per year interest is paid by the issuing organization. If the market price of the bond should decline to $50, the person paying $50 still receives the $8 per year return; hence the interest return rises to 16 percent. Conversely, if the market price of the bond increases, say, to $200, the person receives a 4 percent return.

In the case where the interest rate is relatively high and people wish to hold less money than is actually supplied, they attempt to get rid of this money by the purchase of securities (including bonds). As they compete for the available bonds, the price of bonds increases and the interest return declines. The opposite occurs when the interest rate is relatively low, say at i_0. Now people wish to hold more money than is being supplied. They attempt to remedy this situation by selling off some bonds in exchange for money. As a result bond prices decline, and the interest rate increases.

Notice that in both of these disequilibrium situations the change in the interest rate, either a rise or a fall, changes the preference of people for holding their assets as money. As the interest rate declines, the amount of money people wish to hold comes closer and closer to the amount actually supplied. Similarly, as the interest rate increases, people desire to hold less and less of their wealth as money until the amount they desire to hold exactly coincides with the amount actually supplied. Thus the interest rate serves as the mechanism for equilibrating the desired holdings of money (money demand) with the actual holdings of money (money supply).

By now you probably recognize that unless the interest rate corresponds to the intersection of the demand and supply curves for money, there will always be pressure on it to change. Thus the interest rate that corresponds to this intersection, such as i_e in Figure A–3, is referred to as the equilibrium rate of interest in the monetary sector.

Keep in mind here that this equilibrium rate of interest relates to these particular money demand and supply curves. If one or both of the curves should shift, there would be a different equilibrium rate of interest. We are particularly interested in the shift of the money-demand curve caused by a change in income or NNP. This brings us to the derivation of the *LM* curve.

The *LM* Curve

In the preceding section we derived one possible equilibrium rate of interest. But as soon as we consider many possible equilibrium levels of NNP, as shown by the *IS* curve, we must also consider many possible equilibrium rates of interest. We can follow a procedure very similar to that used in constructing the *IS* curve and construct a line showing the relationship among various levels of equilibrium NNP and the corresponding equilibrium rate of interest. In this case we will choose various possible levels of equilibrium NNP to obtain a series of possible equilibrium levels of the interest rate as determined in the monetary sector of the economy.

In constructing this relationship we will assume a constant (nonshifting) supply of money. (Later on we will see what happens when the supply of money does shift.) Each of the demand curves for money shown in Figure A–4(A) corresponds to a given level of NNP, as denoted in parentheses. At a relatively low level of NNP, such as NNP_0, the demand for money will be low, as illustrated by D_0, and as a result the equilibrium interest rate will be low. As we choose higher levels of NNP, denoted by NNP_1 and NNP_2, the corresponding demand for money increases to D_1 and D_2 and the resulting interest rate increases to i_1 and i_2, respectively.

FIGURE A–4   Relationship between NNP and the equilibrium rate of interest—the *LM* curve

If we plot the equilibrium rates of interest shown on the vertical axis of Figure A–4(A) against the corresponding levels of NNP, we obtain an upward-sloping line as illustrated by Figure A–4(B). This line or relationship is commonly referred to as the *LM* curve. It is so named because every point on the curve represents an equilibrium between the demand for money (sometimes called the liquidity preference curve, or *L* for short) and the supply of money (or *M* for short). Thus it has come to be known as the *L = M* curve, or just *LM*. The main thing to keep in mind is that the *LM* curve traces out a series of many possible equilibrium rates of interest for many possible levels of equilibrium NNP. The upward-sloping nature of the line reflects the idea that higher levels of NNP result in higher rates of interest, given the supply of money. To summarize this section, we can say that the *LM* curve is derived by choosing alternative levels of NNP and then plotting the equilibrium rates of interest as determined by the demand for and supply of money. A summary of the derivation of both the *IS* and *LM* curves is presented below:

IS : Interest rate → Aggregate demand → Equilibrium NNP
LM: Equilibrium NNP → Demand for money → Interest rate

Overall Equilibrium

Before we put the more complete model together to establish overall equilibrium, a word should be said about the interest rate. Actually there are many interest rates existing in the economy, depending on the type of loan or securities under consideration. The interest return on securities that are relatively risk-free to buyers, such as government bonds, understandably will be lower than the interest rate paid by private borrowers for high-risk ventures. Thus in the more complete model the interest rate utilized in constructing the *LM* curve is not likely to be the same as that faced by potential investors as reflected on the *IS* curve. However, this divergence of interest rates generally is not considered a major drawback to building the model because, if one were to adjust the interest rates for such things as differences in risk and the duration of time the money is tied up, the rates should converge toward a common value. Also, the absolute level of the interest rate is not as critical to the model as what happens when the rate changes. In this regard, there is reason to believe that the various interest rates tend to rise and fall together.

We know now that there are many possible equilibrium levels of NNP as shown by the *IS* curve, and many possible equilibrium rates of interest as shown by the *LM* curve. The question is, Which of the many possible equilibrium NNP values and interest rates will actually prevail? Of the many possible equilibrium NNP values and interest rates, there is only one of each that gives rise to an overall equilibrium—that which corresponds to the intersection of the *IS* and *LM* curves. Unless that particular combination exists, forces will be set in motion that will change both the equilibrium NNP in the goods and services sector and the equilibrium interest rate in the monetary sector. Probably the best way to understand the meaning of overall equilibrium is to deliberately choose a situation that does not represent overall equilibrium and then see what happens.

Suppose the interest rate happens to be relatively high, as illustrated by the 14 percent interest rate in Figure A–5. At the 14 percent interest rate, the

FIGURE A-5   Arriving at overall equilibrium

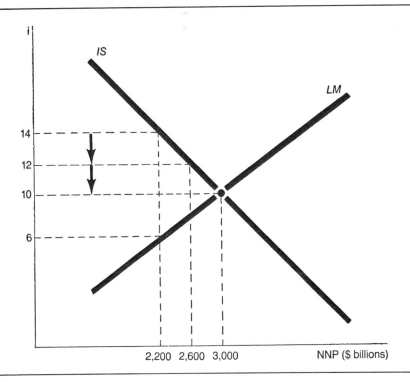

equilibrium NNP as determined by the simple model is relatively low. Let us say that this NNP as read off the *IS* curve is $2,200 billion. But if NNP is only $2,200 billion, the equilibrium rate of interest in the monetary sector is 6 percent, as read off the *LM* curve. In other words, if the level of NNP is $2,200 billion, the demand for and supply of money results in a 6 percent equilibrium rate of interest. Hence, at the actual 14 percent interest rate, the quantity of money supplied is greater than the quantity demanded. As a result, people will try to get rid of "excess" money by attempting to purchase securities. As the price of securities is bid up, the interest rate declines.

As the interest rate begins to fall, the level of investment increases, causing the equilibrium NNP in the goods and services market to increase. Suppose the interest rate goes down to 12 percent. Now the equilibrium NNP, as determined by the simple model and shown by the *IS* curve, rises to $2,600 billion. Will this be the overall equilibrium? Not yet. As shown by Figure A-5, this combination is closer to the overall equilibrium, but still the NNP is too small to give rise to a 12 percent rate of interest in the money market. Thus the interest rate falls some more. It keeps on falling until the equilibrium NNP, as determined by the simple model, rises enough to cause the demand for money to increase until the equilibrium rate of interest in the money market is exactly equal to the actual rate that determines the equilibrium NNP. In this example that rate of interest is 10 percent. At the 10 percent rate of interest, the equilibrium NNP, as determined by the simple model in the goods and services sector and reflected by the *IS* curve, is $3,000 billion. And the $3,000 billion level of

NNP is large enough to result in a money-demand curve that gives rise to a 10 percent equilibrium rate of interest in the monetary sector. Hence the 10 percent and $3,000 billion represent simultaneous equilibrium values in both sectors. Now there is no pressure causing either the interest rate or the equilibrium NNP to change. The system is in overall equilibrium. As mentioned, the overall equilibrium corresponds to intersection of the *IS* and *LM* curves, shown by Figure A–5.

The same reasoning can be used to arrive at the equilibrium by choosing a relatively low rate of interest and then working upward. You might try this on your own.

Although Keynes presented all the ingredients and the rationale for this more complete model in his book, another English economist, J. R. Hicks (a recent Nobel Prize winner), should be credited with formulating the *IS* and *LM* curves.[2] Alvin Hansen, an American economist, also was influential in making these relationships explicit.

Shifts in the *IS* Curve

Now that we have developed the more complete *IS-LM* model and determined the equilibrium NNP, the next task is to investigate how changes can take place in the equilibrium level of income or NNP. Basically these changes can occur because of shifts in the *IS* curve, the *LM* curve, or both. Let us consider the *IS* curve first.

Recall that the *IS* curve is derived from the simple model. A shift in the *IS* curve will take place if there is a shift in one or more of the three components of aggregate demand (consumption, investment, and government spending) that is not related to changes in the interest rate.[3] For example, an increase in aggregate demand may occur if the government decides to increase its spending at any given level of NNP. As illustrated by Figure A–6(A), the increase in government spending shifts aggregate demand upward, causing equilibrium NNP as determined by the simple model to increase from NNP_0 to NNP_1. How does this shift in aggregate demand affect the *IS* curve? Bear in mind here that the interest rate is held constant, say at i_0. At interest rate i_0, the level of NNP on the *IS* curve should increase from NNP_0 to NNP_1. We can conclude therefore that the new *IS* curve should lie to the right of the original curve, as shown by Figure A–6(B). This shift to the right is referred to as an increase in the *IS* curve because equilibrium NNP would increase if the *LM* curve were superimposed on this diagram. Similar shifts of the *IS* curve would occur if any of the three components of aggregate demand were to change, except if the change were due to a change in the interest rate. In the latter case we would just move to different points on the *IS* curve.

Shifts in the *LM* Curve

Recall that the *LM* curve is derived from the demand for and supply of money diagram. A shift in the *LM* curve will occur if there is a shift in the

---

[2] J. R. Hicks, "Mr. Keynes and the 'Classics': A Suggested Interpretation," *Econometrica* 5 (1937), pp. 147–59.

[3] A change in the interest rate is reflected by a movement along the *IS* curve, not by a shift in the curve.

FIGURE A–6   Illustrating the effect of an increase in aggregate demand on the *IS* curve

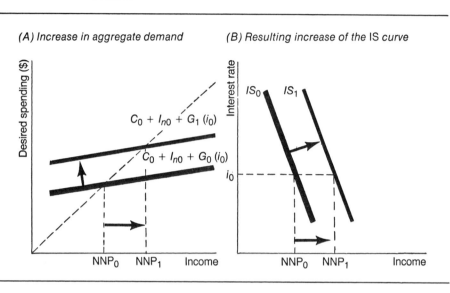

(A) Increase in aggregate demand

(B) Resulting increase of the IS curve

demand for money (at any given level of income), the supply of money, or both. Let us consider the demand side first. Suppose, for example, that people decide to increase their demand for money at any given income level. This is illustrated in Figure A–7(A) by a shift in the money demand curve from D_0 to D_1. Given the supply of money, the equilibrium rate of interest increases from i_0 to i_1. (Bear in mind that the demand for money is drawn for a given level of NNP, say NNP_0.) As a result of the shift in the demand for money, the equilibrium

FIGURE A–7   Illustrating the effect of an increase in the demand for money on the *LM* curve

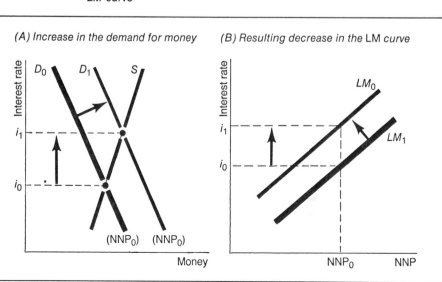

(A) Increase in the demand for money

(B) Resulting decrease in the LM curve

rate of interest corresponding to NNP_0 increases from i_0 to i_1 on the *LM* curve diagram. We can conclude, therefore, that an increase in the demand for money (at a given income) causes the *LM* curve to decrease. This is regarded as a decrease because equilibrium NNP would decrease if the *IS* curve were superimposed on the diagram.

A shift in the supply of money also will shift the *LM* curve. In Chapters 11 and 13 it will be explained how the Federal Reserve System is able to change the money supply and bring about such a shift. For now, let us suppose that the Federal Reserve increases the money supply, which is to say that the money supply curve shifts to the right, as illustrated by Figure A–8(A). Given the

FIGURE A–8 Illustrating the effect of an increase in the supply of money on the *LM* curve

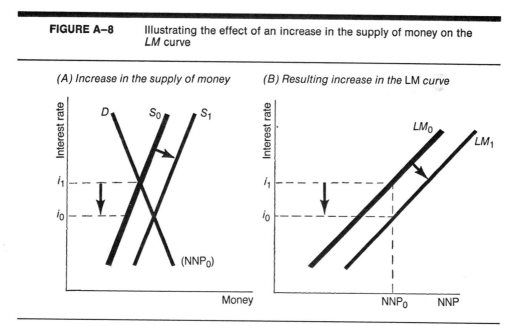

(A) Increase in the supply of money   (B) Resulting increase in the LM *curve*

demand for money, the increase in the supply of money will lower the equilibrium rate of interest from i_1 to i_0 on the *LM* curve diagram for a given income level, say NNP_0. (Remember that the money demand curve is drawn for a given income level.) We can conclude, therefore, that an increase in the supply of money results in an increase in the *LM* curve, as shown by Figure A–8(B). By the same token, a decrease in the money supply, that is, a shift to the left of the money supply curve, has the result of decreasing the *LM* curve or shifting it to the left.

Shifts by the *IS* and *LM* curves, of course, result in changes in the equilibrium level of NNP as determined by the *IS-LM* model. An increase in either *IS* or *LM* causes the equilibrium NNP to increase, whereas a decrease (shift to the left) by either curve causes the equilibrium NNP to decrease.

Advantages of the *IS-LM* Model

The *IS-LM* model has a couple of advantages over the simple model. First, it takes into account the effects of interest rate changes that result from shifts in aggregate demand. For example, suppose government spending is increased and causes aggregate demand and NNP to increase. We know from the demand and supply diagram for money that an increase in NNP causes the demand for money to increase. This in turn results in an increase in the interest rate. But an increase in the interest rate reduces private investment and consumption from their original levels. Thus the net increase in the equilibrium NNP for a given increase in government spending shown by the *IS-LM* model is smaller than that shown by the simple model.

In terms of the *IS-LM* diagram, the horizontal shift to the right by the *IS* curve is exactly the same as the increase in equilibrium NNP shown by the simple model. But you will notice that the equilibrium NNP in the *IS-LM* model does not increase as much as the horizontal shift of the *IS* curve as long as the *LM* curve is upward sloping (you might try this with a diagram of your own). This means that the government spending multiplier is smaller in the *IS-LM* model than in the simple model.

A second advantage of the *IS-LM* model is that it can be used to sort out the conditions under which fiscal and monetary policies will be effective or ineffective. These conditions are reflected in the slopes of the *IS* and *LM* curves. Fiscal policy (changes in government spending or taxation) shifts the *IS* curve. If the *IS* curve is steeply sloped and the *LM* curve is relatively flat, the horizontal shift by the *IS* curve will change the equilibrium NNP by almost as much. This means that fiscal policy is effective in changing the equilibrium NNP. Conversely, if the *IS* curve is flat and the *LM* curve is steep, a given horizontal shift in the *IS* curve will not change the equilibrium NNP very much. In this case, fiscal policy is ineffective.

The slope of the *IS* curve depends on how much investment and consumer spending change in response to a change in the interest rate. If consumer and investment spending change a lot in response to a change in the interest rate, the *IS* curve will be flat, and vice versa. You can prove this to yourself by choosing a given change in the interest rate, say from i_1 to i_0, and then observing what happens to the equilibrium NNP in the simple model, first when aggregate demand shifts a lot and second when it shifts just a little. In the first case, where consumers and investors are highly responsive to changes in the interest rate, you should obtain a flat *IS* curve, whereas in the second case the *IS* curve should be steep.

The slope of the *LM* curve depends mainly on the slope of the demand-for-money line. The slope of this line reflects how responsive people are to changes in the rate of interest in deciding how much money they desire to hold. If the demand-for-money line is steep, it implies that people do not change their desired holding of money very much when the interest rate changes. A steep demand-for-money line, in turn, results in a steep *LM* curve. You can prove this to yourself by drawing two demand and supply-of-money diagrams, one with a steep money-demand line and the other with a flat line. Next, change NNP by a given amount in both diagrams, say from NNP_0 to NNP_1. Recall that the increase in NNP shifts the demand-for-money line to the right. (Be sure to make the horizontal shift the same in both diagrams.) Notice in the steep demand-for-money diagram that the equilibrium rate of interest increases a large amount for the given change in NNP. This in turn causes the *LM* curve to rise sharply for this given movement along the horizontal axis, which means that the *LM* curve will be steep also.

The effectiveness of monetary policy (changes in the supply of money) also is determined by the slopes of the *IS* and *LM* curves. If the *IS* curve is flat and the *LM* curve is steep, a given horizontal shift in the *LM* curve will change the equilibrium NNP by nearly the same amount. In this case monetary policy is effective. Conversely, if the *IS* curve is steep and the *LM* curve is flat, monetary policy will be ineffective. These relationships are summarized below.

— *IS* steep, *LM* flat: Fiscal policy effective.
— *IS* steep, *LM* flat: Monetary policy ineffective.
— *IS* flat, *LM* steep: Fiscal policy ineffective.
— *IS* flat, *LM* steep: Monetary policy effective.

MAIN POINTS OF APPENDIX

1. The *IS* curve is derived by choosing alternative interest rates and plotting the corresponding levels of the equilibrium NNP as determined by the simple model.

2. The *LM* curve is derived by choosing alternative levels of NNP and plotting the corresponding equilibrium rates of interest as determined by the demand-for and supply-of-money diagram.

3. Overall equilibrium in the *IS-LM* model corresponds to the intersection of the *IS* and *LM* curves.

4. If the actual rate of interest is higher than the equilibrium rate, people will be holding more money than they wish to hold. As they attempt to get rid of their excess cash by purchasing securities, the price of securities is bid up and the interest rate declines.

5. A decrease in the interest rate increases the equilibrium NNP in the goods and services market, which in turn increases the demand for money.

6. An increase in the demand for money increases the equilibrium rate of interest in the money market, bringing the equilibrium rate up toward the actual rate of interest.

7. Overall equilibrium occurs when NNP_e corresponds to i_e in the monetary sector and i_e corresponds to NNP_e in the goods and services sector.

8. The *IS* curve will increase in response to an increase in aggregate demand that is not caused by a decrease in the rate of interest.

9. The *LM* curve will decrease in response to an increase in the demand for money.

10. The *LM* curve will increase in response to an increase in the supply of money.

11. If the *IS* curve is downward sloping and the *LM* curve is upward sloping, the spending multipliers will be smaller in the *IS-LM* model than in the simple model.

12. Fiscal policy will be effective if the *IS* curve is steep and the *LM* curve is flat.

13. Monetary policy will be effective if the *IS* curve is flat and the *LM* curve is steep.

QUESTIONS FOR THOUGHT AND DISCUSSION

1. Derive an *IS* curve.

2. Derive an *LM* curve.

3. Explain how the overall equilibrium interest rate and NNP are obtained if the actual interest rate is higher than its equilibrium level.

4. Show how the *IS* curve shifts in response to an increase in aggregate demand that is not caused by a decrease in the rate of interest.

5. Show how the *LM* curve shifts in response to an increase in demand for money that is not caused by an increase in NNP.

6. Show how the *LM* curve shifts in response to an increase in the supply of money.

7. Show how the responsiveness of consumers and investors to changes in the rate of interest affects the slope of the *IS* curve.

8. Show how the responsiveness of money holders to changes in the rate of interest affects the slope of the *LM* curve.

9. Why are the spending multipliers in the *IS-LM* model smaller than those in the simple model?

10. What condition makes for a steeply sloped *IS* curve? A flat *IS* curve?

11. What condition makes for a steeply sloped *LM* curve? A flat *LM* curve?

12. In the context of the *IS-LM* model, under what conditions will an increase in government spending have the greatest effect on equilibrium NNP? An increase in the money supply?

CHAPTER 7

THE RATIONAL EXPECTATIONS HYPOTHESIS

In economics, as in the other sciences, theories are tested by their ability to explain and predict events. Theories which fail this test are either discarded or modified. The Keynesian models presented in the preceding chapter are examples of economic theories that have been put to the test and found wanting. Recall from the discussion in Chapter 6 that, if equilibrium NNP does not correspond to the level of NNP which represents full employment, there will be either unemployment or inflation. During the early 1930s, when Keynes constructed the theory, the big problem, of course, was unemployment. Then, during the World War II years, inflation became the main economic concern. In the postwar years up until the late 1960s, unemployment again became an important economic issue. However, starting in the late 1960s and extending throughout the 1970s, a new phenomenon appeared on the economic scene: the simultaneous occurrence of both unemployment and inflation—commonly referred to as "stagflation." This label describes a stagnant, slow-growing economy with both high unemployment and inflation. The Keynesian models did not predict the occurrence of stagflation and cannot explain it. Therefore economists have gone back to the "drawing boards" in recent years in an attempt to construct new theories which are better able to deal with present-day realities.

One of these theories, which will be discussed in this chapter, is called the *rational expectations hypothesis.*

The core of the rational expectations idea is that people try to maximize their utility, that is, act rationally, given the information at their disposal. The rational expectations hypothesis does not say that the information available to people at any given time is perfect in terms of being accurate or complete. No human being has perfect foresight. But the theory does argue that people do learn from their mistakes and, when new information becomes available, they will modify their behavior in order to better their lot in life. In and of itself the idea of rational behavior is not a new or startling concept in economics. A large part of the body of economic theory is built on this foundation. The theory of rational expectations extends the basis for rational behavior to include expectations of future conditions as well as knowledge of current conditions. Thus far in this text we have encountered several economic theories which assume rational expectations on the part of economic agents (people). It will be useful to examine how established theory says expectations are formed and used before we apply the rational expectations hypothesis to the problems of unemployment and inflation.

FORMATION OF EXPECTATIONS

Expectations of what the future holds influence behavior in just about every aspect of our lives. We wear a raincoat or carry an umbrella if we expect rain; we check a book out of the library if we expect it to be interesting or useful; students prepare for an exam if they expect one to be given, and so forth. In this section the main focus will be on how expectations are formed in the economic sphere.

According to established economic theory, in making economic decisions people utilize information on current economic conditions and on expected future conditions. This idea was first encountered in Chapter 2. Recall that one of the five demand shifters indicated that the current demand for a good or service will depend in part on the expectations of consumers regarding future prices and incomes. For example, if consumers expect the future price of a good to be higher than the current price, many will likely increase their current demand in order to take advantage of the better buy at the present. To believe that people would not do so would be irrational, because one would thus assume that people do not desire to obtain the most for their money.

Probing a bit deeper into the process, one might ask, How do consumers form their expectations? In part, expectations of future conditions may be formed from trends in the recent past. If the price of an item has been increasing for several months and there is no reason to expect a reversal of the trend, consumers may expect the trend to continue, at least for a short period. Of course, the same expectation can be formed from just the opposite trend. If the price of an item has been declining for several months and consumers observe that it is much lower than normal, they may expect the trend to reverse and the price to rise in the near future. Thus it is not always correct to assume that past trends will continue. Indeed, if consumers observe that the price of an item has been stable for an extended period, they may use this information to form an expectation of a rising price in the future. This situation might occur if other prices have been rising while the price of the item in question has remained constant.

In addition to past trends, expectations of future prices will be formed on the basis of information that becomes available to people at the present. To continue the demand example, people are likely to expect higher future prices of a good if its supply is interrupted. For example, a war in the Middle East which disrupts petroleum shipments will almost certainly lead to higher expected prices of petroleum products, and the expectation will in all probability turn out to be correct. Other information, such as government or industry reports, also will influence expectations. The U.S. Department of Agriculture, for example, periodically issues crop and livestock reports which provide information on production and stocks of agricultural commodities. A report which shows an abnormally small crop or poor yield is likely to cause an increase in expected future prices of the item.

Consumer behavior is influenced also by expected future income. If unemployment is increasing, it is reasonable to expect that some families will reduce current spending even if their income remains the same, because of the increased probability that one or more family wage earners will be laid off and the family income reduced. The permanent-income hypothesis introduced in the preceding chapter also is based on expected future income. If a family expects its real income (money income adjusted by the CPI) to increase in the future, the family is likely to increase its current spending even before the higher income is realized. By the same token, a family that enjoys a windfall gain at the present is unlikely to increase its current spending by an equal proportion on goods that are immediately consumed because of the expectation that future income will not be as high.

Expectations probably are even more important on the supply side of the market because production decisions frequently have a long-term impact on output and income, particularly when they require new investment. Recall from the discussion of supply in Chapter 2 that expectations of producers regarding future prices form an important supply shifter. Most of the work on expectations in microeconomics has focused on the supply side of the market.

Producers form expectations in about the same manner as consumers, using information from past trends, current developments, and published reports. Indeed, most large firms either employ economists to forecast market trends or buy this information from consultants. Again, the process of forming supply expectations is much more complex than simply extrapolating past trends into the future. As in the case of demand, it is possible to form an expectation of a price increase from either a rising, a falling, or a stable price. Much depends on the nature of additional information which producers have at their disposal.

The quality or accuracy of information will have an important bearing on what expectations are formed. To take an extreme case, if economic agents feel that the information coming to them about current and future conditions is inaccurate or not much better than a pure guess, they may choose to disregard it altogether. In order for information sources to influence expectations, they must have a better track record than being right 50 percent of the time. For example, if a forecast of wheat prices a year in advance underestimates the actual price 50 percent of the time and overestimates it the other 50 percent, producers can do as well flipping a coin.

It is interesting to note that if economic agents base their expectations on forecasts, their action may cause the forecasts to be wrong even if they are based on accurate information. For example, if a forecast predicts a high price for wheat next year and the majority of wheat producers respond by increasing their output of wheat, the actual price of wheat could turn out to be much lower than anticipated. If this happens repeatedly, the rational producer may choose to do just the opposite of what the forecast indicates. Of course, if enough producers do this, the forecast could turn out correct but for the wrong reasons. Forming expectations is a very tricky business.

There is, of course, information that is designed to deliberately mislead people. A salesperson who misrepresents a product would be an example. After being fooled once or twice, most people soon learn from their experience, however.

ADAPTIVE VERSUS RATIONAL EXPECTATIONS

While the idea that people behave rationally in forming their expectations is embodied in most economic theory, until recently economists have not been able to incorporate this assumption into the measurement of human behavior. The problem is that it is not possible to look into the minds of people and measure what they are thinking about the future. This problem is particularly important in the case of supply. The production of virtually all products takes time, and producers cannot be absolutely certain what price will prevail when the time comes to sell their output. But in order to be willing to invest resources in production, producers must have some idea of at least a likely range of prices that might prevail when the product is sold. The formation of expectations of the future prices is especially difficult for agricultural products because of the lengthy period it takes to produce them and the variability of most agricultural prices.

In statistically estimating supply curves of the type presented in Chapter 2, a common technique has been to assume that the price producers expect to receive for their product is equal to the actual price received in the preceding period. It is common to use a one-year lag so that last year's actual price is taken as the expected price for the current year. It is widely recognized that many things can happen between the time the products were sold last year and when producers form their expectations about this year's price, but it is argued that last year's price still is a better proxy of expected price than the price received when the products are sold.

The use of last year's price as a proxy for the expected price and the movement to equilibrium in the market are sometimes illustrated by what has come to be called the cobweb theorem. This idea is illustrated by Figure 7–1.

To understand how the cobweb works, let us begin by assuming that in year one, quantity produced is equal to Q_1. This small quantity was forthcoming because of the previous year's low price, P_0, which is taken to be equal to the expected price in year one. When Q_1 is produced, the actual price in year one turns out to be P_3. Buyers bid the price up to this level because of the small quantity. According to the cobweb, producers now use P_3 as the expected price in planning production in year two. Because of this relatively high expected price, producers expand output to Q_3 in year two. However, the large output causes actual prices to fall to P_1 in year two. Now producers use P_1 as the expected price in year three, resulting in output Q_2. In year three, actual price rises to P_2, etc. Notice that price and quantity eventually converge to the equilibrium. A shift in demand, supply, or both would start the process over

FIGURE 7–1   The cobweb theorem

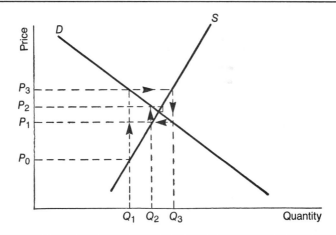

again. Notice also that, in order for price and quantity to converge to equilibrium, the supply curve must be steeper than the demand curve.

It should be noted that in the cobweb theorem producers act in a very mechanistic fashion, something like robots. They never learn from their mistakes. If price was high in the preceding year, they always expect it to be high in the current year, and vice versa. But one can argue that producers are more intelligent than this, at least those who survive and stay in business. After a few years, most would learn that it is not rational to assume that price will remain high for two years in a row when it has never done so in the past. Even if one makes the highly unrealistic assumption that producers are not capable of learning from their past mistakes, some perceptive individuals could rapidly get rich by learning the price pattern. They could buy when the price is low, store the commodity for a year, and sell when the price is high. (The same thing could be accomplished without storage by use of the futures market.) At any rate, if enough people did this the extra demand during periods when price was expected to be low would serve to keep the price from falling, and the extra supply in ordinarily high-price years would keep the price from rising, at least as high. Hence the pattern would be broken. Essentially, the cobweb model implicitly assumes irrational behavior on the part of producers in the formation of expectations because it rules out learning from past mistakes. This assumption is inconsistent with the basic assumptions underlying the construction of the demand and supply curves where rational behavior is assumed. (This is explained more thoroughly in Chapters 2 through 8 of the companion micro text.)

In an effort to introduce somewhat more realism than is implied by the cobweb theorem, economists have frequently utilized adaptive expectations models. The pioneering work on adaptive expectations models was done by Marc Nerlove in the 1950s.[1] Much of the early efforts were directed at agricultural commodities.

---

[1] See Marc Nerlove, "Adaptive Expectations and Cobweb Phenomena," *Quarterly Journal of Economics* 73 (May 1958), pp. 227–40.

Without going into great detail, the adaptive expectations model allows for decision makers to choose a price other than a product's past value in forming expectations of its future price. In particular, the expected price in the current year is equal to last year's expected price plus (or minus) an adjustment factor times the difference between last year's actual price and last year's expected price. The general formula of a simple adaptive expectations model is

$$P_t^e = P_{t-1}^e + \gamma (P_{t-1} - P_{t-1}^e)$$

where:

P_t^e = this year's expected price.
P_{t-1}^e = last year's expected price.
γ = adjustment factor.
P_{t-1} = last year's actual price.

As an example, suppose two years ago producers expected the price of wheat to be five dollars per bushel in the following year (last year), but the actual price last year turned out to be four dollars per bushel. According to the adaptive expectations model, the expected price for this year's crop will be $5.00 + 0.5($4.00 − $5.00) = $4.50 if the adjustment factor is one half, or 0.5. The adjustment factor is estimated statistically from the data and can be any number from zero to one. If it is equal to zero, decision makers do not change their minds on account of past errors in predicting future prices. If the adjustment factor is equal to one, past errors cause decision makers to change their minds about the future price by an amount equal to the difference between last year's actual and last year's expected price. If the cobweb model were employed, the expected price in year t would be the actual price that prevailed in the previous year—$4.00 in this example. The cobweb model is just a special case of the adaptive expectations model in which the adjustment factor equals one.[2]

It should be noted that the adaptive expectations model still treats decision makers as robots, albeit somewhat more intelligent robots than according to the cobweb theorem. The adaptive expectations model presented above maintains that producers always change their expectations by a constant fraction of the difference between P_{t-1} and P_{t-1}^e, regardless of new information that they come across. One can argue that decision makers are more intelligent than this, for the assumption implies that they do not learn from past mistakes. In other words, there is no feedback mechanism in the adaptive expectations model that allows economic agents to change their expectations in response to new information. An important source of new information is the pattern of errors made in past predictions. If decision makers are systematically wrong for several periods, we would expect them to discover the systematic part of their error and adjust to it.

A noneconomic example may help clarify the point. Suppose you have a course where the teacher habitually shows up late for class, although not every day. Some days he is on time, some days he is 5 minutes late and other days he is up to 10 minutes late. If you come to class on time, you waste time when the teacher is late. However, if you are late you miss part of the class if the teacher

---

[2] This can be seen mathematically. If $\gamma = 1$, then $P_t^e = P_{t-1}^e + (P_{t-1} - P_{t-1}^e)$, which reduces to $P_t^e = P_{t-1}$.

is on time. If you followed the cobweb rule in deciding on what time to come to class (the time the teacher arrived for the preceding session) you would almost always be unnecessarily early or late for class, and neither result appeals to you. In fact, such behavior would be irrational. Therefore you search for some pattern in the teacher's time of arrival.

Suppose after several weeks you notice that the teacher is on time on Mondays, close to 5 minutes late on Wednesdays, and up to 10 minutes late on Fridays (assume the class meets three times per week). It is reasonable to believe that you and the other students in the class would adjust to this pattern and time your own arrivals close to the arrival of the teacher. If the teacher's time of arrival on Wednesdays and Fridays fluctuates a little around the 5- and 10-minute marks, you may not arrive exactly on time, but your errors would be less than if you followed the simple cobweb rule of arriving for class at the time when the teacher arrived the class before.

Now suppose about halfway through the term the teacher's tardiness pattern changes, so that he now arrives only 5 minutes late on Fridays instead of the normal 10 (perhaps someone complained). After a couple of weeks, you also adjust your arrival pattern to more closely correspond to that of the teacher. If an adaptive expectations model based on the first few class periods were used to predict student behavior later in the term, particularly after the instructor changed his time-of-arrival pattern, it would not do a very good job of predicting. The rational expectations model is designed to allow people to learn from systematic errors in their past behavior. They may still make mistakes, but such mistakes will come from random or unsystematic variation in the outcome; in statistics this is referred to as "white noise"—it cannot be predicted or expected.

In addition to the information obtained from the systematic component of past mistakes, people can also change their behavior in response to new information they obtain about future events. If, for example, the government announces that the price of wheat will be supported at $6.00 per bushel, and producers have no reason to doubt the government's policy, virtually all producers will base their production decisions on this $6.00 price. The adaptive expectations models will have them changing their expected price by some fraction of the difference between last year's price and the expected $6.00 price. In this example, last year's price is irrelevant. In the example of the tardy professor, if this person is replaced halfway through the term by someone who has a reputation for punctuality, it would be rational for students to immediately change their expectations regarding the class starting time in response to this new information, instead of following the adaptive expectations framework for several days after the new person arrives.

The idea of rational expectations was first put forth by John Muth in 1961.[3] Muth's early work dealt mainly with modeling price movements in markets. Specifically, he constructed a model in which the adjustment coefficient (the γ in the adaptive expectations model presented earlier) depended upon the responses of consumers and producers to price movements. By so doing, he was able to allow consumers and producers to react the same way to *expected* price movements as they did to *actual* price movements, thereby making expecta-

[3] John F. Muth, "Rational Expectations and the Theory of Price Movements," *Econometrica* 29 (July 1961), pp. 315–35.

tions models consistent with the wider body of economic theory which, by and large, also impose the rationality assumption.

Muth's idea of rational expectations lay dormant for nearly 10 years. While the idea is conceptually appealing, mathematically and statistically it is a rather complex theory. It was not until the idea was applied to problems of macroeconomic policy that it finally took root in the economics profession. The pioneering work on rational expectations as it applies to macroeconomic policy should be credited to three individuals: Robert Lucas, Jr., of the University of Chicago, and Thomas Sargent and Neil Wallace, both of the University of Minnesota. Other economists who have made important contributions to the theory in later years include Lars Hansen, Robert Baro, Stanley Fischer, Bennett McCallum, Kenneth Wallis, Robert Hall, John Taylor, and Gregory Chow.[4]

THE PHILLIPS CURVE

In order to see more clearly how rational expectations applies to macroeconomic policy, it is necessary to introduce at this point the relationship between unemployment and inflation that has come to be known as the Phillips curve. A. W. Phillips, an English economist, observed in the 1950s that in the United Kingdom during the 1864–1957 period the annual rate of change of money wage rates was inversely correlated with the level of unemployment.[5] In other words, during the years when money wages were rising relatively fast, the level of unemployment was comparatively low, and vice versa. Professor Phillips hypothesized that when the demand for labor is high and relatively few people are unemployed, employers will bid wage rates up in their attempt to hire more workers. On the other hand, he argued, when business is slow and the demand for labor is declining, money wage rates will rise little if at all. Phillips also argued that workers and unions will be reluctant to take wage cuts during times of depressed business activity. Consequently, employers have little choice but to lay off workers during these periods, resulting in relatively high rates of unemployment. Because of the alleged stickiness of wages when the demand for labor is declining, Phillips postulated that the relationship between rates of change of money wages and unemployment would be curvilinear when shown on a diagram. In other words, when the labor market is depressed a small reduction in the rate of change of money wages would precipitate a relatively large increase in unemployment. The kind of relationship Phillips had in mind is depicted by Figure 7–2.

In the years following the publication of Phillips's article, economists modified the Phillips curve slightly by substituting the rate of change of prices, i.e., the inflation rate, for the rate of change of money wage rates. Because the two variables are highly correlated, the basic shape of the curve remains about the same as that shown by Figure 7–2. Nowadays when economists speak of the

---

[4] A collection of papers on rational expectations by these and other authors appears in Robert E. Lucas, Jr., and Thomas J. Sargent, eds., *Rational Expectations and Economic Practice,* vols. 1 and 2 (Minneapolis: University of Minnesota Press, 1981). The reader is warned that an understanding of these papers requires a high level of understanding of economics, mathematics, and statistics. For a less technical paper on rational expectations, see Mark H. Wiles, "The Future of Monetary Policy: The Rational Expectations Perspective," *Quarterly Review,* Federal Reserve Bank of Minneapolis 4, no. 2 (Spring 1980),pp. 1–7.

[5] A. W. Phillips, "The Relation between Unemployment and the Rate of Change of Money Wage Rates," *Economica* 25 (November 1958), pp. 283–300.

FIGURE 7–2   The original Phillips curve

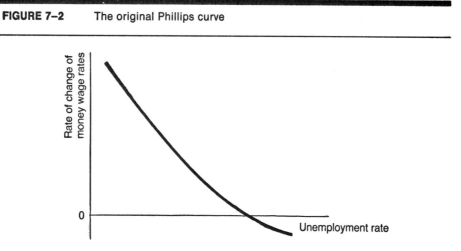

Phillips curve, they invariably refer to the inflation-unemployment relationship.[6]

During the late 1960s and 1970s, the Phillips curve was used a great deal by economists to show the trade-off between inflation and unemployment. According to the Phillips curve, if a nation was willing to accept some inflation it could keep its unemployment rate low. On the other hand, if stable prices are of a high priority, a country must be willing to live with higher unemployment.

The Phillips curve became very popular with economists who advocated activist fiscal policies, that is, Keynesians, for it gave them a relationship that could serve as a guide to policy actions. If the Phillips curve is true, then it should be possible to "fine tune" the economy by policy action to achieve a specific goal of unemployment and inflation. For example, if society wishes to lower the rate of unemployment, then the Phillips curve indicates just how much the inflation rate will have to be increased to achieve the desired objective. The Keynesian models provided a framework for accomplishing the objective.

The simultaneous growth of both unemployment and inflation during the 1970s in the United States as well as in many other countries began to cast doubt on the validity of the Phillips curve and on the Keynesian models. Attempts to stimulate the economy through expansionary fiscal and monetary policies had only a temporary effect on unemployment and in the long run succeeded only in driving up the rate of inflation. (These policies will be described in later chapters.) The relationship between the rates of inflation and unemployment for the United States over the 1950–84 period is shown in Figure 7–3. Notice that it is possible to trace out a line resembling a Phillips curve from the observations of the 1950s and 1960s. No doubt these observations gave economists confidence in the stability of the Phillips curve. But as the nation moved into the 1970s, the relationship began to break down. If one

---

[6] Actually this relationship was first observed in 1926 by Irving Fisher. See Irving Fisher, "A Statistical Relation between Unemployment and Price Changes," *International Labor Review* (June 1926), reprinted in *Journal of Political Economy* 81, no. 2 (March–April 1973), pp. 496–502.

FIGURE 7–3   Relationship between annual percentages change in the consumer price index and the rate of unemployment, United States, 1947–84

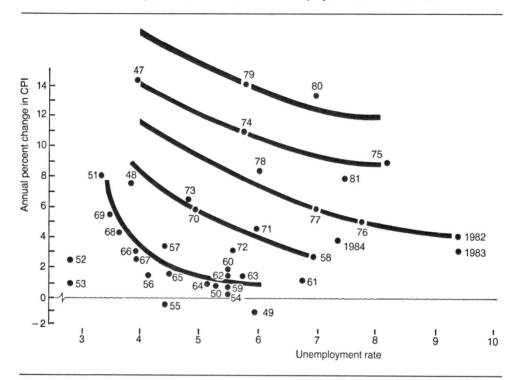

takes a little "artistic license," it is possible to represent the observations from the 1970s and 1980s as being along a number of higher Phillips curves. During the 1970s there were many attempts to rationalize the apparent upward shift of the Phillips curve. Reasons such as the Arab oil embargo, poor crop years in the United States and USSR, and failure of the anchovies to swim to their appointed place in the ocean at their appointed time resulting in higher prices of fishmeal and protein feeds, were given for the unusual location of the Phillips curve during the early to mid-1970s. But as these conditions disappeared in the late 1970s and the Phillips curve did not shift down to its original location, more and more economists came to believe that the Phillips curve is not a stable relationship between inflation and unemployment, as originally believed. Of course, some economists never believed the Phillips curve represented a stable relationship, at least in the long run. This takes us to the "natural rate hypothesis."

THE NATURAL RATE HYPOTHESIS

Professor Milton Friedman in his presidential address to the American Economic Association in December of 1967 predicted that expansionary monetary policy could have only a temporary effect on unemployment, not a permanent effect.[7] Friedman argued that there is a "natural rate of unemployment"

[7] Milton Friedman, "The Role of Monetary Policy," *American Economic Review* 58 (March 1968), pp. 1–17.

to which the economy will always move. This argument has come to be known as the "natural rate hypothesis." (The reasons for a natural rate of unemployment were discussed in Chapter 3.) Friedman pointed out that the natural rate is not a fixed number for all times or all countries. High levels of legislated minimum wages, unemployment compensation and welfare programs, and strong unions, for example, will give rise to a higher natural rate of unemployment than in their absence.

Friedman's argument for the temporary effect of monetary policy on unemployment was based on expectations. To begin, suppose the government attempts to stimulate the economy by increasing the rate of growth of the money supply. (How an increase in the money supply is perceived to affect the economy is explained in Chapter 10. The procedures for increasing the money supply are presented in Chapter 13.) The initial effect will be to increase money incomes and spending, with most of the initial effect on real output rather than prices. Then, as the unexpected increase in demand is felt in the market, the prices of goods and services begin to rise. To employers this means that real wages paid to employees begin to fall because, as Friedman argued, the prices of the goods sold increase initially more than wages do. This improves the net earnings of business firms and provides an incentive for them to hire more workers, thereby reducing unemployment. However, it will not take long before employees catch on that the prices of things they buy have gone up more than their wages. Consequently employees and their union representatives will press employers for real wage increases in order to regain at least what they have lost. However, when real wages increase, most likely after increased strike activity, and business earnings are reduced, unemployment increases back to where it was before the stimulus was put into effect.

The opposite process takes place if the government attempts to reduce inflation by decreasing the rate of growth of the money supply. Now there is a decrease in the growth of demand for goods and services, resulting in a reduction in the prices of many items. Since money wages are not likely to decline immediately, real wages paid to employees rise, causing reduced profits to business and a reduction in employment, i.e., increased unemployment. The fact that businesses are likely to experience increased inventories of unsold goods at this time also will result in increased layoffs and more unemployment. As unemployment continues and wage demands soften, real wages decline back to their original levels, thereby helping to restore profits and stimulating employment.

One of the main points of Friedman's argument is that the government cannot permanently affect the level of unemployment. If it wants to reduce unemployment, for example, over a long period of time, the government will have to stimulate the economy more and more in order to prevent it from slipping back to its natural rate of unemployment. In order to maintain a low level of unemployment, the government will have to accelerate the rate of inflation to higher and higher levels. At some point, of course, inflation becomes intolerable, and the expansionary policy is abandoned.

THE LONG-RUN PHILLIPS CURVE

Friedman's argument about the eventual return of the economy to its so-called natural rate of unemployment led to the construction of the long-run Phillips curve. The long-run Phillips curve is a vertical line extending up from a

point on the horizontal axis that corresponds to the natural rate of unemployment. In deriving this curve it will help to refer to Figure 7–4. In the long-run
Phillips curve diagram there can be an infinite number of individual short-run
curves, each corresponding to a certain expected rate of inflation. To keep the
example manageable, only five inflation rates are considered—6, 8, 10, 12, and
14 percent. The natural rate of unemployment in this example is taken to be 5.5
percent.

FIGURE 7–4   Derivation of the long-run Phillips curve

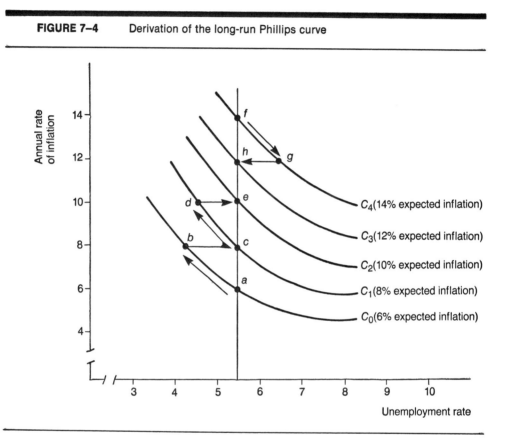

To begin the derivation of the long-run Phillips curve, let us assume that the
current level of unemployment is 5.5 percent and that the government wishes to
reduce it to a lower figure. Also assume that the current rate of inflation is 6
percent, which places the country at point *a* on Figure 7–4. The government
now, in an attempt to stimulate the economy, increases the rate of growth of
the money supply. This causes an unexpected increase in prices for goods and
services, lower real wages, and reduced unemployment. Thus the economy
moves up along curve C_0 from point *a* toward point *b*. Now let us suppose that
the government, seeing the reduction in unemployment, stabilizes the growth
of the money supply, causing the rate of inflation to stabilize at 8 percent per
year. The economy then comes to rest at point *b*.

Wage earners and unions now observe that prices of goods and services
have increased faster than their wages. Consequently they press employers,
under threat of strike, to increase wages faster than the inflation rate in order to
catch up. As real wages increase, unemployment increases, and the economy

moves from point b toward point c. As people come to expect the higher, 8 percent rate of inflation, the short-run Phillips curve shifts from C_0 to C_1. The government can achieve another temporary reduction in unemployment if it causes another unexpected spurt in the rate of inflation, say to 10 percent per year. Now the economy moves from point c to point d and then back to e as real wages catch up and people come to expect the new higher rate of inflation (10 percent). The short-run Phillips curve will now be at C_2. Similar expansionist policies would move the economy up to C_3 and C_4 (12 and 14 percent expected inflation rates).

At some point it is likely that society will begin to view inflation as the overriding problem and call on the government to take steps to reduce it. As explained earlier, a reduction in the rate of growth of the money supply causes a reduction in the growth of the demand for goods and services, relative price reductions, increased inventories, higher real wages, and higher unemployment. In terms of Figure 7–4 this corresponds to a movement from point f to point g if the inflation rate is 14 percent. If the government, seeing the increased level of unemployment, backs off on its restrictive monetary policy so that the rate of inflation stabilizes at 12 percent, unions and employees will soften their wage demands, real wages will decrease to their former level, and unemployment will ease back down toward its natural rate. As people come to expect a 12 percent inflation rate, the short-run Phillips curve shifts down to C_4 and C_3, and the economy comes to rest at point h. Further contractions will shift the economy down to still lower short-run curves.

If one were to repeat the expansion and contraction process over and over again, and the number of resting points, such as a, c, e, f, and h increased, it would become evident that they traced out a vertical line extending upward from the natural rate of unemployment on the horizontal axis. This line is called the long-run Phillips curve because it represents points where the economy comes to rest after its long-run adjustment.

Notice that, according to the natural rate hypothesis, the level of unemployment in the economy depends, not on the rate of inflation, but rather on *changes* in the rate of inflation. Thus it is possible for an economy to experience high rates of unemployment even though it has a high rate of inflation, particularly if the government has recently taken steps to reduce the inflation rate. This situation depicts the U.S. economy in the early 1980s and also characterizes many of the less developed countries. By the same token, an economy can enjoy low rates of inflation and low unemployment at the same time once it has stabilized the price level. Also note that if the short-run Phillips curves are curvilinear, as shown in Figure 7–4, the reduction in unemployment achieved by jacking an economy up the long-run Phillips curve will be less than the increased unemployment suffered on the way down the long-run curve. Thus the economy suffers more unemployment in the long-run by stimulating the economy and then squeezing out the inflation than by not doing anything.

Although the natural rate hypothesis admits to a trade-off between unemployment and inflation in the short run, in the long run there is no trade-off. In a sense this is a more optimistic view of the economy than was implied by the original Phillips curve, which led economists to believe that only one of the twin goals of full employment and stable prices was possible at a time. In another sense it is more pessimistic because it implies government policy cannot have a lasting effect on employment and is likely to cause more unemployment than by doing nothing.

THE RATIONAL EXPECTATIONS ARGUMENT

By and large the rational expectations hypothesis as it applies to macroeconomic policy has grown out of the two articles mentioned earlier, by John Muth and Milton Friedman. Muth's rational expectations idea has been brought to bear on Friedman's natural rate hypothesis. Much of the important work of Lucas, Sargent, Wallace, and others has been to integrate the two ideas, give them a rigorous analytical framework, and push them to their logical conclusions. If one were to represent the rational expectations idea on a diagram, the long-run Phillips curve derivation presented in Figure 7–4, in reference to the natural rate hypothesis, probably is the easiest to work with. While there are some subtle differences between the natural rate and the rational expectations explanations of how business and labor react to changes in government policy, the general outcome is similar for both.

In the rational expectations framework, the availability of information and the ability of decision makers to acquire new information play central roles. Let us begin once again at point a in Figure 7–4. In an attempt to reduce unemployment, the government stimulates the economy, say by increasing the rate of growth of the money supply. Prices start to rise. According to the rational expectations hypothesis, business firms have better information on prices in their own industry than on the general level of prices. They mistakenly interpret the increase in prices they observe as coming from an increase in demand for their specific products. Consequently, firms hire more employees in an effort to increase output, and in the process they reduce unemployment. At first employees also mistake the price increases as being specific to their own industries and willingly take job offers thinking that the increase in money wages is an increase in real wages. Thus the economy moves upward on the short-run Phillips curve C_1 from point a to point b. But soon business and labor discover that the increase in prices and wages is general to most industries. Business firms find they are no better off than before, because their costs have risen. Labor discovers the purchasing power of wages declining and presses for wage increases sufficient to at least offset the increase in the general level of prices. When the dust settles, both business and labor find that they are no better off than they were originally at point a. Thus the economy moves from point b to point c. The only thing that has changed is the inflation rate which is now higher because of the government attempt to stimulate the economy.

The next time the government attempts to reduce unemployment, there is less chance to fool employers and employees into thinking that the price increases are specific to their industry. Now people will keep an eye on prices and costs in the general economy. If business firms come to expect higher costs along with higher prices of their products, they are not so likely to increase production, as occurred along the short-run curve C_1. Similarly, employees are not likely to be so willing to increase work if they expect their real wages to decrease rather than increase. And labor unions are likely to become more militant in their wage demands in order to keep their members from falling behind, as occurred in the initial attempt to stimulate the economy.

After business and labor become accustomed to repeated attempts by the government to stimulate the economy, they are likely to build this experience into their expectations. At the first hint of further stimulus, they simply take action that nullifies the stimulus. Business raises prices to take into account expected inflation, with little or no consequences for output or hiring. Employees get on the same escalator regarding wage demands, and soon there is no incentive for employers to take on additional employees. Just as students would soon catch on to the time of arrival of the tardy professor in the example mentioned earlier, it is no less surprising that business and labor would catch on to systematic attempts by the government to stimulate the economy. In terms of Figure 7–4, the short-run Phillips curve would shift upward more and more quickly as people came to expect increased inflation.

After repeated attempts to stimulate the economy, the government at some point is likely to change its priority to fighting inflation rather than unemployment. However, if business and labor come to expect inflation, they will build this expectation into their pricing policies and contractual arrangements. Business firms will continue to increase the list prices of their products to keep pace with expected inflation. But if the rate of growth of the money supply is reduced, the growth of demand for goods and services also will be reduced. As a result there will be increased inventories of unsold goods, and some goods will have to be sold at prices lower than expected. In turn, profits will decline, output will fall, and layoffs will occur. This undesirable outcome is magnified in the labor market. Unions, becoming accustomed to higher and higher rates of inflation, press for continued wage increases to keep pace with inflation. Because of the unexpected decline in the growth of the money supply, growth in demand for goods and services will slow down, as will the rate of increase of the price level. Consequently, real wages will increase, business will suffer reduced profits (or larger losses), and unemployment will grow. It may take many months for expectations to be revised to take account of the new anti-inflationary policy of the government.

The problem is further compounded if people become reluctant to believe what the government tells them. For example, during the 1970s the Nixon, Ford, and Carter administrations all promised the people that within a matter of a few years they would balance the budget and inflation would subside. The people soon learned that, at least during the 1970s, what the politicians said and what they did were two different things. Consequently it has become much more difficult to change people's expectations from the inflationary psychology that built up in the 1970s. The people who expected inflation and reacted accordingly came out the best.

POLICY IMPLICATIONS

The rational expectations hypothesis leads one to very different policy recommendations than the Keynesian models. Recall that the Keynesian theory provides the framework for activist money and fiscal policies, especially the latter. When unemployment threatens, the Keynesian models call for fiscal policy which includes increased government spending or decreased taxes, particularly the former, in order to increase aggregate demand and stimulate spending. The opposite is called for during inflation. In both instances, the Keynesian models assure us that unemployment or inflation can be eliminated by the appropriate government policy.

The rational expectations hypothesis, in contrast, suggests that government fiscal and monetary policies at best will have only a temporary impact on unemployment and at worst can end up causing more inflation and unemployment than are prevented. In order for expansionary monetary policy to have an impact on unemployment, it must be unexpected by economic agents. Once adjustments are made to the policy, the country reverts back to the natural rate of unemployment. Thus the government must be able to fool the people in order to have even a temporary impact on unemployment. Such is very unlikely, because if the government persists in trying to reduce unemployment, its actions become systematic and no longer fool people.

Once an inflationary psychology has built up, it becomes very difficult to bring inflation under control without causing much unemployment. Advocates of the rational expectations hypothesis argue, however, that inflation can be brought under control without causing high unemployment if the government announces in advance its policy of reducing the growth of the money supply so that people will not be taken by surprise. They point to the success of Germany in the 1920s in bringing its hyperinflation under control without causing widespread unemployment. The German government simply announced what it was going to do and did it—that is, it scrapped the old money and started over with a new monetary standard. In the German case, the people appeared to change their inflationary expectations quickly because something had to be done and they had no reason to believe the government would not do what it said. In the United States, however, during the late 1960s and 1970s, the government probably made hundreds of announcements that inflation would be brought under control but did not follow through on any of them. Small wonder that people in the United States doubted government announcements about future policy to stop inflation.

It is interesting to note that, according to the rational expectations hypothesis, the government must fool the people about its policy intentions in order to reduce unemployment even temporarily. But in order to stop inflation without causing widespread unemployment, the government must announce its intentions in advance and convince people that it will do what it says.

THE NEW CLASSICAL ECONOMICS

As explained in the preceding section, the implication of the rational expectations hypothesis is that the government should refrain from activist monetary and fiscal policies. Engaging in such policies will initially have only a temporary impact in reducing unemployment, and after the policies are expected no impact will be attained. Once the inflation rate has increased and people come to expect it, it is very hard if not impossible to reduce inflation without causing unemployment. Thus in the long run the government can end up doing more harm than good to the economy, i.e., causing both inflation and unemployment.

The policy implications of the rational expectations hypothesis are very similar to those of classical economics. Recall that Adam Smith and those following in his footsteps advocated a minimum of government intervention in the economy, although they were more concerned with achieving long-run economic growth than in preventing short-term unemployment. At any rate, the rational expectations hypothesis has been called the new classical economics, in part because of its implications for limited government intervention in the economy. Another similarity between the two schools of thought is that both believe money is neutral. To the classical economists, money was a veil;

the absolute amount of money in an economy should have no effect on real output, although they recognized that changes in the quantity of money are likely to influence prices in the long run and possibly real output in the short run. The same conclusions stem from the rational expectations theory. This is not to say that money is viewed as being unimportant; to the contrary, the vital role of money in facilitating transactions and saving as well as its impact on the price level are widely recognized by economists.

One might go so far as to say that the rational expectations hypothesis has the potential of becoming one of the most important developments in macro-economic theory to come on the scene in the economics profession in a long time, ranking up with the quantity theory of money and the Keynesian models. If it becomes widely accepted by the profession and policy makers, government policy in the future is likely to be profoundly affected. A major strength of the rational expectations hypothesis is that it is based on a sound theoretical foundation, sharing with the main body of economic theory the assumption of rational behavior by people. In contrast, certain aspects of the Keynesian models assume irrational behavior on the part of economic agents.

MAIN POINTS OF CHAPTER 7

1. The Keynesian models did not predict and cannot explain the simultaneous existence of unemployment and inflation during the 1970s and early 1980s.

2. The core of the **rational expectations** argument is that people try to achieve the greatest good for themselves using the information at their disposal.

3. The main body of economic theory assumes rational behavior on the part of economic agents.

4. Expectations are found from past trends as well as from current information and experience.

5. In estimating supply curves it has been common to use last year's actual price as a proxy for the current year's expected price. The cobweb model illustrates this technique.

6. Adaptive expectations models imply irrational behavior because they do not allow for learning on the part of decision makers. Errors resulting systematically from past behavior represent an important source of information.

7. In John Muth's rational expectations model, consumers' and producers' responses to *expected* price changes depended on their responses to *actual* price changes.

8. The original **Phillips curve** was a relationship between the rate of change of money wages and the rate of unemployment. Current representations of the Phillips curve show the relation between the rate of inflation and the unemployment rate.

9. According to the short-run Phillips curve, the higher the rate of inflation, the lower the rate of unemployment. Phillips argued and presented evidence to show that the line tracing out the relationship between inflation and unemployment is curvilinear, implying that at relatively low rates of inflation, unemployment is highly sensitive to a change in the rate of inflation.

10. The short-run Phillips curve appealed to economists who advocated activist fiscal policies because it provided clear choices between unemployment and inflation and indicated how various combinations of the two could be obtained.

11. The simultaneous growth of unemployment and inflation during the 1970s cast doubt on the stability of the Phillips curve and the validity of the Keynesian models.

12. According to the **natural rate hypothesis** government attempts to stimulate the econ-

omy by expansionist monetary policies can have only a temporary impact on unemployment. After a period of adjustment, the economy will revert back to its "natural" rate of unemployment.

13. The underlying argument of the natural rate hypothesis is that an unexpected increase in demand for goods and services stemming from expansionist policies will raise prices, thus lower real wages, and therefore stimulate hiring, which reduces unemployment. But when employees discover what has happened they will press for wage increases in order to recover their loss of real income, and as a result unemployment increases.

14. In the event of contractionary policies put into effect to control inflation, the unexpected decrease in the growth of demand for goods and services causes lower than expected prices, higher real wages and greater unsold inventories of goods, thereby causing increased unemployment.

15. The natural rate hypothesis can be depicted by the long-run Phillips curve, which is a vertical line extending up from the natural rate of unemployment. In the long-run Phillips curve diagram, each short-run Phillips curve corresponds to a given expected rate of inflation.

16. The **rational expectations hypothesis** as it applies to macroeconomics combines John Muth's argument on rational expectations and Milton Friedman's natural rate hypothesis. The graphical representation of the rational expectations hypothesis is given by the long-run Phillips curve.

17. According to the **rational expectations hypothesis,** expansionary policy causes businesspeople and employers initially to believe that the resulting increase in demand is specific to their industries rather than a general increase because they have better information on prices and sales in their own industries than for the economy as a whole. Consequently, unemployment is reduced temporarily. But when real wages and costs increase, production and employment revert back to their former levels. Similarly, policies which attempt to reduce inflation will increase unemployment if they are unexpected because they will lead to an increase in real wages and unsold goods.

18. The more frequently the government attempts to stimulate the economy, the more such activity becomes expected and the smaller its effect on employment.

19. Once people come to believe that inflation will continue, attempts to reduce inflation in all likelihood will cause increased unemployment. This situation depicts the late 1970s and early 1980s.

20. In contrast to the Keynesian models, the rational expectations hypothesis implies that expansionist policies will have an impact on unemployment only if they are unanticipated. In other words, in order for expansionist policies to be effective they must continually fool the general public. And once an inflationary psychology is built up, it is virtually impossible to reduce inflation without causing unemployment. Thus, attempts to stimulate the economy end up causing both inflation and unemployment.

21. The rational expectations hypothesis is sometimes called the **new classical economics,** in part because of its policy implication for limited government intervention and because it maintains that money is neutral—that is, the absolute quantity of money affects the price level but not the real output of the economy, at least in the long run.

QUESTIONS FOR THOUGHT AND DISCUSSION

1. Why has the validity of the Keynesian models been increasingly questioned in the economics profession?

2. How do people form expectations of future events?

3. *a.* How do people form expectations in the cobweb model?
   b. What is implied about the intelligence of producers in the cobweb model?

4. How are expectations formed in the adaptive expectations model? What does this model imply about the intelligence of decision makers?

5. What is shown by the original Phillips curve? How does it differ from the more recent formulation?

6. What is the natural rate hypothesis? What is its underlying rationale?

7. Using the natural rate hypothesis, derive the long-run Phillips curve from several short-run Phillips curves.

8. According to the natural rate hypothesis, is it possible for a country to experience a high rate of inflation and high unemployment at the same time? Explain. How about low inflation and low unemployment?

9. How does the rational expectations differ from the natural rate hypothesis in regard to the construction of the long-run Phillips curve?

10. According to the rational expectations hypothesis, when does the government have to fool the people in order to carry out its policy objectives? Explain.

11. According to the rational expectations hypothesis, when does the government have to convince the people it will do what it says in order to carry out its policy objectives? Explain.

12. Why is the rational expectations hypothesis sometimes called the new classical economics?

CHAPTER 8

SUPPLY SIDE ECONOMICS

Because of their emphasis on aggregate demand, the Keynesian models presented in Chapter 6 have been referred to as demand side economics. In recent years there has been a renewed emphasis on the importance of production and supply in achieving full employment and stable prices. The rather broad collection of ideas that have been put forth in this area has come to be known as supply side economics. The core of the supply side argument is that high marginal tax rates constitute a strong disincentive to work and invest, thereby leading to a stagnant, high-unemployment, inflationary economy. Supply siders also argue that excessive government regulation of business firms has increased the cost of doing business and dampened economic activity. Third, they advocate a return to the gold standard as a means of curbing inflation and stimulating employment.

While the main difference between Keynesians and supply side advocates centers on the two groups of decision makers (consumers versus producers), it also may be said that the Keynesian models deal mainly with short-run business cycle fluctuations in the economy, whereas the supply side arguments dwell more on longer-run economic growth issues. This is not to say that the supply side economics completely ignores short-run unemployment and inflation problems. For if real economic growth can be sustained, these short-run problems are likely to be less severe than would be the case in a low- or zero-growth economy. Also in contrast to the Keynesian view, supply side economics does not advocate "fine tuning" the economy by periodically changing tax rates. In this regard, the supply side argument is similar to the conclusions drawn from the rational expectations hypothesis.

Although the term *supply side economics* came on the scene during the 1970s, the recognition that high taxes can stifle economic activity goes back to the time of the classical economists. For example, David Hume in his essay *Of Taxes,* published in 1776, wrote, "tis to be feared that taxes all over Europe are multiplying to such a degree as will entirely crush all art and industry." In fact, the classical economists could be called the original supply side economists because of their emphasis on economic growth and their concern over the detrimental effects of high taxes and government intervention in the economy. Because modern supply side economics is a relatively recent development, there is not yet a large body of literature available on the topic, although this situation is likely to change in the 1980s.[1]

THE LAFFER CURVE

The diagram that has come to be closely associated with supply side economics is the Laffer curve. This diagram, popularized by a U.S. economist, Arthur Laffer, depicts the relationship between income tax rates and income tax revenues. Specifically, it says that as tax rates rise above zero, initially the tax revenue collected by the government increases. But as tax rates continue to increase, at some point the tax revenue collected will reach a maximum. After that point, further increases in tax rates will cause tax revenues to decline. At the extreme case, when tax rates reach 100 percent, the revenue collected will fall to zero because no one will work, at least for money, if 100 percent of his or her earnings is taken by the government. The Laffer curve is shown on Figure 8–1.

At the relatively low tax rate T_1 shown on the vertical axis, tax revenue equals R_1. As the tax rate increases to T_2, tax revenue continues to increase and reaches a maximum at R_2. However, with further increases in the tax rate, the revenue collected by the government begins to decline. Notice that the revenue collected at the high tax rate T_3 is the same as the revenue collected at the low rate T_1. Thus, according to the Laffer curve, two different tax rates will yield the same given amount of revenue for the government. Obviously, if the government wishes to maximize tax revenue it will choose tax rate T_2. Of course, there is no reason why a country would necessarily want to maximize the tax revenue of the government.

Supply side advocates argued that in the United States during the 1960s and 1970s the income tax rate increased to the point where the country was on the upper, backward-bending part of the Laffer curve. Consequently, they argued that high taxes stifled economic growth and resulted in high unemployment in the late 1970s and early 1980s.

It should be pointed out that the tax rate which maximizes tax revenue is not necessarily 50 to 60 percent, as illustrated by the diagram. This rate is what the people want it to be and is likely to vary by time and place. During wartime,

---

[1] Two books which cover the broad outline of supply side arguments are Jude Wanniski, *The Way the World Works* (New York: Basic Books, 1978), and George Gilder, *Wealth and Poverty* (New York: Basic Books, 1981).

FIGURE 8–1 The Laffer curve

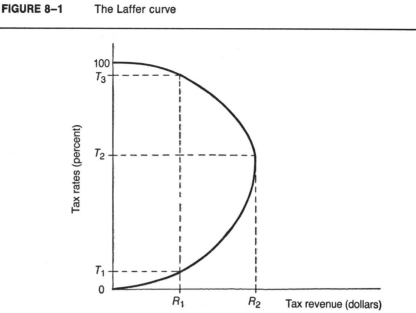

for example, the maximum revenue rate may be quite high as people continue to work out of a sense of patriotic duty to aid the war effort. In another time, the maximum revenue rate may be lower, especially if the government becomes unpopular or if people do not believe they are receiving good value from their tax dollars.

The shape of the Laffer curve should also vary by the governmental unit. The maximum revenue rate is likely to be lower for a local or state government than for the federal government because it is easier for people to leave high-tax communities or states than it is to leave the country. Also, the length of time people have to adjust to a tax change should affect the shape of the curve. Immediately after a tax increase, for example, the revenue collected is likely to increase. But after a period of time, which may be several years, people adjust their work habits and spending decisions to the new higher rates, and tax revenue can decline to a point lower than the original level.

TAX RATES VERSUS TAX REVENUES

The main purpose of the Laffer curve is to highlight the difference between tax rates and tax revenues. An increase in the former does not necessarily lead to an increase in the latter. Thus it is very important for a government to know where on the Laffer curve the country or state is located. If it is on the upper portion of the curve, an attempt to increase tax revenue, say to avoid a deficit, will have the opposite effect. In this situation an increase in tax revenue will be forthcoming only if the government decreases tax rates. This idea motivated the Reagan administration to push for tax rate reductions in the early 1980s.

The relationship between tax rates and tax revenues is easiest to understand by considering a simple example—that of a toll bridge. At a relatively low toll, say five cents per crossing, the revenue collected will be some positive value because most people who desire to use the bridge will not be deterred by this modest toll charge. If the toll is raised to 10 cents per crossing (assume no inflation), the revenue is likely to increase but may not double if some people decide to use the bridge less often. As the toll continues to increase (in real terms), say to $0.25, then to $0.50, $0.75, and $1.00, people will begin to conserve more and more on their crossing. Some will find jobs on the same side of the river where they live or decide it does not pay to shop across the river. At some point, the decline in number of people using the bridge will more than offset the increase in the toll rate, causing the revenue obtained to decline. At some extremely high toll, such as $100 or $1,000 per crossing, the toll revenue would likely fall to zero as people either stopped crossing the river or found some other way to cross that avoided the toll, most likely the latter.

TAXES AND WORK

The impact of increasing tax rates on economic activity and tax revenue in a state or the national economy is of course more complex than the toll bridge example, but it follows a similar principle. Economists have long been aware that taxes affect decisions to work and invest. Consider first the work decision. A person's time can be divided into two parts: work for monetary reward, either self-employed or for an employer, and all other activities, which for lack of a better label shall be called nonmonetary activities. The second category, which takes up three quarters or more of the time of most people, includes more than leisure as traditionally defined. It includes everything from eating, sleeping, rest, and recreation to work for one's self or family, doing such things as preparing meals, taking care of children, repairing house, car, or appliances, and even producing goods or services to be bartered for other goods or services but not sold for money in the market. How much time a person devotes to work for money and how much to nonmonetary activities depends in part on each person's tastes and in part on the opportunity cost of each. In analyzing the effects of changes in taxes, it is most accurate to assume that tastes do not change, particularly for society as a whole. This allows us to see how taxes can change the allocation of time to the two categories of activities.

In order to see how taxes can affect the allocation of time, it is first necessary to define the opportunity cost of each. The opportunity cost of working for monetary reward is the satisfaction or utility given up by not being able to devote as much time to other activities—the satisfaction given up by not having as much time to travel, pursue hobbies, spend with one's family, fix the car, shop for bargains, and so forth. Similarly the opportunity cost of nonmonetary activities is the income given up by not devoting as much time to work. For most people it is not the income per se that is valued but what it will buy—food, clothing, shelter, and the host of other things that money can be exchanged for.

In order to see how income taxes affect the allocation of time between work and nonmonetary activities, it will help to begin with a hypothetical situation where there are zero taxes. Assume also that the individual is maximizing utility with the before-tax allocation of time. (The conditions for maximizing utility from a given amount of time are set out in the companion micro text in Chapter 13, The Economics of Education.) Now suppose an income tax is imposed that gives the individual in question a marginal tax rate of 50 percent, so that the opportunity cost of allocating an extra hour to nonmonetary activities is reduced by one half. In other words, the price of the utility obtained from an extra hour of nonmonetary activities is reduced by 50 percent. If the demand curve for the utility gained from nonmonetary activities is downward sloping, a reduction in its price will prompt the individual to buy more of this utility, which means that the person will buy less utility from the income from work. The net result of the increase in income taxes is to cause people to reallocate time away from work toward other, nonmonetary activities. The opportunity for making this kind of decision appears to be greatest for so-called secondary wage earners—married women, teenagers, and people of retirement age. These groups have somewhat more flexibility than primary wage earners or full-time workers in deciding how many hours per week to work, or whether they will join the labor force. However, primary wage earners do have some discretion on how many hours they will work per year by the amount of overtime, absenteeism, and time between jobs that they choose to take. Since secondary wage earners make up about one half of the labor force in the United States, the potential impact of taxes on work can be substantial. In a later section more specific information is presented on the effects of taxes on employment behavior.

A similar situation results from an increase in sales or excise taxes. The only difference is that these taxes reduce the utility of an extra hour of work by decreasing the goods and services that a given amount of untaxed income will buy rather than by decreasing the income itself. But the end result is still the same; the opportunity cost or price of the utility obtained from nonmonetary activities is reduced.

The relative amounts of time allocated to work and nonmonetary activities can also be affected by payments from the government to individuals. Included in these payments are unemployment compensation and the money received through the various welfare programs. Money received from these payments in effect is a substitute for money obtained from work. Moreover, such money is an attractive substitute because a person does not have to give up nonmonetary activities to obtain it. In other words, if one has a choice of receiving money from work which carries an opportunity cost, that is, the time that cannot be devoted to nonmonetary activities, or receiving it from government programs, which for many people does not require much of an opportunity cost, it is rational for a person to take the latter.[2] In fact, most of these government payments will be forthcoming only if a person is not working. Granted there is a time limit on how long a person can collect unemployment compensation, so that the incentive to return to work is eventually restored. But by lengthening the unemployment period such payments still decrease the average amount of time that people will want to work per year in the total economy.

It is interesting to note that money collected through taxes and paid out in the form of unemployment compensation and welfare benefits acts as a double disincentive to work. Recall that taxes lower the opportunity cost of nonmonetary activities, which leads to a greater allocation of time to these endeavors and less time for work. In addition, money obtained from government payments is for many people a cheap substitute for money received from work,

---

[2] For some people the social stigma of being on welfare represents an opportunity cost of collecting this money, and as a result they may not take advantage of the programs.

which again causes people to reallocate time away from work-for-pay activities. Thus taxes cause both taxpayers and certain tax receivers to allocate less time to work, at least in the above-ground, monetized economy.

Although the tendency to substitute nonmonetary activity time for work time when taxes are increased reduces measured GNP and tax payments from what they would otherwise be, it does not follow that the standard of living falls in the same proportion as GNP. At least some of the extra time spent away from work yields utility which is not reflected in GNP. Also the work that one does for one's self or family, such as repairing the car or appliances, has value that is not reflected in GNP. Indeed higher tax rates are conducive to do-it-yourself activities. If a person's marginal tax rate is 50 percent, for example, one has to earn an extra $200 to pay for a $100 repair bill. Thus if a person is reasonably handy, it may well be cheaper in terms of opportunity cost to do the repair at home rather than hire someone else to do it.

High rates of taxation also provide a strong incentive to enter the so-called underground economy. One technique is to barter at least part of what a person produces for part of what one buys. For example, an auto mechanic may repair the plumber's car in exchange for plumbing services. No money changes hands; no taxes are paid. Both receive more net satisfaction for their work time. Although such behavior is illegal in the eyes of the IRS, it does result in a greater quantity of goods and services than would otherwise be forthcoming. At the present time, at least, barter without reporting the value to the IRS is relatively minor compared to other types of tax evasion. Perhaps most significant is the sale of goods and services without reporting the income. The incentive to enter this market is great; for example, a person in the 50 percent tax bracket can clear twice as much from an extra $100 of sales than someone operating within the confines of the law. Finally, there is the incentive to "fudge" on reporting income and expenses, which becomes progressively stronger as tax rates increase. High tax rates therefore tend to cause more and more people to become lawbreakers.

TAXES AND INVESTMENT

The total output of goods and services in any economy depends on the amount of labor that is put forth and the amount of capital which people have to work with. Investment is the process of producing capital. Part of the total investment in any country is devoted to replacing capital that has worn out or become obsolete, and part adds to the total stock of capital. Unless investment is large enough to replace old capital and also add to the total capital stock, there is little hope of achieving economic growth and improving the society's standard of living, particularly among poor people. Recall as well that investment requires saving. If people spent all of their income on consumer goods and services, there would be no resources left to produce capital goods. The act of saving releases resources for the production of capital.

According to the 1972–73 expenditure survey conducted by the U.S. Department of Labor, the percent of income spent on current consumption decreases (percent saved increases) as the level of income increases (Table 8–1). Indeed, at the lowest income level the amount spent on current consumption is nearly double the level of disposable income. In contrast, at the highest income level, people spend just a little over half their disposable income on consumer

TABLE 8–1 Average family disposable income, current consumption expenditures, and percent consumed by selected income level, United States, 1972–73 expenditure survey

Pre-tax income level	Average family disposable income	Consumption expenditures	Percent consumed
Less than $3,000	$ 1,637	$ 3,211	196
$7,000 to $7,999	6,716	6,501	97
$12,000 to $14,999	11,485	9,388	82
$20,000 to $24,999	18,371	13,027	71
$25,000 or over	30,460	17,290	57

Source: U.S. Department of Labor, Bureau of Labor Statistics, *Handbook of Labor Statistics*, December 1980, pp. 368–74.

goods and save the remainder. Supply siders argue, therefore, that high-income people play an important role in the economy by providing much of the nation's funds for investment. However, supply side advocates point out that the nation's personal income tax falls especially hard on high-income people, which in turn reduces saving and investment from what it would be if marginal tax rates were lower.

The figures presented in Table 8–2 show the average federal income tax payment by income level for 1981 in the United States. Notice that the percent

TABLE 8–2 Federal income tax payments as a percent of taxable income, 1981

Adjusted gross income bracket	Percent of taxable income paid as federal income taxes
Under $10,000	8.4
$10,000–$19,999	13.7
$20,000–$29,999	17.2
$30,000–$39,999	20.2
$40,000–$49,999	23.4
$50,000–$99,999	29.3
$100,000 and over	45.6

Source: U.S. Department of Commerce, Bureau of the Census, *Statistical Abstract of the United States*, 1984, p. 328.

of adjusted gross income paid as federal income taxes increases substantially from the lowest to the highest brackets. This occurs because of the progressive nature of the U.S. income tax. (A progressive tax is one where the tax rate increases at higher income levels. A more thorough discussion of progressive taxes is presented in the following section in this chapter.) At any rate, supply siders argue that the relatively large proportion of income taken by federal income taxes from the upper-income families substantially reduces the total saving of these people, which in turn reduces the funds available for investment.

Supply side advocates point out that during the 1970s the United States had the highest marginal income tax rates of the major noncommunist industrialized nations and also had the lowest percent of GNP devoted to investment. Figures on the percent of GNP devoted to investment for seven of the major industrialized nations are presented in Table 8–3. Notice that the United States ranked

TABLE 8–3   Percent of GNP devoted to investment: An international comparison

| | Gross investment as a percent of GNP | | |
Country	1960	1970	1980
Japan	34.3	38.9	33.0
France	22.9	25.9	23.1
Canada	23.3	21.3	23.4
West Germany	27.2	27.8	25.1
Italy	23.8	23.0	21.1
United Kingdom	18.4	19.4	16.5
United States	18.3	17.5	17.1

Source: World Bank, *World Tables* (Baltimore: The Johns Hopkins Press, 3d ed., 1983), pp. 222–59.

last among these seven countries (except for 1980 when the U.S. rate exceeded the U.K. figure), and that the U.S. proportion of gross investment in GNP averaged just a little over half the Japanese rate over the period.

Supply side proponents argue too that the existence of high income tax rates on high incomes not only reduces the amount of money available for saving but also reduces the incentive to save from the disposable income that remains. To see why this is so, it is first necessary to call to mind that the payoff from investment is by no means a sure thing. There is always the risk that the venture may fail and the investor suffer the loss of not only the anticipated returns from the investment but also the principal itself. Thus every investor must weigh the expected gains against the possibility of loss.

The higher the income tax on expected gains, the lower the net after-tax return from any investment. But if the investment should fail and the investor suffer the loss of some or all of the money invested, the taxes saved from other income will be less than the extra taxes paid if the investment had been a success. In a sense, the "deck is stacked" against the investor. High tax rates reduce expected gains more than they reduce expected losses. A numerical example may help to illustrate this point. Suppose a potential investor who is in the 40 percent tax bracket from existing income sees an opportunity of making $100,000 before taxes by investing $100,000. He anticipates that his chances of success are 50-50. Suppose also that, if the project succeeds, the $100,000 gain will be taxed at the 50 percent bracket. Thus, if the project succeeds, the investor can gain at most $50,000 after taxes. But if the project fails and the $100,000 are lost, the net after-tax loss will be $60,000 ($100,000 × the 40 percent tax rate on the reduction in total income). Therefore, progressive marginal tax rates reduce expected gains more than expected losses, which in turn discourages risk taking and investment.

Advocates of supply side economics argue that this characteristic of the tax system, which discourages risk taking, biases existing investment toward relatively safe, but low-return investments. And such investments tend to be found in old, established firms or industries. They also argue that new firms and industries provide the greatest share of new jobs in the country and are the main source of economic growth. Consequently, if this argument is correct, high rates of taxation not only reduce total saving and investment but also cause existing investment to have a smaller contribution to jobs and growth than would be the case if taxes were lower.

Supply siders also argue that the large growth in government regulations during the 1970s had a dampening effect on investment in new firms and industries. For one thing, buying the legal expertise necessary to cope with the host of complex regulations and to fill out the great number of forms and reports may not be economically feasible for a small firm. This circumstance puts large established firms at a competitive advantage. And according to figures put out by the Small Business Administration, between 1969 and 1976 over 86 percent of the new jobs in the United States came from small firms. Even for the large established firms, the high cost of testing new products and waiting for more government testing, may have biased investment away from development of new products.

The antibusiness climate that prevailed in the federal government in general and the Justice Department in particular during the 1960s and 1970s is cited as another drag on the U.S. economy, reducing growth in jobs and output. An example of this antibusiness climate is the monopolization suit filed by Attorney General Ramsey Clark against IBM during the last hours of the Johnson administration in early 1969. The suit continued during the Nixon, Ford, and Carter administrations before being dropped during the early part of the Reagan administration; it piled up over 104,000 pages of transcript and millions of dollars of legal fees. The IBM legal fees, of course, have been passed on to buyers of IBM products in the form of higher prices, while taxpayers have borne the $13.4 million bill for the government lawyers. But perhaps more important, such suits may have had the effect of causing successful firms to hold back on their expansion plans and as a consequence reduced the creation of new jobs as well as dampening economic growth.

PROGRESSIVE TAXATION

As mentioned, progressive taxes are those which tax higher-income people at higher rates than their low-income counterparts. Proportional taxes tax everyone at the same rate, while regressive taxes tax low-income people at higher rates than high-income taxpayers. In the United States and most other noncommunist countries, income taxes are progressive. Because of the concern over the effect of high marginal tax rates on economic activity by supply side economics, it will be useful to examine in some detail the case for progressive taxation. It may come as a surprise to learn that the case is not as strong as most people may at first suppose.[3]

---

[3] See Walter J. Blum and Harry Kalven, Jr., *The Uneasy Case for Progressive Taxation* (Chicago: University of Chicago Press, 1963).

In the United States the first progressive tax on incomes was imposed during the Civil War. The tax was imposed as an emergency war measure and was intended to be temporary. While the progressive provision of the tax was repealed at the end of the war, the income tax itself remained a few more years, until 1872. It was not until 1913, after the passage of the 16th Amendment, that the United States became committed to a progressive income tax. Most of the controversy over the adoption of the income tax focused on whether it was constitutional to tax income rather than on the progressive feature of the tax itself. Even nowadays we occasionally hear of someone who refuses to pay income tax on the basis that it is unconstitutional. But the courts have pretty much settled the issue in the affirmative, that is, it is constitutional.

A progressive income tax can be attained in one of three ways. First, the tax will be progressive if the marginal tax rate increases at higher income levels. The tax rate on the last dollar of income is referred to as the marginal tax rate. Second, the tax will be progressive even though the marginal tax rate is constant if income below a specified level is not taxed. For example, at a constant tax rate of 20 percent and a $2,000 income exemption, the total tax on a $10,000 per year income would be $1,600 while the tax on a $100,000 income would be $19,600. Thus the flat rate tax becomes mildly progressive, with a 16 percent average rate on the $10,000 income and 19.6 percent on the $100,000 sum. The third way is a combination of the first two; this characterizes the U.S. income tax at the present. It should be understood, of course, that higher-income people pay more total taxes under a proportional income tax and would likely pay more even under a regressive income tax, although the latter could be made so steeply regressive that total tax payments decreased with income.

In adopting various taxes, most societies have attempted to follow certain guidelines or principles in an effort to make taxes as fair and equitable as possible. One such guideline is the equal-sacrifice principle. There are various ways of interpreting this principle. A literal interpretation would be that each person should bear an equal sacrifice in the payment of taxes. Of course, a tax system where everyone paid the same amount of money as taxes would be highly regressive because high-income people would pay a much smaller proportion of their income as taxes than low-income individuals or families. Thus the literal meaning of the equal-sacrifice principle cannot be used to justify progressive taxes.

In applying the equal-sacrifice principle to taxes, it has been commonly argued that a dollar given up in taxes by a high-income person requires less sacrifice on the part of that person than is required of a low-income individual giving up the same amount. Therefore, for sacrifice to be equal, the high-income individual should give up more total dollars in taxes than a poor person. The validity of this argument requires two assumptions. First it assumes a *diminishing marginal utility of money*. In other words, it is assumed that each additional dollar of income adds less and less to the utility or satisfaction of a person. The diminishing marginal utility of money, which cannot be proven, should not be confused with a similar concept in economics that can be shown to be true, namely, the diminishing marginal utility of a good. As defined in the companion micro text, this latter concept says that, beyond some point, the consumption of additional units of a good or service, holding constant other goods and services, will yield smaller and smaller amounts of satisfaction. The diminishing marginal utility of money is different because money is infinitely flexible and can be used to buy more of every good or service. Second, the argument assumes that a poor person receives more satisfaction from an extra dollar of income than a rich person does. Since economists generally agree that an interpersonal comparison of utility cannot be made, there is no way to prove the validity of the second assumption either.

Even if one grants the possibility of a diminishing marginal utility of money and that a poor person receives more satisfaction from an extra dollar than does a rich person, the justification of a progressive tax by the equal-sacrifice principle also requires that satisfaction per dollar of additional income diminishes more than proportionately to the increase in income. If satisfaction per dollar falls only in proportion to income growth, the equal-sacrifice principle could justify only a proportional income tax.

A second principle on which to base a tax system is that taxes should be determined by benefits received from government; the more benefits a person receives the more taxes he or she should pay. The question is: Do benefits received from income taxes paid to the federal or state governments differ among income groups? In the case of national defense one might argue that people benefit equally because everyone's freedom and liberty receive equal protection. In the case of welfare benefits, the poor are supposed to be the main beneficiaries, although there are certain groups of relatively high-income people that have benefited from these programs, namely, government bureaucrats, medical doctors, and lawyers. At any rate it is not the intention of welfare programs to aid the rich. All in all, there is no indication that the income tax system is based on the benefits-received principle. This principle is used, however, in the assignment of many other taxes, such as gasoline taxes for maintaining roads and various user fees for the use of government goods and services. Here there is an attempt, at least, to make payments in proportion to benefits received.

Probably the main argument used to justify the progressive income tax is the desire on the part of the majority of people to obtain greater equality in the distribution of income and wealth. By taking proportionately more money away from high-income people, society is able to reduce the inequality of income and wealth from what it would otherwise be. If some of this money is used to benefit poor people in the form of welfare payments, for example, the income distribution is further equalized. While the majority of people may view a more equal distribution of income as being more "fair" than a less equal distribution generated by free-market forces, the use of a progressive income tax to obtain a more equal distribution poses something of an ethical problem for a democracy. Voters through their elected representatives decide on their preferred income distribution. But in a democracy the majority rules. Since high-income people are a minority group, the majority has the power to confiscate the income and wealth of this minority. In the United States Constitution and subsequent amendments, much care is taken to safeguard the rights and property of minority groups—except the high-income minority. This is a rather significant oversight because the confiscation of income and wealth of the high-income minority is likely to affect the economic health of the majority. High-income people tend to be the highly trained and talented professionals and entrepreneurs who contribute much to society's output of goods and services. Reducing their incentives to work and invest can become a particularly heavy drag on the economy, and everyone may end up being worse off. The recognition of this fact by the majority may temper their desire to tax high incomes even more heavily.

Another characteristic of the U.S. income tax is that it is applied very unevenly across the population. Some income is taxed twice, some is not taxed at all, some is taxed at high rates, and some at low rates. This situation is undesirable because it creates distortions and inefficiencies in the economy and also tends to erode the public's willingness to pay the tax because of a growing feeling that not everyone is treated alike, which of course is true.

A major distortion is caused by the double taxation of dividends earned on corporate stock. First the corporation pays a tax on the earnings of equity capital—that is, the earnings on capital owned by stockholders. Then when stock dividends are paid out to stockholders, these people pay tax on the dividends through the personal income tax. For example, if a corporate firm earns an additional $100 from equity capital and the marginal tax rate is 46 percent for the firm and 50 percent for the stockholder, the total tax on this extra $100 is $100 × 0.46 + $54 × 0.50 = $73.00. Hence the marginal tax rate is 73 percent; for the $100 earned by equity capital with these marginal tax rates, the stockholder receives $27.00 and the federal government $73.00. When the same income is taxed twice, even modest marginal tax rates can add up to a rather large percentage of total income paid in taxes.

On the other hand, income from money invested in municipal bonds is not taxed at all in the federal income tax and is not to be subject to state income taxes if the bonds were issued in that state. In this case, the entire $100 of interest earned on these bonds goes to the bondholder regardless of that person's income tax bracket. Therefore, high-income people have a particularly strong incentive to invest in public works projects rather than new capital in the business world. There is nothing wrong with public works projects, but the tax system leads to an overinvestment in this area relative to investment in private firms.

The progressive nature of the personal income tax also means that high-income people receive a smaller net after-tax return from savings than their low-income counterparts do. Since high-income people save a relatively high proportion of their income during any given year (Table 8–1), high taxes on this income become a strong disincentive to save. In fact, as the tax rates on savings increase, people begin to discover that money spent on luxury cars, yachts, vacation homes, jewelry, etc. may yield a greater return in terms of utility than money saved and invested through the stock market. For example, suppose a high-income person considers the option of investing $1 million in a business firm through the purchase of stock versus the same amount in a luxury home. If the business firm can manage a 10 percent return on the investment, it will earn $100 thousand per year. Suppose also that the money is invested in a large firm so that the corporate income tax is 46 percent and that the firm declares the remaining $54 thousand as a dividend (actually, some of the profit will likely be kept as retained earnings). If the investor is in the 50 percent marginal tax bracket, only $27,000 is left as after-tax earnings. This amounts to a 2.70 percent after-tax return on capital. If the individual lives in a state with an income tax, the return is even lower. Bear in mind too that the investment is subject to risk; the firm could lose all or part of the money invested. The saver may decide that the certain and untaxed satisfaction received from the luxury home is greater than the expected satisfaction that could be received on the uncertain after-tax income. One might be tempted to conclude that the existence of luxury items is an indication that taxes on high-income people are still not high enough. But it may indicate the opposite, namely, that taxes on money earned in the business sector are so high that relatively little is given up by spending one's money on luxury consumption items, particularly if they are a good hedge against inflation.

A SIMPLIFIED CASH–FLOW INCOME TAX

In addition to the distortions and inefficiencies created by the current income tax code, it has become an extremely complex set of rules and regulations. Each year millions of dollars and labor hours are spent searching for loopholes in the tax law and in just filling out the tax forms. While the expenditure of these resources is perfectly rational for individuals and business firms, particularly for high-income people with high tax rates, it amounts to pure waste for the country. Nothing is produced by these activities. The differential treatment received by different people under the tax law also creates resentment because of the belief that the tax is unfair. For example, large business firms and high-income people have ways of legally reducing their taxes that are for the most part not available to hourly wage earners. Most people probably would prefer a tax system where all income was taxed alike so that no one would receive special favors. By taxing all income, the tax rates could be lower and still generate the same revenue.

A simplified tax code could tax all cash income received by households at the same rate regardless of source, whether wages, capital gains, or other kinds of income. It also could tax all incomes at the same rate regardless of size, that is a flat-rate tax. Whether such a tax would be politically feasible is open to question, because of the apparently widespread belief that high incomes should be taxed at higher rates than low incomes. Also there would likely be widespread support for some reduction in taxable income according to number of dependents and the amount given to churches and charitable institutions. Of course, the greater the amount of income shielded by exemptions, the higher the rate must be on the remaining income to generate the same revenue from a given output of total income.

The cash-flow principle could simplify the tax code on business earnings even more. The tax could be computed on the difference between gross sales and out-of-pocket expenses incurred in the production of goods and services during the year in question. There would be no need to construct complicated depreciation schedules. If a firm purchases a $100,000 asset to be used in the business and pays for it by contributing $25,000 of its own money plus $75,000 of borrowed funds, the firm would deduct $25,000 as expenses from its gross sales during the year of purchase. The amounts paid in interest and principal in future years would be deducted as expenses during those years. When an asset is sold, the money received from the owner's equity would be counted as ordinary income and taxed accordingly. In the case of installment sales, only the money actually received each year would be taxed.

By appealing to fairness and efficiency, one might argue that dividends paid out by corporations to their stockholders should not be counted as taxable income to the corporations. Otherwise, as pointed out earlier, these dividends are subject to double taxation; once through the corporation and once through the stockholders. Whether the government, even a conservative administration, would be willing to give up the revenue from the corporate income tax is open to question. However, the importance of this tax as a revenue source has declined, particularly after the tax cuts of the first Reagan administration were legislated. In 1984 the corporation income tax contributed about 10 percent of federal tax revenue, down from 16 percent in 1974. The corporate income tax rate was reduced in an attempt to stimulate investment.

In 1984 the federal government collected $385 billion in personal and corporate income taxes. A flat rate tax of about 11 percent on all income generated in NNP ($3,430 billion) would have yielded about the same revenue.[4] (This revenue would be generated by only a single taxation of stock dividends.) Some progressivity could be achieved by exempting a minimum level of income from taxation, say $1,000 for individuals and $2,000 for families. Still more progressivity could be obtained, of course, by raising tax rates on higher incomes, depending on society's wishes.

An argument that is frequently used against a simplified, flat-rate income tax system is that the government can use differential tax rates or special exemptions to influence the allocation of resources. For example, if the government wishes to promote home ownership it can allow the deduction of interest paid on home loans in calculating one's tax liability. Or if more investment in urban infrastructure is desired, income obtained by interest earned on municipal bonds may not be taxed at all.

A close examination of this argument reveals, however, that it has little economic merit. It is true that differential tax rates do influence the allocation of the nation's resources, pulling more resources into areas where taxes are low, while decreasing spending on investment in high-tax areas. The error of the argument is that if people regard certain products as desirable, such as home ownership or infrastructure, they already have an incentive to invest in these areas. By using tax incentives the government distorts the economy by causing too many resources to be allocated to the favored areas. It can be shown that such distortions reduce the total value of goods and services obtained in the economy from a given amount of resources.[5]

SUPPLY SIDE EVIDENCE

Supply side advocates argue that a reduction in marginal tax rates on middle- and high-income people would stimulate work and investment, leading to a more healthy, growing economy with lower rates of unemployment than existed during the 1970s. They also argue that the increased economic activity resulting from lower tax rates could actually increase government tax revenues from those now collected by the higher tax rates. Is there any evidence to suggest that these arguments are valid? The early advocates of supply side economics generally appealed to historical evidence to support their argu-

---

[4] It should be recognized that NNP includes the implicit rental value of owner-occupied housing and of food produced and consumed on farms. The former is not taxed and the latter is very hard to tax. Thus, the revenue would be somewhat less than this unless double taxation of dividends were retained.

[5] The proof of this proposition is given in advanced public finance or welfare economics courses.

ments. In more recent years, rigorous analytical studies have emerged as further tests of the supply side hypothesis.

United States

Probably the example used most frequently by supply side advocates is the Kennedy administration tax cuts during the early to mid-1960s. In the years immediately preceding the tax cut, the U.S. economy had suffered from what at that time were considered high rates of unemployment and low economic growth. After the tax cuts were put into effect, the unemployment rate declined and the rate of economic growth increased. In fact, the mid-1960s are now looked upon as something of a "golden age" as far as the economy is concerned. Unemployment was low, there was substantial economic growth resulting in higher incomes for poor people and a reduction in poverty, and the price level was relatively stable. The economy then started to deteriorate when income taxes were raised during the latter part of the Johnson administration in an attempt to raise revenue to finance the Great Society programs and the economic cost of the Vietnam War. It is argued that throughout the 1970s, when people were pushed into ever higher tax brackets because of inflation, the economy became more and more sluggish, exhibiting relatively low real growth along with high rates of inflation and unemployment. While it is widely believed that the Kennedy administration tax cuts did much to stimulate the economy in the early 1960s, there is another factor, namely the more than doubling of the rate of growth of the money supply (to be discussed in Chapter 13), which can also help explain the improvement in the economy at that time.

Jude Wanniski, one of the original supply side advocates, argues that the stock market crash of 1929 and the ensuing Great Depression were caused by the passage of the Smoot-Hawley Tariff Act of 1930. This act raised the import tariffs on many commodities in an attempt to reduce foreign competition and preserve jobs. Although the stock market crash came before the act's passage, Wanniski argues that the market anticipated the passage and crashed when it became certain that President Hoover would sign it.[6] It is argued that high import tariffs damaged the U.S. economy because they decreased imports, and when other countries sold less to the United States, they had fewer dollars with which to buy goods from the United States. Hence the business community suffered losses in sales. Whether the Smoot-Hawley Act had so large an impact as to cause the Great Depression is open to question. During 1929 exports accounted for only 4.5 percent of United States GNP. Later in this book (Chapter 13), an alternative explanation is given for the Great Depression.

In the realm of more recent experience, the tax rate reductions put into effect during the first Reagan administration and the subsequent economic recovery have been used as evidence supporting the supply side theory. It is also pointed out that when the marginal tax rate was reduced to 50 percent from 70 percent the proportion of income paid as taxes by the $50,000-per-year and above income people actually increased. This suggests that the U.S. economy was on the backward bending portion of the Laffer curve. Moreover, supply siders have used this evidence to argue for still further tax cuts, with the

---

[6] For a detailed account of the events leading up to the Smoot-Hawley signing, see Wanniski, *The Way the World Works*.

objective of bringing the top marginal rate down to 25 or 30 percent in order to stimulate the economy even more and to reduce the deficit.

In a recent study of the U.S. labor market, Professor Jerry A. Hausman of the Massachusetts Institute of Technology estimated that taxes and welfare payments have significantly reduced the hours worked of U.S. workers.[7] In comparison to a no income tax case, Hausman estimated that the federal income tax alone caused married male workers in the $8,000 to $12,000 income level to work 8 percent less per year. (These figures are for 1975.) In the case of married women, a 1 percent increase in taxes results in about a 1 percent decline in hours worked per year. The progressive income tax is especially burdensome for married couples, where both husband and wife work, because their combined income pushes them into a higher tax bracket than if each were single. Consequently, there is less of an incentive for one of them to work, at least as much as would otherwise be the case.

Supply side advocates also have compared unemployment rates and growth experience between states to shed light on the impact of taxes on economic activity. Massachusetts, which has one of the highest state tax rates in the country, is frequently singled out for comparison. Although Massachusetts ranks high among states in before-tax per capita income and has a highly educated populace, prestigious educational institutions, and a small minority population (3 percent black), its record of economic growth and its ability to provide jobs for its young people are far from enviable. During the 1970s its rate of growth of employment was less than half that the rest of the country in spite of relatively large infusions of federal tax funds via CETA and other programs to provide jobs. In contrast, the neighboring state of New Hampshire, which has less wealth and human capital but ranks among the states with the lowest tax rates, led the nation in the rate of new-job creation during the same period. The well-known growth of new industry and jobs in the sun-belt states, which traditionally have had low taxes, also can be cited as supporting the supply side argument. While this evidence is a strong indication that people do respond to taxes in deciding where to live or where to locate new industry, one should bear in mind that what is true for a state need not necessarily hold true for the country. Part of the response to lower taxes consists of moves between states on the part of people and industry. This response is not generally available to the nation as a whole. Part of this theoretical difficulty can be overcome by comparing nations in regard to differences in taxes and growth.

Other Countries

If the supply side argument is correct, one should observe a negative correlation between economic growth and taxes. Nations achieving the highest growth rates should be those experiencing the lowest taxes. The evidence presented in Table 8–4 appears to support this hypothesis. The left side of the table lists seven countries that were among the slowest growing nations in the world during the 1970s in terms of real GNP per capita, whereas those on the right were among those with the most rapid growth rates. The level of taxation is measured by the percentage of central government spending in GNP. Since

---

[7] Jerry A. Hausman, "Labor Supply" in *The Supply Side Solution*, ed. Bruce Bartlett and Timothy P. Roth (Chatham, N.J.: Chatham House Publishers, Inc., 1983), pp. 224–56.

TABLE 8–4   Growth rates and taxation

Low-growth countries			High-growth countries		
	Growth rate*	G/GNP†		Growth rate*	G/GNP†
Jamaica	−2.8%	30.6%	Brazil	5.4%	17.7%
Mauritania	−0.5	47.3	Cameroon	4.1	16.9
Niger	−0.3	25.5	Japan	3.5	14.7
Papua New Guinea	0	37.3	Paraguay	6.3	11.2
Sierra Leone	−1.0	27.7	Singapore	6.8	18.2
Zaire	−3.2	40.0	South Korea	6.0	16.3
Zambia	−2.7	51.1	Thailand	4.3	14.8
Average	−1.5	37.1		5.2	15.7

* Annual percent rate of growth in real GNP per capita, 1970–81.
† Central government expenditures as a percent of GNP, 1975.
Source: World Bank, *World Tables*, 3d ed., 1983.

part of the taxes of central governments may be hidden in the form of inflation (a tax on money) or in profits received from the purchase and sale of commodities, expenditures probably are a more accurate measure of government involvement in the economy than conventional taxes, especially in the less developed countries (LDCs). At any rate, the percent of central government expenditure in GNP in these high-growth countries is less than half of what it is in their low-growth counterparts. By way of comparison, the United States achieved a 2 percent rate of growth in per capita real GNP during this period and the federal government's expenditure figure is 24.1 percent. Thus the United States was about halfway between the two groups of countries shown in Table 8–4.

It should be recognized, of course, that other factors, such as government trade and price policies, foreign exchange rates, and political stability, can have an important bearing on growth, or the lack of it. Thus it is possible to find two countries with about the same degree of taxation but growing at substantially different rates, or for two countries to grow at different rates but have the same degree of taxation. One has to interpret the evidence given by tables such as 8–4 with some caution. Sorting out the effects of taxation from other factors requires rather sophisticated economic analysis. An example of such a study is that done by Charles E. Stuart on the Swedish economy.[8]

Sweden is well known for having high and steeply progressive tax rates along with a very generous welfare system. Between 1959 and 1980 the marginal income tax rate on the average Swedish wage earner increased from 50 to 80 percent. During this period the real per capita growth of GNP declined from 3.7 percent per year in the 1960s to 1.4 percent per year in the 1970s. In his analysis Stuart found that the high tax rates reduced the amount of time allocated to full-time jobs, where the income had to be declared for tax purposes, and increased the time devoted to household activities and part-time work for cash or barter, where the income was undeclared and therefore evaded taxation, illegally of course. In other words, the high tax rates have driven Swedes

[8] Charles E. Stuart, "Swedish Tax Rates, Labor Supply, and Tax Revenues," *Journal of Political Economy* 86, no. 5 (October 1981), pp. 1020–38.

more and more to the underground economy, in effect turning people into lawbreakers. Stuart also estimated that tax revenue for Sweden would be maximized at the 70 percent marginal tax rate. Thus the Swedish government, which imposed an 80 percent marginal tax rate at the time, could actually have increased tax revenues by reducing tax rates. In other words, according to the Stuart study Sweden was in the upper, or backward-bending, portion of the Laffer curve in the early 1980s. Finally, Stuart was able to explain about 75 percent of the decline in the Swedish growth rate by the increase in taxes over the period.

A GOLD STANDARD

Advocates of supply side economics also favor a return to a gold standard. As will be explained in later chapters, this would be one way of avoiding inflation. And inflation probably is the worst enemy of supply side economics, for it has the tendency to push people into higher marginal tax brackets, which in turn nullifies supply side policy.

A gold standard exists when a nation backs up its paper money totally or partially with gold. This means that the amount of paper money issued by the government cannot expand unless the nation acquires more gold to back it. In effect a gold standard in the United States would keep the dollar price of gold constant in the gold market. It is important to recognize, however, that keeping the price of gold constant by government decree is not a true gold standard. Between 1934 and 1971, the United States maintained the price of gold at $35 per ounce, but during this period the quantity of paper money increased nearly 14 times while the physical quantity of gold in U.S. reserves declined by about one half. If the price of gold had been free to find its own value in the market during this period, its price would have increased steadily as it did in Europe during the post–World War II period. On the surface it may have looked as if the United States were on a gold standard during this period, but it was not, by any stretch of the imagination. In order to be on a true gold standard, the *free-market price* of gold must not increase. Then paper money would be "as good as gold."

Proponents of a gold standard argue that the most practical way for the nation to go on a gold standard would be to peg gold at its existing price and issue only the amount of money required to hold the free-market price of gold constant at that level or within a fixed range. For example, if the market price of gold were $400 per ounce at the outset of the program, the gold price might be maintained between $390 and $410 per ounce. As the economy grew over time, additional paper money would be needed to finance transactions. If the dollar price of gold began to fall slightly, it would be an indication that dollars were becoming more valuable relative to gold. This would mean that people desired more dollars relative to the gold in existence. The government would then issue more dollars until the downward pressure on the dollar price of gold disappeared. Conversely, if the dollar price of gold began to rise, it would be an indication that people desired fewer dollars in relation to gold, and the government could relieve the upward pressure on the gold price by slowing down the growth in the money supply. In this way paper money would retain its value relative to gold.

The major consequence of a gold standard would be to impose a rigid discipline on government fiscal and monetary policy. Under a gold standard the government would no longer be able to print money to finance deficits, which would in turn greatly diminish its ability to increase spending without increasing tax revenue. (The process of printing of money to finance deficits will be described in Chapter 13). The end result would be to stabilize prices because of the limits imposed on the growth of the money supply.

Although most people view a stable price level as a desirable goal, there is still much opposition to a gold standard. For one thing, it would remove much of the discretionary power of government to spend without raising taxes. Those who prefer a more activist fiscal policy understandably do not wish to be held back by such a tight rein. Other opponents of a gold standard argue that instability in the gold market would give rise to instability in the economy. For example, if there were an increase in the demand for gold in the world market, or a decrease in supply, there would be upward pressure on its price. In order to keep the dollar price of gold from rising, the United States would have to restrict the supply of dollars, which in turn would be likely to reduce economic activity and cause unemployment. Conversely, a decrease in the world demand for gold, or an increase in supply, would cause downward pressure on its price. In this case the U.S. government would have to increase the supply of dollars to keep the dollar price of gold from falling, and in so doing the government would cause inflation at home.

A BALANCED–BUDGET AMENDMENT

Although anything is possible, it is not likely that the United States will soon go on a gold standard. There is another development, however, that could impose an even harsher discipline on the government as far as deficit spending is concerned, namely, a balanced-budget amendment to the constitution. As currently written, such an amendment would require Congress to issue a statement of planned outlays and receipts prior to each fiscal year. Such a statement would say that planned outlays do not exceed planned receipts. In other words it would force Congress to consider where the money would come from before it spent it. In the case of extraordinary circumstances, planned outlays could exceed planned receipts if approved by three fifths of the vote of each house of Congress.

Proponents of a balanced-budget amendment argue that the federal government will never balance its budget unless it is forced by law to do so. They maintain that Congress operates in an environment that makes it almost impossible to curtail spending. Congress is constantly petitioned by many relatively small special-interest groups to grant them special benefits. The electorate as a whole generally does not have the time or interest to oppose such favors, since each program may add only a small amount to taxes. Thus Congress is faced with many pressures to increase spending without much offsetting pressure to limit it. Even in Congress, opposition to increased spending is small because of the system whereby lawmakers help each other out. By voting for someone else's special benefit, each lawmaker in turn can expect other lawmakers to return the favor when something is asked for that person's state or district. And whenever there is even a small cut in some special program, it receives much adverse publicity in the media, which lawmakers try very hard to avoid. A balanced-budget amendment would force Congress to consider where the money to pay for a program will come from at the same time it considers the proposal—something that rarely has been done in the recent past.

MAIN POINTS OF CHAPTER 8

1. The core of the **supply side** argument is that high marginal tax rates have reduced incentives to work and invest, thereby reducing economic growth and leading to a high-unemployment inflationary economy.

2. The **Laffer curve** depicts the relationship between tax rates and tax revenues. According to the Laffer curve, an increase in relatively low tax rates will increase tax revenue, but at some point tax revenue will reach a maximum and further increases in tax rates will reduce revenue.

3. Taxes on income affect the allocation of time by reducing the opportunity cost of nonmonetary activities. This reduction occurs because taxes lessen the quantity of real goods and services obtainable by devoting an extra hour to monetary activities. Consequently, when taxes are increased, satisfaction will be maximized only if there is an increase in nonmonetary activities and a decrease in work. The same effect occurs with sales or excise taxes.

4. Money or goods received through welfare programs are for many people a preferred substitute to money received from work because they do not involve an opportunity cost. Hence taxes and welfare both reduce work incentives.

5. High tax rates provide a strong incentive to operate in the barter or underground economy and to deal in illegal goods and services.

6. Investment requires saving, and the rate of saving is highest among high-income people. High taxes on high incomes therefore significantly reduce funds available for investment.

7. The United States ranks lowest among the major industrialized noncommunist nations in the proportion of gross investment in GNP.

8. High marginal tax rates reduce incentives to invest in risky ventures because such taxes cause the possible gain to become smaller than the possible loss.

9. Supply siders argue that the disincentive to invest in risky ventures substantially reduces the growth of new firms and industries, which are where most of the job creation occurs. Also, the antibusiness climate during the 1970s and the large number of regulations pertaining to business firms may have dampened the growth of new firms and jobs.

10. The **progressive income tax** cannot be justified on the principles of equal sacrifice or benefits received. It probably is based mainly on the belief by the majority of people that high-income people should be made to pay a larger proportion of their income as taxes in order to achieve more equality of incomes and wealth.

11. In the United States, the high-income minority is unique among minorities in that it has little protection under the Constitution or laws against discrimination by the majority.

12. Under the U.S. income tax laws, dividends paid by corporations to stockholders are subject to double taxation, whereas interest received from municipal bonds is not taxed at all. The result has been greater incentives to invest in public works projects than in the business sector, particularly for high-income people.

13. High marginal tax rates on high income are likely to lead to the purchase of luxury consumption goods whose services are not taxed rather than to investment in the business sector.

14. The U.S. income tax could be greatly simplified and made more fair by taxing all income equally regardless of source and by adopting a simple cash-flow format.

15. A principal drawback of a progressive tax schedule is that it pushes people into higher tax brackets during inflation, thereby leading to greater pressure to create loopholes in the tax law.

16. The stimulus received by the U.S. economy during the Kennedy administration tax cuts and the dampening effect of the Smoot-Hawley Tariff are frequently cited to support the supply side argument for tax cuts.

17. In the United States, low-tax states have grown more rapidly and provided more new jobs than those with high rates of taxation.

18. It is possible to find in the international economy examples of nations with low rates of taxation that have been more successful in achieving economic growth than high-tax nations.

19. A detailed study of the Swedish economy revealed that high taxes have reduced work for pay and decreased tax revenue from what it would have been with lower rates of taxation.

20. A **gold standard** could be achieved by maintaining a fixed free-market price of gold in terms of paper money. The use of a gold standard would impose a severe discipline on monetary and fiscal policy but would have the effect of stabilizing prices and wages, thereby preventing an increase in income taxes through "bracket creep."

21. A **balanced-budget amendment** would require Congress to issue a statement of planned outlays and planned receipts prior to each fiscal year. Planned outlays could exceed planned receipts only if approved by three fifths of both houses of Congress.

QUESTIONS FOR THOUGHT AND DISCUSSION

1. What are the three main arguments of supply side economics? Which of these has received the most attention?

2. Outline the main differences between supply side economics and Keynesian economics.

3. *a.* Draw two Laffer curves for the country, one showing the short-run effects of a tax increase, the other showing the effects over the long run.
   b. Draw two Laffer curves, one for the country as a whole, the other for an individual state.

4. *a.* Explain how an increase in income tax rates affects the allocation of time between monetary and nonmonetary activities.
   b. Explain how welfare payments affect the allocation of time between monetary and nonmonetary activities.

5. How do high marginal tax rates effect the incentives to invest in risky ventures?

6. *a.* What is the difference between a progressive, a proportional, and a regressive income tax?
   b. Under a flat-rate, or proportional income tax, high-income people will pay the same amount of tax as poor people. True or false? Explain.
   c. Is it possible for a flat-rate tax to be progressive? Explain.
   d. Under a regressive tax is it possible for high-income people to still pay more taxes than poor people? Explain.

7. *a.* What assumptions must be made in order to use the equal-sacrifice principle to justify a progressive income tax?
   b. How do most countries justify a progressive income tax?

8. If all income were taxed equally with no exemptions, what level of flat-rate tax would be needed to generate the same income tax revenue as the federal government received last year?

9. In the United States, some income is taxed twice and some is not taxed at all. Name these incomes, and describe the effect this tax policy has on investment.

10. What effect does inflation have on income tax rates under (1) a flat-rate tax and (2) a progressive tax? What tax would be most appealing to supply side advocates? Explain.

11. Cite some examples used by supply side advocates to support their argument for tax reductions.

12. *a.* What is a gold standard, and what effect would it have on the economy?
   b. Describe the main features of a balanced-budget amendment. How would it affect the economy?

CHAPTER 9

THE AGGREGATE DEMAND–AGGREGATE SUPPLY MODEL

In the preceding three chapters, several divergent theories of the macroeconomy have been presented. The Keynesian models focused attention on the demand side of the economy, including the three main groups of demanders—consumers, investors, and government. The natural rate and rational expectations hypotheses stressed the rational behavior of individuals in the economy and their ability to learn from past mistakes and not be fooled repeatedly. Finally, the supply side theory, as its name implies, emphasized the importance of production and supply in achieving full employment along with the desirability of low marginal tax rates as a means of accomplishing this goal. In this chapter we will present a model that bears some similarity to the Keynesian model but is a bit more flexible. The model will be used mainly to draw a comparison between the three theories presented so far. It is generally referred to as the aggregate demand–aggregate supply model.

AGGREGATE DEMAND

Aggregate demand in this model is defined as a relationship between the general price level as measured by a price index such as the CPI and the level of real output in the economy. The latter value is the nominal or monetary value of GNP or NNP deflated by a price index such as the CPI. Although the name is the same as the Keynesian aggregate demand, it is a different concept. In the Keynesian aggregate demand the price level is not taken into account; it is simply how much the three groups of demanders desired to buy at various income levels. The aggregate demand concept of this chapter bears somewhat more resemblance to the market demand curve presented in Chapter 2, although it is not by any means the same thing as this concept. With the market demand curve the price of only a single commodity is allowed to vary while all other prices are held constant. With this aggregate demand curve all prices and wages are assumed to change at the same time by the same proportion.

Similar to the market demand curve of Chapter 2, the aggregate demand curve slopes down and to the right when the price level is represented on the vertical axis and real output on the horizontal plane (Figure 9–1). This implies

FIGURE 9–1   Aggregate demand

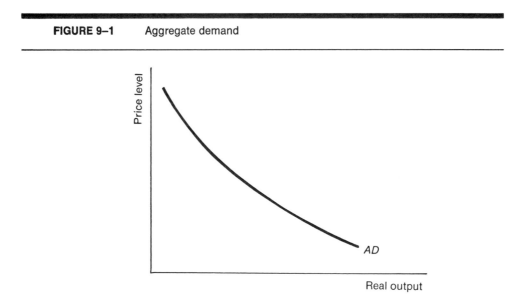

that when the price level is high, relative to some base year, society will demand a smaller quantity of consumption and investment goods than when the price level is relatively low. Consumption and investment goods include the goods purchased and distributed by government.

Two arguments have been used to justify the downward-sloping character-istic of aggregate demand: (1) the interest rate argument and (2) the real balance effect. According to the interest rate argument, an increase in the price level decreases the *real* value of money in the economy. For example, if the price level doubles and everything else remains unchanged, the purchasing power of the stock of money in existence is reduced by one half. In this case it takes twice as many dollars or units of money to finance a given amount of invest-ment or the purchase of consumer durables. The resulting "scarcity" of money causes the interest rate to increase, thereby decreasing the rate of investment and/or spending on consumer durables. As spending on these items is reduced, the real output of the economy declines. Conversely, at low price levels the real value of the money stock is increased. Therefore it takes fewer units of money to finance a given expenditure. As money becomes more "plentiful" in real terms the interest rate declines and spending is stimulated.

The real balance effect, sometimes called the Pigou Effect, after the economist who is credited with first thinking of it, also works through the purchasing power of money. When the price level rises, given the stock of money, real wealth of people declines because now each unit of money buys less. As people begin to feel poorer they reduce their rate of purchases of goods and services, and the real quantity of output demanded declines.

The exact slope of aggregate demand depends on the responsiveness of spending to interest rate changes, and to changes in the real value of the stock of money in existence. If these responses are large, the aggregate demand curve will be relatively flat, and vice versa. It is interesting to note that the factors determining the slope of the aggregate demand curve of this chapter have much in common with the determinants of the slope of the *IS* curve in the more complete Keynesian *IS-LM* model (Chapter 6 appendix). Recall that the more responsive investors are to changes in the interest rate, the flatter the *IS* curve. The same is true of aggregate demand in this model.

The slope of the aggregate demand curve is an important consideration because the steeper the slope, the greater the effect that a policy-induced shift in aggregate demand will have on real output. Conversely, if aggregate demand is close to horizontal, a given horizontal shift will have a relatively small impact on equilibrium output. This will become more evident after developing aggregate supply, and discussing the factors that can shift aggregate demand. Of course, the slope of the aggregate supply curve also is an important determinant of the impacts of demand shifts. Let us now consider aggregate supply.

SHORT–RUN AGGREGATE SUPPLY

It is necessary to divide the discussion of aggregate supply into two components: (1) short-run aggregate supply and (2) long-run aggregate supply. A short-run aggregate supply curve also is defined as a relationship between the price level and the real output of goods and services in the economy. With the price level represented on the vertical axis and real national output on the horizontal, it is hypothesized that, at least over some range, this curve will slope up and to the right (Figure 9–2). Although it has the same general shape as well as the same name as the Keynesian 45-degree line, it is a completely different concept. As you recall, the 45-degree line is simply an identity between how much producers expect to sell and how much they place on the market. Price is not a part of that model. The aggregate supply curve of this chapter also is a completely different idea than the market supply curve of Chapter 2. With that supply curve the price of one good or service is allowed to vary while all other prices are held constant. In this aggregate supply curve, all prices and wages vary at the same time by the same proportion.

To see how this supply curve differs from the other two, it is necessary to understand the economic rationale underlying its hypothesized upward slope. Consider first an increase in the general price level. If the aggregate supply curve slopes up and to the right, it is an indication that the real output of goods and services increases when the price level increases. In order for this to occur,

FIGURE 9–2   Short-run aggregate supply

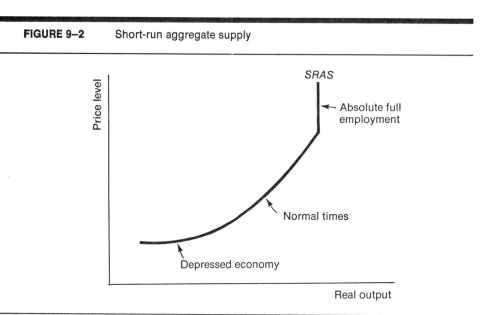

owners of productive resources, mainly labor and owners of capital, must believe that they are better off with higher prices than with lower prices, or they would not offer a greater quantity of their resources on the market as the price level increased. They see their nominal wages and profits increasing but do not perceive the increase in the prices of goods and services they purchase. Hence they become willing to supply more resources and thereby increase output. Economists refer to this behavior as a "money illusion." Of course, this implies irrational behavior on the part of resource owners but let us go along with the assumption for the time being.

The short-run aggregate supply curve is usually drawn to slope upward at an increasing rate with the lower left end rather flat and the upper right end vertical, as in Figure 9–2. This shape is intended to reflect the change from a depressed, high-unemployment economy when the price level and real output are relatively low to a situation of absolute full employment. At the lower end of the curve, a slight increase in prices is thought to bring forth a relatively large increase in output as resource owners anxiously look for an opportunity to put their unemployed resources to work. As the price level continues to increase, fewer idle resources exist, and increases in real output become more and more difficult to obtain. Finally, at some point where the curve becomes vertical, all resources are fully employed and working as hard as physically possible. At that point no further increases in real output are possible, even at higher and higher prices.

SHORT–RUN EQUILIBRIUM

The next step is to combine aggregate demand with short-run aggregate supply and arrive at a short-run equilibrium price level and national output. Since both curves are drawn with price on the vertical axis and quantity on the horizontal, we can superimpose them on the same diagram, as in Figure 9–3.

FIGURE 9–3   Short-run equilibrium

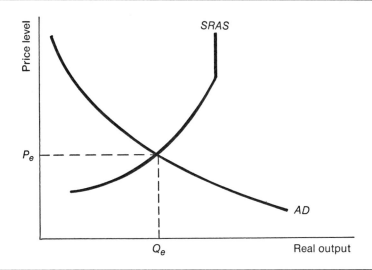

As is evident from the diagram, the equilibrium price level and quantity of real output correspond to P_e and Q_e, respectively. If the price level is above P_e, quantity demanded of goods and services is less than the quantity supplied. Hence there will be unsold goods and the price level will decline, causing a decrease in production of goods and services. At some point when the price level declines enough, aggregate demand just equals short-run aggregate supply and equilibrium is attained. The economic rationale for the movement is the same in the market demand and supply model of Chapter 2. Similar reasoning is applied if the price level happens to be below equilibrium, except now aggregate demand would exceed short-run aggregate supply, a shortage of goods and services would prevail, and the price level would be forced upward, as occurs when there is a shortage in any given market.

SHIFTS IN AGGREGATE DEMAND

Once an economy established an equilibrium position, will it remain there for all time to come? No. The aggregate demand and short-run aggregate supply curves can be expected to shift to new positions, thereby establishing new equilibria. The growth in population, for example, can be expected to shift aggregate demand to the right. At any given price level more people will demand more goods and services. By the same token, as the productive capacity of the economy increases due to a growth in the labor force and capital, the short-run aggregate supply will be located further to the right. (It is best to think of the short-run aggregate supply curve as existing at a particular location at a point in time rather than a gradual shifting over time because, after a period of time has elapsed, it can no longer be regarded as a short-run curve.) But this model is not intended to show the gradual growth of the economy. Rather it is constructed to analyze the short-run shifts in the two curves resulting from policy changes and other phenomena.

FIGURE 9–4   Shifts in aggregate demand

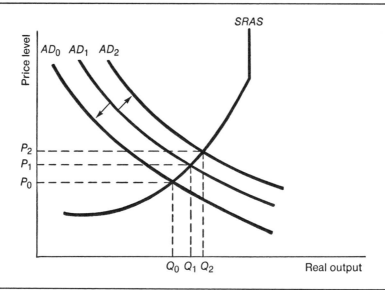

First, let us consider shifts in aggregate demand. For the most part these shifts occur for the same reasons that caused shifts in the aggregate demand curve of the simple Keynesian model. For example, if consumers suddenly became pessimistic about the future and decreased their rate of spending, there would be a shift to the left as shown by the change from AD_1 to AD_0 in Figure 9–4. As another example, if the government suddenly increases its rate of spending for one reason or another, aggregate demand would increase, (shift up and to the right) say from AD_1 to AD_2 in Figure 9–4.

Probably the main reason for developing this model is to illustrate the effects of changes in government policies on output and prices. Similar to the Keynesian models of Chapter 6, this aggregate demand and aggregate supply model implies that this economy can find itself in an equilibrium level of output that is insufficient to generate full employment. For example, suppose Q_2 in Figure 9–4 represents an output level that gives rise to full employment of the labor force. (This may entail some natural unemployment, say 5 to 6 percent of the labor force.) But the level of aggregate demand is such as to give rise to AD_1 and national output Q_1. According to this model, the government can stimulate the economy, say by a spending increase or a tax decrease, causing aggregate demand to increase until it reached AD_2 and full employment. The model also shows some increase in the price level as a result of the shift from AD_1 to AUC_2.

By the same token, this model has been used to show why inflation occurs and how it can be brought under control. If for some reason the aggregate demand curve continues to shift to the right and reaches the vertical portion of aggregate supply, the only effect of an attempt to stimulate the economy will be increased inflation. To control inflation, according to this model, the aggregate demand curve must be constrained from continuing its shift to the right.

SHIFTS IN SHORT–RUN AGGREGATE SUPPLY

When discussing the short-run aggregate supply curve, bear in mind that the time period under consideration is relatively short—too short for people to realize they are laboring under a money illusion. Thus the normal growth of the economy resulting from a higher population and a larger amount of capital cannot be shown on this curve. The main factors shifting short-run aggregate supply are changes in physical resources. These are frequently referred to as "supply side shocks." An example of a decrease (shift down and to the left) in short-run aggregate supply would be a prolonged and widespread drought which resulted in a massive crop failure (water is an important resource). Another example that is often used is the cut-off of oil imports from the OPEC nations in the 1970s. Again, oil is an important resource. Still another is the destruction of productive capacity through war, or some other disaster such as flood or earthquake. All of the above circumstances would cause a decrease, or shift to the left in short-run aggregate supply, as shown by the shift from $SRAS_1$ to $SRAS_0$ in Figure 9–5.

FIGURE 9–5   Shifts in short-run aggregate supply

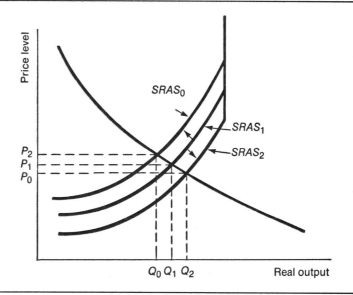

Examples of an increase, or shift to the right, of the short-run aggregate supply curve includes the return to a normal situation after the above shocks have disappeared. Other examples might include the discovery of a significant new oil field, a breakthrough in technology, or a rapid increase in labor force participation. All of these examples can be illustrated by a shift from $SRAS_1$ to $SRAS_2$ in Figure 9–5.

The effects on the economy of shifts in short-run aggregate supply are similar to what would be predicted by the market demand and supply model of Chapter 2. A decrease in the $SRAS$ curve causes an increase in the price level and a decrease in the level of output in the economy. Conversely, an increase, or shift to the right of the curve, causes the equilibrium level of prices to decline and output to increase.

LONG–RUN AGGREGATE SUPPLY

Recall that the main assumption underlying the short-run aggregate supply curve is the presence of money illusion. As prices and wages increased, people at first believed they were better off because they saw their wages increasing but did not take into account that the prices of the goods and services they purchased also increased. The long-run aggregate supply is defined as the relationship between the price level and real output when there is no money illusion. The length of time it takes to go from a short-run to a long-run aggregate supply curve is not universally agreed upon. Those who believe that people generally are not well informed about the relationships between wages and prices, mainly Keynesians, believe that it can last for several years. Others, particularly the rational expectations people, argue that this time period is very short, and grows shorter after one or two attempts have been made to stimulate the economy by government action.

The shape of the long-run aggregate supply curve can best be determined by drawing it on a diagram, as in Figure 9–6. Suppose we begin at the short-run

FIGURE 9–6   Derivation of long-run aggregate supply (LRAS)

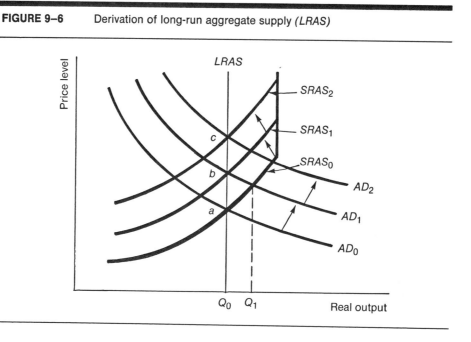

equilibrium denoted by point a as determined AD_0 and $SRAS_0$. Also suppose that the corresponding level of real output, Q_0, is less than the level that would generate full employment. In an attempt to stimulate the economy, the government shifts aggregate demand to the right by a spending increase or a tax cut. In the short run, when people are reacting to a money illusion, they increase real output to Q_1. But now in the long run, when the money illusion no longer exists, they will not produce any more under a higher price level than under a lower one. This means that the increase in the price level causes short-run aggregate supply to shift to the left enough to intersect AD_1 at the same level as the original output, Q_0. This is denoted by point b in Figure 9–6. The same process could be repeated where aggregate demand is shifted to the right again, say to AD_2. The higher level of prices coupled with an absence of a money illusion causes the short-run aggregate supply to shift to $SRAS_2$, and a new equilibrium point is reached at c. If we connect points a, b, and c, we obtain a vertical line which is the long-run aggregate supply curve. Thus the long-run aggregate supply curve, which is the supply curve without the assumption of a money illusion, is a vertical line.

The implication of a vertical long-run aggregate supply curve is that the government cannot bring about a lasting increase in real output and employ-ment by stimulating the demand site of the economy. Recall that this is the argument put forth by the natural rate and rational expectations hypotheses. At the beginning of the process there may be some short-run increase in real output until people realize that the prices of consumer goods are increasing as much as wages. The rational expectations theorists argue, however, that when people catch on to what the government is trying to do, this time lag soon becomes so short as to be imperceptible.

SHIFTS IN LONG–RUN AGGREGATE SUPPLY

As its name implies, the long-run aggregate supply is a long-run concept. Therefore, as the productive capacity of the economy increases due to popula-tion growth and the increase in capital resources, the long-run aggregate supply curve will gradually shift to the right, as shown in Figure 9–7. Of course, this does not mean that the price level will steadily decline. As the population and per capita income increase, aggregate demand also will increase or shift to the right. (To focus on aggregate supply, shifts in aggregate demand are not shown in Figure 9–7.)

One should not conclude from the preceding discussion that shifts in long-run aggregate supply occur naturally and are out of society's control. The supply side economists argue that tax and regulatory policies of the various levels of government have an important impact on the growth of aggregate supply. If incentives to produce are dampened by high tax rates and excessive government regulation, they argue that growth will be slower than if a more favorable economic environment exists. As opposed to the Keynesians who view government policy as operating mainly in the short run on the demand side of the economy, the supply siders, as their name implies, place the major emphasis on shifts in long-run aggregate supply.

As a related point, one should not conclude that the level of output corre-sponding to a given vertical long-run supply curve always corresponds to full employment. It need not. For example, if tax rates become excessively high and investment is curtailed, the aggregate supply curve may not shift to the right as rapidly as the growth in the labor force. Then the economy will suffer from growing unemployment. But as the rational expectations people and the supply side advocates argue, policy which operates on demand side of the

---

FIGURE 9-7   Shifts in long-run aggregate supply

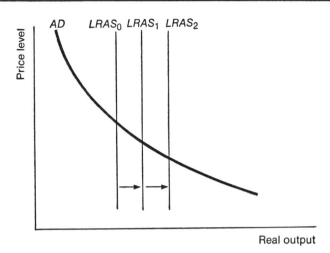

---

economy will not have any lasting effect on employment. They argue that the only thing that will happen through such policies is an increase in the rate of inflation.

MAIN POINTS OF CHAPTER 9

1. **Aggregate demand** is a relationship between the price level and real output. It is drawn as a downward-sloping line, implying that at lower price levels the quantity demanded of goods and services will increase.

2. The two arguments used to justify the downward-sloping shape of aggregate demand are: (1) the interest rate argument and (2) the real balance effect.

3. According to the interest rate argument, a decrease in the price level, other things equal, causes the real value of money to increase. As money becomes more plentiful in real terms, the price of money, or interest rates, declines. The decrease in interest rates in turn stimulates spending on investment goods and consumer durables.

4. The **real balance effect,** also known as the **Pigou Effect,** is thought to stimulate spending because of the increase in the real value or purchasing power of money as the price level declines. As the real value of monetary assets increases, people feel richer and increase their spending.

5. The slope of the aggregate demand curve is determined in large part by the responsiveness of consumers and investors to interest rate changes. The steeper is aggregate demand, the greater the impact on real output of a policy-induced shift in aggregate demand.

6. **Short-run aggregate supply** is a relationship between the price level and real output. It is drawn as an upward-sloping line, implying that at higher price levels real output will increase.

7. An upward-sloping short-run aggregate supply curve implies that people have a **money illusion.** This means that people notice the rise in their wages and in the prices of

goods and services they sell but do not notice the increase in prices they pay. The money illusion is thought to make people work harder and produce more in response to a higher price level.

8. The **short-run aggregate supply curve** is frequently drawn with a relatively flat portion to the lower left, a portion in the middle which increases at an increasing rate, and a portion on the upper right that is vertical or close to it.

9. This shape of aggregate supply is intended to convey the idea that, at low levels of output and periods of high unemployment, a small increase in the price level brings forth a relatively large increase in output. As the absolute full-employment level is approached, greater and greater price increases are required to have any effect on output. The vertical portion represents absolute full employment where no amount of a price increase will increase real output.

10. The short-run equilibrium price level and level of real output correspond to the intersection of aggregate demand and short-run aggregate supply.

11. Shifts in the aggregate demand curve can occur for the same reasons that cause shifts in the aggregate demand curve of the simple Keynesian model. They include changes in the spending decisions of people and/or changes in government policies which affect either the spending of individuals or the spending of government itself.

12. Shifts in short-run aggregate supply, sometimes called **supply shocks** can occur because of changes in the amount of resources available to society. Decrease in short-run aggregate supply can come from abnormally bad weather, other natural disasters, war, or an abrupt reduction in imports such as the Arab oil embargo of the 1970s. Reasons for an increase in the curve include new resource discoveries, abnormally good weather, and a sudden increase in labor force participation of people.

13. The **long-run aggregate supply curve** is a vertical line drawn under the assumption of no money illusion. This means that people do not view an increase in the price level as advantageous because they are aware that the prices of goods and services they buy also have increased.

14. A vertical long-run aggregate supply means that government policy action which shifts aggregate demand has no effect on real output or employment.

15. Increases in long-run aggregate supply occur because of growth in the productive capacity of the economy. Supply siders argue that government tax and regulatory policies can affect the growth of capital and willingness to work, thereby affecting long-run aggregate supply and employment.

QUESTIONS FOR THOUGHT AND DISCUSSION

1. *a.* What is aggregate demand?
   b. Why is it thought to slope down and to the right?

2. *a.* What is short-run aggregate supply?
   b. What assumption is necessary to obtain an upward-sloping short-run aggregate supply curve? Explain.

3. Using the aggregate demand and short-run aggregate supply model, show how government tax and spending policies can increase the level of real output and reduce unemployment.

4. Using the aggregate demand and short-run aggregate supply model, show the effect of an oil embargo on the price level and the quantity of real output. What would such a phenomenon be called?

5. *a*. What is the main difference between the short-run and long-run aggregate supply curve?

   b. Derive the long-run aggregate supply curve.

6. Using the aggregate demand–aggregate supply model, illustrate the main arguments of:

   a. The Keynesians.

   b. The rational expectations people.

   c. The supply side advocates.

PART IV

MONEY AND BANKING

CHAPTER 10

MONEY AND THE NEW QUANTITY THEORY

Attention is now turned to money and the banking system. In this chapter we consider the role of money in the economy. After examining the characteristics and functions of money, we will see how money and prices are related and then present a simple model for predicting the effect of changes in the money supply on the price level and value of income or output in the economy. This model, which was first developed by the classical economists, is known as the *quantity theory of money*. Later in the chapter the model is refined a bit and referred to as the *new quantity theory of money*.

CHARACTERISTICS OF MONEY

Perhaps the first thought that comes to our minds when we consider money is the image of currency and coins in our billfolds or purses. Further reflection might bring to mind the money in our checking and savings accounts at the bank. Of course, from our knowledge of history, we know that people have utilized a variety of objects as money. What was used depended mainly on the resources and technology available at the time. Primitive tribes that "lived off the land" generally utilized certain bones of agreed-upon animals, stones, beads, or other objects that were not overly abundant in nature.

With the coming of animal domestication and agriculture, we read of animals such as cattle or goats, or crops such as wheat, being used as money. Then the precious metals, particularly gold and silver, came into use as money. These examples by no means exhaust the list. It is interesting to note, for example, that even cigarettes were used as money in some prisoner-of-war camps during World War II.[1]

One desirable characteristic of money is that it be made out of material that is relatively cheap to produce. The more resources a society must employ to produce money, the less there are available to produce the real goods and services that sustain life and make it more interesting and enjoyable. For example, if the people of the world insisted on using a costly material such as gold as the only legal form of money, a significant share of the world's population might find it individually profitable to spend their time and effort producing money, that is, mining. But from society's standpoint the efforts of these people would be for naught. The world would lose the goods and services that these people and their capital resources could have produced instead.

Considering the relatively high cost of mining and processing gold or any other metal for money, it is fortunate that paper money has come into such widespread use. The cost in terms of resources used for the paper and printing may add up to only a few dollars for millions of dollars produced. If a society decided that the face value of its money should be equal to its value as a commodity, then producers of the money (for example, miners) would have an incentive to spend up to a dollar's worth of resources to obtain an extra dollar of the money. Of course, the main motivation for adopting paper money probably came more from a desire for greater convenience than to reduce costs to society.

Going further, modern societies have devised other ways to cheapen the resource cost of money and increase its convenience. Checking account money is a good example. Of course, like the adoption of paper money, the coming of checking accounts probably was motivated more by the increased convenience to the individual than by a decreased resource cost to society. As a result of a desire for still greater convenience, money as we know it today may someday become obsolete. We will return to this topic in a following section.

Another desirable characteristic of money is that it be reasonably durable, yet easy to carry around. No material, of course, is perfect in this regard. Cast iron may be durable, but it makes for a weighty change purse. Gold fares rather badly on both counts. Being a rather soft metal, it is not extremely durable, and the fact that it is a metal makes it heavy to carry around. In this regard, paper would have to rank ahead of gold as a desirable form of money.

Although money should be cheap and easy to manufacture, it should at the same time be very difficult to duplicate or counterfeit. Gold ranks high on this point, which probably explains its popularity in medieval times. Of course, when gold coins came into use, the possibility of "sweating" was introduced. People soon found that small particles of gold could be removed from gold coins simply by shaking them in a bag. And by melting the particles together,

---

[1] For an interesting article on the use of cigarettes as money in a World War II P.O.W. camp, see R. A. Radford, "The Economic Organization of a P.O.W. Camp," *Economica* 12 (November 1945), pp. 189–201. Note how prices varied directly with the supply of cigarettes.

one might obtain, for example, 51 coins from a bag of 50. This same problem occurred in prisoner-of-war camps where cigarettes were used as money. Here the men found that by rolling a cigarette between thumb and forefinger some tobacco could be extracted without noticeably altering the form of it. Thus, some could smoke their money and have it too.

FUNCTIONS OF MONEY

The fact that money has existed as long as human beings have populated the earth ought to tell us that money is useful. The word *useful* in this case does not refer to the goods and services that money "buys." Rather it refers to the fundamental reasons for a society to utilize something called money. Money is useful for three basic reasons: it serves as (1) a medium of exchange, (2) a standard or measure of value, and (3) a store of value.

Regarding the first use, if it were not for the concept of money we would have to operate under a barter system. In other words, each person would have to exchange the goods or services he or she produces directly with another person for the goods or services desired. A little reflection will impress upon us how incredibly inefficient a barter system would be. For example, an economics professor would have to exchange lectures for food, clothing, and other goods and services—not a very easy task if owners of food or clothing did not want to listen to economics lectures. The example becomes even more absurd when we consider what the producers of jet liners or guided missiles would exchange for the things they desire. The lesson is clear: Were it not for money, people would have to spend much of their time shopping rather than producing, and as a result society's output would be reduced drastically. Thus, if money did not exist, someone would have to invent it.

Money is useful also to measure the value or price of things. With a barter economy we would have to remember the price of each good or service in terms of every other good or service. For example, one economics textbook might be exchanged for a pair of gloves, three textbooks for a pair of shoes, and so on. Thus each good or service would in fact have thousands of prices, the amount of every other good or service that is worth the same as the good or service in question. It does not take long to realize that even in a relatively primitive society, the task of determining prices would be next to impossible without a common denominator—money. With money, each good or service has only one price, its price in terms of the monetary unit.

Most people like to put away part of the fruits of their labor for future use. Thus money is useful as a store of value. Without money we would have to save material objects? But what would these objects be? Obviously they could not be things that deteriorated or depreciated with time, or else time would erase our savings. Also they should not be items that are costly to guard and store, or else a major part of our efforts would be devoted to guarding our savings rather than producing and enjoying life. Money, of course, is a convenient object to save; it does not deteriorate with reasonable care, and it is relatively costless to store.

WHAT GIVES MONEY PURCHASING POWER?

We know, of course, that paper money and coins are worth only a small fraction of their face value as a commodity. A $10 bill, for instance, is worth only a fraction of a cent in the used-paper market. But at a store it can be exchanged for a good deal more than that, even at today's inflated prices. The same is true of coins.

In fact, it would not be desirable for the commodity value of money to approach or exceed its face value. This happened in the early 1960s with respect to silver nickels. Higher silver prices drove their price up in the market until the value of the metal in a nickel coin was about seven cents. It soon became apparent to some enterprising people that a profit could be earned by melting down nickels and selling the metal in the market, perhaps even back to the government. Thus, money that is worth more than its face value tends to disappear from circulation.

Also, as mentioned earlier, if the commodity value of money approaches its face value, it is an indication that the money is far too costly to produce. If a nickel is worth seven cents, this is an indication that society is devoting seven cents worth of resources to produce each nickel—not a very good buy for society.

But we are still faced with the question. Why can paper money, which has virtually no value in itself, be used to purchase valuable goods and services? We might be tempted to say that the gold in Fort Knox provides a backing and hence a value to our paper money. Before the price of gold was allowed to rise in the 1970s, each dollar outstanding was backed by just a little over one cent of gold. Indeed, if all the gold in Fort Knox were to disappear, and no one knew about it, paper money would no doubt go on being used just as before.

It might be argued that confidence in the government that issued the money gives paper money value. But one can find instances in history where governments have disappeared, yet their money continued to be used and retained its value. For example, the money issued by the old czarist government in Russia continued to be used by the Russian people long after this government disappeared. Moreover, the old czarist money retained its value while the money issued by the new Communist government lost value.[2]

The real reason paper money has value is because people *accept* it as having value. You accept paper money in payment because you know that other people will accept this money when you wish to buy something. Thus it is the acceptance of paper money by both buyers and sellers of goods and services that gives value to this money. If for some reason a sizable fraction of people decided that they would no longer accept paper money as payment, it soon would go out of circulation. However it would have to be replaced by something else, since a modern economy really could not function without some form of money.

GRESHAM'S LAW

It is possible, of course, for a society to utilize more than one form of money, providing both are accepted by the people. A curious situation can prevail, however, when one form of money becomes less valuable than another. For example, consider the case where both gold coins and paper are used as money. Now suppose the quantity of paper money expands relative to

---

[2] Causing inflation was a way the government could confiscate the wealth of people who held money rather than tangible property.

the amount of gold coins. If the government attempts to hold the value of paper money constant relative to that of gold, people, sensing that paper is becoming more plentiful and less valuable, will likely attempt to get rid of their paper money and hold on to their gold. Consequently gold will tend to disappear from circulation. This phenomenon is known as Gresham's law—bad money drives out good money. In order for Gresham's law to be valid, however, it is necessary for the government to maintain a fixed rate of exchange between the "good" and "bad" money. If paper were allowed to find its own rate of exchange with gold in the market, becoming less valuable as its supply increased, then both gold and paper would continue to be exchanged because people would be willing to part with gold if its value increased—that is, they could obtain more paper money per ounce of gold.

A CASHLESS SOCIETY

As noted, money has taken many different forms throughout history. Even within fairly recent times we have seen a gradual transition from the use of currency to demand deposits, or checking account money. And within recent years, the credit card has become a convenient tool for making small purchases. However, the use of credit cards does not rule out the use of checks or currency. It is just a means of paying for several purchases with one check or cash payment.

A truly cashless society would be one step removed from the credit card society of today. Each person might have to present the equivalent of a credit card or some form of identification when making a purchase. But instead of billing the customer at a later date, the procedure would be to deduct the amount of the purchase from the buyer's bank account at the moment of purchase. In this situation there would be little need to carry cash or to have a checking account. Bills would be paid by a simple subtraction of numbers. Similarly, people would receive their income when employers or buyers of services credited or added the appropriate amount to a person's account.

Although such a procedure would characterize a cashless society, it would not imply a moneyless society. The numbers that would be added to or subtracted from accounts would still be given in terms of dollars. But the dollars would not be green pieces of paper or coins. Instead they would be just numbers in people's accounts, and these accounts would be found in the memory cores of computers utilized by financial institutions. Thus the concept of money would still be used, although its form would change from tangible objects, that is, paper and metal, to intangible numbers in people's accounts.

Whether we will experience a cashless society in our lifetime will depend on the cost and convenience of such a monetary system. If some technical problems can be solved, and if people accept it, we may see a gradual transition to this kind of monetary system. The reason for this change is really no different than that for changes in the past. The printing press made it possible for paper money to come into existence. A highly organized and coordinated banking system makes checking account money possible. And the computer may bring forth a cashless society. Of course, the use of coins and currency may still prove to be the best way to handle small, day-to-day purchases made through vending machines, at lunch counters, and so on.

DEFINITIONS OF MONEY

Throughout the remainder of the discussion of money and monetary policy we will refer often to the "quantity of money" in the economy. It is necessary, therefore, to define what is included in this quantity. In the context of macroeconomics there are two widely used definitions of money. One, known as the *narrow definition,* is defined as currency (including coins) outside of banks plus checking account deposits. Economists often refer to checking account deposits as demand deposits. The narrow definition is commonly abbreviated as M_1. In recent years M_1 has been further subdivided into M_{1a} and M_{1b}. The category labeled M_{1a} includes noninterest bearing checking account deposits, whereas M_{1b} adds to M_{1a} the interest bearing NOW accounts and automatic transfer service (ATS) accounts whereby banks automatically transfer funds from saving to checking when checks are written against the latter accounts. The second definition of money, known as the *broad definition,* or M_2, includes currency outside of banks plus checking account deposits plus savings account balances. This definition includes the money market funds that became popular in the late 1970s and early 1980s because of the attractive interest rates they offered. An even *broader definition,* known as M_3, includes M_2 plus deposits at nonbank thrift institutions. These are the institutions which sell savings certificates and the like but do not offer checking account services. A summary of the various definitions of money is presented below:

M_{1a} = Currency plus noninterest bearing checking accounts
M_{1b} = M_{1a} plus interest bearing checking accounts
M_2 = M_{1b} plus savings accounts in commercial banks and money market funds
M_3 = M_2 plus deposits in nonbank savings institutions and large time deposits

To obtain an idea of the relative magnitudes of the four measures, the values for December 1984 are presented below:

M_{1a} = \$412 billion
M_{1b} = \$554 billion
M_2 = \$2,376 billion
M_3 = \$2,987 billion

Notice that the interest bearing accounts are several times larger than ordinary checking account deposits. Certainly in times of inflation, when money is continually losing value, it pays people to keep as much money in interest earning accounts as is possible. For most people the small amount of time to transfer funds from savings to checking is well worth the effort.

It depends somewhat on individual preference as to what definition of money is utilized in discussion. When reference is made to the "money supply" in the media, it generally refers to M_{1b}, unless otherwise stated. The use of this narrow definition of money can be misleading, however. During the late 1960s, 1970s, and 1980s people have increasingly put their money in interest bearing accounts, especially into the money market funds during the later part of the period. Use of the narrow definition of money therefore understates the growth of liquidity in the country because it does not reflect this switch between different types of deposits. Consequently, in the following discussion whenever reference is made to the "quantity of money" or "money supply" it will refer to M_2, the broad definition of money. For the most part the money in savings deposits and money market funds is highly liquid, or available, for spending. Some of the money market funds even allow depositors to write checks against their accounts. The money in M_3 is not quite as liquid because savings certificates are purchased for specified periods.

To obtain an idea of the relative magnitudes of the two main measures of money, M_1 and M_2, over the long run, their totals for selected years from 1929 to 1984 are presented in Table 10–1. Notice the substantial growth in both M_1

TABLE 10–1 Quantity of money in the United States, selected years, 1929–84 ($ billions)

Year	M_1	M_2
1929	$ 26	$ 46
1939	36	51
1949	111	148
1959	141	298
1969	206	590
1974	278	909
1979	389	1,499
1980	415	1,633
1981	442	1,797
1982	484	1,965
1983	525	2,196
1984	554	2,376

Sources: 1929–39: Milton Friedman and Anna Schwartz, *A Monetary History of the United States, 1897–1960* (Princeton, N.J.: Princeton University Press, 1963), Table A–1; 1949–84: *Economic Report of the President*, 1985, p. 303.

and M_2 during the World War II years and again during the 1970s. Note in particular that between 1974 and 1984, M_2 nearly tripled—the highest rate of growth since the World War II years.

Although not shown in Table 10–1, it should be pointed out that currency (including coins) makes up a small portion of the nation's money supply. In 1984 currency accounted for only 7 percent of total M_2. It should also be explained that the currency totals include only that which is outside of banks, that is, money held by individuals and business firms. If currency inside of banks were counted as part of the nation's money supply, some would be counted twice. For example, if a person deposited $100 in currency in a savings account, this $100 would be double counted if the currency inside the bank were included in the nation's money supply. Consequently, currency inside banks is not counted in either M_1 or M_2. This is not to say, however, that banks keep a dollar of currency on hand for each dollar of checking or savings deposits. We will come back to this point in the next chapter.

MONEY AND PRICES

Although money is a common object and prices are something that we deal with just about every day, most people probably do not tie the two together. A moment of reflection will reveal that the money price of an object is the number of units of money that must be exchanged in order to buy it. In other words, a $100 price on a new coat means that 100 pieces of paper called dollar bills (or their equivalent) are to be exchanged for the coat. With this simple idea in mind, one can more closely relate the quantity of money in existence with the prices of goods and services.

Consider as a simple example an economy that produces only one product, say 1,000 bushels of wheat per year. Also assume that this simple economy has 1,000 pieces of paper in existence that it calls money. Finally, assume that *all* the money in existence is exchanged once each year for *all* the wheat produced annually. (This is what money is for—to be used in exchange for goods and services.) Under these assumptions, each bushel of wheat will be changed for one piece of paper called a dollar bill. In other words, the price of wheat in this case must be $1 per bushel. Under these assumptions there is no way the price of wheat could be any different than $1.

Now suppose that the quantity of money in existence doubles to $2,000 but the quantity of wheat produced remains the same at 1,000 bushels. Under the conditions stipulated in the preceding paragraph, where all money is exchanged once for all the wheat that is produced, two pieces of paper called dollar bills will now be exchanged for each bushel of wheat. In other words the price of wheat now must be $2 per bushel. The relationship among the quantity of money, the output of wheat, and the price of wheat is summarized in the table.

Quantity of money	Output of wheat	Price of wheat
$1,000	1,000	$1
2,000	1,000	2

VELOCITY OF MONEY

In the simple example utilized in the preceding section, it was assumed that each unit of money (dollar) was spent once each year on the output forthcoming in that year. In reality each dollar is generally spent more than one time per year. This fact does not invalidate the point made by the preceding example, but as we shall see shortly, the number of times each dollar or unit of money is spent each year also has an important bearing on the price level. This brings us to velocity.

The *velocity of money* is defined as the average number of times each dollar is spent each year. Much of the money that people receive is not held for an entire year. In fact, when people receive income they generally put the money in the bank, where most of it is soon spent to make purchases or pay bills. The people who in turn receive this money can be expected to do likewise. Hence, each dollar is likely to change hands several times per year. Granted some money that is placed in long-term savings may be kept for many years before it is spent, but on the average, money is continually changing hands.

The actual velocity for the country can be computed by dividing the total income of the country by the quantity of money in existence. A commonly used measure of income for this purpose is GNP.[3] To obtain velocity, GNP can be divided by either the narrow or broad definitions of money. Naturally, dividing GNP by the narrow definition of money results in a larger velocity figure than dividing by the broad definition because the denominator is smaller in the former case. The velocity figures for the United States from 1929 to 1984 (for selected years) are presented in Table 10–2.

TABLE 10–2   Velocity of money in the United States, selected years, 1929–84*

Year	Definition of Money	
	M_1	M_2
1929	3.9	2.2
1939	2.5	1.8
1949	2.3	1.7
1959	3.5	1.6
1969	4.6	1.6
1974	5.2	1.6
1979	6.2	1.6
1980	6.3	1.6
1981	6.8	1.6
1982	6.4	1.6
1983	6.3	1.5
1984	6.6	1.5

* GNP divided by the corresponding quantities of money from Table 10–1.

From the figures in Table 10–2 we see that under the narrow definition of money each dollar in 1984 changed hands about seven times. Of course, not all purchases are made from cash or checking account balances. It is common for people to draw money out of savings accounts for making large purchases or paying taxes. Using the broad definition of money, which includes savings account money as well as currency and checking account balances, yields a somewhat smaller velocity. On the average, each dollar in this case changed hands about 1.5 times during 1984.[4]

THE QUANTITY EQUATION OF EXCHANGE

Recall that in calculating velocity, a measure of income (GNP) is divided by the quantity of money. It will be helpful to break down the measure of income, or GNP, into two components: price and quantity; that is, the total value of output (or income) in the economy is equal to the price (or cost) of each final good and service times its quantity. Using P to represent the prices of all goods

---

[3] Because we are interested in total income or spending, GNP, rather than NNP, is used to compute velocity.

[4] Strictly speaking these are income velocity figures because GNP is a measure of income. It is also possible to use total value of sales in the numerator. The resulting figure in this case would be called *transactions velocity*. See Irving Fisher, *The Purchasing Power of Money* (New York: Macmillan, 1913).

and services and Q to represent all the quantities, we can write the expression for calculating velocity, as follows:

$$V = \frac{\text{GNP}}{M} \quad \text{or} \quad V = \frac{P \times Q}{M}$$

By multiplying both sides of the computational formula given on the right by M, we obtain:

$$M \times V = P \times Q$$

The second formula is commonly known as the *quantity equation of exchange.* It says that the quantity of money in the economy multiplied by its velocity equals the total value of income (or output) in the economy during a given year. The equality always holds true because velocity is free to take on any value that satisfies the equation. As a result, the equation is often called an *identity* because the right side always equals the left side.

The quantity equation of exchange has long been used by economists to illustrate what happens to prices (P) and/or value of output $(P \times Q)$ when there are changes in the quantity of money (M) or in velocity (V). A few examples will illustrate the point. Using some specific numbers, suppose we start with a situation where $M = 500$, $V = 2$, $P = 1$, and $Q = 1,000$.

1. Double M, no change in V and Q. This situation corresponds somewhat to the simple wheat economy example given in a previous section, except in that example the velocity is assumed to be one. If money is doubled to 1,000, velocity remains constant at 2, and Q stays at 1,000; the only thing that can happen is for P to double, as shown below:

	M	V	P	Q
a.	500 × 2 =	1	×	1,000
b.	1,000 × 2 =	2	×	1,000

This example could represent an economy at full employment where M is increased but Q cannot increase because resources are being fully utilized.

2. Half M, no change in V. In this case all that can be said is that the right-hand side of the expression will decline by half. In cases where the quantity of money has decreased, such as during the Great Depression, the first effect seems to be a decline in output (Q). Then as surpluses of goods and services build up and unemployment drags on, prices and wages begin to fall:

	M	V	P	Q
a.	500 × 2 =	1	×	1,000
b.	250 × 2 =	500		

3. Double V, no change in M and Q. This case is similar to part 1 above in that a doubling in the rate at which people spend money has the same effect as a doubling of the quantity of money—that is, to double the price level:

	M	V	P	Q
a.	500 × 2 =	1	×	1,000
b.	500 × 4 =	2	×	1,000

Of course, judging from the figures in Table 10–2, it would be highly unlikely that a nation would experience a change in velocity of this magnitude, at least velocity calculated from the broad definition of money.

A decrease in velocity would have the same effect on the value of output as a decrease in the quantity of money (Part 2), so it is not necessary to restate this case.

In most economies, the quantity of money is not likely to double or halve, at least over short periods of time. The same is true of velocity. Nor is it likely that the total output *(Q)* of the economy will remain constant for long. The usual case is for *M* to increase over time along with an increase in *Q*. In addition, we may expect to observe some changes in *V*, especially under the narrow definition of money.

Problems occur when the growth of *M* either speeds up or slows down in comparison to the growth in *Q*. If *M* begins to grow rapidly and *V* does not decrease, the quantity equation, along with experience, tells us that the price level will increase; that is, inflation will occur. In fact, *V* in this case is likely to increase, making the inflation problem even worse, as will be explained later in the chapter. By the same token, a decrease in the growth of *M* compared to *Q* is likely to result in a "sluggish" economy with an above-average unemployment rate. Really severe unemployment problems can be expected if *M* declines in absolute terms as in the Great Depression. To add to the misery, a decline in *M* is likely to bring forth a decrease in *V* as well.

Probably the most serious limitation of using the quantity equation of exchange to predict price and output changes from changes in the quantity of money is the necessity of assuming a constant velocity. In recent years considerable work has been done to better understand why velocity might change and to predict such changes. The outcome of this recent work is sometimes called the "new quantity theory of money," as opposed to the old quantity theory which assumed velocity to be a constant.[5]

In order to understand why velocity may change from one year to the next, it is necessary to understand why people hold part of their assets or wealth in the form of money. Each person's assets or wealth can be divided into two categories: monetary assets (money) and nonmonetary assets. The latter includes securities, such as stocks and bonds, as well as all personal property, such as real estate, cars, clothes, appliances, and books. From personal experience we know that every person owns some of both kinds of assets. There may be a few unusual people who have most of their assets in the form of money and a few of the opposite kind who own mostly nonmonetary assets, but most of us fall somewhere between these two extremes. The question is: Why do we hold part of our wealth as money but nowhere near all of our wealth as money? The answer is to be found in the relationship of the benefits of holding money and the cost of holding money.

BENEFITS OF HOLDING MONEY

The benefits of holding money can be summarized by two words: convenience and security. Because most people tend to make purchases on a continu-

---

[5] See Milton Friedman, "The Quantity Theory of Money: A Restatement," in *Studies in the Quantity Theory of Money,* ed. Milton Friedman (Chicago: University of Chicago Press, 1956).

ing basis while getting paid only periodically, it is more convenient to hold a certain amount of money to make these purchases than to sell off assets whenever a purchase is to be made. For example, it would be very inconvenient for people to sell nonmonetary assets every time they wished to buy lunch, gas for their car, movie tickets, or the many small purchases people make each week. Nor would it be very convenient for people to make all their purchases at one time, say right after payday. Instead most of us prefer to spread our purchases out over a period of time, and as a result we need to hold some money in order to make these purchases.

As mentioned, a second major benefit of holding money is that it provides security. We never know, for example, when a sudden toothache will necessitate an unplanned trip to the dentist or a flat tire on the car will require an unforeseen purchase at a service station. Hence, most of us like to have a few dollars available to avoid financial embarrassment in case of unforeseen situations. Also, it is desirable to have some money on hand to take advantage of exceptional bargains. If we knew in advance just how much we would spend in the coming year we would not have to hold as much in reserve.

Business firms also hold a certain amount of money in the form of either cash in their vaults or deposits in banks. From the standpoint of business firms, money can be looked upon as a factor of production that saves on other services, particularly labor. For example, without a cash reserve, each payday someone in each firm would have to take the time to sell enough of the firm's assets, such as stocks or bonds, in order to acquire the necessary cash to pay its employees. Thus holding part of the firm's assets in cash or money also proves to be convenient for the business firm and increases its productivity. Also, firms, like individuals, may desire to have ready cash available either as a reserve against contingencies or to take advantage of exceptional bargains that come along.

COST OF HOLDING MONEY

Although most people prefer to hold a part of their assets in the form of money, no one would want to hold all of his or her assets in this form. If an individual did, the person would not have any clothes to wear, no personal belongings, house, car, etc. It soon becomes evident that holding all of one's wealth in the form of money is not desirable. Thus, all people must decide what part of their wealth, or income equivalent, they will hold as money and what part they will hold as so-called earning assets, such as securities (stocks and bonds), or directly usable items, such as house, car, appliances, and personal belongings. In making this decision a person must balance the benefits of holding money (convenience and security) against the cost of holding money. An individual will choose to hold a greater proportion of his or her wealth in the form of money only if the added return outweighs the cost. In the previous section we considered the benefits of holding assets in the form of money; in this section we consider the cost.

Offhand one might say that the cost of holding money is negligible because banks are willing to guard money for free and, in the case of savings accounts, even pay people for the privilege of providing the storage service. But the cost of holding assets in the form of money is not the storage cost. Rather it is the *opportunity cost*—what the money could earn if it were converted into so-called earning assets, such as stocks and bonds, real estate, machines, consumer durables, and personal belongings. The returns from stocks and bonds can be easily measured in terms of dividends and interest. The returns become somewhat more difficult to measure for physical assets, such as real estate and machines, although most owners of such assets probably have some idea of the rate of return on their investment. It is still more difficult to measure the returns on consumer durables and personal belongings, such as house, appliances, car, clothes, and shoes. Although most people probably do not bother to convert the value of the services provided by consumer durables or personal belongings into a monetary value, they still are likely to have a fairly good idea of how useful such assets are in providing services. For example, we may infer that the transportation service provided by the car is more valuable to car owners than the convenience and security provided by the same amount of money; otherwise, they would not have decided to own the car as opposed to holding money.

Because of the difficulty of measuring the value of the services provided by real assets, the cost of holding money has commonly been approximated by the interest return on securities, such as stocks and bonds. The higher the interest return on securities, the higher is the cost of holding money. If one includes savings accounts as part of money (the broad definition), this part of a person's monetary assets also earns interest. Hence, the net cost of holding money in this form is the difference (if any) between the interest (or dividend) return on securities and the interest earned by money in a savings account.

The existence of inflation also has a bearing on the cost of holding money. As explained in Chapter 3, inflation depreciates the value of money. Hence inflation makes it more costly to hold money in relation to other assets that increase in value with the price level, such as real estate. During inflation the money rate of interest on securities is likely to rise, so part of the cost of inflation is already taken into account by the higher interest rate. However, usury laws and the uncertainties over what the actual rate of inflation will turn out to be during any given year may keep the interest rate from increasing by the full extent of the rate of inflation, at least in its early stages.

THE PROPORTION OF INCOME HELD AS MONEY

Every person who earns an income or owns some assets must continually weigh the benefits of holding money against the cost of holding money. If the benefits outweigh the costs, it behooves a person to convert a bit more of his or her assets to money and a little less to nonmonetary forms. Moreover each payday a decision must be made regarding how much of a person's paycheck will remain in the form of money and how much will be converted to other assets. Of course, some assets, such as groceries, gasoline, and movie tickets, are used up in a relatively short time, while others, such as car, clothes, real estate, and stocks and bonds, may be around for years or even a lifetime.

A useful number to compute is the equivalent proportion of annual income held as money. For example, if you earn a $20,000-per-year income and you own $10,000 of money (M_2), then you hold the equivalent of half of your annual income as money. It turns out that in deriving the quantity equation of exchange we in effect computed the reciprocal of the proportion of annual income held as money. Recall that the quantity equation of exchange is written as:

$$M \times V = P \times Q$$

If we divide both sides of this equation by V, we obtain:

$$M = \frac{1}{V} \times P \times Q$$

A commonly used symbol for $(1/V)$ is K. Substituting K for $(1/V)$, we have:

$$M = K \times P \times Q$$

Notice that K is the equivalent proportion of income held as money. For example if $P \times Q$ for the country is $2,000 billion and M is $1,000 billion, then K is 0.5, or half. This says that people are holding the equivalent of half of their annual income as money. Notice also that V is equal to 2 in this example. Of course, the K value also can be computed for an individual. What proportion of your annual gross (before-tax) income do you hold in the form of money on the average? For the nation as a whole it is about 0.67 when using the broad definition of money (M_2). If we can determine what might cause people to change the proportion of income held as money, then we have at the same time identified the factors that can cause the velocity of money to change, because velocity is just the reciprocal of K.

FACTORS AFFECTING THE PROPORTION OF INCOME HELD AS MONEY

As stated earlier, people hold money because of the benefits of holding money. They do not as a rule hold all of their assets as money, however, because of the cost of holding money, namely the income or services that must be given up by not owning so-called earning or nonmonetary assets. It seems reasonable, therefore, that if the cost of holding money changes in relation to the benefits derived from holding money, then people may change the proportion of their income held as money—the K value. Two major factors are considered important in explaining why people may change the proportion of their income held as money.

1. Interest rate changes. As mentioned, the cost of holding money is approximated by the interest return on earning assets, such as stocks and bonds. If the interest (or dividend) return on stocks and bonds increases, for example, then the cost of holding assets in the form of money will increase. In other words, by holding money a person will be giving up more income from nonmonetary assets when their interest return is high than when the return is low. If the cost of holding money goes up because of an increase in the interest return on earning assets, then people may decide to hold a smaller proportion of their income as money. This means that K would decrease and V increase.

Just how responsive people are to interest rate changes in deciding how much money they desire to hold is still an unsettled issue among economists. Some economists argue that people do not change the amount of money they desire to hold very much when the interest rate changes, whereas others believe people are relatively responsive to this factor. This issue turns out to be rather important because if people are not responsive to interest rate changes, then changes in the money supply that may cause interest rates to change will not have much effect on K or V. This means that the quantity equation of exchange will be an accurate predictor of what happens to $P \times Q$ when there are changes in M. We will come back to this point in Chapter 13 on monetary policy.

2. Changes in expectations of future unemployment and inflation No one knows the future with certainty, but most people probably have some expectation of what the future may bring at least in regard to unemployment and inflation. For example, if people expect an increase in unemployment, it is reasonable to believe that at least some will attempt to build up their monetary holdings in order to have something in reserve when times become hard. This in turn means that an expectation of higher unemployment in the future should cause K to increase and V to decrease. The opposite may occur if people come to expect a higher rate of inflation in the future. As explained in Chapter 3, money is not a desirable asset to own during inflation because inflation reduces the purchasing power of money. We might expect therefore that people will try to reduce the proportion of income held as money during a time when inflation threatens. As a result K would decrease and V increase.

The preceding discussion is summarized in the following table.

Conditions	K	V
Increase in interest rate	Decrease	Increase
Expected increase in unemployment	Increase	Decrease
Expected increase in inflation	Decrease	Increase

It is interesting to note that the expectation of an increase in unemployment rates, which may cause a *decrease* in V, by itself is enough to cause an *increase* in actual unemployment. If M is constant, $P \times Q$ must decline if V declines. In the case of an expectation of inflation, the resulting *increase* in V is enough to cause an *increase* in $P \times Q$, with most of the increase coming in P if the nation is at or near full employment. These changes in expectations have the effect of causing even more severe unemployment or inflation problems than would be caused by a change in M alone, say through government policy. For example, when M declined during the Great Depression, $P \times Q$ declined by an even greater proportion because of the expectation of higher unemployment and the resulting decrease in V. Similarly, during high rates of inflation the price level generally increases more than the increase in M because of the increase in V. However, during the 1970s there was no significant upward trend of V in the United States in spite of inflation. In 1983 there was a slight decrease in the U.S. velocity. This is consistent with the new quantity theory; as people became more concerned about unemployment, they attempted to increase their monetary assets, leading to a decrease in V and an increase in M. In countries that have experienced really high rates of inflation, say 100 to 500 percent per year, it has been common to observe an increase in V, which pushes prices up more than in proportion to the increase in M, at least in the early stages of inflation.

HOW MONEY AFFECTS THE ECONOMY IN THE CONTEXT OF THE NEW QUANTITY THEORY

From our knowledge of the quantity equation of exchange, it is evident that a change in M must change $P \times Q$ in the same direction, providing V does not change in the opposite direction; this is a mathematical necessity. It is important also to understand the economic logic underlying this phenomenon.

Suppose we begin at an equilibrium position where people are holding the amount of money they desire to hold. For example, if people desire to hold half of their annual income in the form of money ($K = 0.5$) and the actual amount of M in existence is $1,000 billion, then income, or $P \times Q$, will be $2,000 billion.

Now let us suppose that the government for one reason or another increases the actual quantity of money by $100 billion. Remember that every dollar in existence must always be held or owned by somebody. If income is $2,000 billion and people continue to desire to hold the equivalent of half of their annual income in the form of money, it follows that because of the $100 billion increase in the quantity of money, some people must be holding more money than they desire to hold at this level of income. In other words, the increase in the quantity of money causes an imbalance between the *desired* holdings of money and the *actual* amount of money in existence.

What can people do to make the desired K equal to actual K? One thing they can do is to try to convert this "excess" money into securities, such as stocks and bonds. The increased demand for stocks and bonds will cause an increase in their prices, but the increase in the prices of stocks and bonds will cause a decrease in their interest rate. The relationship between the price of a security and its interest return is easiest to see for a bond. A bond that carries a face value of, say, $100 while stipulating a 10 percent rate of interest return always pays $10 per year to the owner regardless of the actual selling price of the bond. (Bonds can sell for a premium over the face value or at a discount below the face value.) If the market price of the bond is bid up to $200, then its interest return is reduced to 5 percent ($10/$200).

However, before securities prices and interest rates change very much, it is expected that people will buy other assets, such as real estate, automobiles, appliances, gold, education, medical care, and travel experiences. As the interest return on securities declines, these other assets become more attractive. Therefore it does not take much of a decrease in the interest return on securities for people to start to increase their purchases of other assets.

Notice, however, that the increased rate of purchases of the other assets mentioned previously has the effect of increasing $P \times Q$ for the economy. In other words, as people come into the market to buy additional goods and services, the prices and/or quantities of these items increase, thereby increasing $P \times Q$. If people still desire to hold the equivalent of half of their annual income in the form of money, then $P \times Q$ will increase until people are able to re-establish their equilibrium. In the example given, $P \times Q$ would increase to $2,200 billion because of the increase in M to $1,100 billion, thereby re-establishing their desired K of 0.5. It is not possible to say how much of the increase in $P \times Q$ comes in the form of increased prices and how much in the form of larger real output (Q). If the economy is at or near full employment, most of the increase will be in P. If there is unemployment or idle resources, both P and Q probably will increase, but there is no way of telling how much each will change. The only thing we can say for sure is that $P \times Q$ will increase by $200 billion up to the $2,200 billion level. The preceding discussion can be summarized by the following chain of causation:

> Increase $M \rightarrow$ Increase in actual K over desired $K \rightarrow$ Increase in
> demand for and price of securities $\rightarrow$ Decrease in interest rate $\rightarrow$
> Increase in purchase of other assets $\rightarrow$ Increase in $P \times Q \rightarrow$
> Return to equilibrium of actual K with actual desired K

Of course the opposite results occur when M is decreased. You might try to reason out this process on your own.

One might argue that the decrease in the interest rate caused by the increase in the price of securities makes people *willing* to hold more money because the cost of holding money now has decreased. If people willingly increase their desired holding of money by $100 billion, then there will be no increase in $P \times Q$. The only thing that will happen in this case is an increase in desired (and actual) K to 0.55 ($1,100/$2,000) or a decrease in V to 1.82. However the relative stability of V during the 1929–84 period in the face of large increases in the quantity of money (Tables 10–1 and 10–2) and sharp fluctuations in the interest rate suggests that V does not change in the opposite direction of M.

It is possible, of course, for people to change their desired level of K. In this case $P \times Q$ can change without a change in M. For example, if people expect an increase in unemployment, they may try to increase their holdings of money in order to have something in reserve. However, if the government does not increase the actual amount of money in the economy, all people cannot increase their holdings of money. If one person succeeds in holding more money, someone else must end up holding less. What happens in this case is that $P \times Q$ decreases as people reduce their rate of purchases of goods and services in an attempt to increase their monetary assets. Eventually $P \times Q$ decreases enough to increase the actual K up to the higher desired K level. As mentioned in the preceding section, such a phenomenon is most likely to occur when M itself is reduced as in the Great Depression. Conversely, K is most likely to decrease (V increase) during extreme inflationary times as people try to get rid of money due to its decrease in value. However, in this case, if one person succeeds in converting money to nonmonetary assets, someone else ends up holding more money. But people still can decrease K by spending money more rapidly (increase V), thereby increasing $P \times Q$. Therefore, a change in M is most likely to result in a change in K in the opposite direction, thereby accentuating the unemployment or inflation problem brought on by the initial change in M. Or one could say that a change in M is most likely to cause a change in V of the same direction, thereby accentuating the impact of the initial change in M. The relationship between changes in M and changes in the desired K is summarized below:

> Increase $M \rightarrow$ Increase inflation $\rightarrow$ Increase in cost of holding
> money $\rightarrow$ Decrease in desired $K \rightarrow$ Increase in $P \times Q \rightarrow$ Still
> more inflation

> Decrease $M \rightarrow$ Increase unemployment $\rightarrow$ Increase in desired
> $K \rightarrow$ Decrease in $P \times Q \rightarrow$ Still more unemployment

MAIN POINTS OF CHAPTER 10

1. Throughout history humans have utilized a variety of different objects as money. What was used depended mainly on the technology and resources available at the time. Money should be relatively cheap to produce, reasonably durable, and hard to duplicate.

2. From the standpoint of total society, money has three main functions. It serves as (1) a medium of exchange, (2) a standard of value, and (3) a store of value. Money can be thought of as a tool that enhances the total output of society. Without money people would be required to spend a large share of their time shopping rather than producing.

3. Even though paper money has no value as a commodity, it can be used as a medium of exchange if the majority of people in society are willing to accept it in payment for goods and services.

4. In years to come we may experience a trend toward a cashless society in which income and expenditures are characterized by bookkeeping entries rather than an exchange of paper or metal. This does not mean, however, that we will have a moneyless society. The monetary unit will continue to be used but will change in form from tangible paper or metal to intangible numbers in the memory cores of computers.

5. Narrowly defined, the quantity of money includes currency plus demand deposits. Under the broad definition, the quantity of money includes currency, demand deposits, and time deposits, the latter includes money market funds.

6. The price of a good is the units of money that are exchanged for it. The more money in existence relative to real goods and services, the more units will be exchanged for each good or service.

7. The **velocity of money** is the average number of times each dollar changes hands, or is spent, each year. Velocity of money for the country can be computed by dividing a measure of income, such as GNP, by the quantity of money in existence; that is:

$$V = \frac{P \times Q}{M}$$

8. The **quantity equation of exchange** is obtained by multiplying both sides of the velocity formula by M—i.e., $M \times V = P \times Q$. The quantity equation of exchange says that the quantity of money times velocity always equals the value of money income or output.

9. An increase in M while holding V and Q constant must result in an increase in the price level.

10. A decrease in M while holding V constant will reduce the money value of income by a decrease in P, Q, or both. Most likely Q would decrease before P.

11. Changes in V have the same effect on the value of money income as changes in M, although changes in V have not been nearly as great as changes in M.

12. A major limitation of using the quantity equation of exchange to predict changes in P or Q from changes in M is the necessity of assuming a constant velocity.

13. By dividing both sides of the quantity equation of exchange by V, we obtain the equation $M = (1/V) \times P \times Q$ or $M = K \times P \times Q$ where K is equal to $(1/V)$. Another way to interpret K is that it is the fraction of money income held as money. The new quantity theory is concerned with explaining and predicting changes in velocity and K.

14. If we can determine why people desire to change the proportion of income held as money, then we can explain and predict changes in the velocity of money.

15. People hold part of their wealth in the form of money because of the convenience and security that money provides.

16. People do not hold all of their wealth in the form of money because of the cost of holding money.

17. The cost of holding money is equal to the earnings that a person could obtain by owning nonmonetary assets.

18. The two main factors affecting changes in the proportion of income held as money are (1) changes in the interest rate and (2) changes in the expectations of future levels of unemployment and inflation.

19. An increase in the interest rate should decrease K and increase V.

20. An expectation of higher unemployment in the future should increase K and decrease V.

21. An expectation of higher inflation in the future should decrease K and increase V.

22. An increase in M causes an increase in $P \times Q$ by causing an imbalance between actual K and desired K. As people increase their rate of spending in an effort to bring actual K down to the level of desired K, $P \times Q$ increases.

23. The reduction in the rate of interest brought on by the increase in prices of securities could conceivably cause people to willingly hold an increase in M. In this case $P \times Q$ would not change.

24. Before the interest return on securities falls very much because of an increase in M, people will find other assets more attractive and in the process of buying these assets will cause $P \times Q$ to increase.

25. The most common situation is for K to change in the opposite direction from M, thereby accentuating the unemployment or inflation problems brought on by the initial changes in M.

QUESTIONS FOR THOUGHT AND DISCUSSION

1. How has money changed in form from early civilizations to current times? Why has it changed?

2. If money did not exist:
   a. How would people pay for their purchases?
   b. How would prices be quoted?
   c. How would people save?

3. a. Why is a $20 bill which is worth a fraction of a cent on the used paper market worth so much more as money?
   b. If people were free to print their own money on paper, would paper money have any value? Explain.

4. During the post-World War II period, people have turned more and more to the use of credit cards. Does this imply a trend toward a "moneyless" society? Explain.

5. a. What is the meaning of the money price of an object?
   b. What is the relationship between the quantity of money in existence and the level of prices?

6. a. What is the velocity of money, and how is it calculated?
   b. Will velocity vary according to the definition of money? Explain.
   c. Which definition of money will provide the most stable velocity? Explain.

7. a. Derive the quantity equation of exchange from the formula for computing velocity.
   b. According to the quantity equation of exchange, what should happen if:
      (1) The quantity of money is increased during a time of full employment?
      (2) The quantity of money is increased during a time of unemployment?
      (3) The quantity of money is decreased?

8. a. Why do people hold part of their wealth in the form of money?
   b. Why don't people hold all their wealth in the form of money?

9. *a.* How is the proportion of income held as money (the K value) related to the velocity of money?

   b. What factors may cause people to change the proportion of their income held as money?

10. *a.* According to the quantity theory, why does an increase in M cause an increase in $P \times Q$?

    b. Under what conditions could an increase in M not cause an increase in $P \times Q$?

11. According to the quantity theory how do people achieve an equilibrium if they happen to be holding more money than they desire to hold? Less than they desire to hold?

12. *a.* During extreme inflation, it has been observed that P increases more than the increase in M. Is this consistent with the quantity theory? Explain.

    b. During the Great Depression, $P \times Q$ decreased in proportion to the decrease in M. Was this phenomenon consistent with the quantity theory? Explain.

CHAPTER 11

COMMERCIAL BANKING AND THE FEDERAL RESERVE SYSTEM

We now turn our attention from money to the industry most directly involved with this commodity, the banking system. In this chapter we will present a brief description of the banking system in the United States, including both commercial banks and the Federal Reserve System. Particular attention is given to the transactions that take place in commercial banks. We will see how one of these transactions results in the creation of money. In studying bank transactions, it is necessary to utilize the balance sheet. So before undertaking a study of banking, let us review this important accounting tool.

THE BALANCE SHEET

Basically a balance sheet itemizes the assets, liabilities, and net worth of a person, firm, or institution as of a particular point in time. *Assets* are defined as anything of value. A person's assets typically include clothes, car, real estate, appliances, cash, stocks and bonds. A business firm's assets include mainly the real estate and capital equipment that the firm has under its control, together with its monetary assets, such as cash and bank deposits. A commercial bank's assets include many of the same items found in an ordinary business firm. There are some special items among a bank's assets, however, that will come to our attention later.

We should be aware, though, that the asset value of a particular item does not tell us anything about who has ultimate claim on the item. For example, if you "own" a $4,000 automobile but have $2,000 yet to pay on it, you have a $2,000 claim on the auto and the lender has a $2,000 claim. The balance sheet would carry the auto as a $4,000 asset regardless of how much you still owed on it. For this reason it is necessary to know the amount of liabilities and net worth also.

The *liability* figures in a balance sheet indicate the amount owed to creditors. Sometimes the balance sheet will separate short-term from long-term liabilities to indicate how soon the debts have to be paid. For our purposes it will be sufficient to know just that liabilities are debts that will have to be paid sometime in the future. *Net worth* represents the assets owned free and clear by the individuals controlling the assets. Essentially, we can view liabilities as the creditors' claim to the assets in a balance sheet and net worth as the owners' claim to these assets.

As its name implies the balance sheet must always balance; that is, the total value of assets must always equal the total claim on these assets. We are assured that assets always equal liabilities plus net worth because the net worth figure is obtained as a residual by subtracting liabilities from assets. These relationships are summarized below:

$$Assets = Liabilities + Net\ worth$$
$$Net\ worth = Assets - Liabilities$$

A convenient method of presenting the balance sheet is in the form of a T-account. With this format assets are listed on the left side of the vertical line and liabilities and net worth on the right side. The following example illustrates the format of a T-account balance sheet and some typical entries for a college student. Notice that the balance sheet is drawn up at a particular point in time. Typically business firms or institutions compute their balances at the end of the calendar year or fiscal year. The asset figures should reflect the current market value of the items listed, $6,000 in this example. The unpaid balances of two loans outstanding represent the liabilities of the student, $2,000 in this example. The $4,000 net worth figure is found by subtracting the $2,000 in liabilities from the $6,000 assets total.

Balance Sheet of a College Student as of a Point in Time

Assets		*Liabilities + Net worth*	
Automobile	4,000	Bank loan	1,200
Typewriter	400	Loan from parents	800
Clothes	1,600	Net worth	4,000
	6,000		6,000

EVOLUTION OF BANKING

To the average individual, banking is a rather mysterious business. Other than bank employees, relatively few people have an opportunity to see first-hand how banks operate. In the remainder of this chapter we will take a figurative look behind the teller's window in order to better understand banking operations. It will be helpful to begin the discussion with the earliest and simplest kind of banker—the ancient goldsmith. By so doing, we will be able to see more clearly why banks came into existence and obtain a better understanding of what banks do. Understandably, banking was a good deal simpler in those early days. In this section we will use present-day terminology, recognizing that names and words that describe banking activities are different nowadays than in ancient times.

During the early period of civilization, gold and silver were the predominant forms of money. Those who were fortunate enough to accumulate a sizable amount of these metals were confronted with the problem of keeping it safe from those who were bent on redistributing the wealth of the land— i.e., thieves and robbers. It should not be surprising then that the ancient goldsmith emerged as the person best able to store money for safekeeping. Since the basic raw material used in his business had to be closely guarded anyway, the goldsmith no doubt found it profitable to take in other people's gold for safekeeping in return for a fee. Of course, at the time of deposit the customer had to be given a receipt indicating the date and amount of deposit. Understandably, this receipt had to be presented when the depositor wished to reclaim the gold.

In providing a storage service the goldsmith's place of business became, in effect, a warehouse for gold. It also became the forerunner of the modern bank. The goldsmith accepted deposits of money and paid them out again on demand. This describes in large part the activities of a modern bank. However, present-day banks also make loans. Let us see how this activity might have emerged.

It probably did not take long for the more perceptive goldsmiths to discover that during any one day the gold withdrawn was in large part offset by the gold deposited. During some days withdrawals may have exceeded deposits by a small amount, or vice versa, but on any given day, the goldsmith was not likely to have all his gold withdrawn, unless his reputation suddenly became suspect. We know, too, that gold is a completely homogeneous commodity: that is, an ounce of gold is the same no matter who deposits it. Hence, the actual gold that was withdrawn during any one day probably was the same gold that had come in through deposits on that very day or the day before. Because gold is homogeneous, there was no need for the goldsmith to dig to the bottom or to the back of his vault to locate gold deposited months or years before. At any rate, the perceptive goldsmith deposited months or years before. At any rate, the perceptive goldsmith undoubtedly noticed that a relatively large share of his gold deposits was lying in the vault gathering dust.

Let us say, for example, that only about 20 percent of his gold was actively used to pay withdrawals on days when deposits were unusually low. For all practical purposes the remaining 80 percent of the gold was never used. In fact, it no doubt was considered a hindrance, since it required more space and provided a greater temptation for would-be robbers.

There always have been people who were in need of loans for various and sundry purposes. Without people or institutions that specialized in making loans, borrowers had to prevail upon friends or relatives. For the very poor who had only poor friends or relatives, there was little chance of obtaining credit. It took people awhile to get used to the idea of paying interest, however.

And without interest to compensate for waiting and for the risk involved, there is not much incentive to lend money.

Once the payment of interest, in one form or another, became socially acceptable, the goldsmiths discovered a grand opportunity to benefit both themselves and their customers. By lending out some of the unused gold, they provided a source of credit for people who wanted to make a fairly large purchase, such as a business, a cart, or an animal. These people were certainly helped because the loans enabled many of them to purchase resources that increased their earning power and standard of living, just as is true today. The goldsmith benefited because of the interest income he earned from his loans. Finally, his depositors benefited because they could now be paid for depositing gold rather than having to pay for the storage service.

So far we have followed the evolution of banking through two steps. First, institutions evolved to satisfy the demand for storage services by people who had accumulated money. Second, these institutions, goldsmiths in the main, discovered that daily deposits and withdrawals normally came close to canceling each other out. Thus, goldsmiths could lend out part of their deposits, keeping only a part on reserve. Today we refer to this procedure as *fractional reserve banking*.

It will be helpful to represent each of these steps on a balance sheet. To simplify the procedure, we will ignore the items not directly connected with the transactions we are interested in, such as the assets representing physical facilities and net worth. The balance sheet on the left below represents the deposit of $1,000 in gold. (In ancient times, of course, the dollar had not been conceived, but we will use it in our example because it is the monetary unit most familiar to us.) The physical commodity gold becomes an asset to the goldsmith because it is now under his control. On the right side of the T-account we must represent the claims to this gold. Since the gold was owned entirely by the depositors, the entire claim to the gold is represented by the receipts given out by the goldsmith. These receipts, therefore, were liabilities to the goldsmith because he eventually would be called upon to pay out this amount in gold.

The right-hand balance sheet illustrates the lending out of part of the gold on deposit. In this example we show a $500 loan. The promissory note, or whatever the borrower gave the goldsmith at the time the loan was made, becomes an asset to the goldsmith. This is offset on the asset side by a $500 reduction in the gold item because it is taken out by the borrower. Note that total assets remain unchanged at $1,000; only the form is changed. The liabilities side remains unchanged in both form and total.

Deposit of $1,000 in Gold		Lending $500 of the Original $1,000 Deposit	
Assets	Liabilities + Net worth	Assets	Liabilities + Net worth
Gold 1,000	Receipts 1,000	Gold 500 Note 500	Receipts 1,000
		1,000	1,000

An additional step toward banking as we know it today was taken when depositors began to use their deposit receipts as money. It is fairly easy to see how this practice came into being. Visualize yourself as living in that time with, say, $500 of gold on deposit at the local goldsmith. Suppose you decided to trade in your old chariot for the latest model. Suppose also that the new chariot cost you $500 in gold plus your trade-in. You could, of course, make a trip to the goldsmith to draw out your $500 in gold. But the chariot dealer would just have to return to the goldsmith the same day with the same gold for redeposit. Both you and the chariot dealer could save a trip to the goldsmith if you just endorsed your deposit receipt over to the chariot dealer, instructing the goldsmith to pay him the $500 on demand.

The practice of exchanging deposit receipts instead of gold resembles a well-known practice in use today—namely, that of exchanging checks instead of the actual currency on deposit in banks. Thus, the deposit receipt was the forerunner of the present-day check. Of course, the check is a bit more convenient because it can be made out in any denomination. Eventually, people realized this, and as a result deposit receipts were made more flexible. With more widespread use, receipts, or checks, became a widely accepted form of money.

So far we have taken the goldsmith analogy to the point where it is just one step removed from the modern bank. The evolutionary process became complete when goldsmiths began to give out deposit receipts instead of gold when making loans. It is easy to visualize how this practice got started. Suppose, in the $500 loan example, that the person who took out the loan immediately redeposited the gold in the goldsmith's vault. The goldsmith then would have to give this person a deposit receipt. After all, we would not expect the borrower to want to carry gold around any more than the people who originally deposited it. Moreover, as deposit receipts became a commonly accepted form of money, it would be foolish to risk losing the gold that had been borrowed when pieces of paper would serve the same purpose.

For borrowers who did not want to take the gold with them, it was natural that the physical removal and immediate redeposit of gold at the time loans were transacted should be eliminated. Now all the goldsmith had to do was fill out a deposit receipt that borrowers could take with them. Notice, however, that this procedure results in a somewhat different balance sheet than resulted from the more primitive loan transaction shown earlier, where the borrower took the gold with him. The following balance sheet illustrates the case where $500 of the original $1,000 deposit was loaned out, but instead of physically removing the gold, the borrower accepted a deposit receipt.

Lending Out $500 of the Original $1,000 Deposit and Issuing Deposit Receipts to the Borrowers

Assets		Liabilities + Net worth	
Gold	1,000	Receipts to depositors	1,000
Note	500	Receipts to borrower	500
	1,500		1,500

Notice here that if receipts to borrowers are considered money, then the goldsmith, or lending institution, in fact created money by making loans and issuing these receipts. We will discuss this phenomenon in more detail a bit later when we look at the transactions of a modern commercial bank.

We have now taken the goldsmith to the point where he was doing essentially the same things as the modern commercial bank does. First he took in deposits; second, he made loans; and third, he issued and honored deposit receipts that in effect became money. Let us now take a brief look at the commercial banking system as it exists today in the United States.

COMMERCIAL BANKS

By commercial banks we have in mind those institutions that among other things offer checking account services. This category does not include savings and loan associations or mutual savings banks. Although these institutions accept deposits and make loans, they do not offer checking account services. As we will see later, the latter characteristic in conjunction with the fractional reserve requirement has an important bearing on the money supply.

As of December 31, 1982, there were 14,963 commercial banks in the United States. Those that received their charter from the federal government are called national banks, and those operating under a state charter are known as state banks. All of the national banks are required to hold membership in the Federal Reserve System; that is, they must buy stock in the system. Each state bank is free to choose whether or not it wishes to be a member of the Federal Reserve System. Of all commercial banks, only 5,619 were members in 1982. At the same time, we should point out that most of the larger state banks are members, so the major share of the deposits in the country (71 percent in 1980) come under the jurisdiction of the Federal Reserve System.

All member banks are required to hold a certain fraction of their deposit liabilities on reserve as cash in their vaults or on reserve in the Federal Reserve bank in their district. This fraction, often called the *reserve ratio,* varies between demand and time deposits and by size of deposit. The highest ratio, 16.25 percent, applies to demand deposits in large "reserve city banks" having demand deposits over $400 million. Small "country banks" with demand deposits of less than $2 million are required to maintain just a 7 percent ratio. Intermediate size banks must maintain ratios between these two extremes depending on their size; in general, the larger the size of the bank, the higher the required reserve ratio is. The reserve ratio for all passbook savings deposits is 3 percent regardless of size of the bank. The reserve ratio for savings certificate deposits varies from 1 to 6 percent depending on maturity; the longer the maturity, the lower the ratio is. Bear in mind that a reserve ratio of 16.25 percent, for example, means that the bank must keep at least $16.25 on reserve either in its own vaults or in its Federal Reserve bank for each $100 of demand deposits on their books. The other figures have a similar meaning. The Federal Reserve Board of Governors has the authority to change these reserve ratios over a fairly broad range, although this power is seldom used. We should point out, too, that nonmember state banks also must maintain reserves against their deposits. These reserves are kept in the reserve city banks, which tend to be located in the financial districts of large cities. In a sense, these large reserve city banks act as Federal Reserve banks for the smaller "country" banks.

It is probably assumed by many people that legal reserve requirements were set up to protect depositors. No doubt they have this effect but an equally valid reason for having legal reserve requirements is to provide a means for the Federal Reserve system to have some control over the maximum amount of bank loans and thus over the maximum quantity of money in the economy.

Similar to the goldsmith, in the process of making loans, commercial banks actually create money.

Before discussing commercial bank transactions, it is necessary to have some understanding of the Federal Reserve System. We will see that many commercial banks' transactions directly affect one or more Federal Reserve banks.

THE FEDERAL RESERVE SYSTEM

Between 1776 and the early 1900s banking in the United States was a highly decentralized and relatively unregulated industry. While the banking industry was a source of considerable controversy over this period and attracted its share of unscrupulous people, commercial banks should receive at least part of the credit for the tremendous growth and development that the United States experienced during its first 150 years. Banking institutions evolved and changed to meet the needs of the people not only in the new lands that were settled but also in the new industries that came into being during this time. This is not to say that the United States experienced smooth, uninterrupted growth during its first century and a half of existence. Indeed, as history books record, many "panics" or recessions occurred along the way. When the country was largely agricultural, crop failures, bumper harvests, and the normal cyclic behavior of the livestock industry introduced an element of instability in the economy. Of course, other nonagricultural industries also experienced periods of rapid growth and decline which introduced another element of instability.

Although banks should not be held responsible for the normal growth and decline of other industries, it became evident that they did not help maintain a stable economy and may have contributed to the instability. For example, during expansionary periods banks faced a strong demand for their loans. As a result banks obliged by increasing loans. But as we will see shortly, this action increased the money supply, which augmented the boom and ensuing inflation. On the other hand, during recessionary periods, banks, along with businesspeople, became pessimistic about the future and as a result reduced their loans outstanding. This in turn reduced the money supply, which contributed to a still further reduction in economic activity.

During certain periods within the year the banking community also experienced shortages and surpluses of money. As a current example, during the Christmas shopping season the volume of business activity rises substantially and more money is needed to carry out these transactions. Unless there is a corresponding increase in money supply, money becomes "scarce" and interest rates rise. As a result there may be an unnecessary curtailment of economic activity. Similarly, during slack periods of the year, mainly during the first quarter, the supply of money that would fulfill the demand without a rise in interest rates during the peak season would be too large, resulting in unnecessary instability in the money market.

Because of these seasonal fluctuations in the demand for money, it became clear that the country needed an agency that could provide an "elastic" currency, that is, a money supply that could expand and contract with the seasonal fluctuations in the economy. Thus, the need for a central bank became evident because of the "perverse elasticity" of money that accentuated booms and recessions and also because of the need for a greater elasticity of the money supply during peak and slack periods within the year.

Between 1873 and 1907 the United States experienced five serious panics with many bank closings. Following the 1907 panic congress brought forth the Federal Reserve Act which was signed by President Woodrow Wilson on December 13, 1913. This act created the Federal Reserve System. Understandably, there was a great deal of reluctance on the part of bankers to create a strong, centralized banking authority located in Washington or New York. Yet the inadequacy of a completely decentralized banking system was recognized. As a result the Federal Reserve System was set up as somewhat of a compromise between a more centralized government bank, such as the Bank of England or Bank of France, and a totally private banking system.[1]

To maintain some form of decentralization, the country was divided into 12 Federal Reserve districts, each having a Federal Reserve bank. Several of the Federal Reserve banks have one or more branches located in other cities of the district. The Federal Reserve System is supervised by a seven-member Board of Governors located in Washington, D.C. The Board of Governors is assisted by a Federal Advisory Council and a Federal Open Market Committee. As the name implies, the Advisory Council advises the Board of Governors on monetary policy. The Open Market Committee buys and sells securities, which, as we will see later in the chapter, affects the quantity of money in the economy.

Federal Reserve banks are sometimes called quasi-public banks because they are owned by member banks but controlled by the Board of Governors. The Board of Governors is really a government agency, because the members are appointed by the president of the United States.

Federal Reserve banks also have been called "banker's banks" because they perform essentially the same functions for commercial banks as commercial banks do for private individuals. You and I, for example, cannot walk into a Federal Reserve bank and make a deposit or negotiate a loan. But these services are available to commercial banks that are members of the Federal Reserve System. We will see later why a commercial bank might be in need of a loan. The U.S. Treasury also maintains a deposit in the Federal Reserve System, so in a sense the "Fed," as it is often called, serves as the bank for the federal government.

We can obtain a better idea of the economic characteristics of the Federal Reserve System by looking at the balance sheet for the entire system, shown below.

On the asset side, the largest item is securities. Mainly these are U.S. government bonds issued by the Treasury. The Open Market Committee is continually buying and selling securities, which we will see has an important bearing on the quantity of money in the economy. Gold certificates represent the stock of gold held by the U.S. government. The loans item represents short-term credit extended to commercial banks that are members of the Federal Reserve System for the purpose of bolstering their reserves.

---

[1] For a detailed description of the Federal Reserve System and its functions, see U.S. Board of Governors of the Federal Reserve System, *The Federal Reserve System: Its Purposes and Functions* (New York: AMS Press, 1976).

Consolidated Balance Sheet of the Federal Reserve System as of December 31, 1984 ($ billions)

Assets		Liabilities + Net worth	
Cash	0.4	Reserves of member banks	21.8
Gold certificates	11.1	Treasury deposits	5.3
Securities	160.9	Federal Reserve notes	168.3
Loans to banks	3.6	Other liabilities and	
Other assets	31.2	net worth	11.8
	207.2		207.2

Source: *Federal Reserve Bulletin*, March 1985.

On the right side of the balance sheet the three items listed represent liabilities of the Federal Reserve. Commercial banks that are members of the Federal Reserve System are required to keep a certain fraction of their deposit liabilities on reserve, either in their respective Federal Reserve banks or as vault cash in their respective banks. Member bank reserves represent liabilities of the Federal Reserve System because these funds are in a sense held in trust for the commercial banks and may be relinquished at any time. Treasury deposits represent the checking account money that the federal government has on deposit for the purpose of paying its bills. Federal Reserve notes, the largest single liability item, is the official name of the paper currency used today in the United States.

COMMERCIAL BANK TRANSACTIONS

In order to understand how the banking system can alter the quantity of money in the economy, it is first necessary to understand the nature of transactions that take place within the banking community. We already have caught a glimpse of the banking world in our discussion of the goldsmith at the beginning of the chapter. As we proceed, you will probably note a strong resemblance between the modern commercial bank and the ancient goldsmith. It will be easier to understand banking transactions if we start with the most basic—the deposit of cash by a customer—and then move on.

1. Deposit of $10,000 cash by a customer. Suppose, to make the example more meaningful, you decide to open up a bank. After receiving your charter, you rent some facilities and obtain some of the basic equipment used by a bank, which among other things might include a vault and some conservative clothing. On your first day of operation a local business person brings in $10,000 in cash and wishes to establish a checking account in your bank.

Our main interest at this point is how this transaction affects your balance sheet. The $10,000 in cash that has come under your control becomes an asset of your bank. In the following balance sheet we refer to this cash deposit as total reserves. Of course, we know a balance sheet must balance, so at the same time there is a corresponding increase in the liabilities side. This is accomplished by increasing the demand deposit (checking account) item by $10,000. Bear in mind that demand deposits represent a liability to you because you may be required to pay this amount to your customer at any time. To simplify the arithmetic, assume the required reserve ratio is 0.20, or 20 percent, so that, along with the $10,000 increase in demand deposits, your required reserves increase by $2,000 (0.20 × $10,000). Thus, out of the $10,000 deposit of cash, $2,000 is taken up by required reserves and the remaining $8,000 becomes "excess reserves." (In the following balance sheets we show only the changes that take place, in order to concentrate on the particular transaction at hand.)

Deposits of $10,000 in Cash by a Customer

Assets	Liabilities + Net worth

Total reserves (cash) + 10,000
  Required reserves
    +2,000
  Excess reserves
    +8,000
	Demand deposits + 10,000

Notice in this transaction that you have not yet created any money. The cash that has come into your bank is now removed from the money supply (only cash outside of banks is considered part of the quantity of money) but this has been offset by the increase in demand deposits. The quantity of money in the economy has changed in composition, from cash to demand deposits, but not in total amount.

2. Deposit of required reserves in Federal Reserve bank. Assume you are a member of the Federal Reserve System and decide to deposit the entire amount of required reserves in the Federal Reserve bank in your district. In this transaction, only the Federal Reserve balance sheet is affected, because your reserves remain the same. You still have $10,000 in total reserves: $2,000 in the Federal Reserve bank and $8,000 in your vault.

Federal Reserve Balance Sheet
Deposit of $2,000 Required Reserves
in the Federal Reserve Bank

Assets		Liabilities + Net worth	
Cash	+2,000	Member bank reserves	+2,000

3. A $1,000 check is drawn on your bank. It is reasonable to suppose that your depositor will begin to write checks against her account. Suppose she buys $1,000 worth of supplies and pays for the purchase by writing a check. Naturally, the supplier will soon after deposit this check in his account, which we will assume is in some other bank (call it Bank B). We will see that this transaction affects the balance sheets of three banks: your bank (call it Bank A), the Federal Reserve, and Bank B.

Your depositor, of course, must have her checking account balance reduced by the amount of the check. But how will you know she has written a check? The procedure followed is for Bank B to first add $1,000 to the supplier's checking account and offset this by adding $1,000 to the reserve entry in its balance sheet. Then the check goes to the Federal Reserve bank, which adds to or credits Bank B's reserves by $1,000 and subtracts from or debits your reserves (Bank A) by a like amount. This service that the Fed provides for its members is often referred to as a "clearinghouse" function. The Federal Reserve bank then sends the canceled check back to you, which informs you that your depositor should have her checking account reduced by $1,000 and that your reserves in the Federal Reserve are reduced by the same amount. Last you send the canceled check back to your depositor, so she knows her account has been reduced. The entire transaction of the effects of a $1,000 check drawn on Bank A is summarized by the balance sheets below:

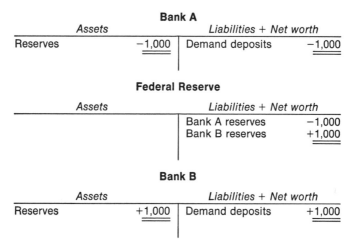

Bank A

Assets		*Liabilities + Net worth*	
Reserves	−1,000	Demand deposits	−1,000

Federal Reserve

Assets		*Liabilities + Net worth*	
		Bank A reserves	−1,000
		Bank B reserves	+1,000

Bank B

Assets		*Liabilities + Net worth*	
Reserves	+1,000	Demand deposits	+1,000

Note that all three balance sheets continue to balance after the transaction is complete. In fact it is always a good idea to represent commercial bank transactions by balance sheets because they provide a good check on one's accuracy. If the balance sheets do not balance after working through the transaction, you can be sure you have made an error. Unfortunately, the converse is not true; erroneous balance sheets can still balance.

Assuming that the original $10,000 depositor is the only person who has put money into your bank, the $1,000 check has reduced your total demand deposits and reserves to $9,000. With a 20 percent reserve ratio, this means that your required reserves drop slightly, to $1,800, and that your excess reserves are reduced to $7,200 ($9,000 − $1,800). Of course, it is reasonable to believe that before long your depositor also would bring checks into your bank that were drawn on other banks. These checks would replenish your reserves at the Fed and increase your bank's demand deposits.

So far we have not created any new money. The practice of writing checks just transfers demand deposits from one bank to another. In the above example, your bank lost $1,000 in demand deposits, but Bank B gained a like amount.

MONEY CREATION

Being a banker, you naturally are eager to make loans because the interest return on money lent out is a prime source of income for most banks. The first question is: How much can you loan out? Let us suppose that checks coming into your bank have offset checks going out. Thus, your balance sheet shows $10,000 in demand deposit liabilities and $10,000 in total reserves as illustrated in the top balance sheet that follows. The required reserve ratio of 0.20 tells you that 20 percent, or $2,000, of the $10,000 demand deposits must be kept on reserve either in your vault or at the Federal Reserve bank. Thus, the remaining 80 percent, the $8,000 excess reserve, represents the value of new loans that can be made to the public.

Consider next what happens when a likely prospect comes along in need of an $8,000 loan, say, to build an addition to his home. He signs a promissory note agreeing to pay you certain specified interest and payments on the principal. In return you set up a checking account for him. The moment you set up this checking account, you in effect create $8,000 in additional money. After all, demand deposits are money. Thus, banks create money by making loans.

So far you have added $8,000 to the demand deposits item in your balance sheet. Now you have a total of $18,000 in demand deposits in your bank, backed up by $10,000 in reserves. This situation is depicted in the middle balance sheet below. But notice that at this point you still have excess reserves. Under the 0.20 reserve ratio you are required to have only $3,600 in reserves, but you still have $10,000. What happened? Did we make a mistake?

The answer is no, because as soon as this $8,000 loan is spent (checks are written against it) you must expect that these checks will be deposited in some other bank. And, as you recall from the check-writing transaction of the previous section, a check drawn against your bank reduces your reserves at the Fed by the amount of the check. Suppose, then, that the entire loan is spent by writing a single check, say, in payment to a contractor. If the contractor deposits this check in another bank, Bank B, the Fed reduces your reserves by $8,000 (you better be sure you have $8,000 at the Fed) and increases the reserves of Bank B. The end results of the loan process, as it affects your bank, is shown on the bottom balance sheet.

Initial Situation

Assets			Liabilities + Net worth	
Reserves		10,000	Demand deposits	10,000
Required reserves	2,000			
Excess reserves	8,000			

Loan Is Made

Assets			Liabilities + Net worth	
Reserves		10,000	Demand deposits	18,000
Required reserves	3,600			
Excess reserves	6,400			
Note		8,000		
		18,000		18,000

Loan Is Spent

Assets			Liabilities + Net worth	
Reserves		2,000	Demand deposits	10,000
Required reserves	2,000			
Excess reserves	–0–			
Note		8,000		
		10,000		10,000

In this example, we assumed that the demand deposits were created at the time of the loan. We could have assumed instead that the borrower took the money in cash, say, 80 crisp $100 bills. You still would have created $8,000 in additional money, because cash inside banks is not considered part of the money supply whereas cash outside banks is a part of the money supply. Eventually, of course, the contractor who received the $8,000 would take it to a bank for deposit, thus exchanging cash for demand deposits. So we end up at the same place regardless of whether we assume the loan goes out as a check or as cash.

MULTIPLE EXPANSION

The story of your loan does not end when the $8,000 check is cleared against your bank. Let us now go to Bank B, the contractor's bank. When the check has cleared, the Fed increases Bank B's reserves by $8,000 and at the same time Bank B's demand deposit item is increased by the same amount. But if Bank B receives $8,000 in new demand deposits and reserves, we know part of this $8,000 will be excess reserves. Operating under a reserve ratio of 0.20, 20 percent of the $8,000, or $1,600, represents required reserves. The remainder, $6,400 in this example, is excess reserves available to be loaned out.

In order to focus entirely on the $6,400 loan that Bank B can make, let us omit the other items on its balance sheet. The top balance sheet that follows represents the influx of new reserves into Bank B because of the $8,000 check. The middle balance sheet shows the immediate effect of making the loan, and the one on the bottom shows the end result after the loan is spent. Notice in this case that Bank B has created $6,400 in new demand deposits by making the loan.

So far, in these first two rounds of the multiple expansion process, a total of $14,400 in new money has been created—$8,000 with your original loan and $6,400 with Bank B's loan. There is no reason why the multiple expansion process has to stop here. We could carry it on to Bank C and then round after round to infinity. But by now you probably see what is going on. When a check comes into a bank, the bank acquires some excess reserves, which enable it to increase its loans. Of course, the amount of the loan and the demand deposits created become smaller and smaller the further the process is carried. The multiple expansion is summarized in Table 11–1.

TABLE 11–1   Summary of the multiple expansion process

	New total reserves	Excess reserves, loans made, dollars created
	Bank A, $10,000	$ 8,000 = 1 × $8,000
	Bank B, 8,000	6,400 = 0.80 × 8,000
	Bank C, 6,400	5,120 = $(0.80)^2$ × 8,000
	.	.
	.	.
	.	.
	To infinity	$40,000

Receipt of $8,000 Check

Assets			Liabilities + Net worth	
Reserves		8,000	Demand deposits	8,000
Required reserves	1,600			
Excess reserves	6,400			
		8,000		8,000

Loan Is Made

Assets			Liabilities + Net worth	
Reserves		8,000	Demand deposits	14,400
Required reserves	2,880			
Excess reserves	5,120			
Note		6,400		
		14,400		14,400

Loan Is Spent

Assets			Liabilities + Net worth	
Reserves		1,600	Demand deposits	8,000
Required reserves	1,600			
Excess reserves	–0–			
Note		6,400		
		8,000		8,000

You probably noticed a similarity between the multiple expansion process here and the multiplier discussed in Chapter 6. Rather than carrying the process out to infinity, which becomes a bit tedious before long, we can use a simple formula to determine how much the money supply will eventually increase. Recall from Chapter 6 the following expression:

$$1 + X + X^2 + X^3 + \cdots + X^n = \frac{1}{1 - X}$$

In this case, $X = 1 - R$ where R is the reserve ratio. Thus,

$$\frac{1}{1 - X} = \frac{1}{1 - (1 - R)}$$

But

$$\frac{1}{1 - (1 - R)} = \frac{1}{R}$$

because the ones cancel out.

Therefore, to find the ultimate expansion of the money supply stemming from an influx of new excess reserves, we multiply the original increase in excess reserves by (1/Reserve ratio). In the example $R = 0.20$, so the "money multiplier" is (1/0.20) or 5. Thus the sum of the right-hand column in Table 11–1 is equal to (1/0.20) × $8,000, or $40,000.

We should at the same time remember that the multiple expansion process can work in reverse; that is, a decrease in excess reserves can bring about a multiple contraction of the money supply. For example, suppose the borrower pays back the $8,000 loan. You decrease his checking account by $8,000 and give him the note. Now you have "destroyed" $8,000. If you do not relend the $8,000, the total money supply in the country will decline by $(1/R) \times \$8,000$. This happens because Banks B, C, D, etc., lose reserves as checks are drawn against them. In the process they lose reserves and must contract their loans outstanding also. Lest you receive the impression, however, that the entire banking system revolves around your bank, remember that every commercial bank in the country has the same option of renewing or not renewing loans.

It is necessary to mention also that the full multiple expansion or contraction takes place only if the participating banks are "fully loaned up" at all times; that is, they keep no excess reserves. In reality, though, most banks try to retain some excess reserves rather than operating right at the margin, so to speak. Generally, if banks face a strong demand for loans and high interest rates can be obtained, they tend to operate with less excess reserves than when the loan business is sluggish and interest rates are low. If a bank happens to find itself with less than the legal reserves, it can in an emergency borrow from the Federal Reserve bank in its district although the Fed tends to discourage habitual borrowers.

Bear in mind that the multiple expansion or contraction process is not likely to approach an infinite number of rounds. However, the major change in the money supply comes during the first few rounds. In the example above, the first three rounds alone created $19,520, or almost half the ultimate expansion. At any rate, the multiplier of $(1/R)$ provides an upper bound to how much the money supply will expand or contract for a given change in excess reserves. At the same time it is important to recognize that in working through the multiple expansion process, we used a required reserve ratio of 0.20 purely to simplify the arithmetic. The actual ratio is much lower than this, particularly for time deposits. The time deposit reserve ratio of 3 percent gives rise to a $33 maximum expansion in the money supply for each $1 increase in excess reserves. As mentioned in the previous chapter, time deposits, or savings account money, constitute the largest component of the money supply. Hence, the actual money multiplier is likely to be considerably larger than the value of five we have been working with.

BOND PURCHASES

A commercial bank with excess reserves on its books may choose to purchase bonds rather than make direct loans to individuals or business people. Most banks in fact like to diversify their portfolios and purchase a variety of earning assets with their excess reserves. Government bonds—federal, state, or municipal—are a popular investment for banks. The bonds may be purchased directly from the issuing agency or from a second party who happens to be holding them. Either way, the purchase of a bond by a bank has the same effect as making a loan—it creates money.

This will be easiest to see if we go back to our original example before your bank made the $8,000 loan. Instead suppose that you had purchased $8,000 in bonds held by a woman who wanted to use the money for a new car. Once you have the bonds, you pay her the cash, give her a certified check, or create a checking account in her name. In any case, you have created $8,000 in new money. As soon as the woman spends the $8,000, another bank is likely to experience an increase in its deposits and excess reserves, and off we go again on the same multiple expansion process. Thus, the purchase of bonds from an individual by a commercial bank increases the nation's money supply the same as if the bank made loans.

SUMMARY OF COMMERCIAL BANK TRANSACTIONS

In this chapter three basic bank transactions have been discussed. These are summarized below, along with each one's effect on the nation's money supply.

Transaction	Change money supply?
Depositing currency	No
Writing checks	No
Making loans (or buying bonds)	Yes

AN IMPLICATION OF FRACTIONAL RESERVE BANKING

By now you probably realize that a bank does not hold in cold storage, so to speak, all the money that has been brought in for deposit. A certain fraction, the required reserves, must be held; but the remainder, or excess reserves, can be used to make loans or purchase bonds. As pointed out at the beginning of the chapter, a bank is able to operate with fractional reserves because on any one day deposits and withdrawals tend to cancel out. During a normal day the difference between deposits and withdrawals may not exceed 2 or 3 percent of a bank's total deposits. Hence, if a bank has 15 to 20 percent of its deposits on reserve there generally is no danger of running out of cash.

There have been times, however, when depositors became fearful that their banks would close and they would lose their hard earned cash. In the early 1930s, for example, when a rumor started in town that the bank was about to close, depositors rushed in to draw their money out. When this happened it was inevitable that the bank would close because no bank retained all the money that had been deposited. Therefore, if a significant fraction of a bank's depositors wanted their money, the bank had no choice but to close its doors. If enough of a bank's depositors became convinced that a bank was going to fail, it failed.

After the financial crisis of the early 1930s the Federal Deposit Insurance Corporation (FDIC) was set up. As of 1985 each depositor is insured up to $100,000, so there is no need for most people to fear losing their deposits. From time to time we still hear of people keeping their money in a mattress or some such hiding place because they distrust banks. No doubt a good share of this distrust was built up during the Great Depression.

FEDERAL RESERVE TRANSACTIONS

In our discussion of the Federal Reserve system we noted that the Open Market Committee is continually buying and selling securities in the market.

We will now see that these transactions are an important determinant of the supply of money in the economy.

First let us consider the sale of a $1,000 bond to a bond dealer. To pay for the bond, the dealer writes out a $1,000 check against his or her account in a commercial bank. When the check clears, the Fed deducts $1,000 from the bank's reserve account and in turn the bank deducts this amount from the dealer's checking account. The initial result of a Federal Reserve sale of a $1,000 bond to a bond dealer is illustrated below:

Commercial Bank

Assets		Liabilities + Net worth	
Reserves	−1,000	Demand deposits	−1,000

Federal Reserve Bank

Assets		Liabilities + Net worth	
Securities	−1,000	Bank reserves	−1,000

Notice first that the bond sale by the Fed immediately reduces the money supply by $1,000 because demand deposits are reduced by this amount. But we should be aware that commercial bank reserves also are reduced. If the reserve ratio is 0.20, required reserves decline by $200 and excess reserves go down by $800. From our discussion of the multiple expansion and contraction process, we know that this $800 decline in excess reserves will result in an ultimate contraction of (1/0.20) × $800 or $4,000 in the economy, in addition to the initial $1,000 decline, making a total decrease in money of $5,000.

The opposite happens, of course, when the Fed purchases bonds in the open market. Here a $1,000 purchase immediately increases commercial bank reserves and demand deposits by $1,000. After the multiple expansion process has run its course, the initial $800 increase in excess reserves allows the money supply to increase by another $4,000, making a total increase of $5,000.

The main point to keep in mind here is that a Federal Reserve sale of a bond reduces the money supply and a purchase tends to increase money. Intuitively these transactions make sense. An open-market sale injects bonds into the private economy but in exchange pulls money and reserves out. Conversely, an open-market purchase pulls bonds out and in exchange injects money or reserves into the economy.

Whether or not the full multiple expansion or contraction process takes place depends a great deal on the action of banks and the general public. This is especially true on the expansion side. For example, suppose the Fed wants to increase the money supply through an open market purchase. But if banks are reluctant to make loans or if people are reluctant to borrow, the money supply may expand relatively little. Yet experience has shown that open-market operations do in fact change the money supply in the desired direction.

MAIN POINTS OF CHAPTER 11

1. The **balance sheet** itemizes the assets, liabilities, and net worth of a person, firm, or institution. Assets include anything of value, liabilities represent the claims of creditors against the assets, and net worth represents the owner's claim to the assets. Assets always equal liabilities plus net worth, because net worth is computed as the difference between assets and liabilities. Thus, Assets = Liabilities + Net worth because Net worth = Assets − Liabilities.

2. Goldsmiths who provided places of safekeeping for money were the forerunners of modern bankers. Because deposits came close to offsetting withdrawals on any given day and because gold or money is a homogeneous commodity, only a small fraction of the total gold deposits actually changed hands during a day's business. Hence, goldsmiths found that part of their gold deposits could be loaned out. This was the beginning of fractional reserve banking.

3. To avoid carrying gold, people soon began to exchange deposit receipts in place of gold. This was the beginning of checking account money or demand deposits.

4. We can identify three steps in the evolution of banking: first, the deposit of money or gold for safekeeping with goldsmiths; second, the lending out of gold because only a small fraction was actively in use; and third, the gradual acceptance of deposit receipts as money.

5. As of December 31, 1982, there were 14,963 commercial banks in the United States. Although a majority of the state banks are not members of the Federal Reserve System, the largest ones do belong, so the largest share of the deposits in the country is under the jurisdiction of the Fed.

6. Each commercial bank is required to hold a certain percentage of its deposits on reserve as cash in its own vault, in the Federal Reserve bank of its district, or in a reserve city bank. The percentage of deposits that must be held in reserves is known as the **reserve ratio.** These reserves are intended to protect depositors, but perhaps more important they provide a control for the Fed over the maximum amount of loans that can be made by commercial banks.

7. The Federal Reserve System was established in 1913 to prevent unwanted expansions and contractions of money and credit during boom and recession periods, respectively, and also to provide for an "elastic" currency because of seasonal fluctuations in business activity within the year.

8. The Federal Reserve System consists of 12 Federal Reserve banks, one in each of the 12 districts, and a number of branch banks. The system is controlled by the seven-member Board of Governors appointed by the president of the United States.

9. A deposit of cash by a customer in exchange for demand deposits does not change the total quantity of money in the economy; it changes only the form in which money is held from cash to demand deposits.

10. When a check is drawn on Bank A and deposited in Bank B, the demand deposits and total reserves in Bank A are drawn down by the amount of the check, but these items are increased by the same amount in Bank B. Thus, there is no change in total bank reserves or in demand deposits outstanding.

11. Commercial banks create money by making loans because the borrower receives demand deposits or cash that later can be spent. When the loan is spent and deposited in another bank, this amount adds to the second bank's deposits and total reserves. Part of these reserves becomes excess reserves on which the second bank can make loans, etc. The maximum multiple expansion that can take place is equal to $(1/R)$ times the initial increase in excess reserves. The same formula applies to a multiple contraction brought on by a reduction in excess reserves.

12. The purchase of a bond by a bank has the same effect as making a loan. Money is created in exchange for the bond. The same multiple expansion process takes place.

13. One implication of fractional reserve banking is that only a small proportion of a bank's total deposits is available for withdrawal on a given day.

14. The sale of bonds by the Federal Reserve to bond dealers or commercial banks has the effect of pulling money out of the private economy and reducing reserves. Hence, there is a multiple contraction of the money supply. On the other hand, the purchase of bonds by the Federal Reserve (either from banks or dealers) serves to inject additional money and reserves into the economy, thereby allowing a multiple expansion of the money supply.

QUESTIONS FOR THOUGHT AND DISCUSSION

1. *a.* Construct a balance sheet for an individual from the following information: house, $80,000; car, $5,000; loan on house, $50,000; loan on car, $2,000; money in bank, $2,400; other assets, $3,000.
   b. Why should a balance sheet always balance?

2. *a.* How was it possible for the goldsmith to loan out part of the gold on deposit?
   b. How did this practice benefit all parties concerned—i.e., depositor, goldsmith, and borrower?

3. *a.* Why was it more convenient to use deposit receipts than gold to pay for purchases?
   b. What modern commercial instrument took the place of the early deposit receipt as a medium of exchange?

4. Why was the Federal Reserve System established?

5. *a.* Using a balance sheet, show what happens when an individual deposits $100 in his or her checking account at a commercial bank.
   b. How much of this $100 could the bank lend out if the reserve ratio were 0.15?

6. *a.* Using balance sheets, show what happens when an individual writes a $100 check on his or her account. Include the deposit of the check in the recipient's account.
   b. Is any money created in the above transactions? Explain.

7. *a.* Construct a balance sheet for a commercial bank showing that it has $10 million in deposit liabilities and $10 million in total reserves.
   b. How much could the bank lend out if the required reserve ratio were 0.20?
   c. If the bank makes the loan stipulated in part *b* above, how much, if any, new money is created? Explain.
   d. How much new money could be created by the banking system from the original excess reserves if all banks are fully loaned up?

8. Using a balance sheet, show why the purchase of a $1,000 bond by a bank from an individual is similar to making a $1,000 loan to an individual from the standpoint of creating new money.

9. If all the people who had checking accounts in a certain bank tried to close them out on the same day, it is not likely that the bank could satisfy their demands from its existing reserves. True or false? Explain.

10. *a.* During the Great Depression many banks were forced to close because they could not pay out to their depositors the amounts that had been originally deposited. What effect did such action have on the nation's money supply? Explain.
    b. How might the Federal Reserve have prevented these failures?

11. *a.* Using balance sheets, illustrate the purchase of a $1,000 bond by the Federal Reserve from a bond dealer.
    b. What effect, if any, would this transaction have on the nation's money supply?

PART V

POLICIES AND PROBLEMS

CHAPTER 12

FISCAL POLICY AND PROBLEMS

In this chapter and the next we will draw upon much of the material covered thus far to discuss and evaluate government policies that have been utilized in attempts to prevent or at least mitigate the problems of unemployment and inflation. We will see that, in certain instances, the implementation of these policies can in fact cause unemployment and/or inflation. There are two broad categories of such policies: fiscal and monetary. We turn first to fiscal policy.

Although "fiscal policy" has become something of a household phrase, it will be useful nevertheless to define its meaning in rather precise terms. We will define *fiscal policy* as the attempt by government to promote full employment without inflation through its spending and taxing powers. Throughout this chapter, then, we will be primarily interested in the effects of government spending and taxation on the level of output and employment in the economy. Considerable attention will be given to the problems of achieving full employment without inflation by the use of fiscal policy.

EVOLUTION OF FISCAL POLICY IN THE UNITED STATES

In preface to the discussion of fiscal policy, we should make it clear that the deliberate attempt by government to promote full employment by its spending and taxing powers is a relatively recent phenomenon. It began during the early years of the Franklin Delano Roosevelt administration, as evidenced by the creation of the public works programs instituted to create jobs and stimulate economic activity.

Yet a close reading of the record reveals that the idea still had a long way to go.[1] Although President Roosevelt endorsed the public works programs, he was not entirely convinced that a big public spending program was the answer to the country's unemployment problem. For example, upon seeing a list of projects under a $5 billion spending program, President Roosevelt proceeded to rip the list to pieces in the presence of his cabinet, indicating that many of the projects were impractical or useless.[2] Roosevelt agreed in May 1933 to a $3.3 billion spending program as a compromise between the $5 billion proposal and the $1 to $1.5 billion suggested by him.

It is also interesting to note that President Roosevelt appeared quite concerned about balancing the budget at that time. To meet the growing federal deficit, Roosevelt asked for and received tax increases in 1935 and 1936. Granted the 1935 tax increase was directed mainly at high-income persons and large corporations in an attempt to reduce the concentration of wealth; but the 1936 increase was more clearly sold on the basis of raising additional revenue.

It is not likely that we would see a tax increase today if the unemployment rate were 15 to 20 percent as it was in the mid-1930s. Of course, this is not to say that Roosevelt would have adhered to the same policy today had he been able to benefit from the 50 years of hindsight available to us. We have learned a great deal during the past half-century about how the economy operates, but, as will become evident, we still have a lot to learn.

The passage of the Employment Act of 1946 represents another significant milestone toward the establishment of a deliberate and conscious set of spending and taxing policies aimed at promoting full employment without inflation. In this act Congress declared that it was the responsibility of the federal government to promote the maximum employment, production, and purchasing power of the economy. The act also established a Council of Economic Advisors to assist the president on economic policy and a Joint Economic Committee of Congress to investigate economic problems of national interest.

BUILT-IN STABILIZERS

Before discussing the deliberate changes in taxes and spending that can be undertaken by the government to promote full employment without inflation, it is necessary to call attention to fiscal policy measures that have been built into our economic system. These policies specify that government spending or tax

---

[1] Herbert Stein, *The Fiscal Revolution in America* (Chicago: University of Chicago Press, 1969) gives a comprehensive review of the development of fiscal policy.

[2] Ibid., p. 53.

changes will take place automatically in response to upturns or downturns in economic activity.

Two important automatic spending measures are unemployment compensation and the various welfare programs. Although these programs probably were put into effect to redistribute income from middle- and high-income peo· ple to those with low incomes, they also have the effect of reducing the severity of economic fluctuations in the economy. For example, as unemployment rises and family incomes fall, the influx of money through unemployment compensation prevents a more drastic decline in economic activity. Then, as the economy recovers and people return to their jobs, a reduction in unemployment compensation helps to hold down inflationary pressure in the future period. Thus unemployment compensation is in effect an automatic or built-in stabilizer for the economy. Welfare programs have a similar effect of injecting more money when more people are out of work and incomes are down.

The progressive income tax, which is another device for redistributing income, also has a stabilizing effect on the economy. As explained in the supply side chapter, a *progressive income tax* taxes high-income people at higher *rates* than low-income people. In times of inflation, for example, more people are pushed into higher tax brackets. Consequently more money is pulled out of the economy than would occur with a proportional tax, and as a result there is less inflationary pressure than there would otherwise be. The opposite occurs during recessions, when people with reduced incomes are taxed at lower rates, thus leaving them more money to spend than if they were taxed at higher rates. We can say, therefore, that the progressive income tax is a built-in stabilizer because it pulls proportionately more purchasing power out of the economy during inflationary times and leaves proportionately more in during recessions. Granted inflation and recessions still occur, but they should not be as severe as they would be without the built-in stabilizers.

Built-in, or automatic, stabilizers often are referred to as *nondiscretionary fiscal policy* because they operate without specific congressional edict. The built-in stabilizers were originally created by an act of Congress, but once they have been instituted, Congress does not have to pass further legislation in order for them to operate.

Most of our discussion in this chapter will dwell on so-called *discretionary fiscal policy*. Here we have in mind tax or spending policies designed to deal with specific problems during specific periods of time. The 1982 income tax cut is an example of such a policy. By cutting taxes the government allowed the people to keep a little more money that they could spend in order to stimulate economic activity and reduce unemployment. Other examples of discretionary fiscal policies include the public works projects of the 1930s and the start of the superhighway construction program of the late 1950s. Both of these policies were aimed at stimulating business activity so as to reduce unemployment during these periods, although the highway program was sold in part by citing its military significance.

The simple Keynesian model provides a useful frame of reference for beginning the discussion of discretionary fiscal policy. The policy action prescribed by the simple model will be presented, and much of the remaining discussion in the chapter will dwell on the problems inherent in the model and the problems of implementing successful fiscal policies.

FISCAL POLICY IN THE CONTEXT OF THE SIMPLE KEYNESIAN MODEL

In discussing the simple Keynesian model in Chapter 6, it was noted that the equilibrium level of NNP may not coincide with full-employment NNP. If equilibrium occurs at a lower level of NNP than is necessary for full employment, unemployment will develop. Conversely, if equilibrium NNP is greater than the level that corresponds to full employment, inflation will appear.

Let us first consider the problem of unemployment as illustrated by Figure 12–1(A). Suppose that equilibrium NNP is $3,000 billion, but in order for the economy to be at full employment a $3,200 billion NNP is required.[3] The object of fiscal policy, then, is to shift aggregate demand upward so that equilibrium NNP coincides with full-employment NNP. In this example the gap between equilibrium and full-employment NNP is $200 billion. In order to increase (shift up) aggregate demand, the government should increase its spending, decrease taxes, or undertake some combination of the two. If we know how much NNP has to be increased to reach full employment, the simple model can even tell us how much government spending has to be increased or taxes reduced.

Government Spending Multiplier

Recall from the discussion of the multiplier in Chapter 6 that a dollar of new or additional spending will bring forth several additional dollars of spending in the economy. This occurs because spending by one person is income to another, and when people receive income they generally spend part of it. Also recall that the fraction of additional dollars of income that is spent is referred to as the marginal propensity to consume (MPC). In the discussion of the multiplier we saw that the government spending multiplier is equal to $1/(1 - \text{MPC})$. Thus if MPC is 0.75, an additional dollar of new government spending ultimately will bring forth $4 of new spending in the economy, that is, $1/(1 - 0.75) = 4$.

With the multiplier in mind it is an easy step to stipulate how much government spending should be increased to bring the economy from the $3,000 billion level of NNP to the $3,200 billion full-employment level. If each additional dollar of government spending brings forth $4 of new spending in total, the $200 billion increase in NNP can be obtained by a $50 billion increase in government spending. A convenient formula for determining how much government spending has to be increased in order to restore full employment is:

$$\frac{\text{Gap}}{M_g} = \Delta G$$

where the gap is the *difference* between the actual equilibrium NNP and the equilibrium NNP that corresponds to full employment ($200 billion in this case), M_g is the government spending multiplier (4 in this example), and ΔG is the required change in government spending. In this example, a $50 billion increase would shift aggregate demand up enough to push equilibrium NNP ahead by $200 billion, and in so doing restore full employment without inflation (at least according to this model).

---

[3] Full employment in this case is taken to mean 5 to 6 percent natural unemployment.

FIGURE 12–1   Fiscal policy in the context of the simple Keynesian model

(A) Unemployment policy

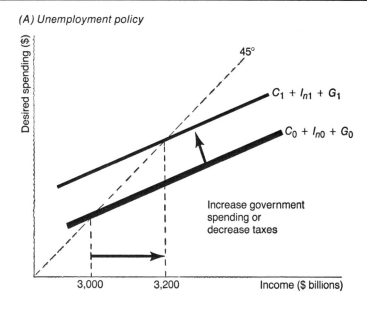

(B) Inflation policy

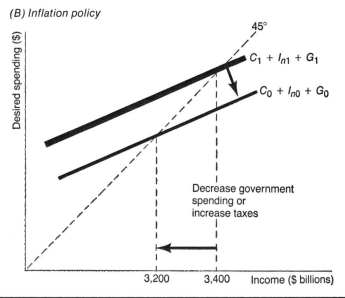

Tax Multiplier

Offhand one might conclude that the unemployment problem in the preceding example could be taken care of by a decrease in taxes of $50 billion. But this is not correct. A $1 billion tax decrease will not have as large an impact on NNP as a comparable increase in government spending. In other words a $1 billion tax decrease will not shift the aggregate demand line up by a full $1 billion, as is the case with a $1 billion government spending increase. Why? To answer this question, it is first necessary to understand that people do not increase their spending by the full amount of a tax cut. The MPC tells us that. For example, if the government reduces taxes by $1 billion, the people will have an additional $1 billion that can be considered as additional disposable income. But it is not likely they will spend the entire $1 billion; they will spend part and save part. If their MPC is 0.75, the people will spend $0.75 billion and save the remaining $0.25 billion. Thus a tax decrease of $1 billion will shift the aggregate demand line upward by only $0.75 billion if the MPC is 0.75.

The fact that people increase or decrease their saving as well as their spending in response to a tax change is the reason the tax multiplier is less than the government spending multiplier. With just a little extra effort we can determine how much less the tax multiplier will be. Perhaps the easiest way to approach this is to compare the multiplier process of a government spending change with a comparable tax change. In Table 12 1 we compare the first three

---

TABLE 12–1   Comparing the multiplier process of a government spending change with a tax change

	$1 billion increase in government spending	$1 billion decrease in taxes
Round 1	$1 billion	$0.75 billion
Round 2	0.75	0.56
Round 3	0.56	0.42
.	.	.
.	.	.
To infinity	.	.
	$4 billion	$3 billion

---

rounds of the multiplier process for a $1 billion government spending increase with that of a $1 billion tax decrease. Notice that on the first round in the government spending column, the entire $1 billion is spent. But in the tax column the first round shows only $0.75 billion being spent. The remaining $0.25 billion is saved. In all subsequent rounds the numbers in the tax column are progressively smaller.

Using the multiplier formula developed in Chapter 6, we see that the total increase in spending in the economy will increase by $4 billion because of the $1 billion initial increase in government spending. However, in the case of the $1 billion tax decrease, total spending increases by only $3 billion. Hence the government spending multiplier is four in this case, and the tax multiplier is three, or one less. Under the assumptions of the simple model, the tax multiplier always will be one less than the government spending multiplier for a lump-sum tax. If we let MPC be 0.80, for example, M_g would be five and M_t (the tax multiplier) would be four. The fact that the tax multiplier is one less than the government spending multiplier can be proven algebraically, but this is best left to an intermediate level macro course.

Now that we know that the tax multiplier is always one less than the government spending multiplier, we can modify the formula that we developed in regard to a government spending change so it can be used also to predict a tax change. Now we have:

$$\frac{\text{Gap}}{M_t} = \Delta T$$

where again the gap is the difference between actual equilibrium NNP and full-employment equilibrium, M_t is the tax multiplier, and ΔT is the required decrease in taxes to restore full employment without inflation.

In the context of the preceding example, the $200 billion gap divided by the tax multiplier of 3 (assuming MPC is 0.75) tells us that taxes should be decreased by $66.7 billion.

Although the discussion in this section has been couched in terms of an unemployment problem, the same procedure can be used to deal with an inflation problem, as illustrated by Figure 12–1(B). In this example aggregate demand intersects aggregate supply at a level of NNP that is $200 billion greater than full employment. As the economy moves past the $3,200 billion full-employment level, the increase in NNP is due largely to an increase in the price level. In other words, inflation occurs. The objective of an anti-inflationary fiscal policy is to shift aggregate demand down by a government spending decrease, a tax increase, or some combination of the two. The same formulas that are utilized to specify the appropriate government spending or tax changes in the unemployment situation can, of course, be used to specify the required government spending decrease or tax increase for the inflation problem. In this case the $200 billion decrease in equilibrium NNP can be accomplished by either a $50 billion spending decrease or a $66.7 billion tax increase.

Balanced-Budget Multiplier

An interesting implication of the government spending multiplier being one greater than the lump-sum tax multiplier is that equilibrium NNP can be increased even if taxes are increased to pay for the added government spending in the case of an unemployment problem. For example, suppose the government increases its spending by $1 billion and at the same time increases taxes by $1 billion so as to maintain a balanced budget, at least for this change in spending. If the MPC is 0.75, the government spending multiplier tells us that the government spending increase by itself will increase equilibrium NNP by $4 billion. But because M_t is one less than M_s (three in this example), the tax increase will reduce equilibrium NNP by $3 billion. Viewing this process as a sequence, the $1 billion government spending increase pushes NNP up by $4 billion, but the tax increase pulls it back by $3 billion, leaving a $1 billion net increase.

If we had increased government spending and taxes by $10 billion, the net increase in NNP would have been $10 billion. Moreover, this would be true regardless of the size of the MPC. It will be helpful to prove this to yourself by choosing different changes in G and T and working out the outcomes under different values of MPC. You will find that the value of MPC does not alter the fact that comparable changes in G and T always change equilibrium NNP by this exact same amount. Economists refer to this phenomenon as the *balanced budget multiplier.* The value of this multiplier is one, because equilibrium NNP changes by one times the initial change in *G* and *T*.

PROBLEMS WITH THE KEYNESIAN MODELS

Using the simple Keynesian model to prescribe policy designed to solve unemployment or inflation problems makes it appear that these problems are relatively easy to deal with. In the face of unemployment, all that is necessary is to shift aggregate demand upward by increasing government spending, decreasing taxes, or both. If inflation is the problem, just the opposite is called for. In fact, the simple model tells us exactly how much government spending or taxes should be changed providing we know where we are in terms of actual NNP and where we would like to be.

Our experience over the last half-century of using fiscal policy to solve unemployment and inflation problems ought to tell us at least one thing: Dealing with these problems in reality is not nearly so easy as the simple model might lead us to believe. The unemployment rate during 1982 and 1983 (9.5 percent) was higher than every year since the Great Depression. The inflation rate during 1979 was as high as it had been since the end of World War II. It does not appear that the ability of the government to deal with unemployment and inflation has improved much since World War II. In asking why this seems to be true, we should first focus our attention on the Keynesian model itself. Does the model really predict what will happen when government spending or taxes change? In other words, do the government spending and tax multipliers accurately predict what will happen to the economy when spending or taxes change? The answer is almost certainly no.

First, we should be reminded of several simplifying assumptions that are made when building the simple model. Recall that investment spending and government spending are assumed to be fixed regardless of the level of income or NNP. The same is assumed for taxes. We know, of course, that these assumptions are not true in reality. However, it is possible to build a mathematical version of the model in which investment, government spending, and taxes vary with income or NNP. The multipliers will be somewhat different in the more sophisticated mathematical version of the model but not so great as to make the simple graphical version useless. Moreover, government economists have long used the mathematical version of the model.

We proceed next to a somewhat more troublesome assumption. In using the simple model, one implicitly assumes that changes in the interest rate that result from changes in government spending or taxation do not affect private consumption or investment spending. Consider, for example, an increase in government spending. If the supply of money is held constant, the resulting increase in NNP can be expected to cause an increase in the rate of interest because people will need more money to transact business. As mentioned, this increase in the rate of interest is assumed not to reduce private spending in the simple model. But it seems reasonable to believe that a higher rate of interest will in fact decrease both private investment and consumer spending. Investment becomes less profitable with higher rates of interest, and consumer goods become more expensive, especially items such as cars and appliances. If the interest rate rises significantly due to an increase in NNP, and consumers and investors are relatively responsive to this increase, it is possible for the decrease in private spending to in large part offset the increase in government spending. In this case the government spending multiplier could be close to zero.[4] Therefore it is not out of the realm of possibility that the government spending (or tax) multiplier is relatively small, at least much smaller than the $1/(1 - MPC)$ figure. If so, then fiscal policy will not have the impact on the economy suggested by the simple model.

A third problem with the Keynesian models is that in using them to predict the effect of, say, an increase in government spending, one must assume that people will continue to spend the same amount as before on private goods. This is a different issue than the interest rate effect discussed in the preceding paragraph. In this case we are saying that an increase in the amount of goods purchased and supplied by the government and then distributed back to the people does not decrease private purchases. One might, of course, question this assumption. For example, if the government increases its spending on such things as food (food stamps), medical care, and housing, it is quite likely that the people who receive these goods will reduce their own purchases of these items. It is possible, therefore, that this trade-off of public for private goods may cause the multiplier to be much smaller than the simple model would imply. The government can reduce this problem by increasing its spending on things that people do not buy for themselves such as streets and highways, waste disposal facilities, and the military. However, there is still the possibility that if the federal government increases its spending on infrastructure, such as streets and highways and waste disposal facilities, state and local governments may decrease their spending on these items, again offsetting the increase in federal spending.

A fourth problem with the Keynesian models is that they do not take into account any change in the price level. For example, in using the models to specify the increase in government spending necessary to bring NNP up to the full-employment level during a period of unemployment, it must be assumed that the only thing that increases is real output. An increase in the price level may occur because of the increased demand for goods and services resulting from the government spending increase or tax decrease. If the price level should increase, then the monetary value (undeflated prices) of full-employment NNP also will increase. This phenomenon is something like a dog (actual NNP) chasing a rabbit (full-employment NNP) with no assurance that the former will catch the latter.

A fifth problem is the required assumption that a decrease in aggregate demand resulting from a decrease in government spending or an increase in taxes does not increase unemployment. Recall that the Keynesian models define inflation as a time when the equilibrium NNP is greater than the actual NNP. The implication is that a decrease in government spending or an increase in taxes will shift aggregate demand downward and bring equilibrium NNP back to full-employment NNP, leaving the economy in the ideal situation of full employment without inflation. However, our experience tells us this is not likely to happen. What is more likely under these circumstances is an increase

---

[4] In the context of the *IS-LM* model presented in the appendix to Chapter 6, the government spending (or tax) multiplier will be relatively small if the *LM* curve is steep and the *IS* curve is flat. On the other hand, multipliers shown by the *IS-LM* model will approach the size of the multipliers in the simple model if the *IS* curve is steep and the *LM* curve is flat.

in unemployment coupled with continuing inflation, at least for a time. To paraphrase the title of a once popular play, "a funny thing happened on the way to equilibrium." We will discuss this problem in more detail in the later section on adjustment problems.

Finally, it should be pointed out that the predictions of the Keynesian models regarding the effects of government spending increases or tax decreases are based on the assumption that the Treasury has the money to carry out these policies. Rarely is this the case, however. The problems of financing a government spending increase or tax decrease will be taken up in a later section of this chapter.

The following is a summary of the various problems and drawbacks of using the Keynesian models as tools to analyze fiscal policy.[5]

1. The simplifying assumptions of constant levels of investment, government spending, and taxes over different income levels.
2. The impact of changes in the interest rate on private consumer and investment spending, which could make the government spending multiplier close to zero.
3. The possibility of public for private trade-offs when government spending is increased to combat unemployment.
4. The assumption of a constant price level when government spending is increased and/or taxes are decreased to combat unemployment.
5. The assumption of no increase in unemployment when government spending is decreased and/or taxes are increased to fight inflation.
6. The assumption that the Treasury has the money either to increase government spending or to decrease taxes.

FISCAL POLICY IN THE CONTEXT OF RATIONAL EXPECTATIONS

In contrast to the Keynesian view, which advocates an activist fiscal policy, the rational expectations hypothesis suggests that at best such policy will provide only temporary help in reducing unemployment or inflation and at worst may end up destabilizing the economy, causing more unemployment and inflation than it prevents.

Consider first an unemployment problem. As explained earlier, the Keynesian model would call for a tax decrease and/or a government spending increase. According to the rational expectations hypothesis, such policy will reduce unemployment only as long as its full effects on the economy are unexpected by the people. If the government announces a tax decrease or government spending increase, labor unions are likely to press for higher wages because of their concern that the added stimulus to the economy will be inflationary. The higher wage demands will in turn offset the possible employment-increasing effects of the fiscal policy.

The rational expectations people maintain that fiscal policy such as tax cuts or government spending increases may have a short-term effect on reducing unemployment provided business and labor are not aware of the inflationary tendencies of fiscal policy implemented to stimulate the economy. But after one

---

[5] All of these problems apply to the simple model, and all but number 2 apply to the more complete *IS-LM* model.

or two attempts to reduce unemployment by such policy, people learn of its side effects and take action immediately to protect themselves against the expected future inflation and in so doing nullify even the short-term employment-increasing effects.

In the context of the long-run Phillips curve diagrams presented in Chapter 7, the initial effect of the unexpected stimulus is to move the economy up along a short-run Phillips curve, reducing the level of unemployment but increasing the inflation rate. Then, as people come to expect a higher inflation rate and as wages catch up to prices, unemployment increases, and the economy moves back to a point on the long-run Phillips curve. As repeated attempts to stimulate the economy become better known to the people and are expected, the leftward movement along a short-run Phillips curve becomes smaller and smaller before the curve itself shifts up to higher expected inflation levels. When this happens, the main impact of attempts to stimulate the economy will be higher rates of inflation rather than reductions in unemployment. This is not to say that an economy will always be exactly on the long-run Phillips curve. But any deviations from the vertical long-run curve will be random disturbances rather than stable trade-offs between unemployment and inflation.

After repeated attempts to stimulate the economy by fiscal policy, at some point, inflation will come to be viewed as the major problem rather than unemployment. Now the situation will call for government spending cuts and/or tax increases. The immediate result of such policy will be to move the economy down along a short-run Phillips curve, causing an increase in unemployment. If the short-run curve is relatively flat, as suggested by Figure 7–3, the rate of unemployment may increase a relatively large amount compared to the decrease in the inflation rate. Perhaps the best example of this phenomenon occurred during the early 1980s, when the Reagan administration attempted to reduce inflation and government spending. The underlying economic consequences of an anti-inflationary fiscal policy are discussed in more detail in the forthcoming section on adjustment problems.

FISCAL POLICY IN THE CONTEXT OF SUPPLY SIDE ECONOMICS

Although there are substantial differences between the rational expectations hypothesis and supply side economics, they do agree on one thing: attempts to "fine tune" the economy by fiscal (and monetary) policy will not bring about the desired effects of achieving full employment with stable prices. As mentioned in Chapter 8, supply side economics recommends a tax reduction during a time of unemployment but not as a short-term fix. Supply side advocates argue that a permanent reduction in tax rates is required in order to stimulate investment because investment decisions are long-term in nature.

A government spending increase, the other possible fiscal policy action to spur employment, would not be recommended by supply side advocates. They point out that taxes are what the government spends. If government increases its spending, taxes must increase, either at the present or at some time in the future. If people make their current spending decisions in light of higher future taxes, little or no stimulus can be expected on account of government spending increases. It will be useful at this point to present a more thorough discussion of the problems of financing a government spending increase and/or a tax cut.

FINANCING PROBLEMS

It used to be argued that the money to finance increased spending or reduced taxes would be collected as increased taxes during inflationary times, when it was presumed that the government would run a surplus. Yet the record reveals that between 1929 and 1984 the federal government incurred deficits—that is, spent more than it took in—in 46 out of those 56 years.[6] Moreover, the average annual deficit was more than three times larger than the average annual surplus. Thus the chance of the government having money on hand to deal with an unemployment problem is not very good. The government could increase taxes if it wished to increase spending, but this would just reduce private spending even more. Also, a tax increase during a time of high unemployment is not likely to be politically feasible. Thus it is likely that during a time of unemployment the government will not have extra money on hand if it wishes to increase spending or cut taxes. What can it do then? Most likely it will spend more than it takes in as taxes, that is, incur a deficit.

There are two ways that the federal government can finance a deficit. First, it can borrow from the people by selling them government bonds. Second, it can "print money." In the second case the Federal Reserve buys bonds that have been issued by the Treasury. When the Treasury receives payment for the bonds, the Federal Reserve adds (or credits) the corresponding amounts to the Treasury's checking account that is in the Federal Reserve bank. The Treasury then proceeds to write checks on the added numbers in its account for the purchase of goods and services. The numbers printed in the Treasury's checking account are as good as new $10 and $20 bills for the purpose of buying goods and services: hence the expression "printing money." In less developed countries, where checking accounts are used less, the more literal meaning of printing money best describes the phenomenon. This practice will be explained in more detail in Chapter 13 on monetary policy.

The manner in which government deficits are financed has important repercussions on the outcome of fiscal policy. If the government sells bonds to the general public, purchasing power is removed from the economy, and people are likely to spend even less, making the unemployment problem worse. Granted, when the money is spent by the government it comes back into the economy, but the increase in government bonds outstanding means that they eventually have to be paid for by increased taxes. As a result people may still reduce their current spending because of the higher tax liabilities. In this case the added government borrowing required to finance additional government spending or reduced current taxes may nullify the desired stimulation of economic activity.

The practice of printing money to finance deficits provides additional stimulus to the economy over and above the added government spending or tax cut. We will consider the outcome of printing money to finance deficits in more detail in Chapter 13 on monetary policy. For now it will be sufficient to say that the additional money is likely to cause inflation. Thus the finance of government deficits by printing money trades one problem for another—unemployment for inflation.[7]

---

[6] *Economic Report of the President,* 1969, p. 297, and 1985, p. 320.

[7] In the context of the *IS-LM* model, an increase in government spending (or decrease in taxes), holding constant the money supply, shifts the *IS* curve to the right. If the money supply increases due to printing money, both the *IS* and *LM* curves shift to the right. Of course, if people reduce current spending due to the higher tax liability that results from the sale of government bonds, there may be little or no shift of the *IS* curve.

The problems of implementing successful fiscal policy include more than problems with the Keynesian models and financing problems. They also include problems of timing, adjustment, and politics. These issues are taken up in the following three sections.

TIMING PROBLEMS

In order for fiscal policy to have its desired effect to combat either inflation or unemployment, the impact of policy action must come at the correct time. In order to obtain the desired effect of fiscal policy, two timing problems must be overcome. The first is the problem of when to undertake needed changes in government spending and taxation in order to stabilize the economy. The second is the lag between the decision to undertake spending or tax changes and the effects of such changes on the economy.

The first problem is really a matter of identifying when the economy is headed for a recession or a round of inflation. This problem exists because the economy tends to fluctuate from year to year in a rather uneven and unpredictable fashion. The difficulty, then, is to decide whether an upturn or downturn is just a minor fluctuation or whether it is the beginning of something big. If the government takes rather drastic measures to curb a recession, for example, at the hint of a slight downturn in economic activity, the result might well be a forthcoming inflationary spiral. Theoretically, then, the government should take antirecessionary measures (a spending increase or a tax cut) when the economy is just beginning to enter a downturn in economic activity, as illustrated by time T_0 in Figure 12–2. By the same token, anti-inflationary measures should be reserved for a time such as T_1. The object is to smooth out the booms and busts, as shown by the dotted line starting at T_0 in Figure 12–2.

If the government is successful in identifying critical turning points in the economy, such as T_0 and T_1, there is still the question of doing something soon enough to have the desired effect. Suppose, for example, that the time span

FIGURE 12–2   Illustrating the problem of the current timing of fiscal policy

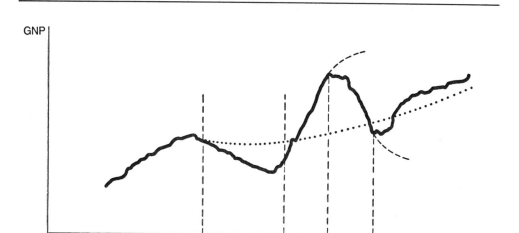

between T_0 and T_1 is three years. If it takes the government two years to push a tax cut through Congress or to decide on new government projects, the actual effect may be just the opposite of what is desired. If the antirecessionary measures do not begin to be felt until around T_1, the result may well be to stimulate the economy in the forthcoming boom period following T_1. As a result, the inflation following T_1 could be even worse than it would have been had no action been taken at all. This is illustrated by the dashed line beginning at T_2. Also, it is not very feasible to shut down government projects that have been initiated during a recession even when an inflationary period looms on the horizon. Hence these additional projects serve to accentuate the forthcoming inflation.

The same problems of timing and effect confront the government when inflation threatens, such as at T_1. Again a tax increase or a spending reduction may require one or two years to pass Congress (especially if there is an upcoming election). As a result the anti-inflationary policy may become a prorecessionary policy and pull the economy into a more severe state of unemployment, as illustrated by the downward-sloping dashed line beginning at T_3.

There is also the problem of predicting when actual government spending or tax changes will have their major effect on the economy. We have implicitly assumed in our previous discussion that the desired effect of policy takes place immediately after action is taken. But this need not be the case. The major problem is that relatively little is known about the duration of lags between government action and its effect. Indeed the lag may change from one year to the next.

ADJUSTMENT PROBLEMS

The underlying reasons for the increase in unemployment when attempts are made to reduce inflation are still not well understood, although one can think of some reasonable, albeit tentative, explanations for this phenomenon. Consider first a decrease in government spending. People who had been producing goods and services purchased by the government suddenly find that their market has dried up. If these people are working for private firms, their employers have little choice but to lay them off unless new markets can be found immediately, which is not likely. The problem is likely to be most noticeable when firms lose military contracts. Because of the specialized nature of these goods, it takes time for such firms to retool to produce for the nonmilitary market. Indeed, just a change in the *kind* of government spending can be expected to have a similar effect because of the time it takes people to find new jobs in expanding industries. When the affected people are employed directly by the government, a similar adjustment must be made. Again there is a period of increased unemployment until they can find new jobs. The release of military personnel after a war accentuates this problem.

An increase in taxes can be expected to have a similar effect. If people have less money to spend, it is likely that they will reduce spending on consumption and investment goods. Again the people who had been producing these goods will be laid off, resulting in increased unemployment.

In addition, one should recognize the likelihood of a multiplier effect. The original people laid off because of a decrease in government spending or increase in taxes no doubt will decrease their spending, which means that people who had been supplying these goods will find their jobs in jeopardy. This does not mean, of course, that people who become unemployed because of a decrease in government spending or increase in taxes will be unemployed permanently. The unemployment occurs because of the time it takes to find jobs in other occupations or localities. In order for these people to find new jobs they may have to accept a relative decline in their wages, which is not easy to take, especially when taxes have increased.

Not only will attempts to reduce inflation by a reduction in government spending or increase in taxes be likely to increase unemployment, but it is virtually certain that inflation will not stop abruptly. It is more likely that inflation will continue for many months or even years, although it is likely to continue at a decreasing rate. The reason inflation persists is likely to be the result of expectations. During inflation people come to expect a continuing increase in the price level. As a result, wages and other contracts are likely to reflect inflationary expectations. For example if prices have been rising at 10 percent per year, wage contracts are likely to build in a 10 percent per year increase just to maintain the purchasing power of employee salaries. The same is true of contracts to supply raw materials or finished goods. With the increase in the unemployment rate and a falling off of demand for certain goods and services stemming from anti-inflationary fiscal policy, there will be a "softness" in the markets for labor and goods. Therefore new contracts are likely to reflect this softness and stipulate a smaller growth in wages and prices. But it may take several rounds of contract renewals over a period of several years to bring wage and price increases down to a noninflationary level.

During contract renegotiations, it also is possible, indeed likely, for wages and prices to be thrown out of balance. If the rate of growth of prices, for example, becomes lower than the growth in wages, real wages will increase, thus lowering profits and causing firms to reduce their output of unprofitable goods. As a result, more unemployment is experienced. On the other hand, if the rate of growth of wages is lower than the growth in prices, we are likely to observe a period of increased strike activity. The imbalance between wages and prices basically is due to an inability to accurately forecast future inflation. This problem can exist even in the absence of an anti-inflationary fiscal policy. One thing is certain, the adjustments in the economy to both inflation and anti-inflationary fiscal policies are very complex. We still have a lot to learn about this process. The main point of this section is that we should expect to experience both unemployment and inflation for a time after attempts are made to control inflation through fiscal policy. This is not to say that the country should abandon anti-inflation policies, but it would be better not to have started the inflation in the first place. Similar adjustment problems occur when monetary policy is used to reduce inflation, as will be pointed out in Chapter 13.

POLITICAL PROBLEMS

By now it probably has become apparent that carrying out a successful fiscal policy requires that some rather complicated economic problems be overcome, including the uncertainty as to whether the Keynesian models really predict what will happen as well as financing, timing, and adjustment problems. It should also be kept in mind that discretionary fiscal policy requires action by Congress and the executive branch of the federal government. Before such action can be undertaken there must be agreement regarding the kind of fiscal policy to be undertaken, how strong it should be, whom it should affect and when it should be undertaken. Considering the differences in viewpoints, between liberals and conservatives, it should come as no surprise that obtaining such widespread agreement poses some rather formidable political problems.

As mentioned in Chapter 1, liberals tend to favor or at least more readily accept increased government spending on goods and services while conservatives prefer a lesser role for government. Thus, during a time of increased unemployment we would expect liberals to favor increased government spending and conservatives to argue for a tax reduction. This difference in philosophy became quite apparent during the late 1970s in the debate over the Kemp-Roth bill. Conservative lawmakers supported the bill, which proposed a significant reduction in federal income taxes, while their liberal counterparts opposed it, arguing that it would cause inflation or cut deep into government spending and services.

Assuming agreement can be reached on the appropriate spending increase or tax cut (in the case of increased unemployment), further decisions have to be made on where the additional spending should take place or whose taxes should be reduced. Most senators and members of Congress, regardless of political affiliation, like to obtain a "fair share" of any increase in government spending for their area or constituents. Understandably, this creates conflict, since the amount of any needed spending increase is not likely to be great enough to be spread across the entire nation.

In regard to a tax decrease, disagreement is likely to arise on who should obtain a tax break and the kind of taxes to be reduced. For example, should we have a proportionate, across-the-board tax decrease, or a tax reduction for only certain income levels, such as low-income people? Or should business firms be given a tax cut, say in the form of accelerated depreciation or investment credits, to stimulate economic activity? It is not likely that liberals and conservatives will readily agree on the answers to these questions.

The political controversy generated by a proposed government spending decrease or tax increase (as would be appropriate during inflation) is likely to be even more intense. Even if there is general agreement on the need for a spending decrease, few senators or members of Congress are going to welcome it for their states or regions, particularly before an election. People whose jobs depend on government spending, or who benefit in some way from this spending, can be very vocal in their opposition to spending cuts. At any rate, it is becoming apparent that it is a good deal easier for government to increase spending than to decrease it.

A proposed tax increase involves similar problems. With the cost of living rising, probably more rapidly than wages during the early stages of inflation, few lawmakers are likely to push for higher taxes and further reduce the real take-home pay of workers. This is particularly true in a period immediately preceding an election. Some people have advocated giving the president power to vary income tax rates, within limits, in order to obtain more flexibility and more prompt action. However, it does not appear that Congress will soon buy such a proposal.

FISCAL INSTABILITY

In the discussion of fiscal policy, the implication is that the economy is unstable and government spending and tax measures are required to offset this inherent instability. For example, if consumers or investors become pessimistic about the future and reduce their spending, the government is presumed to step in and offset the reduction in aggregate demand. Or if people suddenly desire to spend more, and thereby cause inflation, the government is to reduce its spending or increase taxes, again with the objective of stabilizing the economy.

The figures in Table 12–2, which are the annual percent changes in the federal government budget, federal taxes, and private spending, reveal that

TABLE 12–2 Annual percent changes in the federal government budget, federal taxes, and private consumption and investment spending, 1962–84*

Year	G	T	C + I	Year	G	T	C + I
1965	−0.1%	3.7%	9.1%	1975	21.0%	6.1%	6.0%
1966	13.7	12.0	8.7	1976	12.3	6.8	14.0
1967	17.5	14.3	3.7	1977	9.9	19.3	12.8
1968	13.0	2.8	9.2	1978	12.0	12.3	12.0
1969	3.2	22.2	8.8	1979	9.5	16.0	11.8
1970	6.5	3.2	4.6	1980	17.5	11.6	7.3
1971	7.6	−2.8	9.0	1981	14.0	15.9	11.6
1972	9.7	10.8	11.2	1982	10.0	3.1	−2.0
1973	6.5	11.3	11.8	1983	8.4	−2.8	6.3
1974	9.1	14.0	7.2	1984	−5.4	11.0	9.9

* Each figure represents the percent change from the preceding year.
Source: *Economic Report of the President*, 1985, pp. 234 and 317.

federal spending and tax revenues have fluctuated more than private spending. In itself this pattern need not be bad. If the rate of federal spending increases and/or taxes decrease when the rate of private spending is low or declining, a countercyclical pattern of government spending and taxes would be a stabilizing force in the economy. However from the data presented in Table 12–2, there is little evidence to suggest that federal spending and taxes have been countercyclical. One can find years when the rate of growth of private spending was low or declining and government spending growth decreased or federal taxes increased (1967, 1969, and 1974). Also it is possible to find years when the rate of growth of private spending was high or increasing and government spending growth increased or federal taxes decreased (1968, 1971, 1972, and 1978). Perhaps even more important, the substantial increase in the rate of growth of private spending in the 1970s, due mainly to inflation, is not unrelated to the large increases in the growth of government spending during the late 1960s and 1970s, as will be explained in Chapter 13.

On the basis of this evidence, it appears that the economy would have been more stable (suffered less unemployment and inflation) if federal spending and taxes had grown by a constant percent each year, say 3 to 4 percent annually, instead of fluctuating as they did and speeding up in the late 1960s, 1970s, and early 1980s.

Of course one should acknowledge that the federal government may have other goals that are not conducive to a stable economy. During the period covered in Table 12–2, waging the Vietnam War and carrying on the "war on poverty" could be considered two such goals. It is up to the individual to decide whether goals that cause economic instability are worth their price. At any rate, it behooves government decision makers to carefully consider the destabilizing effects of large year-to-year changes in government spending and taxation.

There is also the destabilizing effect of short-run political goals of politicians, namely the desire to get reelected. It is probably true that an incumbent is more likely to be reelected if unemployment is low or declining and taxes are not increasing as rapidly as income. Therefore, politicians have an incentive to increase government spending during election years in an effort to reduce unemployment and "hold the line" on taxes. The propensity of politicians to spend during election years along with their reluctance to raise taxes to cover this spending are reflected by the figures in Table 12–3. Notice that the deficits

---

TABLE 12–3   Deficits of the federal government, 1961–84

Years	Deficits ($ billions)	Years	Deficits ($ billions)
1961–63	5.1	1973–75	21.6
1964	5.9	1976	66.4
1965–67	4.7	1977–79	40.5
1968	25.2	1980	60.0
1969–71	7.5	1981–83	138.2
1972	23.4	1984	185.3

Source: *Economic Report of the President*, 1985, p. 318.

---

have been substantially higher during presidential election years than during the preceding years. The necessity of printing money to finance these deficits causes an increase in the money supply, which in turn leads to more inflation. Then the implementation of restrictive monetary and fiscal policies to deal with the inflation leads to more unemployment. As a result the country ends up with both unemployment and inflation. We will return to the instability problem in Chapter 13.

THE NATIONAL DEBT

A discussion of fiscal policy would not be complete without a consideration of the national debt. Although state and local governments also borrow, we will define the national debt here as debt owned by the federal government. The national debt was incurred because of government deficits. When the government wishes to spend more than it takes in through taxes, it must borrow by selling government bonds to the general public, to state and local governments, and to the Federal Reserve. Thus the magnitude of the national debt is measured by the amount of federal government bonds outstanding.

As shown by Table 12–4 the U.S. national debt amounted to $1,577 billion in 1984. The most rapid increase in the national debt occurred during World War II, when the government issued large numbers of bonds to pay for military

TABLE 12–4   National debt, 1929–84 (constant 1984 dollars)

Year	Total ($ billions)	Per capita ($)	Percent of GNP
1929	101	821	16
1934	231	1,821	46
1939	318	2,426	47
1944	1,233	8,912	101
1949	931	6,236	85
1954	884	5,425	63
1959	854	4,803	51
1964	899	4,684	43
1969	889	4,387	34
1974	1,021	4,816	34
1979	1,190	5,395	35
1984	1,577	6,664	43

Source: *Economic Report of the President*,
1976, p. 195, and 1985, p. 317.

expenditures. In 1984 dollars, the total national debt remained relatively constant during the 1950s and 1960s. However, between 1969 and 1984 the national debt nearly doubled in real terms. On the brighter side, it should be noted that the national debt per capita and as a percent of GNP declined substantially from the end of World War II up until the mid-1970s. However, the percentage increased again during the late 1970s and early 1980s.

In recent years many people have expressed concern about the size of the national debt. We hear phrases such as "the country going broke" or "fiscal irresponsibility" in regard to the growing size of the national debt.

Is the national debt really something to be concerned about? It used to be argued that when government bonds were sold primarily to U.S. citizens the national debt is debt which the government owes to the people. However, because the people "own" the government, it is debt that the people owe to themselves. If the government decided to pay off, say, $100 billion of the national debt, it would increase taxes by $100 billion and immediately pay this amount back to the people. As you can see, this $100 billion dollar payment would not make the nation any "poorer" because the people would still have the $100 billion. Granted, there may be a redistribution of wealth toward former bondholders, but the total wealth of the nation would remain unchanged. Of course, it is not likely the government ever would want to pay off such a large amount of the debt in a short period of time, because such action likely would have a destabilizing effect on the economy.

During the early 1980s the increase in real interest rates attracted foreign buyers of U.S. government bonds. In this case the national debt takes on more of the characteristics of private debt in that paying off the debt removes real wealth from the economy. True, when the debt was incurred, that is, when the bonds were sold, real wealth was transferred into the economy from other countries. Consequently, paying off the debt cancels out the wealth obtained when the debt was incurred. On the other hand, interest payments on the bonds represent a net transfer of wealth out of the country.

Regardless of whether the government bonds are sold to U.S. citizens or to foreign buyers, it is important to recognize that tax money must be raised to pay off the debt. Unless people are informed about their tax liabilities, they may be unpleasantly surprised to see their taxes increasing in order to pay off debt without receiving any increase in the level of public goods or services. In 1984, interest payments on the national debt amounted to over 13 percent of all federal government expenditures. High rates of taxation could in turn reduce the incentives of taxpayers to work and invest and as a result reduce the real output of the economy. In this sense an excessively heavy burden of national debt could drag the economy down to a lower standard of living.

Should this phenomenon become a recognizable problem, the government would be increasingly tempted to print money to finance the deficit, thereby inflating the economy and in so doing reduce the debt in real terms. If the price level should double, for example, the real value of previously sold government bonds outstanding would decline by one half. The losers in this process would be the people or institutions that owned these bonds.

WHO PAYS THE ECONOMIC COST OF WARS?

A major share of the national debt was incurred to finance military expenditure, especially during wars. The fact that the government chose not to finance the entire cost of wars through increased taxes during wars has prompted some people to argue that borrowing to finance part of the cost of war passes this portion of its cost on to future generations. Is this a valid argument?

Perhaps the best way to look at the economic cost of war is in terms of what is given up. During a war the people living at the time must forgo consumer goods and services in order to produce more war goods. This is true regardless of whether the government taxes, borrows, or prints money to finance the war. In taxing or borrowing, the government removes purchasing power from the private sector. This reduces the purchase of nonmilitary goods and services by the public while increasing the wherewithal of the government to buy goods and services. Except for the possible disincentive effects of higher taxes, levying taxes to pay off the bonds after the war does not reduce the amount of private goods available to future generations because they also receive the money from the redeemed bonds. Printing money (the purchase of government bonds by the Federal Reserve) amounts to a more immediate tax on people living during the war. The result of the increase in the money supply is to increase the general price level (cause inflation). As pointed out in Chapter 3, inflation reduces the purchasing power of money held by people, in this case people living during the war. Thus printing money is about the same as levying a tax on money, although it is a somewhat more subtle form of tax. At any rate, the government is able to gain access to goods and services by printing money, and the people who give up these goods are those living during the war.

Even with the extremely high cost of fighting wars, it should be noted that the true economic cost of war is still understated. This occurs because military personnel generally are paid less during a war than what they would have to be paid to willingly engage in that type of work. An all-volunteer army would reflect the true economic cost of a war but it is not likely that taxpayers of any nation would be willing to pay the full cost of supporting a volunteer army during wartime. Hence draftees in a sense pay a disproportionate share of the economic cost of war.

There is one sense in which future generations bear the economic cost of war regardless of how it is financed, and that is because of the reduction of investment during wartime. For example, during the height of World War II, the relatively small amount of gross investment was not large enough to offset the depreciation of capital equipment; so there was a net decline in the nation's capital stock. As a result the nation's productive capacity is somewhat smaller today than it might have been without the war. This effect is, of course, much greater for countries that are ravaged by war.

MAIN POINTS OF CHAPTER 12

1. **Fiscal policy** can be defined as the conscious attempt by government to promote full employment without inflation through its spending and taxing powers.

2. The public works program of the Roosevelt administration represented an early attempt at influencing the level of economic activity by government spending. The Employment Act of 1946 made it the explicit responsibility of government to maintain full employment.

3. **Built-in stabilizers** are fiscal policy measures that go into effect automatically in response to changes in economic activity. They are designed to counteract or smooth out cyclical changes in the economy. Some examples include unemployment compensation and the progressive income tax.

4. In the context of the simple model, unemployment will exist if equilibrium NNP is less than the level of NNP that will generate full employment.

5. According to the simple model the government can eliminate unemployment by increasing government spending and/or decreasing taxes; both have the effect of shifting aggregate demand upward.

6. The formula for determining how much government spending should be increased to eliminate unemployment is

$$\frac{\text{Gap}}{M_g} = \Delta G$$

when the "gap" is the difference between the actual equilibrium NNP and the full-employment level of NNP, M_g is the government spending multiplier, and ΔG is the required change in government spending. The formula for a required tax change is

$$\frac{\text{Gap}}{M_t} = \Delta T$$

where M_t is the tax multiplier and ΔT is the required change in taxes.

7. In the context of the simple model, inflation will occur if the equilibrium NNP is greater than the level of NNP corresponding to the full-employment level.

8. According to the simple model, the government can eliminate inflation by decreasing government spending and/or increasing taxes, both of which have the effect of shifting aggregate demand downward.

9. The same formulas that apply to the unemployment situation can be used to specify the required decrease in government spending or increase in taxes that will eliminate inflation.

10. Under the assumption of a lump-sum tax, the tax multiplier in the simple model is one less than the government spending multiplier. This occurs because the entire change in government spending shows up on the first round of the multiplier process, but in the case of a tax change the first round of the multiplier process is equal to MPC times the tax change.

11. Because the goverment spending multiplier is one greater than the tax multiplier, the so-called balanced-budget multiplier is one, meaning that an equal change in G and T will change NNP by one times that change.

12. The government spending and tax multipliers used in the simple model require the simplifying assumptions of fixed levels of I_n, G, and T.

13. Additional problems with the simple model include the assumptions that private spending does not decrease with an increase in the interest rate caused by increased government spending (or a tax cut), and there is no public-for-private trade-off with increased government spending.

14. In predicting changes in government spending or taxes to deal with an unemployment problem, the simple model requires the assumption of no change in prices.

15. In using the simple model to prescribe changes in government spending or taxes to deal with an inflation problem, it is generally assumed that inflation stops and unemployment does not increase. Neither is likely to be true.

16. According to the rational expectations hypothesis, fiscal policy implemented to reduce unemployment will have its desired effect only if people are unaware of the full effects of such policy. After repeated attempts to reduce unemployment, labor will automatically press for higher wages in the expectation of more inflation in the future, so that the employment effects of government attempts to stimulate the economy will be negligible.

17. Along with rational expectations, supply side economics does not advocate fiscal policy that attempts to "fine tune" the economy. Supply siders argue for tax reductions to achieve higher economic growth and lower unemployment over the long run.

18. The federal government finances deficits by selling bonds to the people and/or to the Federal Reserve. The former action decreases the purchasing power of the private sector, while the latter method increases the supply of money. The latter method is known as "printing money" to finance deficits.

19. In order for fiscal policy to have a stabilizing effect on the economy, it must be timed to counteract recessionary or inflationary tendencies. If fiscal policy has its main effects at the wrong time, it can be destabilizing.

20. A reduction in government spending or an increase in taxes to combat inflation is likely to increase unemployment by requiring some people to relocate to expanding industries and possibly by causing an imbalance between wages and prices.

21. As people come to expect inflation, attempts to reduce it by decreasing government spending or increasing taxes probably will slow down the rate of inflation but not stop it completely, at least for a number of years. During this period the country is likely to experience both unemployment and inflation.

22. To combat unemployment, liberals tend to prefer government spending increases, while conservatives prefer tax cuts. Political disagreements also arise over the size of spending or tax changes and who should benefit.

23. Between 1964 and 1984, federal government spending and taxes exhibited more year-to-year variation than private spending.

24. The absence of a countercyclical pattern of federal government spending and taxation suggests that the economy would have been more stable if government spending and tax revenues had grown by a constant percent per year.

25. The national debt was incurred because of government deficits and is measured by the amount of government bonds outstanding. When bonds were sold primarily to U.S. citizens, it used to be argued that paying off the debt would not reduce the wealth of the country because the money would go back to the people. In more recent years, as more of the bonds were sold to foreign buyers, the national debt took on more of the characteristics of private debt. But regardless of who owns the government bonds, a heavy tax burden to pay off an excessive national debt could reduce the incentives of taxpayers

and as a result lower production and the nation's standard of living. The government would then be increasingly tempted to inflate the economy in order to reduce the real value of the bonds outstanding.

26. Whether wars are financed by current taxation, selling bonds in the open market, or printing money, the economic cost of wars is borne by the people living at the time of the wars due to the reduction in nonmilitary goods and services that can be produced.

QUESTIONS FOR THOUGHT AND DISCUSSION

1. What are the main built-in stabilizers, and how do they operate?

2. *a.* According to the simple Keynesian model, how much would government spending have to be increased if actual equilibrium NNP is $50 billion less than the NNP that would generate full employment? (Assume MPC is 0.80.)

   b. How much would taxes have to be decreased under the same conditions as stipulated in part *a* above?

3. What conditions are required for the multipliers derived from the simple Keynesian model to be correct? Are these conditions likely to prevail? Explain.

4. *a.* In the context of the *IS-LM* model, will the necessary increase in government spending to counteract an unemployment problem be greater than or smaller than the increase stipulated by the simple model? Explain.

   b. What shapes of *IS* and *LM* curves are most condusive to the use of fiscal policy? What underlying conditions give rise to these shapes?

5. *a.* According to the rational expectations hypothesis, what conditions are required for the success of fiscal policy implemented to reduce unemployment? Will these conditions likely prevail? Explain.

   b. What does supply side economics have in common with the rational expectations hypothesis?

6. *a.* What are the various ways of financing an increase in government spending and/ or a decrease in taxes?

   b. What are the consequences of each method?

7. How can bad timing of fiscal policy destabilize the economy?

8. "Inflation contains the seeds of unemployment." True or false? Explain.

9. *a.* Are the personal motives of politicians conducive to a stable or unstable economy? Explain.

   b. On the basis of the evidence, has the federal government been a stabilizing or destabilizing force in the economy? Explain.

10. It used to be argued that the national debt is money we owe to ourselves; therefore, it is nothing to worry about because the nation as a whole will be no poorer if it were paid off. What element of truth is contained in this argument? In what way is it false?

11. "Financing a war by selling bonds transfers the cost of the war to future generations." True or false? Explain.

12. In what way does a military draft cause the true economic cost of a war to be understated?

CHAPTER 13

MONETARY POLICY
AND PROBLEMS

We now come to the second major tool used by the government to promote full employment without inflation—monetary policy. *Monetary policy* is defined as the deliberate action of the government or monetary authority to manage the supply of money and the interest rate with the goal of achieving and maintaining full employment without inflation. In the United States the monetary authority is the Federal Reserve System. An important group within the Federal Reserve System is the Open Market Committee. This committee, which is made up largely by the Board of Governors, is responsible for deciding on the timing and magnitude of Federal Reserve purchases and sales of government securities in the securities market. As we will see shortly, this is the major tool the Fed uses to influence the quantity of money in the economy.

Monetary policy will be analyzed using the Keynesian models, rational expectations, and the new quantity theory. Before turning to the discussion of monetary policy, however, it is necessary to establish the appropriate criterion for initiating and evaluating policy action. Also, it will be useful to review the methods used by the Federal Reserve to change the supply of money in the United States economy.

MONEY VERSUS THE INTEREST RATE

The effect of money and the interest rate on the economy has been subject to a great deal of controversy among economists and government policymakers, extending from the Great Depression up to the present. One major point of contention has been the appropriate indicator for monetary policy. In deciding on the correct monetary policy to follow, should the major indicator be the interest rate or the quantity of money? During much of the history of monetary policy in the United States, it appears that the interest rate has served as the prime guideline for action, although in recent years there seems to have been a shift in emphasis toward the money supply as the appropriate indicator for policy.

If one looks back over time it becomes evident that the money rate of interest tends to rise during inflationary times and to fall during periods of depressed economic activity, such as the Great Depression. For example, from 1929 to 1939, the years spanning the decade of the Great Depression, the money rate of interest on four-to-six-month prime commercial paper decreased from 5.85 percent to 0.59 percent, respectively. In contrast, from 1972 to 1981, a time of inflation, this same rate of interest more than tripled from 4.69 percent to 14.76 percent.[1] Does it follow, therefore, that if the government took action to reduce the interest rate during inflations and to increase it during recessions, these problems would be reduced? No. Such action would make matters even worse. Perhaps the most important thing to recognize here is that the money rate of interest depends very much on inflation or the absence of it. As pointed out in Chapter 3, the interest rate tends to be high during inflation because lenders need to get a higher rate of interest to compensate them for the loss in purchasing power of their money. Also, borrowers become more willing to pay a higher rate because they know they will pay back the loans in "cheap dollars." Conversely, the interest rate becomes lower in periods of relatively stable prices and still lower when prices are declining as in the Great Depression. Now lenders are willing to accept a lower rate of interest because their money will not be depreciating in value when it is loaned out. Also, borrowers are less willing to pay a high rate of interest since they will have to pay back the loans with relatively valuable dollars.

Consider what would happen if the government tried to lower the rate of interest during an inflation by increasing the rate of growth of the money supply. The immediate result probably would be some reduction in the interest rate as money became still more plentiful in the loan market. But in the long run the increase in the rate of growth of the money supply would cause even more inflation. Consequently, interest rates would increase to even higher levels. There is much confusion over the relationship between rates of growth of the money supply and money rates of interest. In the short run an increase in the rate of growth of the money supply may lower interest rates temporarily because of the larger supply of money in the loan market. But the long-run effect of such action will be just the opposite, namely, to increase money rates of interest to still higher levels because of the increase in inflation.

Attempts to raise the interest rate during a recession by reducing the rate of growth of the money supply also would have a destabilizing effect. Initially the

---

[1] *Economic Report of the President,* 1969, p. 290, and 1982, p. 310.

interest rate would increase as money became even more scarce, but then as prices began to fall the interest rates would fall to still lower levels. Of course such a restriction in the money supply would cause even more unemployment. It is not so likely that the government would make the mistake of reducing the rate of growth of the money supply during a recession, at least nowadays.

The preoccupation with the money rate of interest by the Federal Reserve has led to much confusion about the appropriate monetary policy and at times has been used to justify an erroneous policy. For example, during the Great Depression the Fed pointed to the falling money rate of interest as an indication that money was plentiful. We know now that because of the substantial decline in the money supply from 1929 to 1933, money was far from plentiful, as most people who lived during the Great Depression will tell you. The money rate of interest declined during the 1930s in large part because of the decline in the price level.

A similar kind of error was made by the people who called for an increase in the rate of growth of the money supply when interest rates were high during the inflationary years of the 1970s and early 1980s. As will be discussed later in this chapter, there is strong evidence that suggests that the Federal Reserve would have had more success in achieving a stable economy of full employment without inflation if it had tried to stabilize the rate of growth of the money supply rather than the money rate of interest. Of course, if the Fed were successful in stabilizing the growth of the money supply, the interest rate also would become more stable.

PRIMARY TOOLS OF MONETARY POLICY

As mentioned, the Federal Reserve System is the monetary authority in the United States. Since monetary policy is largely a matter of regulating the money supply, let us explore next the tools available to the Fed to carry out this task. Essentially the Fed has three primary tools: (1) open-market operations, (2) changes in the required reserve ratio of commercial banks, and (3) changes in the discount rate that commercial banks pay to borrow from the Federal Reserve.

We already have discussed the effect of open-market operations in Chapter 11, but perhaps a bit of review will prove helpful. Recall that the Fed is continually buying and selling government securities in the bond market. For example, an open-market purchase of a bond leads to an increase in the money supply. In this case the Fed receives the bond, which is not money, and in exchange the seller receives a check (or cash), which is money. Thus, the quantity of money in the economy increases as the result of the open-market purchase. Keep in mind too that the money supply is likely to change by some multiple of the initial bond purchase because of the multiple expansion effect. A similar line of reasoning applies to the open-market sale of a bond by the Fed. Here the Fed receives money, the seller receives the bond, and as a result the money supply is likely to decline by a multiple of the bond purchase. Open-market purchases and sales of bonds are the major tools that the Federal Reserve uses to change the quantity of money in the economy.

We might reasonably ask at this point: How can the Fed be sure that it will always be able to buy or sell the desired amount of bonds? After all, people are not forced to do business with the Fed. The answer is that when buying bonds, the Fed must offer a price that is competitive in the market or else prospective sellers will sell to other buyers. If the bond purchase is extremely large, the Fed may have to increase its bid price in order to induce more sellers to part with their bonds. Similarly, when the Fed sells bonds, it may have to reduce their price to a point that makes the offering attractive to prospective buyers.

As explained in Chapter 10, the price of a bond and its interest return are inversely related. For example, suppose the Federal Reserve sells at $1,000 a bond and as specified on the bond the government agrees to pay 10 percent annual interest to the holder, or $100 per year. Even if the market price of the bond should decline to $500, the $100 annual interest still continues to be paid. Only now the holder of the bond receives a 20 percent return on the money— $100 per year from $500 invested. Thus, a decrease in the market price of bonds implies that their interest return rises. If bonds become cheap enough, the interest return eventually becomes attractive enough for buyers to take the bonds off the hands of the Fed. (Of course, the Fed may suffer a capital loss in the process, but it is not in business to make profits anyway. The Federal Reserve System exists to regulate the money supply and in so doing stabilizes the economy at a level that represents full employment without inflation.) On the other hand, an increase in the price of bonds implies that the interest return of the bonds decreases.

The second major tool that can be used by the Fed to regulate the supply of money is the legal reserve ratio. Recall from the discussion of banking in Chapter 11 that commercial banks are required to hold a certain fraction of their deposits on reserve, either as cash in their own vaults or as money in a reserve account in their Federal Reserve bank (if the bank is a member of the Federal Reserve System). By changing the legal reserve ratio, the Fed can change the amount of bank loans and thus change the amount of money in the economy. Remember that banks create money by making loans.

In the examples in Chapter 11 we assumed for convenience of computation a required reserve ratio of 0.20, meaning that commercial banks are required to keep 20 cents on reserve against each dollar of demand deposits. Thus, $1,000 of total reserves in the banking system can support $5,000 in demand deposits $[(1/R) \times \$1,000]$, assuming the multiple expansion process has run its course and banks are fully loaned up. Now if the Fed should reduce the required reserve ratio to, say, 0.10, this same $1,000 in total reserves could support $10,000 in total deposits. Banks could in this case increase loans and thus increase demand deposits. On the other hand, an increase in the reserve ratio would require banks to contract their deposits for a given amount of reserves.

Notice the basic difference between open-market operations and a change in the reserve ratio. The former is a device to change the total reserves in the banking system while the latter is a means of changing the amount of deposits that can be supported from a given amount of total reserves. However, the Federal Reserve seldom uses its power to change the legal reserve ratio, mainly because it is almost too powerful a tool. Even a very small change in the reserve ratio has rather drastic effects on the banking community and causes large and abrupt changes in the money supply.

The third major tool or device that the Fed can use to change the money supply is a change in the discount rate. The discount rate is the rate of interest that the Fed charges member banks when these banks obtain loans from the Fed to bolster their reserves. Occasionally a commercial bank will find itself dangerously close to the upper limit of its loans (given its reserves) or actually over the limit, especially during peak lending periods. In this situation the commercial bank can temporarily increase its reserves by borrowing reserves from the Fed.

The Fed generally changes the discount rate in conjunction with a large open-market transaction. Suppose there is inflationary pressure in the economy which prompts the Fed to make a large open-market sale in order to reduce reserves and the money supply. The resulting tight money situation and high interest rates provide banks with an incentive to borrow from the Fed in order to maintain reserves so that loans need not be reduced greatly. This is just good business. But to make it less profitable for banks to borrow for reserves, the Fed will raise the discount rate along with the open-market sale. Similarly, when the Fed wants to stimulate bank lending it usually reduces the discount rate to make it more profitable for banks to borrow to obtain reserves.

SECONDARY TOOLS OF MONETARY POLICY

The items discussed in the previous section are the three main tools the Federal Reserve can use to regulate the supply of money in the economy and thus to influence economic activity. The Fed also has a number of other means to influence economic activity that we might mention briefly. First, there is the idea of *moral suasion,* sometimes called *jawbone control.* These terms describe attempts by the Fed to influence commercial bank lending by persuasive means. For example, during inflationary times the Fed might frown on excessive borrowing by a bank that tries to expand its reserves. Similarly, during recessionary times the Fed might extol the virtues of a vigorous lending policy on the part of banks. Perhaps the main drawback of moral suasion is that it does not work very well. When it comes to making a choice between bowing to the wishes of the Fed and maximizing profits, most self-respecting bankers choose the latter.

The Fed also can influence economic activity by what is known as selective credit controls. For example, the Fed regulates the length of the repayment period on installment loans. If people are required to repay a new car loan in, say, 24 months as opposed to 36 months, fewer people tend to buy new cars. Another device is the regulation of margin requirements on stocks. If, for example, the margin requirement is 60 percent, a person need pay only 60 percent of the price of the stock from his or her own money and is allowed to borrow the remaining 40 percent.

MONETARY POLICY IN THE CONTEXT OF THE SIMPLE KEYNESIAN MODEL

The fact that the simple Keynesian model contains no information on the monetary sector of the economy limits its usefulness as a device to analyze the effects of monetary policy. However, it is possible to present an intuitive idea of how monetary policy affects the economy in the context of this model.

It is easiest to trace the effects of a change in the money supply in the simple model if we view the process as sort of a chain of causation. To begin, suppose the Fed makes a large open-market purchase. From our past discussion we know that this action increases money and bank reserves. With increased reserves banks can undertake to expand their loans. After all, banks earn a large share of their income from loans so it would be foolish to hold the extra reserves in "cold storage."

However, in order for banks to induce individuals and businesses to borrow more, they will probably have to lower their interest charges. A reduction in the interest rate provides an incentive for business firms to borrow for new investment projects such as buildings, machines, and equipment. Lower interest rates also provide an incentive for consumers to save less and spend more, particularly on consumer durables, such as autos and appliances. In the simple model this increase in spending would be represented by an upward shift in aggregate demand.

Our knowledge of the multiplier process tells us that new spending will increase by some multiple of the initial increase in consumption and investment and give rise to an increase in equilibrium NNP. We can summarize the chain of causation as follows:

Increase in $M \rightarrow$ Decrease in $i \rightarrow$ Increase in I and $C \rightarrow$ Increase in aggregate demand $\rightarrow$ Increase in equilibrium NNP

Of course, just the opposite would be expected to occur in the case of an open-market sale of bonds. The resulting decrease in money and reserves leads to an increase in the interest rate, other things being equal. Then as investment and possibly consumption decline, aggregate demand shifts down, resulting in a decrease in equilibrium NNP.

The effect of monetary policy can be illustrated on the familiar aggregate demand and supply diagram shown in Figure 13–1. Figure 13–1(A) again represents unemployment. Here the appropriate monetary policy would be to increase the rate of growth of the money supply so that the interest rate declines and shifts aggregate demand upward. In the case of the inflationary situation illustrated by Figure 13–1(B), the appropriate monetary policy would be to reduce the rate of growth of the supply of money, thereby increasing the interest rate, shifting aggregate demand downward, and reducing the equilibrium NNP.

We cannot be as precise in predicting the ultimate effects of monetary policy, however, as we were able to be with fiscal policy. Recall that by using the multiplier, we were able to predict to the exact dollar how much of a tax or government spending change was needed to match the equilibrium NNP with the full-employment level. In order to make such precise predictions for monetary policy, we would need two additional pieces of information. First, we would have to know how much an open-market purchase or sale of bonds would change the interest rate. Second, information would be needed on how much investment or consumption changes in response to a given change in the interest rate.

Economists have been able to gather a little information on the response of investment to changes in the interest rate, although the general area of the relationship between interest rate changes and spending changes is still subject to considerable uncertainty. Even less is known about the impact of an open-market purchase on the interest rate and the process that occurs in the economy when the interest rate changes.

FIGURE 13–1   Monetary policy in the context of the simple Keynesian
model—correcting for unemployment and inflation

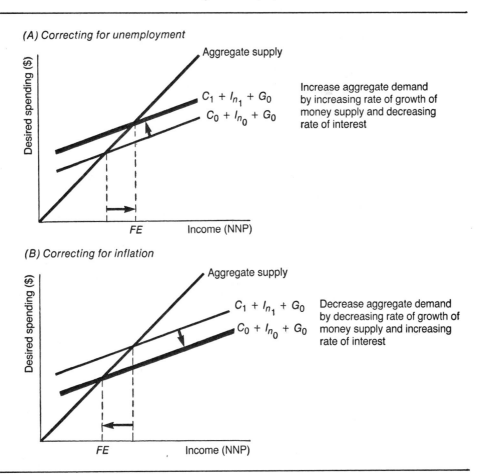

(A) Correcting for unemployment

Aggregate supply

$C_1 + I_{n_1} + G_0$

$C_0 + I_{n_0} + G_0$

Increase aggregate demand
by increasing rate of growth of
money supply and decreasing
rate of interest

Desired spending ($)

FE   Income (NNP)

(B) Correcting for inflation

Aggregate supply

$C_1 + I_{n_1} + G_0$

$C_0 + I_{n_0} + G_0$

Decrease aggregate demand
by decreasing rate of growth of
money supply and increasing
rate of interest

Desired spending ($)

FE   Income (NNP)

PROBLEMS WITH THE KEYNESIAN MODELS

In using the simple Keynesian model to show the effects of monetary
policy, it is important to keep in mind the assumptions that are required in
order for the predicted results to occur. If the assumptions violate reality, the
predicted results may not correspond to what actually happens when monetary
policy is undertaken. The simplifying assumptions of constant levels of investment, government spending, and taxes that were made in building the model do
not, of course, correspond to reality; however, as in the case of fiscal policy,
these assumptions are not looked upon as a serious drawback of the model. As
mentioned in Chapter 12, a mathematical version of the model can be built that
allows *I*, *G*, and *T* to vary with income.

The first problem with the simple Keynesian model is that it poses the
important question of whether changes in the money supply and the resulting
changes in the interest rate really cause a change in consumer and investment

spending, as assumed in the preceding section. One can visualize a situation in which consumers and investors do not respond in any significant degree to these changes in the interest rate. If this should be the case, then monetary policy will be a rather ineffective way to change the equilibrium NNP. Of course, there is the other possibility that consumers and investors are highly responsive to interest rate changes. In this case monetary policy will be a relatively effective way of shifting aggregate demand to obtain a desired level of equilibrium NNP. Unfortunately, from the simple model there is no way of knowing whether the prescribed changes in the money supply will in fact do what is assumed. The more complete *IS-LM* model presented in the appendix to Chapter 6 is able to show explicitly under what conditions monetary policy will be ineffective and under what conditions it will be effective.[2]

The second problem is whether changes in the money supply actually affect the economy in the way the Keynesian models stipulate. Recall that in the Keynesian models, money affects the economy through changes in the interest rate. An increase in the money supply, for example, decreases the interest rate and stimulates investment and consumer spending. This in turn causes aggregate demand to increase along with equilibrium NNP. An alternative explanation for the way money affects the economy is given by the quantity theory of money, which we will review in the following section. At any rate, according to the quantity theory, money has a more direct and more powerful influence on the economy than is implied by the Keynesian models.

A third problem with the Keynesian models when using them to predict the effects of an increase in the money supply during a period of unemployment is the assumption that the price level does not change. Unfortunately there is no guarantee that prices will remain constant when the money supply increases because there is no assurance that the extra money will be spent on goods and services produced by industries where the unemployment exists. When people have more money to spend they are as likely (perhaps more likely) to spend this extra money on goods and services produced by industries where there already is full employment and as a result just bid up the prices in these industries without having much impact on employment, at least until workers can relocate to these expanding industries.

If the price level increases with an increase in the money supply, then the monetary value of full-employment level of NNP also will increase; with the higher price level the same real output that gives rise to full employment represents a higher dollar value. As a result the new equilibrium NNP will not reach the new full-employment level, which in turn will call for still another increase in the money supply (if monetary policy is to be used). As pointed out in Chapter 12, this phenomenon is something like a dog (equilibrium NNP) chasing a rabbit (full-employment NNP) with no assurance that the former will ever catch the latter. The result may just be an inflating of the economy.

The assumption of a fixed level of prices is crucial for the Keynesian models. If the interest rate, which is what stimulates spending in the Keynesian models, is going to decrease with an increase in the money supply, the price level has to remain fixed. If the price level in fact begins to increase, then the

---

[2] In the context of the *IS-LM* model, monetary policy will be ineffective if the *IS* curve is steep and the *LM* curve is flat. Monetary policy will be effective if the *IS* curve is flat and the *LM* curve is steep.

money rate of interest, which is what is used by the simple model, also will increase, as explained in Chapter 3 and discussed again at the beginning of this chapter.

A fourth and perhaps more serious problem with the Keynesian models occurs when the money supply is restricted in order to increase the interest rate and reduce spending during an inflationary period. It is assumed in this case that when equilibrium NNP is reduced so that it coincides with the full-employment level, the only thing that happens is a stabilization of the price level. What is more likely to happen in this case is an increase in unemployment and a continuation of inflation, although at a decreasing rate. The end result is the existence of both unemployment and inflation. Recall that this was common during the 1970s. This problem is not unique to the Keynesian models, it confronts the quantity theory also. Thus we will postpone a possible explanation until the later section on adjustment problems.

The following is a summary of the various problems and drawbacks of the Keynesian models when used as tools to analyze monetary policy. They:

1. Assume that consumers and investors change their spending in response to changes in the interest rate. (This assumption is not required in the *IS-LM* model.)
2. Assume that changes in the money supply affect spending through the interest rate which may not be entirely true.
3. Assume a constant price level when the money supply is increased to reduce unemployment.
4. Assume unemployment does not increase when the rate of growth of money supply is decreased to reduce inflation.

MONETARISTS VERSUS THE KEYNESIANS

It has been common to regard monetarists as economists who believe that consumers and investors are relatively responsive to changes in the interest rate that are brought about by changes in the money supply.[3] In effect this means that changes in the money supply have a pronounced influence on economic activity. However, Milton Friedman, regarded by many as the leading spokesman for the monetarists, points out that the difference between the monetarists and the Keynesians is more fundamental than a difference in viewpoint on the responsiveness of consumers and investors to changes in the rate of interest.[4]

Recall that in the Keynesian models changes in the money supply influence spending because of changes in the interest rate. However, remember from Chapter 10 that in the context of the quantity theory of money, changes in the money supply have a more direct influence on total spending. For example, if people are holding as much money as they wish to hold, an increase in the money supply means that some people end up holding more money than they wish to hold. In an attempt to reduce their "excess" holding of money they may buy securities, bidding up their prices and lowering the interest return on

---

[3] In the context of the *IS-LM* model, monetarists have been described as those who believe the *IS* curve is flat and the *LM* curve is steep.

[4] See Milton Friedman, "Comments on the Critics," *Journal of Political Economy* 80 (September–October 1972) pp. 906–50.

them. This in turn may stimulate new investment as borrowers find credit less costly. But according to Friedman, money holders are not limited to buying securities. They may buy houses, automobiles, appliances, clothing, and other goods in an attempt to rearrange their portfolios away from money toward earning assets. In the process of buying these assets (goods and services), their prices and/or quantities are increased, thereby increasing $P \times Q$ and re-establishing the equilibrium between the desired and actual levels of K in the economy.

To summarize the difference between the Keynesian model and the new quantity theory, one might say that there is more "slippage" between changes in the money supply and the resulting changes in economic activity in the former model. In the Keynesian framework, changes in the money affect spending through changes in the interest rate. In the new quantity theory, money has a more direct influence on spending as people change their rate of spending in an effort to maintain their desired K value.

MONETARY POLICY IN THE CONTEXT OF THE NEW QUANTITY THEORY

Recall from Chapter 10 that the impact of changes in the money supply on the economy is expressed in the quantity theory by the quantity equation of exchange, $M \times V = P \times Q$. The quantity theory is perhaps most useful for identifying the main source of inflation and providing a policy prescription to deal with this problem. According to the quantity equation of exchange, $M \times V = P \times Q$, if M grows more rapidly than Q, inflation is inevitable, providing V does not decrease when M increases. (We will come back to the question of the stability of V in the following section.)

Figures on the relative growth of Q and M in the United States from 1949 to 1984 are presented in Table 13–1. The Q in this table is represented by total real GNP as reported by the Department of Commerce.[5] GNP is converted to an index by dividing the series of numbers by the 1949 value. The index makes it a bit easier to compare the growth of real output with the growth in money over the period. As stated previously, the broad definition of money (M_2) is used as

TABLE 13–1 Indexes of total real output and money in the United States, selected years, 1949–84 (1929 = 100)

Year	Real output	Money	Year	Real output	Money
1949	100	100	1980	299	1,102
1959	147	201	1981	307	1,213
1969	221	398	1982	301	1,326
1974	253	614	1983	312	1,483
1979	301	1,012	1984	333	1,604

Sources: Real output figures from *Economic Report of the President*, 1969, p. 228, and 1985, p. 232. Figures on money from Table 10–1.

---

[5] In this case real GNP is obtained by deflating GNP in current-year prices by the "implicit price deflator" constructed by the Department of Commerce.

the M figure. It is converted to an index also by dividing the series of numbers by the 1949 value of M_2.

As indicated by the figures in Table 13–1, total real output in the U.S. economy increased by 3.3 times between 1949 and 1984. However, the nation's money supply increased more than 16 times during this period. Thus, the nation's money supply grew at a much faster rate than did real output. Since V has remained relatively constant (Table 10–2), the quantity equation predicts that the nation should have experienced inflation, which of course it did. By the same token, the quantity theory suggests that if the nation really wants to stop inflation, then the government must slow the growth of the money supply to the level of the growth of real output in the economy.

One might ask: Why did the government (or the Federal Reserve) increase the money supply so much more than the growth in real output? The most likely reason is the deficit spending of the federal government. We will take up this problem in more detail in a forthcoming section.

If unemployment is the problem, the quantity theory also can be helpful in identifying a possible cause of the problem and providing some insight in what might be done to reduce it. Recall from Chapter 10 that an absolute decrease in the money supply must result in a decrease in $P \times Q$ (GNP) providing V does not increase. As in the Great Depression the most likely result is for Q to decrease first, causing increased unemployment, and then after a time some decrease in the price level probably would occur. The remedy, of course, is to reverse the decline in M and start it growing again. Indeed, the quantity theory suggests that an even better solution is to not allow the money supply to decline in the first place.

An absolute decline in the money supply is relatively rare. A more common problem is for M to grow more slowly than real output is capable of growing, such as occurred in the late 1950s and early 1960s. If the slow growth in the money supply persists long enough, the economy is likely to be sluggish and experience increased unemployment. In this case the quantity theory suggests that the rate of growth of M should be increased to bring it up to the rate of growth of Q that the economy is capable of generating. From 1950 to 1980 total real output in the U.S. economy grew at an average rate of 3.5 percent per year.

PROBLEMS WITH THE QUANTITY THEORY

When using the quantity equation of exchange, $M \times V = P \times Q$, to predict the outcome of a change in M, the crucial assumption is that V does not change in the opposite direction. Recall from Chapter 10 that an increase in the money supply will likely give rise to a temporary situation where people are holding more money than they desire to hold. In attempting to get rid of this extra money they may buy stocks and bonds, which can cause an increase in the price of these securities and in turn cause their interest return to decline. The decline in the interest return on these assets has the effect of reducing the cost of holding money because now less income is given up by holding money. If this decrease in the cost of holding money prompts people to increase their desired holding of money, they may not increase their spending on other assets very much. In this case the increase in M would in large part be offset by a decrease in V. As a result the increase in M would not have much of an impact on either P or Q. On the other hand, if the decrease in the interest return on stocks and bonds is relatively small or if it does not have much effect on the equivalent proportion of income that people desire to hold as money, V will remain relatively constant and the increase in M will cause a nearly proportionate increase in $P \times Q$. The crucial question, therefore, is whether V fluctuates in the opposite direction of M or is relatively stable.

The evidence presented in Table 10–2 suggests that V is relatively stable at least when M_2, the broad definition of money, is used. As mentioned, the broad definition is probably a more accurate measure of money because of the ease of switching money between checking and savings accounts. As shown in Table 10–2, the only decreases in velocity between 1929 and 1984 occurred during the Great Depression and during the 1982–83 recession. The high level of unemployment during these years prompted people to hold a greater proportion of their income as money (increase their K); therefore, velocity declined. The decrease in V served to accentuate the depressing effect of the decrease in the money supply during the early 1930s. The decline in velocity during 1982 and 1983 also had a dampening effect on the economy similar to that which occurred during the early 1930s, although the decline was not as severe in the more recent period. At any rate, the relative stability of V suggests that the quantity equation is a fairly good predictor of changes in $P \times Q$ when there are changes in M.

As explained in Chapter 10, during times of large and abrupt changes in M, V will most likely change in the same direction, thereby accentuating the effect of changes in the money supply. Recall from the discussion of the quantity theory that a decrease in the money supply (or in its rate of growth) and the resulting increase in unemployment are likely to cause people to try to increase their holding of money, thereby causing an increase in K and a decrease in V. The opposite should occur when the money supply is increased enough to cause severe inflation. Now people try to get rid of money, causing a decrease in K and an increase in V. In both cases the effect of the change in M is accentuated rather than nullified.

Of course, even if money has a pronounced impact on the economy, there are still difficulties that will be encountered. Consider first an unemployment problem. The quantity theory suggests that increasing the rate of growth of the money supply will increase GNP. However, in order for unemployment to be reduced, the increase in GNP should come from an increase in real output (Q) rather than an increase in prices (P). The problem is that there is nothing in the quantity theory that guarantees that output will in fact increase. It is entirely possible that the increase in GNP could come primarily from an increase in the price level. This could occur if the added spending that resulted from the increase in the money supply was on goods and services produced in industries having relatively full employment already. The result would be a bidding up of prices in these industries without much impact, at least in the short run, on industries that have most of the unemployment. Unemployment will decrease only if it shows up as an increase in Q. Increasing the rate of growth of the money supply under the above conditions will simply cause inflation without having much impact on output and employment. Recall that this same problem existed for the simple Keynesian model, except in that model prices are *assumed* to remain constant, which of course does not guarantee that they will in fact remain constant.

An even more difficult problem exists when the growth of the money supply is restricted in an effort to control inflation. In this case, increased unemployment is likely to occur while inflation continues, albeit at a decreasing rate. Since this problem also confronts the Keynesian models, we shall discuss it in the following section.

ADJUSTMENT PROBLEMS

Both the Keynesian models and the quantity theory suggest that the appropriate monetary policy during a period of inflation is a restriction in the growth of the money supply. Of course, if the objective were to roll back prices to some previous level, an absolute reduction in the money supply would be required. But knowing what happened the last time the money supply was reduced in absolute terms (we had the Great Depression), such action would not likely be taken, at least consciously. Monetary policy would be considered successful if it succeeded in stabilizing prices at higher levels than previously existed. But even this less ambitious objective is still likely to lead to increased unemployment.

Although past experience strongly suggests that a reduction in the rate of growth of the money supply causes increased unemployment, the underlying reasons for this problem are not well understood. In the context of the Keynesian models, temporary increases in the rate of interest that can result from an unexpected tightening of credit can be one source of the increased unemployment. In this case investment and consumer spending probably will decrease for a time, causing at least a temporary increase in unemployment. Of course, as pointed out at the beginning of this chapter, a decrease in the rate of inflation will eventually lead to a reduction in the money rate of interest. In the context of the quantity theory, a reduction in the growth of money, say, from 10 percent to 5 percent per year when income is growing by 10 percent will result in a situation where people end up the year holding a smaller proportion of their income as money (K) than they anticipated, providing they were in equilibrium before the reduction in the growth of money. This would cause people to reduce their spending in an effort to replenish their monetary holdings, and as a result there would be increased unemployment. Of course, the higher interest rates that result in the short run from the decrease in the growth of the money supply and that serve to depress the economy also are consistent with the quantity theory.

Although unemployment may increase, inflation is most likely to continue, again as our experience with attempting to reduce the 1980 double-digit inflation would lead us to believe. The reasons for the simultaneous existence of unemployment and inflation are best explained by the rational expectations hypothesis.

MONETARY POLICY IN THE CONTEXT OF RATIONAL EXPECTATIONS

Recall from Chapter 12 that, according to the rational expectations hypothesis, government attempts to "fine tune" the economy by means of fiscal policy will at best have only a short-term effect on unemployment and at worst are likely to end up causing inflation and perhaps even more unemployment in the future when the government tries to slow down the inflation. Essentially, the same conclusion holds for monetary policy. The long-run Phillips curve diagram of Figure 7–4 provides the framework for the analysis of monetary policy as well as that of fiscal policy, at least for the rational expectations argument.

Consider first an attempt by government to stimulate the economy by increasing the rate of growth of the money supply. The resulting increase in the price level is at first mistaken by business firms to be an increase in the demand for their particular product. They hire more workers, and the unemployment rate declines temporarily as the economy moves up along a specific short-run Phillips curve. But as wage earners and union leaders recognize that the price increases are widespread across the economy, they press employers for wage increases in order to regain the reduction in real wage rates. The level of unemployment then increases, and the economy comes to rest once again at the natural rate of unemployment but on a higher short-run Phillips curve corresponding to a higher expected rate of inflation. After repeated attempts to stimulate the economy by means of monetary policy, people soon learn what the government is doing and react simultaneously or even in advance of the policy action. In this case the main effect of this policy is to just move the economy up to higher and higher short-run Phillips curves without any pronounced reduction in unemployment even in the short-run.

As pointed out in Chapter 12, sooner or later inflation, rather than unemployment, will come to be viewed as the main problem. Now the government is likely to reduce the rate of growth of the money supply. As the inflation rate subsides slightly, employers mistake the slowing down of price increases as a softness in the demands for their particular products. Consequently, they lay off people and unemployment increases. Then as unions and wage earners slacken their demands for pay hikes, unemployment cases back down to the natural rate after a period of time. But during the adjustment period the economy still suffers from inflation and high unemployment.

Advocates of the rational expectations hypothesis argue that the unemployment consequences of reducing inflation could be mitigated or even eliminated if the government were to announce its intentions of reducing the rate of growth of the money supply. In this case employers need not lay off employees because of the mistaken belief that the demand for their product had decreased, nor would employees press for as large a pay increase because of the anticipated slowing down of inflation. If the government could convince people of its actions so that expectations were altered, the economy could move down along the vertical long-run Phillips curve without experiencing a series of short-run Phillips curves from the corresponding periods of high unemployment.

The problem is to convince people that the government will stick to its announced policy of reducing the growth of the money supply. After the broken promises of several administrations, it is understandable that people have become wary of new promises with no guarantee that the announced action will be carried out. If the federal government would stick to its goal of reducing the rate of growth of the money supply for a period of a year or more, then people might revise their inflationary expectations downward and the economy would move down to a lower short-run Phillips curve. But in the meantime, unemployment is likely to be high.

It is clear from the preceding discussion that the economy would have been better off if monetary expansion had been curtailed in the first place so that inflationary expectations had not been created. As a further consequence unemployment would not have been increased, in an attempt to slow down inflation. Although the rational expectations hypothesis is somewhat more optimistic than the monetarist view in regard to the amount of unemployment caused by a slow down in inflation, both schools of thought advocate a steady growth in the money supply corresponding to the growth in real output of the economy. "Leaning against the wind" is out. Unfortunately, the actual rate of growth of the money supply in the United States during the 1960s, 1970s, and early 1980s has been extremely uneven, as will be pointed out in a following section.

TIMING PROBLEMS

Whatever model one uses to prescribe monetary policy, the problem of timing must be faced. There are two aspects of the timing problem: (1) when to take corrective action and (2) when the action has its impact on the economy.

The first problem stems from the difficulty of discerning a temporary fluctuation in economic activity from the start of a real recession or inflationary spiral. Because of the political implications of rising unemployment or inflation, there is a great deal of controversy regarding the state of the economy. At the first glimpse of rising unemployment, the political party that is not in power generally calls for a change of policies and leadership, claiming that the country is headed for a deep recession. On the other hand, the party in power is likely to argue that the economy is experiencing a temporary downturn and soon will recover to its former state of high employment. It is evident, then, that the monetary authority cannot expect to always please both political parties at once, nor should it try. From this standpoint, it is perhaps fortunate that the Federal Reserve Board of Governors is somewhat of an autonomous body, to some extent shielded from conflicting pressures of the political parties.

But the Fed is still faced with the problem of when to take action. It must be aware, too, that action at the wrong time can be worse than no action at all.

FIGURE 13–2   The timing of monetary policy

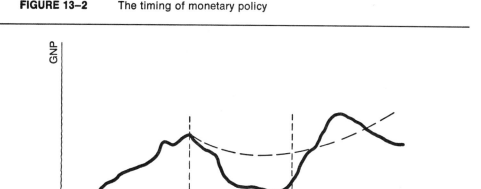

For example, if the Fed steps up the rate of increase of the money supply in a mistaken belief that the economy is headed for a downturn, the result could be a needless inflation in the months and possibly years to come. Or if it sharply curtails the rate of increase of the money supply, thinking that inflation is upon us when it is not, the result may well be a needless increase in unemployment in the future. As illustrated in Figure 13–2, the correct time to undertake an expansion of the money supply or increase its rate of growth—that is, engage in an "easy money" policy—is at time T_0. Or if the economy is headed for an inflationary spiral, such as at T_1, the models imply that the Fed should cut back on the rate of growth of the money supply—that is, engage in a "tight money" policy. The object of these policies, of course, is to smooth out the fluctuations in the economy, as illustrated by the dashed line beginning at T_0 in Figure 13–2.

LAGS IN THE EFFECT OF MONETARY POLICY

The second timing problem mentioned in the preceding section stems from the time it takes for changes in the money supply to affect economic activity. If there is a lag between policy action and its effect, one has to be mindful of the possibility that the impact of the policy will not come at the time desired. For example, suppose the economy is headed for a downturn as illustrated at time T_0 in Figure 13–2. If the increase in the rate of growth of the money supply is not felt by the economy until time T_1, the result may well be a worsening of the inflation problem that the economy will experience after T_1.

Friedman presents evidence that the lags in the effect of monetary policy are both long and variable.[6] In other words, the lag may be 6 to 12 months at one time and 24 to 36 months or longer at another time. The reasons for the long and variable lags are not as yet well understood or agreed upon. One might expect that the lag would have something to do with the time it takes for the multiple expansion (or contraction) process to work itself out through the economy. For example, as banks gain new reserves during an expansionary phase, it takes time to find and screen suitable borrowers. Of course, borrowers also must be willing to take on new debt. If the economy has been in a recession and business people are still pessimistic about the future, they are not so likely to negotiate new loans as during a more optimistic time. Recall that it is the making of loans by commercial banks that results in the multiple expansion. Thus, the willingness of business firms to borrow is likely to influence how quickly an expansionary monetary policy is felt in the economy and how large the impact is on the economy.

In the case of an anti-inflationary monetary policy where the Federal Reserve sells bonds and reduces commercial bank reserves, there seems to be a more immediate reaction in the economy. When loan money becomes scarce, industries that are dependent on borrowed funds, such as construction, seem to be affected quickly and significantly. Layoffs occur, affecting other industries, such as appliance and lumber. Thus, it is not unreasonable to believe that the lag between monetary policy action and its effect may be different both within an expansionary phase and between expansionary and restrictive monetary policies.

---

[6] Milton Friedman, "The Lag in the Effect of Monetary Policy," *Journal of Political Economy* 68 (December 1960), pp. 617–21.

RULES VERSUS DISCRETION: THE FRIEDMAN PROPOSAL

Because of the likelihood of long and variable lags in the effects of monetary policy, Friedman has proposed that the monetary authority would have a greater stabilizing effect on the economy if it would follow a simple rule of increasing the money supply about 4 to 5 percent per year to keep up with a growing economy instead of periodically "stepping on the gas" and then "slamming on the brakes" in response to downturns and upturns in economic activity.[7]

Notice, however, that Friedman is not saying that monetary policy is of little importance. Rather, he is saying that money is so important that large fluctuations in the money supply cause large and damaging fluctuations in economic activity. Friedman argues that following his simple rule would have promoted much more stability in the economy than we experienced with the Fed's attempts to lean against the wind.

MONETARY INSTABILITY

Year-to-year changes in the U.S. money supply (M_2) for the 1959–84 period are presented in Table 13–2. Although more dramatic fluctuations in the

---

TABLE 13–2   Year-to-year percent changes in the U.S. money supply, M_2, 1959–84*

Year	Change	Year	Change
1959	2.1%	1972	13.0%
1960	4.9	1973	6.9
1961	7.4	1974	5.5
1962	8.1	1975	12.6
1963	8.4	1976	13.7
1964	8.0	1977	10.6
1965	8.1	1978	8.0
1966	4.5	1979	7.9
1967	9.2	1980	8.9
1968	8.0	1981	10.0
1969	4.1	1982	9.4
1970	6.6	1983	11.7
1971	13.5	1984	8.2

* December-to-1 December changes in M_2.
Source: *Economic Report of the President,*
1985, p. 303.

U.S. money supply occurred during the 1930s and 1940s, there are still some rather significant fluctuations during the post-World War II period. The quantity theory predicts that the extraordinary small growth of the money supply during the 1959–60 period of 3.5 percent per year should have resulted in a rather sluggish economy with relatively high unemployment during the early 1960s, which in fact occurred. John F. Kennedy's 1960 campaign slogan of

---

[7] Milton Friedman, *A Program for Monetary Stability* (New York: Fordham University Press, 1959).

"let's get this country moving again" was an appropriate one under the circumstances. The more than doubling of the rate of growth of the money supply to 8.0 percent per year during the 1961–65 period probably had something to do with the resurgence of the economy during the mid-1960s, although the well-publicized tax cut is generally given credit for this turn of events. It is interesting to note that it was during these years, 1961–65, when the money supply grew at 8.0 percent per year that the economy enjoyed a period of relatively stable prices and full employment. Perhaps there is a lesson to be learned here.

Moving on to the mid-1960s, the money supply growth began to pick up steam but then started to fluctuate significantly toward the end of the decade. After declining to 4.5 percent in 1966 from 8.1 percent the previous year, the growth of the money supply more than doubled in 1967. An even more dramatic change occurred in 1969 when M_2 growth declined to 4.1 percent, down from a 8.6 percent average the preceding two years.

The early 1970s brought an acceleration in the growth of the money supply to more than 13 percent per year in 1971–72 followed by another decline as the country moved into the middle of the decade. The roller coaster pattern of money supply growth continued as the 1970s drew to a close, with M_2 growth increasing to 13.2 percent per year in the 1975–76 period before dropping back to 8.9 percent growth during the 1978–80 period. As the country moved into the 1980s, the money supply growth continued its fluctuating pattern.

Actually, the year-to-year changes in the money supply understate the true instability because the within-year changes average out. To provide an example of the within-year instability, the month-to-month annual growth rates of M_2 for 1984 are presented in Table 13–3. These rates are the percent changes from the

TABLE 13–3 Month-to-month annual rates of growth of M_2 for 1984

Month	Annual percent change	Month	Annual percent change
January	5.7	July	5.2
February	8.6	August	4.8
March	4.0	September	7.6
April	6.9	October	6.0
May	8.4	November	15.1
June	7.2	December	15.3

beginning to the end of the month multiplied by 12 to put the figures on an annual basis. The monthly figures are what the annual rates of growth would have been if the same rates had prevailed over the entire year. It's evident from Table 13–3 that there is even more instability within years than between years. The within-year instability also causes unnecessary shocks in the economy.

Proponents of the Friedman proposal, which calls for a stable 4 to 5 percent annual rate of growth of the money supply, argue that if this rule had been followed, the nation would have avoided much of the economic instability that occurred and in turn avoided the more severe unemployment and inflation problems. This is a rather strong statement because it implies that past monetary policy has caused more unemployment and inflation than it prevented. In view of the evidence presented in Chapter 12, one might say the same thing for fiscal policy.

HOW FEDERAL DEFICITS CAN CAUSE INFLATION AND UNEMPLOYMENT

For the purpose of exposition it has been convenient to separate the discussion of fiscal policy from monetary policy. However, in reality fiscal policy is likely to have an important bearing on the rate of growth of the money supply. This is particularly true when the federal government runs deficits. If the government incurs deficits in the process of increasing its spending (or cutting taxes), then you recall from Chapter 12 that one way to finance these deficits is to "print money." In this process the Treasury sells bonds, most likely to a bond dealer. When the Federal Reserve clears the check written by the bond dealer, it prints the corresponding figures in the Treasury's checking account at the Fed. The Treasury can then write checks on these added numbers in its account for the purchase of goods and services, the same as if these numbers were new $10 and $20 bills, hence the term *printing money*.

However, it should be recognized that by itself the Treasury's sale of bonds to bond dealers (in effect the general public) does not change the nation's total money supply. The check written by the bond dealer reduces demand deposits and the money supply, but this decrease is exactly offset by the increase in demand deposits that occur when people who sell goods and services to the government deposit the Treasury's checks in their accounts.

The key transaction in the process of printing money to finance deficits is when the Federal Reserve buys bonds back from bond dealers. Now the money supply is increased, not only because of the increase in demand deposits in commercial banks when the Federal Reserve pays for the bonds but, more important, because of the multiple expansion process that occurs due to the increase in excess reserves.

To give an idea of the magnitude of Federal Reserve purchases of government bonds during the late 1960s and 1970s, the Federal Reserve owned $33.6 billion of government securities as of December 31, 1963. Eighteen years later, on December 31, 1981, the value of government securities owned by the Federal Reserve had more than tripled to $124.5 billion. Bear in mind that the increase in commercial bank reserves resulting from the Federal Reserve bond purchases brings forth a multiple expansion of the money supply so the total money supply increase is many times more than the $90.9 billion *increase* in bonds owned by the Federal Reserve.

If velocity is relatively stable, as shown in Table 10–2, then the resulting increase in the money supply invariably causes inflation, providing that money grows more rapidly than real output, which of course it did from 1949 to 1984 (Table 13–1). We should not be surprised, therefore, that the nation experienced relatively high rates of inflation during the 1970s and early 1980s. Indeed, we should be surprised if the nation had not experienced inflation during this period!

One might ask: Why was the Federal Reserve so accommodating to the Treasury, buying its bonds and in the process causing an increase in the money supply? The problem is that if the Federal Reserve did not buy some of these bonds, they would all have to be purchased by private buyers. The savings from individuals and business firms used to buy the government bonds then are no longer available to be used by private borrowers or to purchase stocks in the stock market. In this case the federal government "crowds out" private borrowers and companies wishing to raise capital by selling stocks. The government can do so by offering higher and higher interest rates on government bonds so that savers can be induced to buy these bonds. And this is precisely what the government did during the early 1980s.

The crowding out of private borrowers is particularly hard in the construction and automobile industries, which depend heavily on credit. The slowing down of sales in these industries because of higher interest and tighter credit in turn causes increased unemployment, which is likely to spread to other industries because of the multiplier effect working in reverse. Thus, the Federal Reserve is caught over a barrel. If it buys the government bonds, it causes inflation; if it does not, unemployment increases. During the 1970s, it opted for inflation; in the early 1980s it chose unemployment.

During the second half of the Carter administration and the two Reagan administrations, the Federal Reserve became more determined to slow down the rate of growth of the money supply. As a consequence, more of the government bonds issued to finance the deficit had to be sold in the open market. Interest rates rose dramatically, causing substantial reductions in sales and increases in unemployment, particularly in the automobile and construction industries. Also the higher interest rates attracted foreign funds which in turn led to an increase in the value of the dollar relative to foreign currencies. As will be explained in Chapter 15, the strong dollar encouraged imports and dampened exports, which resulted in increased unemployment in U.S. industry and a depressed U.S. agriculture.

Although the Federal Reserve has frequently taken the blame first for the excessive growth in the money supply during the 1970s and for the high interest rates of the early 1980s, the Congress and executive branch of government should be held accountable for creating the larger deficits that occurred during the 1970s. In the absence of these deficits there would not have been as much pressure on the Federal Reserve to rapidly increase the money supply and then to try to clamp down on its growth. In this regard the Federal Reserve should not be held entirely blameless either. If the Fed had been less accommodating in financing deficits by printing money during the 1970s, it would have imposed greater discipline on Congress and the executive branch of government to live within their means. The higher interest rates and the crowding out phenomenon would have become more pronounced earlier which in turn may have led to a more responsible fiscal policy. Part of the problem may have been the Fed's preoccupation with interest rates. To keep them from rising, the Fed had to accelerate the growth of the money supply during the 1970s in order to flood the credit markets. But eventually, this policy caught up with the Fed in the form of higher inflation and higher money rates of interest. Ultimately, the blame for the large deficits and the resulting inflation and unemployment goes back to the people for desiring more and more government programs without facing up to the fact that these programs have to be paid for by taxes in one form or another (conventional taxes or inflation).

PRICE AND WAGE CONTROLS

During periods of excessive inflationary pressure, many governments have resorted to price and wage controls in an effort to stem the upward spiral of prices. In the United States, price and wage controls have been instituted generally in times of armed conflict in an effort to hold down the increase in prices. The stringent controls instituted during World War II and the somewhat more flexible controls put into effect in August 1971 are two examples. Price and wage controls have precipitated a substantial amount of controversy among economists, political leaders, and the general public. Thus, it will be useful to review some of the arguments in favor of controls, together with some of the problems that controls bring about.

Those who favor price and wage controls tend to place relatively little faith in the ability of traditional fiscal and monetary policies (such as reduced government spending, higher taxes, or tight money) to do the job. Some who favor controls may grant that traditional policy might eventually stem inflation but argue that the time required is too long or the unemployment effects too severe to be acceptable to the general public.

It is argued also that controls can help to break the inflation psychology that people may have acquired during a prolonged period of inflation. If anti-inflationary policies, such as a tax increase or a reduced rate of money creation, accompany the controls, the momentum of inflation is likely to be more quickly checked. In this case unions are not likely to be as demanding in asking for future wage increases and people in general need not be as concerned about getting rid of their cash by purchasing real assets that rise in value with the price level. Thus, pressure for price increases is eased somewhat in both the labor and product markets. With an ease in wage demands, employers are likely to be more willing to retain or hire employees, thus easing the unemployment problem brought on by restrictive fiscal or monetary policies.

Economists who oppose price and wage restraints point out that the imposition of controls does not remove the basic causes of inflation. They argue that inflation is caused basically by excessive growth in the money supply due in large part to deficit spending. Hence, the imposition of price and wage controls may suppress the symptoms of inflation but does not remove its underlying cause.

It is argued that unless price and wage controls are applied universally, those prices or wages that are not affected will grow even more rapidly. In other words, it would be something like squeezing a balloon—if you push in at one place, it will bulge out at another. But if all prices and wages are frozen, then the economy is placed in a sort of straitjacket. That is, there is no way for consumers to provide signals to producers through the price system.

As pointed out in Chapter 2, resources are allocated in a market economy mainly on the basis of market prices. If the price of one product rises relative to others, it is a signal to producers that consumers desire more of this product relative to others. Producers, in attempting to increase profits by producing more of the higher-priced product, at the same time satisfy the desires of consumers. Similarly, if the price of a resource increases, producers have an incentive to economize on its use by substituting lower-priced resources in its place. Thus, the imposition of price and wage controls takes away the allocating function of product and resource prices.

A second problem encountered with price and wage controls is that they result in shortages in the product and resource markets, which in turn lead to rationing and black-market activities. These undesirable side effects of price controls can be demonstrated by the market demand and supply diagram developed in Chapter 2. Recall that one of the main demand shifters is a change in money income. An increase in money income resulting from an increase in the money supply causes the demand for most goods to increase or shift to the right, as shown by Figure 13–3. Recall as well that a major supply shifter is a

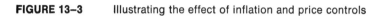

FIGURE 13–3   Illustrating the effect of inflation and price controls

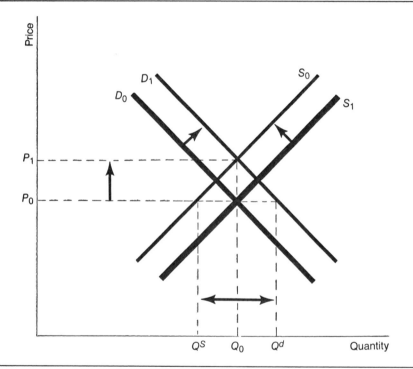

change in the prices of resources. During inflation the increase in prices of labor, capital, and raw materials causes the supply curve of products to decrease—that is, shift to the left. The increase in demand and decrease in supply both contribute to the increase in the market equilibrium prices of goods and services. As shown by Figure 13–3, the new higher price is equal to P_1.

If the market is "frozen" at P_0 or prohibited by law from increasing, a shortage will occur. Notice at the new demand and supply curves that quantity demanded, Q^d, is greater than quantity supplied, Q^s, at the original or controlled price P_0. This in turn creates a shortage equal to the difference between Q^s and Q^d. If wages are controlled also, the shift to the left by the supply curve would not be so large because costs would not increase as much. Of course, the costs of imported raw materials can still increase, which would increase costs for some industries. But even if the supply curve does not shift to the left, there still will be a shortage caused by the difference between Q_0 and Q^d. Because of the resulting shortages, consumers turn to the black market, paying prices higher than the legal maximum. The longer the price controls remain in effect and the wider the gap between Q^d and Q^s becomes, the greater is the incentive to buy and sell on the black market. As the resulting shortages increase, the pressure on market price to increase continues to grow. Eventually, all countries that have attempted to prevent inflation by price controls have been forced to allow prices to rise to their market equilibrium levels.[8] Moreover, when price controls are relaxed, prices tend to shoot up rapidly to catch up to their higher equilibrium levels. Also, the decline in the quantity supplied that occurs during price controls causes prices to rise even more than they would have risen without the controls.

Price indexes, such as the CPI which reflect prices during periods of price controls, of course measure the legal or controlled prices, not the black-market prices. As a result, the removal of price controls and the subsequent upward spurt of the price index may give the appearance that the controls have been successful in preventing inflation, and that the inflation has recurred with the removal of controls. In reality the price index fails to measure black-market prices and the continual upward pressure on prices during the period the price controls are in effect.

Although it is generally not reported in history books, the imposition of the price controls by the commonwealth of Pennsylvania on the commodities purchased by the American Revolutionary Army during the winter of 1777–78 nearly caused the demise of George Washington's army at Valley Forge.[9] Price controls caused severe shortages of food, as farmers either held back the sale of food at prices they considered very unfair or sold the food to the British who paid in gold. The intent of the price controls was to reduce the cost of maintaining the Revolutionary Army. But the result was the near defeat of that army.

MAIN POINTS OF CHAPTER 13

1. During inflationary times, money rates of interest will be high because of the "inflationary premium." If the Federal Reserve attempted to lower interest rates by increasing the money supply, there might be a short-run reduction in interest rates, but then they would be pushed to even higher levels because of the resulting increase in inflation.

2. The relatively low money rate of interest during the Great Depression was due to a decrease in the price level resulting from a decrease in the money supply, not from a "surplus of money."

3. The three main tools that the Federal Reserve has at its disposal to change the money supply include: (a) open-market operations (buying and selling government bonds),

---

[8] For an account of the results of wage and price controls in Western European countries since the end of World War II, see Lloyd Ulman and Robert J. Flanagan, *Wage Restraint: A Study of Income Policies in Western Europe* (Berkeley: University of California Press, 1971). According to the authors, the various wage and price policies in various countries have exhibited a common characteristic: "periods of effectiveness were typically short lived; they were frequently followed by wage and price explosions which sometimes blew up the policies themselves" (p. 223).

[9] Robert L. Schnettinger and Eamonn F. Butler, *Forty Centuries of Wage and Price Controls*, Washington, D.C.: Heritage Foundation, 1979.

(*b*) changes in the required reserve ratio of commercial banks, and (*c*) changes in the discount rate that commercial banks pay the Fed for borrowed reserves.

4. The Fed can increase the money supply by: (*a*) purchasing government bonds from banks, institutions, or the general public; (*b*) reducing the required reserve ratio; or (*c*) reducing the discount rate. The open-market purchase of bonds is the main method of increasing the money supply. A decrease in the money supply is accomplished by selling bonds, increasing the reserve ratio, or increasing the discount rate. The open-market sale is the primary method of decreasing the money supply.

5. The Federal Reserve can always buy the desired amount of bonds by increasing their price. An increase in the price of bonds is equivalent to a decrease in their interest return. The Fed also can sell the desired amount of bonds by decreasing their price, which is equivalent to raising their interest return.

6. Secondary tools of monetary policy include moral suasion and various credit controls.

7. Monetary policy in the context of the simple Keynesian model is accomplished by the following chain of causation: Change in $M \to$ Change in $i \to$ Change in I and $C \to$ Change in aggregate demand $\to$ Change in equilibrium NNP.

8. In the Keynesian models, changes in the money supply are assumed to affect the economy through changes in the interest rate. If investors and consumers are not responsive to interest rate changes, monetary policy will be ineffective, at least according to the Keynesian models. However, it is doubtful that changes in the money supply affect the economy only through changes in the interest rate.

9. In the context of the Keynesian models, an increase in the money supply during a time of unemployment is assumed not to change the price level, which may not be true.

10. Professor Friedman argues that the main distinction between the monetarists and the Keynesians is in the way changes in the supply of money are perceived to affect the economy. According to Friedman, the monetarists view changes in the quantity of money as affecting the asset balance of people, causing them to either (*a*) try to get rid of excess cash by stepping up their purchases of goods, services, and securities (in the case of a money supply increase) or (*b*) try to increase their holding of cash by selling or reducing their rate of purchase of these items (in the case of a money supply decrease).

11. Money supply changes have a stronger and more direct impact on the economy in the context of the quantity theory than in the context of the Keynesian models.

12. With the quantity theory the effect of changes in the money supply (M) is given by the quantity equation of exchange, $M \times V = P \times Q$.

13. According to the quantity theory, if money (M) grows more rapidly than real output (Q), inflation is inevitable providing V does not decrease. In the United States between 1949 and 1984 real output increased 3.3 times while money (M_2) increased over 16-fold.

14. In order to use the quantity equation to predict the outcome of changes in M, a crucial assumption is that V does not decrease when M increases, and vice versa. Except for a decrease in the Great Depression and the 1982–83 recessions, the velocity of money in the United States has remained relatively constant in the neighborhood of 1.6 during the 1929–84 period.

15. In order to reduce unemployment, it must be assumed that an increase in M causes an increase in Q. However, the quantity equation cannot guarantee this outcome.

16. During a time of inflation a reduction in the rate of growth of the money supply is likely to cause increased unemployment while inflation continues, although at a decreasing rate.

17. In the context of the rational expectations hypothesis, increasing the rate of growth of the money supply may result in a temporary reduction in unemployment if employers mistakenly believe that the resulting price increases are specific to their industry. But repeated attempts to stimulate the economy that become expected by the people are

likely to cause price increases without even short-term reductions in unemployment.

18. In attempting to reduce inflation by decreasing the growth of the money supply, unemployment is likely to increase unless the government can convince the people that inflation will in fact subside. However, people are likely to be skeptical of promises to control inflation if past promises have not been carried through.

19. Timing of monetary policy is a problem because of the uncertainty regarding when to undertake policy action and the existence of long and variable lags between changes in the rate of growth of the money supply and their impact on the economy.

20. Because of these timing difficulties, Friedman has proposed that monetary policy would be more stabilizing if the monetary authority would follow the simple rule of increasing the money supply 4 to 5 percent per year to keep step with the growing economy.

21. During the 1959–84 period, the annual rate of growth of M_2 ranged from 2.1 percent in 1959 to 13.7 percent in 1976. During the latter part of the period, the monetary growth rate trended upward, especially during 1975–77.

22. Federal deficits will cause inflation if the Federal Reserve buys bonds issued by the Treasury, that is, prints money.

23. If the Federal Reserve does not purchase government bonds, private borrowers and companies wishing to sell stock are crowded out of the loan and equity markets resulting in high interest rates and increased unemployment, particularly in the automobile and housing industries.

24. Although price controls have at times postponed inflation, they have never successfully prevented inflation. Controls are eventually scrapped because of the resulting shortages and black-market activities.

QUESTIONS FOR THOUGHT AND DISCUSSION

1. During inflationary periods the nominal or money rates of interest tend to rise while during recessions they tend to fall. Would you advocate, therefore, that the Federal Reserve take actions to stabilize interest rates in order to stabilize the economy? Explain why or why not.

2. *a.* What can the Federal Reserve do if it wishes to increase the money supply?
   b. How can the Federal Reserve be sure that it can always buy or sell government bonds?

3. How is an increase in the rate of growth of the money supply perceived to affect the economy in the context of the simple Keynesian model?

4. What shapes of the *IS* and *LM* curves are most conducive to the use of monetary policy for reducing unemployment? What underlying conditions give rise to these shapes?

5. *a.* How is an increase in the rate of growth of the money supply perceived to affect the economy in the context of the new quantity theory?
   b. What conditions are required for the change stipulated in part *a* to be effective?

6. If the country is experiencing a high rate of inflation and the Federal Reserve reduces the rate of growth of the money supply, what are the immediate or short-term effects of this policy likely to be? Long-term effects?

7. *a.* According to the rational expectations hypothesis, is it possible for the government to reduce unemployment by increasing the rate of growth of the money supply? First consider a situation where the policy change is unexpected and then where it is expected.

b. According to the rational expectations hypothesis, is it possible to reduce inflation without increasing unemployment? Explain.

8. Cite the major timing problems which confront the successful implementation of monetary policy.

9. It has been argued that the economy would become more stable if the Federal Reserve Open Market Committee were replaced by a computer. Why?

10. How can federal deficits cause inflation? Unemployment?

11. Should the blame for the rapid increase in the U.S. money supply and the resulting inflation during the late 1960s and 1970s be placed entirely on the Federal Reserve? Explain.

12. *a.* What happens to the market demand and supply of goods during inflation?

b. What happens if the government attempts to control inflation by wage and price controls?

CHAPTER 14

INCOME REDISTRIBUTION: POLICIES AND PROBLEMS

A major part of the discussion in the preceding two chapters dealt with government policies to eliminate, or at least reduce, unemployment and inflation. In this chapter the discussion in large part will dwell on government policies to alter the distribution of income among the people. In a sense the preceding chapters also were implicitly concerned with this issue. Unemployment reduces the income of the unemployed relative to employed people. Inflation also affects the income distribution. People whose incomes rise less rapidly than the price level or who hold assets that do not rise with the price level (money) suffer a reduction in income and wealth in absolute and/or relative terms. In this chapter we will be most concerned with policies to help people at the low end of the income scale—the poor. After an explanation of why incomes differ, we will turn to the problems of identifying the poor and measuring the distribution of income. Then we will look at some of the policies and programs that influence the distribution of income in the United States, discussing particularly how these policies affect the poor.

SOURCES OF INCOME INEQUALITY

It will be useful at the outset to briefly review the reasons why incomes differ among people. Basically, there are two broad reasons: (1) differences in labor earnings and (2) differences in earnings of capital. A more detailed coverage of the labor and capital markets is presented in the companion micro text, but an intuitive explanation of these markets will suffice at this point. Let us consider first the sources of differences in labor earnings. There are two: (1) differences in wages or salaries and (2) differences in hours worked. Wages or salaries differ for a variety of reasons. Perhaps most obvious are differences due to skills. Other things equal, highly skilled people tend to earn higher incomes than those with few skills. Skilled people are more productive than unskilled individuals which makes it possible for them to earn higher salaries, and the extra income compensates for the expense of schooling or training necessary to acquire skills. Of course, innate differences among people allow some to acquire certain skills easier than others. This is especially true in music, art, athletics, and mathematics to name a few. Experience also counts. People with many years of experience tend to earn more than newcomers because of skills acquired through years of experience and/or because of greater responsibility of the job. This is particularly true of highly skilled occupations. In relatively unskilled occupations, experience tends to make less of a difference in wages. Working conditions also influence wages. Jobs which involve harsh working conditions or are located in remote areas generally pay higher wages than those with pleasant working conditions or located in desirable locations. Discrimination can also affect wages, resulting in lower incomes for members of minority groups. Given a person's wage or salary, the number of hours worked also will influence income. Some people moonlight, working two or three different jobs, while others may be content with a part-time job, taking instead satisfaction from more leisure. Of course, there are others who may be unable to find a job because of unemployment or are unable to work because of physical or mental disability.

Differences between people in the amount of capital owned and in the rate of return on capital also create income inequality. People acquire capital by saving part of their income and/or by inheriting it, usually from parents or other family members. For a given rate of saving, a high-income person will acquire more capital than a low-income individual; for a given income, a person who saves a large fraction of that income will accumulate more capital than a spendthrift. In addition, capital is transferred from one generation to another by inheritances, after inheritance taxes, of course. Finally, the income of owners of capital will depend on its rate of return; high rates of return yield a higher income to those people having the necessary skills to manage capital and willingness to put forth the effort. The willingness to bear risk also influences the rate of return or income from capital. High-risk ventures may pay off handsomely or they may fail. Those people with the good luck, effort, and skills to succeed end up with more income than those who fail.

It is evident from the preceding discussion that the natural outcome of a market economy will be one where incomes are distributed unequally. From the beginning of civilization, societies have wrestled with the problems of what and how much, if anything, should be done to bring the income distribution toward more equality. There can never be complete agreement on these questions because people differ in their preferences for social action. Many people argue that society has an obligation to help its less fortunate members and should therefore take some income away from higher-income people in order to bring the poor up to a higher standard of living. Others maintain that it is not equitable to deprive people who wish to work and save their money. Also, supply siders argue that high taxes on high-income people reduce incentives, causing a reduction in GNP which in turn makes everyone worse off.

It is evident, however, that in the United States and perhaps in most countries the majority of people feel that society should take some action to alter the income distribution toward more equality. This desire is reflected by the various government programs and policies designed to take money away from high-income people in order to provide some help to those with low incomes. Much of the discussion to follow will cover these policies and programs along with some of the problems or side effects which they cause.

POVERTY DEFINED

At first glance it may seem odd to be concerned with such a seemingly obvious definition. Surely, you might say, the poor are the people with little money. In general terms you would certainly be correct—additional cash in the pockets of the poor would go a long way in alleviating poverty. But how much additional cash? How low does a family's income have to be before the family is considered poverty stricken?

During 1983 the government considered an income of $10,178 per year to be the "poverty line" for a family of four. A single individual living alone with an income of about half this amount would be considered to be on the edge of poverty. We should remember that the demarcation line that defines the so-called poor is used purely for convenience of definition. A family a few dollars over the line is really not much better off than a family a few dollars below, although the former is not defined as poor, whereas the latter is.

The definition of poverty has changed over the years, partly because of inflation and partly because of general economic growth. In the early 1960s, for example, when the nation became acutely aware of the current poverty problem, a $3,000 income per year for a family of four was considered to be the cutoff point. Back in the late 1920s and early 1930s, families with $3,000 per year income would have been considered well off. The poverty line then was something less than $2,000 per year. If we compare the United States with most other nations, a $10,000 per year equivalent level of purchasing power would be considered quite comfortable. In the less developed countries the equivalent of a $10,000 yearly income in current U.S. purchasing power would be considered a mark of absolute affluence.

It is quite evident, then, that poverty is a relative thing. Its definition depends to a large extent on the public conscience. As the nation's overall average income rises, so does the accepted demarcation line between the "rish" and "poor."

Even recognizing the tendency for the definition of poverty to change over the years and from country to country, the selection of a single number to represent the poverty line is, as you might suspect, a gross oversimplification. Perhaps most important is the need to recognize the variety of circumstances and environments in which people find themselves. For example, we would expect a family with young children to require more income to maintain a certain living standard than a couple with no children.

Looking at Table 14–1, it appears that in spite of the old cliché, two *cannot* live as cheaply as one. However, comparing the single person with the married

---

TABLE 14–1   Estimated annual budget cost for a moderate living standard in urban United States, 1984*

Single person, under 35 years old	$10,307
Husband and wife, under 35 years old:	
No children	13,908
One child under 6 years	17,261
Two children under 6 years	19,250
Husband and wife, 35–54 years old:	
One child, 6–15 years	23,097
Two children, older 6–15 years of age	27,827
Three children, oldest 6–15 years of age	32,007

    * Adjusted 1967 data, using the increase in the consumer price index between 1967 and 1984 as adjustment factor.
    Source of 1967 data *U.S. Statistical Abstract*, 1969, p. 349.

---

couple, it does appear that two living together can live more economically than two living separately, which tells us something about the economic incentive for marriage. Also, as shown in Table 14–1, families with older children have to spend considerably more than families with younger children to maintain the same standard of living.

Although the living costs quoted in Table 14–1 provide for a standard of living much above the poverty level, they do make it clear that different family circumstances require different incomes to reach a comparable living standard. For example, a single person of college age can live moderately well on about $10,000 per year. A family with three children of school age will need more than three times this amount to attain the same living standard.

Place of residence also affects the amount of income required to attain a given living standard. The Social Security Administration has estimated that living costs for farm families are about 30 percent lower than the corresponding figures for urban families, although this estimate probably is too low. The Bureau of the Census estimates farm living costs to be 15 percent lower than the corresponding figure for urban families. Also, living costs in small towns tend to be 10 to 15 percent lower than those in large cities. Probably the main difference is in housing. Housing costs and rents tend to be higher in large cities than in small towns and rural areas.

PERMANENT INCOME

In the discussion so far we have considered income only during a given year. If a family's income is below the poverty line for a particular year, the family is considered poor. But even taking into account the complexities mentioned in the previous section, defining poverty by a single year's income still involves some problems. We must consider as well variation or changes in income. Perhaps the most noticeable problem here is the year-to-year fluctuation in income. Consider two comparable families: one has a steady $12,000 per year income and the other has an income that fluctuates from, say, $6,000 per year to $20,000 per year every other year. Over a period of 10 years, the $12,000 per year family is never included in the poverty group if the cutoff point is $10,178 per year. On the other hand, the second family would fall within the poverty group in 5 of the 10 years, even though its average income over this 10-year period would have been $13,000 per year—$1,000 per year higher than the first family.

Thus, the incidence of poverty, as poverty is currently defined, can be reduced simply by reducing the variability of income. Indeed, the second family actually could suffer an absolute reduction in average income over a number of years and still be defined as "better off" simply because it escapes the every-other-year poverty classification. But it is hard to imagine that the second family would consider itself better off with a $1,000 per year smaller, although less variable, income.

A related problem, and perhaps even more important, is the way in which a family, or person, views its long-term income potential. Many college students, for example, do not consider themselves poverty stricken even though their incomes might place them in this category. They know that in a few years or less, they will be able to enjoy a substantial increase in income. Thus, college students tend to enjoy a much higher standard of living than, say, ghetto dwellers with comparable incomes but little or no hope of ever improving their lot. There can be little doubt, too, that the psychological effect of having a low income is much different for a college student than for a ghetto dweller. The hope of someday breaking out of one's poverty conditions makes these conditions somewhat more bearable. In a sense, poverty is a state of mind as well as the state of one's bank account.

The fact that people tend to look at their long-run earning potential in making consumption decisions probably makes current expenditures on consumption a better measure of poverty than current income. For example, if you have a current income of $6,000 per year but expect to be making $20,000 per year in two years, your current consumption per year is likely to be larger than someone who expects little or no increase in income. The idea that long-run average income, or permanent income as it is called, is an important determinant of current consumption was first expressed by Friedman in his book *The Theory of the Consumption Function*. This idea is generally referred to as the permanent-income hypothesis.

Another reason for paying attention to current expenditures instead of current income as a measure of poverty is to take account of people who live off their savings. This is particularly important for retired people. For example, it is not uncommon to observe an older person or couple selling some property or stocks to pay for medical care, buy a new car, or take a trip. Indeed, people save during their lifetimes for these very purposes. This is not to say, however, that there is no need to be concerned about poverty among older people. The point is that there is a great deal of difference between a couple who has $8,000 per year income and zero savings or wealth, and a couple who has the same income but $100,000 in savings or wealth. The first couple is poor and the second is not, even though both would be included in the poverty class. Of course, one might raise the question: Would it be fair for society to exclude the second family from welfare benefits if it has lived frugally and saved while the first couple did not?

THE DISTRIBUTION OF INCOME IN THE UNITED STATES

As one might expect, poverty is closely related to the distribution of income. If everyone had the same income, the question of poverty would not be likely to come up; everyone would be equally rich or equally poor, whichever you prefer. The fact that incomes do differ means that someone must be on the lower end of the income scale. Therefore, in measuring the extent of poverty it is useful to look first at the distribution of income.

In Table 14–2 we present the percentages of families that fall within six specified before-income-tax brackets for 1950, 1970, and 1982. To make the

TABLE 14–2 Percentage distribution of money income of families in the United States, selected years (constant 1982 dollars)

Annual income level	1950	1970	1982
Under $5,000	15.0%	4.6%	5.0%
$ 5,000 to 9,999	18.6	9.4	10.6
10,000 to 14,999		11.2	12.4
15,000 to 19,999		16.1	12.1
20,000 to 24,999	66.4	10.1	12.3
25,000 to 34,999		27.2	19.5
35,000 to 49,999		12.4	16.0
50,000 and over		9.0	10.9
	100.0%	100.0%	100.0%
Median family income	$13,308	$24,528	$23,433

Source: U.S. Bureau of the Census, *Current Population Reports,* Series P-60, no. 142, "Money Income of Households, Families, and Persons in the United States: 1982," February 1984, p. 39.

three years comparable, the 1950 and 1970 income figures were adjusted for changes in the general price level before the percentages were computed. Thus, any upward movement shown in family incomes is due to real economic growth rather than to inflation.

From the figures presented in Table 14–2, we would have to conclude that the old cliché "the rich get richer and the poor get poorer" does not hold true, at least for the United States during the post–World War II era. The percentage of families below the $5,000 income level decreased from 15.0 percent in 1950 to 5 percent in 1982 (in constant 1982 prices). Even more dramatic is the increase in the proportion of families in the $50,000 and above category—rising from a relatively small proportion in 1950 (exact figure unavailable) to 10.9 percent in 1982 (also in constant 1982 prices). The near doubling of median family income in constant prices during this period reveals the importance of economic growth in bringing low-income people up to a higher standard of living.[1]

---

[1] Median family income is defined as that level of income which 50 percent of the families are below and 50 percent above.

We cannot tell from the overall upward movement of family incomes, however, whether the dispersion of incomes is becoming narrower or whether poor families are getting a relatively smaller slice of the pie. The figures in Table 14–3 provide some indication of the relative distribution of incomes.

TABLE 14–3 Percentage share of total before-tax U.S. money income received by each fifth of families, selected years

Family group	1950	1970	1982
Lowest fifth	4.5%	5.4%	4.7%
Second fifth	11.9	12.2	11.2
Third fifth	17.4	17.6	17.1
Fourth fifth	23.6	23.8	24.3
Highest fifth	42.7	40.9	42.7

Source: U.S. Bureau of the Census, *Current Population Reports,* Series P-60, no. 142, "Money Income of Households, Families, and Persons in the United States: 1982," February 1984, p. 47.

Here we observe that if all families are ranked by income level from the lowest to the highest, the lowest 20 percent received 4.7 percent of the total money income in 1982. However, it should be noted that the lower-income groups increased their share of total income during the post–World War II years. For example, the lowest fifth of the families increased their share of the income pie from 4.5 percent in 1950 to 5.4 percent in 1970. In the relatively high unemployment year of 1982, the share of income going to the poorest families decreased almost to the 1950 level. One should bear in mind, however, that these figures are based on before-tax income. Since the proportion of income left after taxes is smaller for the higher-income people (Table 8–2), figures based on net after-tax income should exhibit less dispersion. At any rate, the figures do reveal the importance of maintaining a high level of employment. When unemployment increases, incomes of the poor decline relative to incomes of the rich.

One should also bear in mind when looking at income distribution figures that the figures do not reflect income in kind, such as food stamps, public housing, and medical care, that is provided to low-income people through various government programs. If the monetary value of this income were added to money income, the distribution of total income would be less unequal than shown in Table 14–3.

THE LORENZ CURVE

Economists have long used a device to describe the nation's income distribution that is perhaps a bit more illustrative than numbers, such as those shown in Table 14–3—a device called the Lorenz curve after the man who developed it. The Lorenz curve is obtained by plotting the cumulative percentage of the nation's income against the cumulative percentage of the nation's families or individuals receiving this income. Generally, income is represented on the vertical axis of the diagram and households or individuals on the horizontal axis, as shown in Figure 14–1.

Perhaps the easiest way to understand the Lorenz curve is to ask: What would the curve look like if the nation's income were distributed in a perfectly

---

FIGURE 14–1   The Lorenz curve

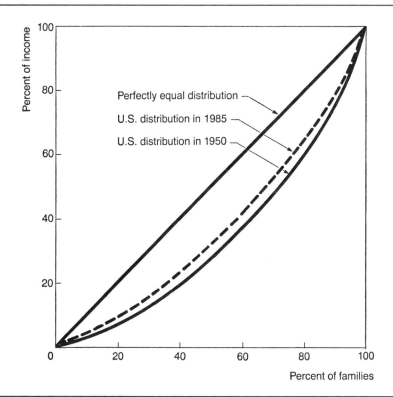

---

equal manner? In other words, suppose everyone received the same income. In this case, 20 percent of the nation's families would receive 20 percent of the income, 40 percent would receive 40 percent of the income, etc. Plotting these figures on a Lorenz curve diagram would result in a straight, upward sloping line, as shown in Figure 14–1.

Of course, no nation exhibits a completely equal distribution of income. The lowest 20 percent of the families generally receive substantially less than 20 percent of the income, whereas the highest 20 percent of the families receive much more than 20 percent of the income. What does the Lorenz curve look like in a situation such as this? If we plot the percentage of income received by the lowest 20 percent of the families, say, in the United States for 1950, we go up on the vertical axis to only 4.5 percent according to the figures in Table 14–3. Proceeding on, we see that the cumulative income of the bottom 40 percent of the families, as shown in Table 13–3 for 1950, amounts to 16.4 percent of the total income for that year. Hence, in plotting this combination, we choose the point that corresponds to 40 percent on the horizontal axis and 16.4 on the vertical axis. If we continue on in this manner for the 60 and 80 percent points on the horizontal axis, we obtain points that also lie below the straight, bisecting line. By connecting these points, we obtain the Lorenz curve. Note that this curve lies below the straight line that depicts perfect equality.

We can conclude therefore that the more unequal the distribution of income, the more curvature there will be in the Lorenz curve. Indeed, if all the income of the country were received by just one family, the curve would be a vertical line extending up from the 100 percent point in Figure 14–1. By the same token, if there is a trend toward a more equal distribution of income, the Lorenz curve will flatten out and move closer to the straight, bisecting line. As mentioned, there appears to have been a trend toward a more equal distribution of income in the United States in recent times. Thus, the Lorenz curve is somewhat flatter now than it was 20 to 30 years ago. This is illustrated in Figure 14–1, where the 1985 Lorenz curve lies closer to the perfect equality line than the 1950 curve.

THE GINI RATIO

Economists sometimes use another term to describe the distribution of income—the Gini ratio or Gini coefficient. The Gini ratio is derived from the Lorenz curve diagram and is defined as the ratio of the area between the Lorenz curve and the perfect equality line to the total area below the perfect equality line. In terms of Figure 14–2, it is the ratio of area A over the total area $A + B$; that is, the Gini ratio is equal to $A/(A + B)$.

FIGURE 14–2   Deriving the Gini ratio

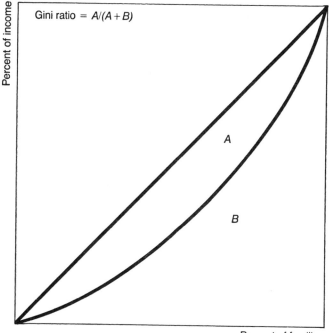

The size of the Gini ratio or coefficient cay vary from zero to one. As a nation moves closer to perfect equality in its income distribution, the Gini ratio will approach zero. This occurs because area A, the numerator in the fraction, becomes smaller and smaller as the Lorenz curve becomes flatter and approaches the perfect equality line. At the extreme of perfect equality, area A disappears or becomes zero, which means that the value of the fraction becomes zero. Conversely, as a nation moves toward complete inequality of the income distribution, the Lorenz curve approaches the boundaries of the rectangle and area B grows smaller and smaller. At the extreme of complete inequality, area B disappears, so the ratio is equal to A/A or one.

Nations that have a relatively low Gini ratio have relative equality in their distribution of income. The advantage of using the Gini ratio is that it enables us to describe a nation's income distribution by a single number rather than a series of numbers, such as in Table 14–3, or a diagram, such as Figure 14–2. Of course, the Gini ratio also can be used to describe the income distributions of smaller groups of people, such as states or municipalities.

POVERTY IN THE UNITED STATES

Before turning to the policies and programs aimed at reducing poverty, it will be useful to take a brief look at the extent of poverty in the United States and how it has changed over the years. Each year the Department of Commerce establishes an income level that represents the dividing line between the poor and everyone else. This income is sometimes called the poverty line. It is determined by the amount of income necessary to purchase the essentials such as food, housing, transportation, and clothing that would provide a family with a "lower" living standard as defined by the Department of Commerce. Of course, this income level varies by family size and place of residence—that is, farm versus city. The poverty line for an urban family of four for selected years is presented in Table 14–4 along with the percentage of families in this category having incomes below that level. The poverty line has been moving upward in recent years primarily because of inflation. It is encouraging to note that the percentage of families falling below the poverty line declined by nearly half between 1959 and 1969. However, relatively little improvement is evident be-

TABLE 14–4 The U.S. poverty line and percent of families below the line, 1959–1983 (defined for urban families of four people)

Year	Poverty line (current dollars)	Percent of families below poverty line
1959	$2,973	22.4%
1964	3,169	19.0
1969	3,743	12.1
1974	5,038	11.6
1979	7,412	10.7
1983	10,178	12.3

Source: U.S. Bureau of the Census, *Current Population Reports*, Series P-60, no. 145, "Money Income and Poverty Status of Families in the United States: 1983" (Washington, D.C.: U.S. Government Printing Office, August 1984), p. 3.

tween 1969 and 1979. In fact between 1979 and 1983 there was some regression, because of the recession and increased unemployment during the early 1980s.

It is important to recognize, however, that the incidence of poverty (percentage of families falling below the poverty line) varies considerably between different families according to circumstances. As shown in Table 14–5, poverty

---

TABLE 14–5 Selected characteristics of families in relation to the incidence of poverty, 1983

Selected characteristic	Percent below poverty line
1. Race and sex of Householder:	
White—all families	9.7%
White—female head	28.3
Black—all families	32.4
Black—female head	53.8
2. Age of Householder:	
15 to 24 years	29.5
25 to 34 years	16.2
35 to 44 years	12.0
45 to 54 years	8.8
55 to 59 years	8.5
60 to 64 years	8.7
65 and over	8.7
3. Educational attainment of Householder:	
Elementary	16.8
High school	10.5
College	4.7
4. Size of family:	
2 persons	10.1
4 persons	11.7
6 persons	21.5
7 persons or more	36.3
5. Employment status of Householder:	
Employed	7.2
Unemployed	36.2

Source: U.S. Bureau of the Census, *Current Population Reports,* Series P-60, no. 145, "Money Income and Poverty Status of Families in the United States: 1983" (Washington, D.C.: U.S. Government Printing Office, August 1984), p. 27.

---

is most prevalent among minority families, families having a female head, those having a head under 25 years of age, families headed by a person with a low level of schooling, families with many children, and families where the head is unemployed.

IMPLICIT PROGRAMS THAT HELP THE POOR

Before considering the more explicit poverty or income redistribution programs, we ought to mention that the extent of poverty is influenced a great deal by other circumstances in the economy as well.

1. General economic growth. Although we do not generally consider economic growth as a program to help the poor, there can be no doubt that the across-the-board increase in incomes has greatly reduced the extent of poverty in the United States and in the other more highly developed nations of the world. This is clearly shown in Table 14–4, where the incidence of poverty during the 1960s was reduced by about half. Remember, too, that these figures are based on a current definition of poverty. Had we used the poverty definition from the 1930s the incidence in 1983 would have been even lower, indeed almost nonexistent.

2. A full-employment economy. Since poor people make up a disproportionately large share of the unskilled labor force, a rise in unemployment hits poor people hardest. In the discussion of unemployment in Chapter 3, it was pointed out that the unskilled tend to be the first laid off. The unemployment rate among blue-collar workers rises faster than that for all workers during a recession, in spite of the fact that the blue-collar category includes many skilled artisans who do not face as great a threat of layoffs. Thus, during recessions the poor tend to be hurt the most.

3. A stable price economy. The presence of an unexpected high rate of inflation also hurts the poor; indeed it is likely to *make* some people poor. Those who keep a relatively large share of their assets in the form of cash, savings deposits, bonds, or life insurance policies are, of course, made relatively poorer by inflation. Contrary to popular opinion, poor people tend not to be large debtors. Because unexpected inflation helps debtors at the expense of creditors, the poor as a group tend to end up relatively worse off during inflation. Retired people living off monetary savings or relatively fixed incomes also experience a reduction in the purchasing power of their already low incomes.

4. Public education. Although we may not think of public education as a policy or program to help the poor, there can be no doubt that such has been the case. The relationship of education to poverty is very clear. If we take a cross section of poor people, we find them in many different situations. Some are white, others black; some live in big cities, others in small towns or on farms. We find the poor in every region of the country and from divergent backgrounds. Indeed, the poor are far from a homogeneous group. If we tried to find a common characteristic that fitted most poor people, aside from a lack of money, probably the closest we could come would be their low level and poor quality of education.

The relationship between income and education is illustrated by Table 14–6. Here we see that median income is over three times larger for families where the major wage earner has four or more years of college than for those families where the breadwinner has less than eight years of schooling.

The mere fact that income bears a close positive relationship to education does not guarantee, of course, that large numbers of poor people can use education to escape from poverty. Education is a very costly activity and not many poor people could afford to purchase much if they had to pay the full cost. Thus, if education is to be a major means of escape from poverty, a large share of its cost must be borne by the public. In public elementary and high schools the entire operating costs are financed by tax revenues. In public colleges and universities student tuition generally covers a third or less of the operating costs of the institutions, with tax revenue covering most of the re-

TABLE 14–6   Relationship between income and education in the United States, 1982

Educational level	Median annual income
Less than 8 years	$12,047
8 years	15,251
1 to 3 years high school	17,517
4 years high school	23,837
1 to 3 years college	27,440
4 or more years college	38,255

Source: U.S. Bureau of the Census, *Current Population Reports,* Series P-60, no. 142, "Money Income of Households, Families, and Persons in the United States: 1982," February 1984, p. 98

mainder. There can be little doubt that the long history of public education in the United States has contributed to the upward mobility of people coming from poor families, resulting in a more equal income distribution. If all education had to be paid for by the parents of school-age children and young people, children from low-income families would have less chance of breaking out of the low-income level. This is not to say that publicly financed education should result in perfect equality of income, but it should be regarded as a major factor that moves the income distribution in the direction of more equality.

The use of publicly financed education has become a widely accepted means of achieving more income equality probably because it tends to provide equality of opportunity as opposed to equality of income. Taxpayers seem more willing to help people who in turn will help themselves than to transfer income directly to low-income people who many taxpayers may believe are unwilling to work and improve their lot in life.

In spite of generous public support of educational institutions in the United States, it has been argued that the poor and lower middle class still subsidize the college education of higher-income people. The argument has some validity. Low-income people pay taxes to support public colleges and universities but utilize these institutions to a much smaller extent than the higher-income people. This is especially true for poor people among minority groups.

One way to make higher education more accessible and responsive to poor people is for the government to directly support or subsidize people (students) rather than educational institutions. One proposal is to give students vouchers that they could "spend" at the educational institution of their choice. This would have the advantage also of creating some competition between educational institutions, which in turn should promote greater efficiency and higher quality of services provided.

Recently a number of states have ruled it unconstitutional to finance public schools by property taxes because of the resulting inequality in educational opportunity. A high-income community will tend to have a higher tax base, and as a result more income is generated to operate the school system than in a poor community. Financing schools by means of a state or federal income tax would remove some of the inequality brought on by financing public schools through local property taxes.[2]

Indeed, it can be argued that schools in poorer communities should be even better than schools in high-income communities in order to make up for some of the environmental disadvantages experienced by children in poor families and neighborhoods. It is becoming more evident that the attitude of parents toward education and the opportunities that children have for out-of-school learning are important determinants of future earning potential.

EXPLICIT PROGRAMS TO HELP THE POOR

In addition to the points mentioned in the previous section, there are other programs and policies designed to alter the income distribution toward more equality.

1. Minimum wage laws. Since poor people tend to be on the low end of the wage scale, minimum wage laws affect the poor primarily. At first glance it may appear that minimum wage laws are a boon to poor people. After all, if a poor person cannot be paid less than $3.50 per hour, say, income will be higher than if the person's wage were $2.50 per hour. What is often forgotten, however, is that the higher minimum wage can benefit poor people only if they are working. If the market wage is lower than the minimum wage, the inevitable result will be a reduction in the employment opportunities for people at the low end of the wage scale, mainly teenagers and unskilled workers. As wages increase because of minimum wage legislation, employers find it more profitable to substitute machines for labor, thereby eliminating some low-paying jobs. It can be argued, therefore, that minimum wage laws work to the detriment of low-income people by making it more difficult for them to find jobs. The high rate of unemployment among teenagers is a case in point.[3]

2. Farm programs. Since poverty has been and still is relatively prevalent on farms and in rural areas, various farm programs have been designed to bolster farm incomes. In large part these programs have taken the form of supporting the prices of various agricultural products above their free market levels. Again, it may appear reasonable to believe that such a program would benefit poor farmers. If a farmer can receive $5 per bushel for wheat, for example, his income ought to be higher than if $4 per bushel were received. But one of the problems of such a program is that the setting of a support price higher than the market level reduces the quantity demanded of farm products (which includes foreign buyers as well). Thus, the government may have to set limits on how much farmers can produce in order to keep the surpluses at manageable levels. At any rate, the nation ends up using scarce resources to produce products that no one wants to buy.

An even more important problem of farm programs is that they end up

---

[2] Of course, owners of real property would benefit from a reduction in property taxes because of greater reliance on income taxes.

[3] For further discussion of the effects of minimum wage laws, see Chapter 11 (The Labor Market) of the companion micro text.

helping large, high-income farmers to a much greater degree than they help small, poor farmers. A little simple arithmetic makes this point clear. A small farmer who produces 100 bushels of wheat for sale will gain $100 extra income if the price of wheat is raised from $4 to $5 per bushel by the support price. But the large farmer who sells, say, 40,000 bushels of wheat per year gains $40,000 in extra income from the program.

The amount of government program benefits on a per farm basis for 1978 is presented in Table 14–7. Adding the direct payments to farmers to the benefits

TABLE 14–7   Government program benefits to farmers in 1978 (dollars per farm)

Source of benefit	Size of farm (crop acres)			
	Less than 70	220– 259	1,000– 1,499	2,500 and over
Direct payments	$365	$2,684	$14,282	$35,955
Price benefits	195	1,375	7,258	22,000
Less income foregone on set-aside acres	293	2,244	6,235	13,694
Net benefits per farm	267	1,815	15,305	44,261

Source: William Lin, James Johnson, and Linda Calvin, "Farm Commodity Programs: Who Participates and Who Benefits," U.S. Department of Agriculture, Economic Research Service, Agricultural Economic Report no. 474, September 1981, p. 25.

obtained by the higher prices resulting from farm programs and subtracting the income forgone by not being able to farm set-aside acres, we see that the smallest category of farms received on the average $267 per farm in 1978, whereas the largest category received $44,261 per farm. It is clear that farm programs have contributed to a more unequal distribution of income in agriculture.

While on the topic of farm income, the idea of parity price should be explained. The *parity price* of a commodity is the price that farmers would have to receive for that item in order for it to have the same purchasing power as in some base period. For example, if the price of wheat in the base period was $1 per bushel and the prices of goods and services that farmers buy increased by eight times from the base period to the current year, then the 100 percent of parity price of wheat in the current year would be $8 per bushel. In using the parity concept, the 1910–14 base period invariably is used. The use of this base is not purely accidental because these years have come to be known as the "golden age of agriculture." During this period agricultural product prices were relatively high in comparison with the prices of goods and services purchased by farmers.

The goal of some farm groups is to raise farm prices to 100 percent of parity. In other words, they would like a given "bundle" of farm products to be able to buy as much now as in 1910–14. Since that time, it has been rare for farm products to approach 100 percent of parity. In the post–World War II years, farm products have commonly sold in the range of 60 to 90 percent of parity.

Aside from the fact that 1910–14 was an unusually profitable period for agriculture, one might think that the goal of 100 percent of parity would be a reasonable one to strive for. However, this goal has not been attainable during the post–World War II period, and it is not likely it will be attained in the foreseeable future. The main reason is that the index of prices paid by farmers, constructed by the U.S. Department of Agriculture, does not fully reflect quality improvements in the inputs purchased by farmers. Consequently, this index is biased upward which in turn has the effect of making the 100 percent of parity price too high. At a full 100 percent of parity, farmers would be able to buy more goods and services per unit of product than in the 1910–14 period. An attempt by the government to support farm product prices at 100 percent of parity would inevitably result in large surpluses of unsold products. In the case of dairy products, price supports at levels below the 100 percent of parity market still have resulted in huge surpluses of dairy products. The consequences of price supports are discussed more thoroughly in Chapter 8 of the micro text.

3. Welfare programs. Included under this general heading are a variety of programs specifically designed to help poor people, such as the Aid to Families with Dependent Children (AFDC), hospital and medical care for the poor, school lunches, food stamps, and public housing. Although these programs undoubtedly help the poor, they have undergone a growing amount of criticism in recent years. In spite of substantial increases in per capita real income over the past 10 to 15 years, welfare programs have been increasing and costing more and more each year. Moreover, taxpayers complain that not enough of the welfare funds reach poor people; too much is eaten up by highly paid administrators in the welfare bureaucracy or goes to high-income professionals, such as physicians and lawyers. The present welfare programs also give rise to a number of undesirable side effects.

For example, there is the built-in incentive for breaking up families. Poor families with several children find that the income of the wife and children can be doubled in many instances if the husband leaves home and the family goes on welfare. Consider, for example, a man with a wife and two children who earns $600 per month. If the husband and wife separate for one reason or another, the wife may then become eligible for welfare payments under the AFDC program. In many states the welfare payments would be as high as the husband's take-home pay. As a result the family (husband plus wife) could double its income by the husband leaving home. This provides a rather strong incentive for families to separate, at least for the purpose of applying for welfare. It also acts as a strong disincentive for families to reunite once they have separated.

In addition, the program takes over the support of many children born to unmarried mothers. This is not to say that *all* single-parent families have resulted from a desire to benefit from the program. But the large increase in single-parent families coinciding with the inception of the AFDC program makes it hard to believe that the program is neutral in its effect on family behavior. Any program that increases the number of children growing up without both parents while shifting the cost of rearing them to society leaves a great deal to be desired.

4. Social security and unemployment insurance. These two programs are more straightforward and less controversial than the ones we have just discussed. Perhaps the major criticism of the social security program is that it has elements of a 100 percent tax phenomenon. If a retired person wants to supplement his or her income with part-time work, the individual must be careful not to earn over the allowable maximum, or else the social security benefits will be lost. If these benefits are lost, it is equivalent to a 100 percent tax on wage income over the cutoff point. Surprisingly, there is no limit on the amount of income that can be earned from capital in being able to qualify for benefits.

5. Progressive income tax. Although the federal income tax provides the major share of revenue for the federal government, the fact that tax rates increase with income also makes it an income redistribution device in that it takes relatively more income away from high-income people than from those with low incomes. The justification for the progressive income tax was presented in Chapter 8. A couple of additional points might be made here. In recent years there has been more skepticism about how effective the progressive income tax is as a device to redistribute income. If supply side economics is correct and high marginal tax rates inhibit economic growth, the poor are likely to suffer more than high-income people. Unskilled people tend to be the first to be laid off and last to be rehired. Moreover, when the economy is sluggish, there may be less chance for poor people to move up to better-paying jobs.

A second and somewhat more subtle point is that the removal of relatively more income from high-income families by a progressive income tax reduces the family's ability to redistribute income among its own members. When families redistribute income among their own members, there appears to be a tendency for the low-income members to receive more help than those with high incomes. This practice has the effect of making the income distribution somewhat more equal than it would otherwise be. Thus, it is not clear how much more income is redistributed by progressive taxation.

THE NEGATIVE INCOME TAX

First proposed by Milton Friedman in his 1962 book, *Capitalism and Freedom,* the negative income tax has been called a number of things including "income maintenance" or a "family assistance plan." The proposal is surprisingly simple. If society is really serious about helping poor people and wants to help them in the most efficient way possible, the best way is for the government to supplement their incomes by a so-called "negative tax"—a payment from the government to the poor.

Perhaps the easiest way to understand how the negative income tax plan might work is to look at a specific example. Suppose that under the ordinary income tax schedule, a family of four could earn up to $10,000 per year without paying any federal income tax. Let us consider the case of a poor family of four with a total income of $6,000 per year. This family would file an income tax return reporting that it had an income deficit of $4,000. Let us assume that the negative tax rate or the refund rate is 50 percent. In this case the family would receive a $2,000 check (0.50 × $4,000) from the government, which in a sense is a negative tax. Thus, the family would end up with a total income of $8,000: $6,000 from its initial income plus $2,000 in negative taxes.

It is important to recognize, too, that the negative tax rate must be something less than 100 percent. In other words, the government would not make up the entire difference between a family's initial income and the zero tax income ($10,000 in our example). For example, suppose the family had an opportunity to earn an extra $1,000, so that its initial before-tax income would increase to $7,000. With a $3,000 deficit, the government would mail a check for $1,500, giving the family a total income of $8,500: the initial $7,000 plus the $1,500 negative tax. In this second case the family's after-tax income would have increased to $8,500. If the government had made up the entire difference between the $10,000 base and the family's actual income, the total income would have been $10,000 in both cases. Thus, there would be no incentive for the family to earn additional income if it remained below $7,000. But as long as the negative tax rate is less than 100 percent, the family still has an incentive to earn money on its own. Of course, the negative tax rate and the base zero tax income can be set at any level desired as long as the rate is kept below 100 percent. The 50 percent rate and $10,000 income are just examples. Additional refinements could be built into the plan, such as allowing deductions from actual income for such things as medical expenses above a certain level before calculating the negative tax.

The arguments in favor of the negative tax are quite convincing. First, it would be possible to eliminate or at least reduce the variety of present programs that are overburdened with administrative expense and often treat different groups very unequally. The negative income tax would not suffer from either of these shortcomings. Second, poor people would not have to suffer the indignities and degradation that they are now subject to in the welfare schemes that label the poor in full view of their neighbors. Also, programs that dole out a few dollars for this and a few dollars for that treat the poor as if they were second-class citizens who could not be trusted with money. To be poor is bad enough, but to suffer the indignities of the present welfare setup is more than some can bear.

Of course, the negative income tax scheme does present some problems. Probably the major concern of middle- and high-income taxpayers is that the assurance of a guaranteed annual income might prompt people with low-paying jobs to simply quit working and live off the taxes of employed people. However, the less than 100 percent negative tax rate feature would mitigate this problem somewhat, since a family always would have a higher net income by working than by not working. Indeed, the AFDC and social security programs are as open to this criticism as the negative tax scheme. Granted there are likely to be some people with low-paying second jobs who would quit such jobs if their income were supplemented. This would increase full- or part-time employment opportunities for teenagers and college students, however.

The way in which people might spend the money received from negative tax payments also troubles some people. What is to stop poor people from buying alcohol, football tickets, and color television sets with their extra income (i.e., from acting like middle-class Americans)? Our willingness to provide welfare for low-income people appears to be influenced by what the recipients get from the welfare. Necessities such as food, clothing, and shelter are most desired, as evidenced by the food stamp, AFDC, and public housing programs.

Yet this is a somewhat naive approach. If a poor family receives $100 worth of food stamps or subsidized housing, this leaves $100 more of its own money with which to buy such nonessentials as mentioned above. Also, providing welfare "in kind" rather than in money is not likely to maximize the welfare of the recipients for a given budgetary cost. Items that are given free or at a reduced price will of course be accepted but may not be what the family would have bought had they received an equivalent amount of cash. If what they would have bought is different, we can infer that the payment in kind is less desirable than the cash. For example, which would you prefer: $10,000 worth of low-income housing or $10,000 in cash? The provision of low-income housing also has a tendency to create ghettos, something that could be avoided if low-income people were given an equivalent amount of money and were free to live where they chose.

The cost of a negative income scheme is regarded by some as being out of the realm of possibility. Naturally, if the minimum income level were set high, the cost would be high. But this is not the question. The relevant question is whether the amount society decides to spend on welfare, say, $200 billion, can be more efficiently spent by the current setup or by the negative tax scheme. There can be little doubt that the negative tax scheme would be much more efficient and equitable. We could avoid a large part of the welfare bureaucracy that has grown up over the years, giving this money directly to poor people. Moreover, we could be sure that the poor would indeed receive the benefits, and in ways that would not degrade them or label them as second-class citizens.

If a negative income tax plan were ever put into effect, it would be important to design it in such a way that families would not have an incentive to separate, such as occurs under the AFDC program. One way of removing such an incentive would be to require the husband to pay as taxes the equivalent of his wife's negative tax payment when he files his income tax at the end of the year. In this case the family would receive the same income regardless of whether they stayed together or separated. In fact there would be an incentive to stay together in this case because a family living in one location should be able to live more economically than one living in two locations.

MAIN POINTS OF CHAPTER 14

1. People have different incomes because of differences in time worked, wages earned, and capital owned. Wages differ because of differences in skill requirements, experience, working conditions, and discrimination. Also, the existence of risk means that successful people in the professional or business world end up earning more than those who are unsuccessful. The amount of capital owned depends on income differences, the willingness to save by forgoing current consumption, and inheritance from parents.

2. The definition of poverty depends to a large extent on the average income and wealth of the population. The higher the income, the higher is the line of demarcation between rich and poor.

3. The family income necessary to rise above the poverty classification also depends on size of family and place of residence.

4. The extent of poverty in any one year depends on the long-run expected income as

well as current income. The idea that current consumption depends on long-run expected income is known as the permanent income hypothesis.

5. The percentage of families under the $5,000 per year income level has fallen from 15.0 percent in 1950 to 5 percent in 1982 in constant 1982 dollars.

6. During the past 30 years the before-tax income distribution in the United States has tended toward greater equality.

7. The **Lorenz curve** shows the percentage of total income received by a certain percentage of the population. A straight-line diagonal Lorenz curve illustrates perfect equality. The more curvature of the Lorenz curve, the more unequal is the distribution of income.

8. The **Gini ratio** is the ratio of the area between the actual Lorenz curve and the perfect equality line to the total area under the perfect equality line. A Gini ratio of zero denotes complete equality of income, whereas a ratio of one denotes complete inequality.

9. In the United States poverty is more prevalent among black families, young families with a female head, families whose head has a low level of education, large families, and those where the head is unemployed.

10. Because of general economic growth, the percentage of families defined as poor declined by nearly half between 1959 and 1969. However, relatively little improvement is shown after 1969.

11. In the United States the poor benefit greatly from programs or policies not designed specifically as poverty programs. These include: (*a*) general economic growth, (*b*) full employment, (*c*) stable prices, and (*d*) public education.

12. Other programs or policies designed to more specifically help poor people include: (*a*) minimum wage laws, (*b*) farm programs, (*c*) various welfare programs, (*d*) social security and unemployment insurance, and (*e*) the progressive income tax.

13. The farm program and traditional welfare programs have come under increasing criticism in recent years because of their high cost and undesirable side effects on both the poor and the rest of society.

14. **Parity** is defined as the purchasing power of agricultural products in comparison with that which existed in 1910–14. The goal of 100 percent of parity is not likely to be attained over a long period because the index of prices paid by farmers is biased upward due to quality improvements in the inputs bought by farmers.

15. Under the negative income tax plan, families below a specified income level would receive a "negative tax," or payment, from the government.

16. An important feature of the negative income tax plan would be a negative tax rate of less than 100 percent. This would allow families to increase their total incomes without having their negative tax payments decreased by a like amount. Hence, there would still be an incentive for poor people to improve their incomes on their own.

17. A major concern of people about the negative tax scheme is its adverse effect on work incentives. Also, some raise objections that the money will not be "wisely" spent and that the scheme would be too costly for taxpayers.

QUESTIONS FOR THOUGHT AND DISCUSSION

1. *a.* Why are incomes distributed unequally?
   b. What would happen if society attempted to obtain perfect equality in the distribution of income?

2. Because of year-to-year changes in weather and prices, the income of farm families tends to be more variable than the income of nonfarm people. Would this characteristic have any bearing on the incidence of poverty in rural areas during any given year? Explain.

3. *a.* Should people who have lived frugally all their lives and amassed considerable savings be excluded from welfare benefits if their income places them in the poverty class after they have retired? Defend your position.

    b. Should people who have squandered their money on high living during their working years rather than saving for old age be eligible for welfare benefits after they have retired? Defend your position.

4. Between 1959 and 1969 the percentage of families below the poverty line in the United States was reduced by nearly half. From 1969 to 1979 there was very little change in the percentage of families below the poverty line. What may account for the difference between these two periods?

5. Most full-time college students earn a level of income (through part-time and/or summer work) that places them in the poverty class. Yet most college students probably do not consider themselves poverty stricken. Why not?

6. *a.* According to the official income statistics, the rich are getting richer and the poor are getting poorer. True or false? Explain.

    b. Why do the official income distribution figures likely understate the equality of income in the United States?

7. What evidence might be used besides income data to obtain an idea of the dispersion of incomes among the people in a community or country?

8. Using a Lorenz curve illustrate what you believe to be the income distribution among college students as compared to the income distribution for society at large. Which group would have the highest Gini ratio?

9. *a.* What are the characteristics of a family that stands the greatest chance of being poor?

    b. What characteristic is most commonly shared by poor people (besides not having money)?

10. *a.* How would funding of public education by the "voucher system" change public schools?

    b. Who would favor and who would oppose such a system?

11. List the major consequences or side effects of the following programs to help low-income people.

    a. Minimum wage laws.

    b. Farm price support programs.

    c. AFDC program.

    d. Social security.

    e. Progressive income tax.

12. *a.* List the main advantages of the negative income tax scheme.

    b. Why has it not attracted more public support?

PART VI

THE INTERNATIONAL ECONOMY

CHAPTER 15

INTERNATIONAL TRADE AND FINANCE

Our discussion thus far has centered mainly on the national economy. In this chapter and the next we will broaden our perspective somewhat and look at the international economy. We begin with a discussion of trade between nations, that is, international trade, and then in the next and final chapter, we address the issue of economic growth and development primarily in relation to the world's less developed countries (LDCs).

In the discussion of international trade we should bear in mind that nations exist because of artificial boundaries that humans have devised. Were it not for border guards, barricades, and checkpoints, we could travel across national boundaries without being aware that we had done so. The artificial and temporary character of nations or national boundaries is aptly illustrated by their continual formation and dissolution throughout history. For example, we now think of East and West Germany as separate countries, whereas just a few decades ago they were a single country. What was once trade between two people or two business firms now has become international trade between people located in different countries.

The main point to be made here is that international trade is just trade between two people, business firms, or groups of people who happen to find themselves enclosed within different national boundaries. Too frequently we lose sight of this simple fact and consider international trade as trade between two countries or governments. Of course, governments have a great deal to say about whom we buy from and sell to, and at what price, as we shall see more vividly later in the chapter.

THE BASIS FOR TRADE

Perhaps the easiest way to understand the basis of all trade is to consider why each of us as an individual engages in trade. If people did not trade with each other, everyone would have to be self-sufficient. However, the extreme inefficiency of self-sufficient people is well documented throughout history, starting with the cave dwellers. It did not take people, even the most primitive people, long to discover that by specializing in one or a few activities, their total productivity could be increased greatly. For example, in tribal societies it is well known that certain people made the utensils, others hunted, and still others cared for the domestic animals and crops. These people knew that the output of the entire tribe was increased when even a modest amount of specialization took place.

The opportunity to increase output also accounts for present-day trade between people, whether it be people in the same neighborhood or people of different regions of a country or different countries. In the United States, for example, it would be foolish for people in the northern part of the nation to attempt to grow their own citrus fruits; the output of the entire nation is increased when people in the South and West produce the nation's fruit, part of which is traded with the people of the North for items produced there. A trade barrier between North and South surely would reduce the output of the entire country, because each region would have to undertake production for which it is not well suited. The same reasoning applies to trade between countries. (In the discussion that follows we will speak of international trade as trade between two countries. But keep in mind that in reality it is trade between people living within different national boundaries). If the United States attempted to produce its own coffee, for example, it would have to forgo the production of a relatively large amount of other products because of the resources that would have to be devoted to relatively inefficient coffee production.

The examples in the preceding paragraph illustrate what is perhaps the most obvious reason for the increase in total output or productivity resulting from trade—differences in climate or natural resources. Citrus fruits and coffee require special climates, so it makes sense to produce these products in the areas that have the appropriate climate. Similarly, the extraction of minerals or petroleum can take place only where nature provides these resources. Other examples include the location of a fishing industry in a specific area due to the proximity to a large body of water, or the existence of lumbering due to abundant tree growth. It would not make much sense for the Great Plains to produce lumber and the Northwest to produce corn, for example.

In addition to differences in the natural endowment, specialization and trade take place because of the past establishment of traditions and institutions that favor a certain industry. For example, Taiwan has become well known for its light manufacturing industries; Germany, for its machines and tools; Sweden, for its high-quality steel; and Switzerland, for its watches. Traditions of workmanship and knowledge are passed down from generation to generation, giving the nation or region a distinct advantage in certain kinds of production.

The existence of a particular industry often gives rise to other supporting industries and institutions. For example, trade centers or markets are established where buyers and sellers can get together. Financial institutions develop that cater to a particular industry because of the specific knowledge required. If a large share of the people are employed by an industry, it is common for the public schools to offer training that is specifically applicable to the industry. Economists refer to the increase in productivity that occurs because of the formation of other supporting industries or institutions as "external economies." In other words, an industry may become more productive as it becomes larger because of the existence of other supporting industries and institutions.

It is sometimes argued that the people of certain regions or nations have some innate ability or characteristic that makes them better suited for certain occupations. For example, the Japanese have gained a reputation for being nimble and able to assemble tiny components of their products. The Germans and Swiss, on the other hand, are often thought of as possessing a characteristic of preciseness that makes them well qualified to produce tools and instruments. It is not clear whether such traits are inherent in the population or learned or acquired through generations of people doing the jobs that require these traits. At any rate, if differences in skills among populations do exist, regardless of whether they are inherent or acquired, it is reasonable to expect that a nation or area will be better off if it accentuates the activities that it does comparatively well.

COMPARATIVE ADVANTAGE

It is fairly easy to see how specialization and trade can be beneficial to areas or nations because of special advantages in the production of certain goods or services. As mentioned, these advantages may stem from climatic conditions, natural resource endowments, human skills, etc. It is possible, however, to find areas or even nations that seem to have been "shortchanged" by nature and as a result do not possess special advantages vis-à-vis other areas or nations. In these cases, will there be any incentive for the more productive nations to trade with their less productive neighbors? After all, in order to have trade between two nations, or even two people, it is necessary for both to gain from the transaction. If one trader gains and the other loses, the loser will refuse to trade.

We are indebted to one of the classical economists, David Ricardo, for first shedding light on this question. Using the production of cloth and wine in Portugal and England as an example, Ricardo demonstrated that even though Portugal might be able to produce each unit of wine and cloth more "efficiently" than England, it still was to the advantage of Portugal to engage in trading these two commodities with England. The incentive for trade to take place in this situation is much less obvious than the examples we discussed earlier, where each country has a natural advantage in one of the commodities.

The key to understanding the basis for trade in this latter situation is found in the concept known as "comparative advantage." Perhaps the easiest way to understand this concept is to construct a simple example. Let us use the United States and the United Kingdom as our two countries, and wheat and wool as our two products. If you wish you may assume that the United States is more efficient in both, or vice versa. We will see a bit later that any difference in the level of absolute efficiency between the two countries does not affect the problem.

In Table 15–1 we present some possible levels of output for each commodity in each country. Notice that when wool is increased in each country the

TABLE 15–1	Examples of production possibilities schedules for wheat and wool in the United States and the United Kingdom (millions of bushels and bales)

| | | United States | | United Kingdom | |
Possibility		Wheat	Wool	Wheat	Wool
A		480	0	120	0
B		320	20	80	10
C		160	40	40	20
D		0	60	0	30

output of wheat declines, and similarly if more wheat is produced the quantity of wool must decline. This tells us that each country has a limited amount of resources and, therefore, each cannot simultaneously increase the production of both commodities. Economists often refer to these figures as production possibilities schedules. If these figures were plotted on diagrams we would obtain production possibilities curves, as discussed in Chapter 1.

Using the figures in Table 15–1, we can calculate the cost of wheat and wool in the two countries. First notice that if the United States wishes to increase its wool output from 0 to 20 million bales, it must give up 160 million bushels of wheat. In other words, each bale of wool costs eight bushels of wheat in the United States. In the United Kingdom we see that each additional bale of wool costs only four bushels of wheat. Thus, in comparing the two countries, we would say that wool is expensive in the United States and cheap in the United Kingdom in terms of the wheat given up to obtain it.

The cost of wool can be obtained in the same manner. Moving up from the bottom of the table, we see that the United States gives up 20 million bales of wool to obtain 160 million bushels of wheat, or 0.125 bale of wool for each bushel of wheat. In the United Kingdom the first 40 million bushels of wheat are obtained by giving up 10 million bales of wool, or 0.25 bale of wool for each bushel of wheat. Thus, we can conclude, in terms of wool, wheat is cheap in the United States and expensive in the United Kingdom. These costs are summarized in Table 15–2.

Because wool is relatively cheap in the United Kingdom compared to in the United States, economists would say that the United Kingdom enjoys a comparative advantage in the production of wool vis-à-vis the United States. Similarly, the comparatively low cost of wheat (in terms of wool) in the United States gives the United States a comparative advantage in the production of this product. Notice that in our derivation of comparative advantage, we did not say anything about the absolute efficiency of wheat and wool production in

TABLE 15–2   Costs of wheat and wool

	United States	United Kingdom
Cost of wool in terms of wheat	8 bushels	4 bushels
Cost of wheat in terms of wool*	0.125 bale	0.25 bale

* Notice that the wheat costs are the reciprocals of the wool costs, and vice versa.

the two countries. The important distinction is the relative efficiency of producing one product versus the other. In the United States, wool production is relatively inefficient (in this example) because a relatively large amount of wheat must be given up to obtain the wool. In the United Kingdom, wheat production is relatively inefficient because much wool must be given up to obtain the wheat.

We can say, therefore, that a nation has a *comparative advantage* in producing a good if, in the process of increasing the output of that good, it *gives up* less of an alternative good than another nation *gives up*. Notice that when we are talking about giving up an alternative good we are in fact referring to opportunity cost—a concept introduced in Chapter 1. In discussing the gains from trade in the following section, the word *cost* refers to opportunity cost— what has to be given up to get more of something else.

THE GAINS FROM TRADE

So far in the example we have illustrated a situation in which the United States has a comparative advantage in wheat and the United Kingdom has a comparative advantage in wool. So what? We will now show that because of comparative advantage, each country, by cutting back on the production of its high-cost product and increasing the output of its low-cost product and then trading part of its "cheap" product, can end up with more of both products. The only thing required for this little "sleight-of-hand" is that the price paid by each country is lower than the cost to produce the item at home.

In our example, the production cost of a bale of wool is eight bushels of wheat in the United States and four bushels of wheat in the United Kingdom. Suppose the two countries could agree on a middle-ground price of, say, six bushels of wheat from the United States for each bale of wool it buys from the United Kingdom. Notice that this is a good deal for the United States, because in order to obtain more wool by producing it domestically, it would have to give up eight bushels of wheat per bale of wool. Similarly, this price implies that the United Kingdom pays one sixth of a bale of wool for each bushel of wheat. This is a good deal for the United Kingdom, because by producing more wheat domestically it must give up one fourth of a bale of wool for each bushel of wheat. Hence there is a mutual advantage for both countries to trade.

Let us now illustrate how both countries can end up with more of both products after trading. As an initial situation, suppose both countries are producing at possibility B shown by Table 15–1. In this situation, the United States is producing 320 million bushels of wheat and 20 million bales of wool, while the United Kingdom is producing 80 million bushels of wheat and 10 million bales of wool.[1] Now let us suppose the United States cuts back on its production of wool by 5 million bales. The 8-to-1 cost ratio tells us that the United States can expand its wheat output by 40 million bushels. Also suppose the United Kingdom cuts back on wheat production by 32 million bushels. The 4-to-1 cost ratio in the United Kingdom tells us that they can expand wool output by 8 million bales. (We will discuss how these changes might be initiated in the section on international markets.)

To complete the example, let us suppose the United States sells 36 million bushels of wheat to the United Kingdom in exchange for 6 million bales of wool. Recall that the agreed-upon price was six bushels of wheat for a bale of wool. After the transaction is complete, note that the United States has 324 million bushels of wheat (360 − 36) and 21 billion bales of wool (15 + 6). The United Kingdom now has 84 million bushels of wheat (48 + 36) and 12 million bales of wool (18 − 6). In other words, both countries now have more wheat and more wool. This delightful phenomenon happened because each country increased the output of the product in which it had a comparative advantage and then each country traded part of this increased output to the other country for the product that it found expensive to produce. The results are summarized in Table 15–3.

INCOMPLETE SPECIALIZATION

In the above example, it turns out that the total output of wheat and wool in the United States and the United Kingdom is maximized if the United States specializes in wheat and the United Kingdom in wool. But in reality, complete specialization would not be likely to take place.

TABLE 15–3   Illustrating the gains from trade

	United States		United Kingdom	
	Wheat	Wool	Wheat	Wool
Before trade	320	20	80	10
After trade:				
Domestic production	360	15	48	18
Add imports		+6	+36	
Subtract exports	−36			−6
Total	324	21	84	12

In order to make this example as simple as possible, we left out a number of complicating factors. Even in a simplified form, international trade examples have a tendency to become complex and confusing. One simplification is that in the production possibilities schedule shown in Table 15–1 we assumed that

---

[1] Keep in mind that these figures represent only an example and are not intended to illustrate the actual production possibilities of these two products in the United States and the United Kingdom.

wheat could be transformed into wool, or vice versa, at a constant cost over the entire range of possibilities. In the United States, for example, we assumed that the cost of obtaining an additional bale of wool was eight bushels of wheat regardless of the amount of each produced. We made the same assumption for the United Kingdom, only here we assumed a constant ratio of 4 to 1.

In reality we would not expect the same cost ratio to prevail over the entire range of production possibilities. For example, in the United States there are certain parts of the country (such as mountainous or hilly areas) where wool production can be carried out without much sacrifice of wheat because wheat could not be grown on the hills anyway. Thus, the first few million bales of wool could be obtained quite economically in terms of wheat given up. But then as more and more of the nation's resources are devoted to wool production, more and more of the productive wheat land is taken over by this activity. Hence, at relatively large amounts of wool produced, additional wool becomes more costly because more and more wheat is given up to obtain the added wool. The same is true for expanding wheat production. Trying to grow wheat in the high mountain plateaus will reduce wool output considerably but would add relatively little wheat output. Hence, wheat becomes expensive.

In this more realistic situation of increasing costs, we would expect that beyond some point it would not pay to trade.[2] For example, the Unites States might continue to produce a little wool domestically because the first few million bales might be produced cheaply (in terms of wheat) as in the United Kingdom. Similarly, the United Kingdom might continue to produce some of its own wheat because certain areas can produce wheat very economically.

We also should consider transportation costs. In order to move the products of one nation to another, additional resources are required to provide the transportation services. With increasing costs, at some point the comparative advantage might become so small that it would not be large enough to offset the added costs of transport. This would be particularly important in the case of heavy or bulky products. We do not observe much international trade in cement blocks, for example.

The absolute size of a country and the per capita income of its inhabitants also can be expected to influence the degree of specialization. As you would expect, large nations such as the United States tend to be much more diverse in terms of climate and natural resources than smaller nations. Much of the trade between states within the United States would be international trade if the country were made up of a number of smaller countries. In addition, a small nation, even if it specializes in a particular product, may not be able to satisfy the total demand of a large high-income nation. Hence, the larger country may have to produce a portion of the product domestically in addition to importing in order to satisfy the total demand for it.

The extent of a nation's trade with other countries is influenced also by political and military considerations. If the government of one nation is not on speaking terms with the government of another nation, trade between the two countries is not likely. It is unfortunate that ideological differences between the political leaders of nations are allowed to determine whether or not the people

---

[2] The production possibilities curves drawn in Chapter 1 illustrate increasing costs. If you plotted the numbers in Table 15-1, you would obtain a straight, downward-sloping line as the production possibilities curve.

of the respective countries can trade with each other. As we saw in Table 15–3, the output available to the people of both nations can be increased because of trade.

National policies aimed at achieving self-sufficiency are common, particularly among developing nations. The implication is that a nation is better off if it produces most of everything it consumes. As we saw in the preceding section, this will not be true if the nation has a comparative advantage in one or more products. Of course, the advantage of trading diminishes a great deal when one trading partner abruptly refuses to buy or sell. This problem has come to the surface a number of times in recent years. For example, the Arab oil embargo caused many Americans, including the president, to believe that self-sufficiency is better than trade because we could at least be assured of supplies. The same was true of other nations when the U.S. government temporarily prohibited exports of certain agricultural products during 1974 and 1975, and again during the Carter administration's embargo of agricultural exports to the Soviet Union. In order for trade to flourish, it must take place under conditions of trust where trading partners allow themselves to be dependent on each other. Unfortunately, in the arena of international politics, trust and the willingness to depend on other nations probably are the exception rather than the rule.

PRIVATE GAINS AND LOSSES FROM TRADE

In our previous discussion we stressed that society as a whole gains when nations tend to concentrate their production on goods and services they produce comparatively well and trade any excess for goods that other nations can produce more cheaply (in terms of other goods given up). However, we should point out that specific individuals or groups within an economy are likely to reap economic gains from trade and other groups are likely to suffer losses.

It is relatively easy to see how profits can be made. Suppose some enterprising American, while reading international price quotations, notices that the price of a bale of wool in the United Kingdom is equal to four bushels of wheat but that it takes eight bushels of wheat to be worth the equivalent of a bale of wool in the U.S. market: What a splendid opportunity to make a profit! The entrepreneur can buy wool in the United Kingdom, offering a bit more than the 4-to-1 ratio. After paying the transport charges, the difference, which might be the equivalent of two or three bushels of wheat for each bale of wool, would be pure profit for the importer of wool.

Of course, the same thing could be done with wheat. The import-export firm could buy wheat relatively cheaply in the United States and sell it in the United Kingdom where it is relatively expensive. Again the difference between the buying and selling prices, less transport charges, would be a pure profit. Indeed, this kind of activity has made millionaires out of a number of people. This is not to say that such import-export activity is harmful. On the contrary, it is very beneficial. The consumers of wool in the United States can enjoy a more abundant supply at a lower price. The same thing is true for the consumers of wheat in the United Kingdom.

There are some additional benefits of opening up trade. The producers of wheat in the United States are likely to enjoy an increased price for their product because of the additional demand of consumers in the United Kingdom. Similarly, wool producers in the United Kingdom are not likely to complain about the stronger demand and rising price for their product. And with these price increases, U.S. wheat producers and U.K. wool producers both will find it profitable to increase output.

If the two governments allow free trade to take place in wheat and wool, before long the relative prices of these two products will come closer together in the two countries. In other words, as more wheat comes into the United Kingdom, the price of wheat relative to wool is likely to fall, say, from four bushels of wheat per bale of wool to perhaps five and a half bushels per bale. By the same token, as wool becomes more plentiful in the United States, the wheat-to-wool price ratio will tend to decline from, say, 8:1 to perhaps 6.5:1. However, we would not expect the relative prices to become completely equal in the two countries because of the transportation costs of bringing wool into the United States and wheat into the United Kingdom. Thus, the pure profits of exporters and importers will tend to diminish as trade increases in volume.

However, as mentioned, there are some people who lose because of international trade, at least in the short run. In terms of our example, it is likely that U.S. wool producers and U.K. wheat producers will find the prices of their products declining because of the increased supply from abroad. As a result, people who suffer economic losses from trade may attempt to persuade their respective governments to prohibit or at least limit the import of cheap products from abroad by instituting various trade barriers, mainly import quotas and tariffs. Of course, the advocates of quotas and tariffs have used numerous arguments other than self-protection to justify the existence of trade barriers. Unfortunately many of their arguments are based on questionable economic reasoning. It will be useful to briefly explain the effects of trade barriers and analyze some of the arguments used to justify such barriers.

QUOTAS AND TARIFFS

As the name implies, a *quota* simply limits the amount of a good that can be brought into a country. A quota may be set up to exclude a good entirely or to allow the import of a certain maximum amount per year. A *tariff*, on the other hand, is in effect a tax on an imported good. As a result of tariffs, the prices of imported goods to domestic consumers are increased over what they would otherwise be. And, as you would expect, the higher prices discourage domestic buyers from purchasing imported articles. Thus, quotas and tariffs both have the effect of reducing trade. The following are some of the more common arguments used to justify trade restrictions.

1. Tariffs as a revenue source. Governments, of course, generally are on the lookout for sources of revenue, particularly for ways to "fleece the goose with the least amount of squawking." It might seem logical, therefore, to impose a tax on foreign producers; that is, let foreigners help pay the country's taxes. But in reality the people of the nation imposing the tariff end up paying the equivalent of the tax anyway because of the higher prices that they pay for the imported items. Also, the reduction in imported goods that results from the tariff makes it necessary for consumers of the importing country to use relatively more of the higher-priced domestically produced goods.

2. Tariffs to equalize for low-cost foreign labor. A common argument for tariffs in the United States is that the wages of labor in foreign countries are but a fraction of U.S. wages and, therefore, foreign products can be made more cheaply and drive U.S. products off the market. A basic flaw in this argument is that it makes no mention of why U.S. workers receive higher wages. In market economies the wage of a worker is determined ultimately by his or her productivity. If a person is paid $60 per day, that person has to produce at least $60 per day in order for the person's employer to pay this wage.

Workers in other nations who happen to be paid a fraction of U.S. wages find themselves in this unhappy situation because their output is so small—a fraction of the output of U.S. workers. Mainly this stems from the fact that low-paid foreign workers have a relatively small amount of capital (machines, tools, etc.) to work with. Also, their skills may be less sophisticated than those of U.S. workers. Both of these factors explain why foreign workers, especially those in the less developed countries, earn such low pay. The main point is that well-paid labor does not imply high-cost products. The important factor in determining the cost of a product is the price of labor and capital in relation to their productivities. A U.S. worker may earn three times the pay of a foreign worker, but if the person's contribution to output is more than three times that of the foreign worker, the U.S. worker is actually the cheaper of the two. It appears, however, that during the 1970s wages in the United States increased to such high levels in certain industries that the products of these industries were no longer competitive with those of foreign producers. During the early 1980s, for example, wages plus fringe benefits averaged about $19 per hour in the U.S. auto industry compared to about $8 per hour for Japanese auto makers. Since Japanese automobile factories were even more automated and modern than U.S. factories at that time, it became cheaper to produce cars in Japan than in the United States. An industry can easily lose its comparative advantage if its costs increase more rapidly than costs in other countries.

It is of interest to note also that low-wage countries have gained a comparative advantage vis-à-vis the United States in the production of labor-intensive items such as the assembly of electronic components. Other aspects of production of modern electronic products may still take place in the United States, however, where the technological base still gives it a comparative advantage.

If nations were to impose tariffs to offset lower wages in other countries, trade between countries would be greatly diminished because of the reduction or elimination of comparative advantage. In other words, the argument for a tariff to offset low wages in other countries, carried to its logical conclusion, implies the near elimination of international trade to the detriment of all concerned.

3. The "infant industry" argument. Sometimes nations attempt to justify tariffs on foreign products in order to reduce competition for a newly established domestic industry. The argument is that small industries should be given protection until they can grow large enough to take advantage of economies of scale and thus produce at a lower cost some time in the future.

The problem with this argument is that an industry should not come into existence until it can earn a rate of return on its capital that is comparable to other nonsubsidized industries.[3] If the return on its capital is lower, the economy could enjoy a larger real output by investing in other industries. For

---

[3] A possible exception to this rule occurs when the industry in question results in external effects on other industries—that is, lowers their production costs.

example, if the rate of return on other additional investment in the economy is 15 percent, then the rate of return on the infant industry over the long run should also be at least 15 percent. If it takes a tariff to achieve a 15 percent return, we know that the true rate of return is less than that, indicating that the economy is not investing its resources wisely. If the return is relatively high, as is often implied, then it should not need a tariff to become established. The high profits in the later years should be great enough to compensate for any losses in its early years.

4. Tariffs for retaliation. It has been argued that although tariffs and quotas on imports are undesirable, a nation often is forced to retaliate against other nations that have set up trade restrictions of their own. But it can be argued that a government that retaliates by increasing its tariffs really does not have the economic well-being of its people in mind. The imposition of a tariff by a nation reduces the products coming into that country, thereby reducing the total amount of goods and services available to its people. The fact that one government chooses to reduce the economic well-being of its people is not a good reason for another government to follow suit. Retaliatory tariffs are analogous to two governments trying to best each other, each saying, "I can deprive my people of more things than you can deprive yours of."

5. "Buy American." Quite frequently we see bumper stickers or advertisements urging us to buy American-made products. Apparently, the objective is to keep foreign products out while providing employment for U.S. workers. However, it is necessary to keep in mind that thousands of U.S. workers are employed in industries producing for foreign markets. Unless we buy from other countries, they cannot buy from us. Without trade, some of the workers in export industries would have to find jobs in other industries. So it is not clear that workers in these industries end up any better off in the long run.

The "buy American" slogan also is used as an argument for keeping American dollars at home. Yet, as pointed out in Chapter 10, money is just a convenient tool for exchanging goods and services. The important things are the real goods and services that are available to society, not the number of pieces of paper called money that it has. The amount of money in a society can be increased simply by the government's cranking up the printing presses.[4]

In our discussion so far we have not presented a convincing argument for tariffs and quotas, but we cannot deny that they are extremely popular throughout the world. Thus, there must be some reason for having them. To be perfectly honest, tariffs and quotas can result in a short-term gain for specific industries. In our wheat and wool example, the entrance of foreign wool into the United States or foreign wheat into the United Kingdom probably would have reduced the price of wool in the United States and the price of wheat in the United Kingdom, or at least kept prices lower than they would otherwise be. By placing tariffs or quotas on these products and reducing imports, U.S. wool producers and U.K. wheat producers probably would enjoy higher prices.

Thus, when advocating trade restrictions, industry spokespersons should, to be honest, admit that tariffs or quotas will help them by keeping the prices of

---

[4] Keep in mind, though, that large fluctuations in the quantity of money can have important effects on the real output of an economy.

their products higher than they would otherwise be. Efforts to increase tariffs or lower quotas often increase during downturns in economic activity, as observed in the early 1980s in regard to Japanese cars. The object is to keep out foreign products so as to maintain higher domestic sales. Granted, it is in the interest of industry representatives or union leaders who represent the labor in industries that face foreign competition to try to keep out foreign products. We should not expect businesspeople who face declining sales or union members whose jobs are in jeopardy to think first of society's welfare. But the government should.

It should be stressed also that trade restrictions are likely to provide only short-term benefits to the industries that they are designed to help. In the long run many of the people in the protected industries probably would have been better off to leave and enter industries in which the nation has a comparative advantage. By doing so their incomes might be increased even more because of their greater productivity in other lines of work. Tariffs and quotas often serve to delay adjustments that eventually come about in the long run.

A more subtle, but economically justifiable, argument for a trade barrier on a particular item can be made if a country either buys or sells a large share of the world's production of the commodity in question. The underlying economic rationale for the argument is presented in more advanced international trade courses, but a brief intuitive explanation will be helpful here.

Consider first a nation that sells a relatively large share of the world's output of an item, such as Brazil in the case of coffee. By restricting exports, Brazil is able to significantly decrease the quantity of coffee exchanged on the world market and therefore drive up the price it receives for coffee. As a result Brazil as a country is able to enjoy higher total profits from its export trade.[5] Keep in mind that this is a case of placing a barrier on exports rather than on imports. Most of our previous discussion centered on the latter.

A case can be made for taxing or placing a quota on an import if the nation buys a substantial share of the world's output of the item. In this case the resulting decrease in the quantity imported depresses the world price and as a result the price paid for the item by the importing country will be lower than if free trade were allowed.[6] However, in order for such a situation to arise, the country in question must consume a substantial portion of the world's consumption of the product. Since consumption patterns of nations tend to be more homogeneous than production patterns, it is extremely difficult to find examples where a single importer can have a significant impact on the world consumption of a product. Certainly this argument could not be used to justify the major portion of import trade barriers that nations have set up.

We should caution, too, that in the cases of these justifiable export or import barriers, the benefits will extend only so far. By placing the barrier too

---

[5] For those who have had microeconomics, the objective is to equate marginal cost with marginal revenue, analogous to the behavior of an imperfectly competitive firm on the selling side. See Chapter 10 of the companion micro book. If free export is allowed by a number of firms, price and quantity will correspond to the intersections of marginal cost (supply) and demand facing the country. Profits will be increased by restricting exports to the point of intersection between marginal cost and marginal revenue.

[6] In this case, the objective is to purchase the quantity corresponding to the intersection between marginal resource cost and demand, as in the case of a monopsonist (see Chapter 11 of the micro text). If free trade is allowed, the quantity imported will correspond to the intersection of supply and demand.

high, the nation can be made worse off than it would have been with no barrier at all. It should also be kept in mind that the barriers just discussed are justifiable only from the standpoint of the country in question. Those nations that must pay a higher price for products they buy or receive a lower price for products they sell do not, of course, benefit from such barriers.

DUMPING

Occasionally a nation will try to sell more of its products abroad by setting the export price lower than its domestic price, with the government reimbursing producers for the difference. This practice has come to be known as "dumping" and has been associated in the post-World War II years with agricultural products produced by the United States and some of the other more highly developed nations. In their attempt to support prices of a number of agricultural products, the governments of these nations have been forced to buy the resulting surplus.[7] Then in an attempt to dispose of the surplus, the government sells it abroad at a reduced price or gives it away, usually to developing nations. The U.S. Public Law 480 program is a good example.

At first glance it might appear that such a practice works to the advantage of all concerned. Consumers of the developing countries receive free or low-priced food, which in many cases has helped them avoid starvation or at least severe malnutrition, and the governments of the developed nations have been able to put the surplus to good use. But there have been a couple of undesirable side effects. First, producers of comparable products in other exporting nations suffer a reduction in the demand and price of their products. For example, Canadian wheat producers do not greet subsidized wheat sales by the United States with much enthusiasm.

A second problem, and perhaps even more important, is that producers in the recipient nations face a depressed market for their output because of the free or cheap products coming in under such programs. This in turn tends to retard the development of domestic agriculture in the recipient nations.

In more recent years the charge of dumping has been levied against other developing nations by certain groups in the United States because of a belief that these nations have been selling manufactured products on the U.S. market at prices lower than their production costs. Such a practice would not likely persist however. Firms do not stay in business very long by selling below cost. Of course, their own governments could subsidize these firms by making up the difference between their domestic price and the U.S. price, except now their taxpayers would end up subsidizing U.S. consumers. Again such a practice is not likely to enjoy much popularity among foreign taxpayers, even though U.S. consumers should not complain.

U.S. TRADE

It will be of some value to look briefly at the magnitude and characteristics of U.S. trade with other nations. The figures in Table 15–4 provide an indication of the magnitude of U.S. exports and imports. In most years since the

---

[7] A surplus results because market price is maintained higher than equilibrium price. This is just the opposite of the problem of shortages caused by price controls. For additional discussion, see Chapter 8 of the companion micro book.

TABLE 15–4   U.S. exports and imports of merchandise, selected years (1982 prices)

Year	Exports ($ millions)	Imports ($ millions)	Imports as a percent of GNP
1930	$ 18,597	$ 14,691	3.4%
1940	23,423	14,920	2.7
1950	33,287	29,967	3.2
1960	52,121	39,434	2.9
1970	86,921	81,403	4.2
1980	260,432	284,184	9.2
1982	212,275	243,952	7.9

Source: *U.S. Statistical Abstract*, 1969, p. 783, and 1984, p. 834.

Great Depression, the United States has exported a larger value of merchandise to other countries than it has bought from them. However, this pattern changed in the 1970s when U.S. imports exceeded exports by a substantial amount, due mainly to the increase in prices of oil imports.

Also noticeable is the small quantity of imports relative to GNP at least before 1970. Even in 1982 imports were less than 10 percent of GNP. Most Americans, it appears, do "buy American." In fact, U.S. citizens consume a small share of their total goods and services in the form of imported items compared with most other nations of the world. We should not conclude from these figures, however, that Americans are more isolationist or distrustful of foreign goods than other people. For it is necessary to bear in mind that the United States is a large and diverse nation compared with most other countries. A good deal of the trade that takes place between regions or states in the United States would be considered international trade in other countries. It is interesting to notice, however, that the share of imports in GNP increased substantially between 1970 and 1980.

Table 15–5 provides some information on the major items traded by the United States. Notice in particular that manufactured items, including chemi-

TABLE 15–5   U.S. exports and imports, 1982

	Exports ($ millions)	Imports ($ millions)
Food and live animals	$ 23,950	$ 14,453
Beverages and tobacco	3,026	3,364
Crude materials, inedible, except fuels	19,248	8,589
Mineral fuels and related materials	12,729	65,409
Chemicals and related products	19,891	9,494
Machinery	60,308	39,684
Transport equipment	23,628	33,635
Manufactured goods	16,739	33,148
Other	30,662	36,176
Total	$207,158	$243,952

Source: *U.S. Statistical Abstract*, 1984, p. 833.

cals, machinery, and other manufactured goods, make up about half of all U.S. exports. Mineral fuels (petroleum) now constitute the largest single item on the import side.

It is possible to observe, of course, the same type of item being exported and imported, although not necessarily to or from the same country. For example, the United States may sell electric generating equipment to India and buy similar equipment from West Germany. It all depends on the preferences of buyers in the various importing countries. Also, we should recognize that the large general categories in Table 15–5 include a great many diverse items, many of which are found only in exports and not in imports, and vice versa. Thus, we cannot use these aggregate figures to infer anything about the comparative advantage of the United States over other countries.

The figures in Table 15–6 tell us who the major trading partners of the United States are. Note that there is not much trade with the developing na-

---

TABLE 15–6   U.S. trade statistics by continent and nation groups, 1982

	Exports to— ($ millions)	Imports from— ($ millions)
Africa	$ 10,271	$ 17,770
Asia	64,822	85,170
Australia and Oceania	5,700	3,131
Western Europe	60,054	52,346
North America	52,057	70,094
South America	15,257	14,373
Communist nations or areas	6,554	3,354
Developed nations	122,541	141,594
Developing nations	82,674	99,002

Source: *U.S. Statistical Abstract*, 1984, p. 834.

---

tions as with the more highly developed, industrialized economies, although during the 1970s the value of imports from developing nations increased substantially because of the higher prices paid for crude oil and other raw materials. In spite of the highly publicized grain sales to the Soviet Union, trade with the communist nations still is a small part of the total. By and large the major U.S. trading partners are other countries in North America (mainly Canada), Western Europe, and Asia, primarily Japan.

A simple but often forgotten point is that from the standpoint of the entire world, exports must always equal imports during any given period of time. A dollar of exports by one nation must always be a dollar of imports to another, just as a sale by one person is always a purchase by someone else. Of course, for an individual nation, exports need not equal imports during any given year.

A country is said to have a "favorable" balance of trade if it sells more than it buys from other countries; that is, if exports exceed imports. It is perhaps unfortunate that this term came into such general use because it does not have much, if any, economic justification. As mentioned in Chapter 4, the error of this thinking is made clear by considering the limiting case where a nation sells everything it produces to other countries but buys nothing in return, leaving exactly zero goods and services for the people to consume—not a very "favorable" situation by most definitions.

BALANCE OF TRADE VERSUS BALANCE OF PAYMENTS

In discussing international trade and finance, it is necessary to distinguish between a nation's balance of trade and its balance of payments. The balance of trade can be thought of simply as the difference between exports and imports of merchandise. As shown in Table 15–7, the United States in 1983 imported

TABLE 15–7   U.S. balance of trade and balance of payments, 1983 ($ billions)

Exports of merchandise	+200.3
Imports of merchandise	−261.3
Balance of trade	−61.0
Investment earnings, net	+23.5
Grants, pensions, and other transfers	−2.6
Military transactions, net	+0.5
U.S. government grants	−6.1
Other	+4.1
Balance of payments	−41.6

Source: *Federal Reserve Bulletin*, March 1985, p. A–51.

$261.3 billion of merchandise while exporting $200.3 billion. leaving a balance of trade deficit of $61 billion.[8] However, it should be noted that considerably more money flows between countries than is due to merchandise trade alone. Two important items are U.S. spending on investments in other countries and income from such investments flowing back into the United States. There are also monetary flows because of foreign investment in the United States and income received from this capital. In 1983, the amount of money flowing into the United States because of investments in other countries was $23.5 billion more than the amount flowing out due to foreign investments in the United States. This item along with the "other" category and net military transactions, reduced the balance of trade deficit, leaving a balance of payments deficit of $41.6 billion in 1983.

EXCHANGE RATES

At this point you may ask: How do firms doing business abroad pay or receive payment for the items they buy and sell? An American seller of wheat, for example, would not want to be paid in English pounds because this money would be of little use in the United States. Conversely, sellers of wool from the United Kingdom need to be paid in pounds. This problem is taken care of quite nicely by the financial institutions in the respective countries which are autho-

---

[8] The import and export totals in Tables 15–4, 15–5, and 15–7 do not correspond exactly because of differences in items included in each.

rized by their governments to do business abroad. Some of the large New York banks have checking accounts in the larger London banks, and vice versa. Thus, an English exporter of wool, for example, upon receiving a check from an American import firm drawn on a New York bank, presents this check at a London bank and receives payment in pounds. Ultimately, the account of the U.S. import firm in its New York bank is decreased when the check is returned to the United States.

We must recognize, of course, that American dollars are not exchanged on a one-for-one basis with English pounds or other currencies. The currency of each nation has either an official or a market exchange rate, or both, with the currencies of all other nations. For example, suppose one English pound is exchanged for $1.25 in American dollars. If a New York bank deposits $12,500 American dollars (in check or currency) in a London bank, the account of the New York bank in London is increased by 10,000 pounds.

The *exchange rate,* then, is simply the number of units of one currency that it takes to buy a unit of another currency. For example, if the rate of exchange between the West German mark and U.S. dollar is two to one, it takes two marks to purchase a dollar, or 50 cents to purchase a mark. Or we could say that the exchange rate is the price of one currency in terms of another currency. For each nation's currency, there exists an exchange rate between it and the currencies of other countries.[9]

In order to fully appreciate the role of exchange rates in international trade, it will be necessary to study in somewhat more detail the import and export markets for internationally traded goods and services. After gaining an understanding of these markets, we will be in a better position to understand how exchange rates are determined and why they change.

IMPORT AND EXPORT MARKETS

Recall from Chapter 2 that in each market there is a demand for a good or service and a supply of that good or service. Also recall that we represented demand by a downward–sloping line, indicating that people buy more when price declines (other things being equal). Similarly, supply was represented by an upward–sloping line, which implies that producers place larger quantities on the market at progressively higher prices.

It will be easier to understand international markets if we utilize specific examples. As the two countries, let us consider the United States and West Germany. Also, let us consider two products: U.S.-produced feed grains exported to West Germany and West German-produced Volkswagens imported into the United States. Thus, we will be dealing with two markets in the United States—one from the standpoint of U.S. importers of Volkswagens and the other from the standpoint of U.S. exporters of feed grains. Both the import price of Volkswagens and the export price of feed grains are quoted in terms of dollars. The markets are illustrated in Figure 15–1.

At first glance, the import and export markets appear no different from the domestic markets discussed in Chapter 2. Both demand curves are downward

---

[9] For quotations of recent exchange rates see the *Federal Reserve Bulletin,* published monthly by the Federal Reserve System. Many daily newspapers also report current exchange rates.

FIGURE 15–1   Markets for imports and exports in the United States

---

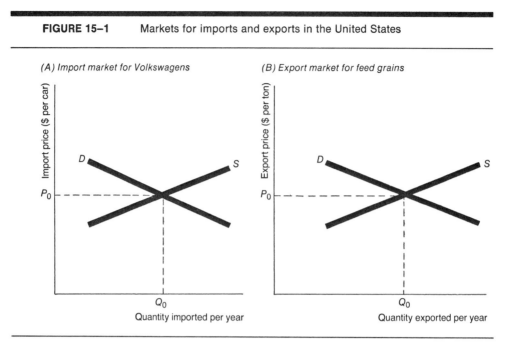

(A) Import market for Volkswagens

(B) Export market for feed grains

---

sloping, indicating that U.S. consumers buy more Volkswagens when their dollar price declines and that German farmers buy more U.S. feed grains when the price they pay declines. Similarly, both supply curves are upward sloping, indicating that at higher prices more Volkswagens will be supplied to the United States and more feed grains to Germany. And each market has an equilibrium price and quantity, as shown on the diagrams.

However, the markets for internationally traded commodities are not quite so simple as domestic markets. The complication enters because of the need to consider the price of each currency in terms of the other—that is, the exchange rate. As we will see in a moment, changes in the exchange rate shift the demand and supply curves of internationally traded commodities and as a result alter the prices paid by consumers of imported items and the prices received by producers of exported goods.

As an example, let us consider the effect of the decrease in the value of the dollar relative to the German mark on the dollar price paid and the mark price received for Volkswagens imported into the United States from West Germany. To make the example a bit more specific, suppose the price of the dollar decreases from four marks per dollar to two marks per dollar. (We will see shortly how this change could come about.) Let the supply curve S_1 in Figure 15–2 represent the supply of Volkswagens for U.S. consumers if the exchange rate is four marks per dollar. This supply curve tells us that Volkswagen is willing to supply Q_1 cars at a price of $6,000 per car. At the four marks per dollar exchange rate, the Volkswagen company receives 24,000 marks per car at the Q_1 level of sales in the United States.

Notice, however, that when the exchange rate falls to 2:1 (two marks per dollar) Volkswagen would have to receive $12,000 per car in order to still receive 24,000 marks per car. In other words, in order for Volkswagen to be

FIGURE 15–2   The effect of a decrease in the exchange rate on the dollar price paid
and mark price received for Volkswagens

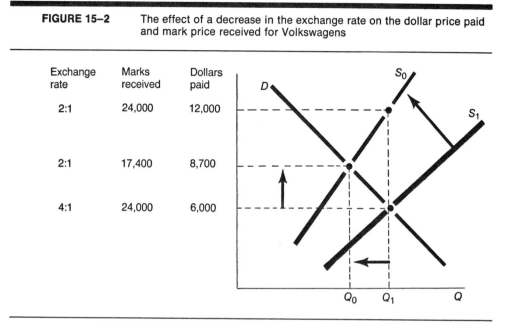

Exchange rate	Marks received	Dollars paid
2:1	24,000	12,000
2:1	17,400	8,700
4:1	24,000	6,000

willing to continue supplying Q_1 cars, the U.S. price per car would have to
increase to $12,000 per car. This means that the supply curve facing U.S.
consumers shifts upward and to the left (decreases) as a result of the decrease
in the exchange rate (shown by S_0 in Figure 15–2).

The decrease in the supply of Volkswagens has the effect of increasing the
dollar price paid for Volkswagens and decreasing the number of Volkswagens
imported, as shown by Figure 15–2. It is important to recognize, however, that
the dollar price paid for Volkswagen does not increase as much as the vertical
shift in the supply curve. This is because the demand curve is downward
sloping. U.S. consumers are not willing to pay $12,000 per car and still buy Q_1
cars per year. The market equilibrium price of $8,700 per car in this example is
what people are willing to pay at the given level of demand and supply.

Perhaps even more surprising, the mark price received by Volkswagen for
each car declines from 24,000 marks at the 4:1 exchange rate to 17,400 at the
2:1 rate. In order for Volkswagen to continue to receive 24,000 marks per car,
the dollar price would have to increase to $12,000, which it does not. Hence,
the decrease in the exchange rate causes an increase in the dollar price paid for
Volkswagens and a decrease in the mark price received by the company. This
is the main reason Volkswagen incurred considerable losses in the mid-1970s,
immediately following the decrease in the value of the dollar.

As one might expect, the decrease in the exchange rate also influences the
demand for U.S. products exported to Germany. Consider as an example the
export demand for feed grains facing U.S. producers. At the original 4:1 exchange rate, the demand for U.S. feed grains is denoted by D_0 in Figure 15–3.
This demand curve tells us that German buyers are willing to pay $200 per ton
at Q_1 tons purchased per year. At the 4:1 exchange rate this translates into 800
marks per ton. When the exchange rate falls to 2:1, German buyers should still
be willing to pay 800 marks per ton for Q_1 tons. But notice that 800 marks per

FIGURE 15–3   The effect of a decrease in the exchange rate on the dollar price received and mark price paid for U.S. feed grains

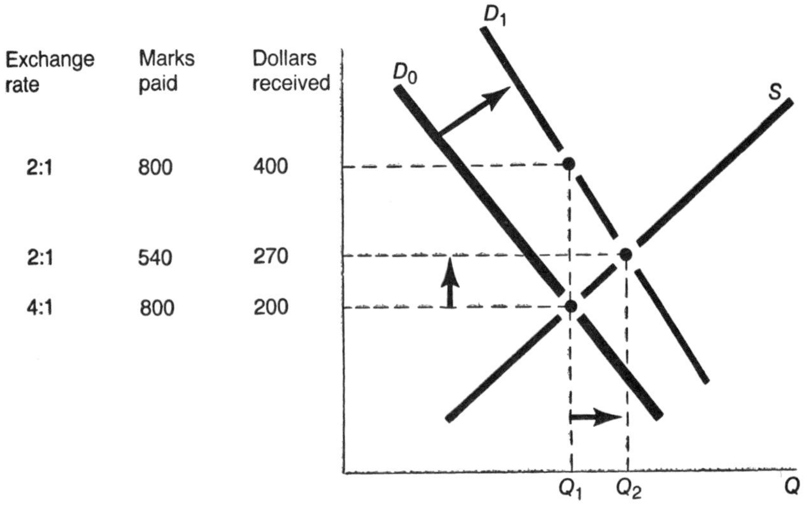

Exchange rate	Marks paid	Dollars received
2:1	800	400
2:1	540	270
4:1	800	200

ton at the $2:1$ exchange rate translates into $400 per ton at Q_1 tons. Thus, the export demand for U.S. feed grains shifts upward and to the right (increases) as the result of a decrease in the exchange rate, as shown by Figure 15–3.

It is also interesting to note that the dollar price received by U.S. producers does not increase by the full vertical shift in the demand curve. If the supply curve is upward sloping, the equilibrium price increases in this example from $200 to $270 per ton. At the $2:1$ exchange rate German buyers are able to purchase Q_2 tons at 540 marks per ton. Thus, the decrease in the exchange rate increases the dollar price received by U.S. producers but decreases the mark price paid by German buyers. This analysis in part explains the strong market experienced by U.S. cash grain farmers in the mid-1970s, following the decrease in the value of the dollar.

In the early to mid-1980s, when the U.S. dollar appreciated relative to the German mark and other currencies, the opposite occurred. Now industries producing the export market, such as agriculture, were placed at a disadvantage. The higher-priced dollar decreased the foreign demand for these industries' goods, causing lower prices and a smaller quantity exported. This phenomenon coupled with the high real interest rates and the decrease in the value of land was especially hard on young farmers just getting established and deeply in debt.

Of course, the strong U.S. dollar of this period benefited U.S. import industries, along with the tourist industry. Supplies of foreign goods and services to U.S. consumers increased, resulting in larger quantities available in the market and lower prices. Tourist travel to other countries also boomed in this period, helped along by lower air fares caused by deregulation of the airline industry. On the other hand, U.S. industries having to compete with imports such as automobiles, textiles, and steel suffered losses and higher unemployment during those years.

The preceding discussion can be summarized as follows: When the currency of a nation appreciates in value, export industries in that nation are harmed because of the decrease in demand for their products abroad; while import industries in the country benefit because of the increase in the supply of products from other countries. The opposite holds true when a nation's currency depreciates in value. Export industries benefit because of the increase in demand for their products abroad, while import industries suffer because of the decrease in the supply of products imported from other countries.

FOREIGN EXCHANGE MARKETS

Since an exchange rate can be defined as the price of one currency in terms of another, it is reasonable to believe that currency prices are determined in foreign exchange markets, similar to the way goods and service prices are determined in goods and service markets. Moreover, we can identify both a demand for and a supply of currencies. In terms of the example in the previous section, there would be a demand for U.S. dollars in West Germany in order to pay for the feed grains imported from the United States. Similarly, there would be a supply of dollars in West Germany from the purchase of Volkswagens by U.S. consumers.

The demand for and supply of U.S. dollars in West Germany is illustrated in Figure 15–4. The price of U.S. dollars is quoted in terms of marks per dollar. The more marks per dollar, the higher is the price of dollars, and vice versa. The quantity axis shows the number of dollars exchanged per year. Notice too that the demand for dollars is represented by a downward-sloping line, indicating that more dollars will be demanded as the price of dollars declines. The supply of dollars is represented by an upward-sloping line, indicating that the number of dollars supplied will increase as the price of dollars increases. Also, there is an equilibrium price and quantity corresponding to the intersection of these two curves.

In order to understand the reason for the downward-sloping demand for dollars and the upward-sloping supply of dollars in Figure 15–4, it is necessary to go back to Figures 15–2 and 15–3. Recall that a reduction in the exchange rate from 4 : 1 to 2 : 1 had the effect of decreasing the supply of Volkswagens and increasing the demand for U.S. feed grains. The decrease in the supply of Volkswagens had the effect of increasing the price but reducing the quantity. As long as quantity decreases more than price increases, there will be fewer dollars supplied to the foreign exchange market after the decrease in the price of the dollar than before the decrease. Because of the many substitutes for Volkswagens in the United States, there is reason to believe that the demand for Volkswagens is relatively flat; that is, people turn to lower-priced substitutes when the VW price increases. As a result we might expect that the curve for the supply of dollars to the foreign exchange market slopes upward and to the right, as shown by Figure 15–4.[10]

---

[10] It is not imperative that the curve for the supply of dollars slopes upward. An equilibrium can be reached in the foreign exchange market even if the supply curve slopes downward, as long as the supply curve is steeper than the demand curve.

FIGURE 15–4   Demand for and supply of dollars in West Germany

---

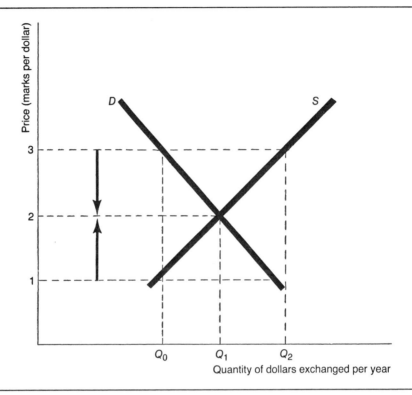

Quantity of dollars exchanged per year

Turning next to the demand for dollars, recall that the decrease in the exchange rate had the effect of increasing both the dollar price and the quantity exchanged of feed grains. Thus, the total number of dollars demanded in the foreign exchange market to pay for the feed grains will be larger after the decrease in the exchange rate. In other words, the demand curve for dollars in the foreign exchange market is expected to slope downward and to the right.

In the example depicted by Figure 15–4 the equilibrium price of the dollar is two marks per dollar. At the relatively high three-mark price, Q_2 dollars are supplied while Q_0 dollars are demanded. Consequently, there will be a surplus of dollars on the foreign exchange market. As German dollar holders place these surplus dollars on the market in an attempt to exchange them for marks, the price of the dollar will have to decline in order to entice holders of marks to exchange marks for dollars. As is true of any market, the surplus causes downward pressure on price. The exchange rate continues to decline until it reaches the intersection of the dollar demand and supply curves. As the exchange rate declines, recall that imports of German products into the United States are reduced and exports of U.S. products into Germany are increased. These changes cause more dollars to be demanded and fewer dollars to be supplied, which brings the foreign exchange market into equilibrium. The opposite would occur if the exchange rate were one to one. Now there would be a shortage of dollars, causing a price increase. The resulting changes in the import and export markets would increase the quantity of dollars supplied and decrease the dollars demanded until equilibrium was again reached.

We should be aware that shifts in the import demand or export supply can occur for reasons other than changes in the exchange rate. For example, inflation in the importing country can increase the import demand for products from abroad. Other things being equal, this will increase the supply of the nation's currency in the foreign exchange market, which in turn will result in a decrease in the equilibrium price of the currency. Thus, it is well to keep in mind that changes in the exchange rate affect the import and export markets, and autonomous changes in the import or export markets in turn affect the foreign exchange market.

It is also necessary to bear in mind that the supply of dollars to foreign currency markets depends not only on merchandise imports into the United States but also on such things as expenditure by U.S. firms for plant and equipment in other countries, expenditures by U.S. tourists, and U.S. military spending abroad. During the 1960s and early 1970s the United States experienced persistent balance of payments deficits resulting in a continued buildup of dollars in foreign countries, particularly West Germany and Japan. As these countries turned in their "surplus" dollars for gold, the United States lost about half of its gold reserves during this period. This brings us to a discussion of the post-World War II monetary system.

THE POST-WORLD WAR II INTERNATIONAL MONETARY SYSTEM

In the previous section we presented the process of adjustment that would occur if the actual exchange rate between two currencies were different from its equilibrium value. In so doing, we essentially showed how market rates of exchange are determined. However, it is necessary to qualify the preceding discussion by pointing out that during the early part of the post–World War II period, the exchange rates between the currencies of the major trading nations were for the most part set by government decree rather than by freely functioning foreign exchange markets. A bit of background will be useful at this point.

In an effort to promote confidence and stability in the international monetary system in the upcoming post–World War II period, a conference of allied nations was held at Bretton Woods, New Hampshire, in 1944. As an outgrowth of this conference, an international organization known as the International Monetary Fund (IMF) was established. Among other things, each member nation of the IMF agreed to maintain specified rates of exchange between its currency and all other currencies. This was to be accomplished by buying or selling its own currency in the foreign exchange market whenever the exchange rate deviated from the "parity rate" by 1 percent, or by making its currency convertible into gold or other reserve assets at the request of another member nation or official institution. As it turned out, countries other than the United States maintained or attempted to maintain the official exchange rate by buying or selling their currencies for dollars, while the United States attempted to maintain a parity between the dollar and gold or other reserve assets tied to gold by offering to sell gold to qualified buyers at a fixed $35 per ounce price. (We will discuss the role of gold and the problem of maintaining adequate reserves shortly.)

The IMF permitted member nations to alter the prices of their currencies in terms of gold (and other currencies) should they encounter a prolonged period of balance of payments disequilibrium. If a nation were running persistent balance of payments deficits, it would be likely to devaluate its currency. More specifically, *devaluation* means that the nation increases the price of gold vis-à-vis its currency. For example, the United States devalued the dollar in 1971 by changing the price of gold from $35 to $38 per ounce, and again in 1973 by increasing the gold price to $42.22 per ounce. Another way of looking at devaluation is that it has the effect of decreasing the price of currency vis-à-vis gold. If other currencies stay tied to gold, it reduces the price of the currency in question relative to other currencies. Recall that this is exactly the same situation we discussed in reference to Figures 15–3 and 15–4. This devaluation has the effect of reducing the supply of imports to a nation while increasing the demand for its exports. And this in turn increases the quantity demanded of the currency in the foreign exchange market while decreasing the quantity supplied, to bring the balance of payments closer to equilibrium.

Occasionally, a nation revalued its currency upward against gold and other currencies, as West Germany, Japan, and a few other nations did in 1971.[11] This has an effect opposite to that of devaluation, in that it decreases the demand for the country's exports and increases the supply of its imported goods.

In practice, member nations of the IMF have adjusted the value of their currencies rather infrequently. Indeed, the United States held to the $35 per ounce gold price from 1934 to August 1971. The rather inflexible exchange rates during the post–World War II period gave rise to a growing balance of payments deficits for the United States, shrinking U.S. gold reserves (from $23 billion in 1952 to $10 billion in 1972) and leaving an increasing number of U.S. dollars in foreign hands. During the 1960s it became increasingly apparent that a realignment of currency values against each other and against gold was the only permanent solution to the disequilibrium in the international money markets. Clearly, the dollar was overpriced vis-à-vis gold and other currencies. Finally, in August 1971 the United States stopped the sale of gold for $35 per ounce and called for a meeting of IMF nations. As a result of this meeting, the dollar price of gold was increased to $38 per ounce. The currencies of the other major trading nations also were appreciated in value relative to the dollar and relative to gold.[12] The realignment of currencies in the 1971 meeting has come to be known as the Smithsonian Agreement.

It was soon evident, however, that the currency and gold price realignment coming out of the Smithsonian Agreement did not bring the IMF parity prices in line with equilibrium prices of currencies in the foreign exchange markets. Indeed, the United States experienced an even larger balance of payments deficit in 1972 than in 1971. This culminated in yet another devaluation of the dollar in 1973, from $38 to $42.22 per ounce of gold.

The second devaluation of the dollar still did not bring the dollar price down to the foreign exchange market equilibrium. The disequilibrium seemed to be widest in the case of the dollar versus the West German mark and the Japanese yen. Even after the second devaluation, the governments of these countries were forced to buy billions of dollars in order to support the mark and

---

[11] In addition to West Germany and Japan, Switzerland, Austria, Belgium, and the Netherlands revalued their currencies upward against gold in 1971.

[12] There were two exceptions. The Italian lira and Swedish krona each declined 1 percent relative to gold.

yen price of the dollar. And each time the United States devalued the dollar, these governments (really, their taxpayers) lost large sums of money. For example, suppose the German government purchased 1 billion U.S. dollars at four marks per dollar in order to keep the price of the dollar from falling below this level. Let us say that after the devaluation of the dollar, the parity ratio became 3.6 marks per dollar. Now the people who sold the 1 billion dollars to the German government had the option of buying them back for 3.6 billion marks. If they did, the outcome was that the German government was left with 400 million fewer marks in its treasury after the U.S. devaluation than before it. The 400 million marks then represented a profit to speculators at the expense of German taxpayers.

Needless to say, any government can soon be expected to grow weary of losing these amounts of money just to support the price of another nation's currency. Hence, it was not long after the 1973 dollar devaluation that most of the major trading nations of the world "floated" their currencies vis-à-vis the dollar—i.e., allowed the dollar to find its own level on the foreign exchange markets of the world. Although the 1973 float technically was a violation of the IMF rules, it had been done before. Canada, for example, allowed the Canadian dollar to float for extended periods during the 1950s and 1960s, and Britain had already floated the pound in mid-1972.

The U.S. dollar, of course, was not always overvalued. Indeed, during the time of the so-called dollar crises in Europe and Japan that we have just discussed, the dollar in some countries was undervalued by the official rate of exchange. This was true in many of the developing countries (especially those experiencing high rates of inflation), the Soviet Union, and its Eastern European satellites. For example, in the 1970s the official exchange rate between rubles and dollars in the Soviet Union was roughly one for one. However, if one knew the right people in Vienna or Moscow, one could obtain about five rubles for the dollar.[13] Thus, the official price of the dollar was set substantially below the price that would have prevailed in a freely functioning foreign exchange market.

The practice of maintaining an artificially low price of foreign currencies can be expected to result in a black market in currencies. For example, it is easy to see how much more a dollar will buy in the Soviet Union if you can obtain five rubles per dollar on the black market as opposed to the one-for-one official rate of exchange. By the same token, Soviet citizens have an incentive to buy these high-priced dollars if they can buy goods on their black market with the dollars that they could not buy with rubles.

FIXED VERSUS FLOATING EXCHANGE RATES

The problems brought on by attempting to maintain official exchange rates that are different from the equilibrium rates established by freely functioning foreign exchange markets have prompted many economists to argue for a system of floating exchange rates. As mentioned, under such a system the price of each currency in terms of other currencies would be allowed to find its own level in foreign exchange markets. Moreover, the price of each currency would

---

[13] This is not meant to encourage such transactions, particularly in the Soviet Union. The penalty for getting caught can be rather harsh.

be allowed to change in response to changes in the demand and supply of the currency in question.

Yet there has been considerable reluctance to turn exchange rates loose. Those who favor a system of relatively fixed rates believe that such a system is more conducive to stability in the international markets than floating rates. As explained previously, a change in the price of a currency causes shifts in the demand and supply for imports and exports. It is argued that these shifts can be disruptive to an economy, especially if foreign trade accounts for a large share of its total economic activity.

In response to this argument, proponents of floating rates grant that a float initially causes shifts in trade patterns if the pegged rates are different from the free-market equilibrium rates. However, this is mainly an adjustment that must take place in order to get the international monetary system's house in order. If rates had not been fixed, this adjustment would have taken place gradually over time. Once the currency exchange market prices approach equilibrium, changes will come mainly in response to changes in the demand and supply conditions of internationally traded goods and services. If the economies of these nations follow an unstable boom and bust pattern, the exchange markets also will follow a similar pattern. But this would not be due to an inherent instability in the foreign exchange markets.

It also has been argued that floating exchange rates tend to result in world-wide inflation as occurred during 1974 just after exchange rates were allowed to float. However, as pointed out in Chapter 1, it is not necessarily true that just because event B occurs after A, then A causes B. In this case the worst inflation occurred just after the abandonment of the fixed exchange rate system. Yet by taking a closer look at the events preceding 1974, we shall see that the attempt to hold to the fixed exchange rates was the more probable contributing factor to inflation.

In the years preceding the float, other governments, particularly West Germany and Japan, supported the price of the U.S. dollar vis-à-vis their respective currencies by purchasing large quantities of dollars that had accumulated in their countries. In the process of buying dollars, these governments injected large amounts of their own currencies into their respective economies. It is only reasonable to expect, therefore, that these countries would experience inflation shortly after these purchases.

Of course, under a system of floating exchange rates a nation that experiences a rate of inflation that is higher than those of its trading partners will experience a decline in the value of its currency in the foreign exchange market because there will be more units of its currency in existence relative to other currencies. This should be looked upon as an advantage rather than a drawback of floating exchange rates. Even though domestic prices will increase during inflation, the prices of goods exported to other nations need not increase (in terms of other nations' currencies) because other nations will be able to buy more units of the inflated currency with each unit of its own currency.

GOLD—THE INTERNATIONAL MONEY

Gold long has been used as an international money to settle accounts between nations. Perhaps the easiest way to see how gold is used is to consider a simple example. Suppose that during a given year U.S. citizens purchase $1,800 million worth of goods and services from West Germany, while Germany buys $1,400 million from the United States. When the books are balanced at the end of the year, financial institutions in West Germany find they have $400 million more U.S. dollars at the end of the year than at the beginning. It is possible that these financial institutions will decide to hold these extra dollars as added U.S. dollar reserves. However, if its dollar reserves are deemed adequate or excessive, the German central bank may decide to exchange these dollars for gold.

Under the rules of the IMF, member nations are obliged to sell gold at the specified price. And this is what the United States did during much of the 1950s and 1960s. Foreign nations accumulated dollars because of the U.S. balance of payments deficits and proceeded to exchange billions of these excess dollars for gold. Moreover, the more certain that foreign dollar holders became that the United States would have to devalue the dollar sometime in the near future, the more incentive they had to exchange dollars for gold. For example, by exchanging $35,000 at the $35 per ounce price, a foreign bank or firm received 1,000 ounces of gold. Exchanging the same $35,000 after the price of gold increased to $38 reduced the gold received to 921 ounces. Thus, if one wanted to exchange surplus dollars for gold, it clearly was better to do it before devaluation than after. As the run on gold continued into the 1970s, the United States government suspended the convertibility of the dollar into gold in August 1971. We should also point out that the U.S. dollar (and to a lesser extent the pound sterling) has been used to supplement gold as international money.

Because of the substantial increase in world trade since the end of World War II, the demand for international reserves also has increased. The supply of gold, on the other hand, grew to a much smaller extent during this time. Thus, the market equilibrium price of gold increased accordingly, breaking the $100 per ounce level in the European gold market in 1973. At that time the official price of gold was $42.22 per ounce in the United States. Because the official price of gold was held substantially below the free-market price in terms of dollars, a "shortage" of gold developed; that is, a greater quantity of gold was demanded than was supplied, at least in reference to dollars.

Because of the large difference between the market price of gold and the official price in the early 1970s, it became apparent that the only lasting solution to the world gold shortage was to allow the price of gold to seek its own market equilibrium. In late 1974, just before it became legal for U.S. citizens to own gold (the first time since 1934), the dollar price of gold exceeded $180 per ounce on the European gold market. Because U.S. citizens turned out to be less inclined to buy gold than many European speculators anticipated, the world market price of gold sagged a bit during the mid-1970s but rebounded to about $800 per ounce before declining to less than half that in the early 1980s.

SPECIAL DRAWING RIGHTS (SDRs)

In an attempt to "demonetize" gold, the IMF created in 1968 a new international money called *special drawing rights* (SDRs), sometimes called "paper gold." These SDRs were created to take the place of gold or other reserve currencies (mainly the U.S. dollar) in settling accounts between nations. The motive here was to create a true international currency that would be free from the influences of private supply and demand fluctuations (as gold) and from changes in domestic monetary policies (as the dollar or pound sterling).

In recent years much of the early enthusiasm over SDRs has faded. When faced with the choice of being paid in gold or pieces of paper printed by the IMF, most creditor nations understandably prefer the real thing. Also, the so-called world gold shortage that existed in the early 1970s has disappeared, as one would expect when the price of gold was freed from its artificially low level. At $400 an ounce, a little gold goes a long way.

MAIN POINTS OF CHAPTER 15

1. International trade is, in reality, trade between people who happen to find themselves within different national boundaries.

2. Trade allows people to specialize in what they do best and hence increases their productive capacity.

3. The most noticeable basis for trade stems from differences in the natural endowment, such as climate, minerals, and water.

4. A nation or area will enjoy a **comparative advantage** in the production of a product if it gives up less of alternative products than do other nations or areas that produce the product.

5. By increasing the output of products in which it holds a comparative advantage and then trading these products for items it finds expensive to produce, a nation can enjoy more of both types of products.

6. Because nations or areas are not homogeneous, we do not observe complete specialization taking place. In other words, because of increasing costs, a nation may lose its comparative advantage in a product as output of the product expands. Also, as comparative advantage becomes less, transport charges may eventually offset the cost advantage, especially for heavy or bulky products.

7. There will be a private incentive for trade to take place as long as an imported item can be purchased at a lower price than it can be sold for in the importing country.

8. As international trade takes place, the people who produce goods and services whose prices are forced down because of lower-priced imports suffer economic losses, at least in the short run.

9. In an effort to limit the import of relatively cheap foreign goods or services, nations have imposed quotas and tariffs. Most of the rationalizations for the existence of trade barriers, however, are based on questionable economic reasoning.

10. **Dumping** refers to the situation where a country sells products on the world market for a lower price than exists in its domestic market, with the difference between the two prices made up by the government.

11. Imports accounted for 8 percent of U.S. GNP in 1982. The largest share of U.S. exports consists of manufactured products, and the largest share of U.S. trade is carried on with the more developed nations of the world.

12. The **balance of trade** refers to the difference in value of exports and imports of merchandise. The **balance of payments** includes the difference between exports and imports but also includes the inflow and outflow of money due to purchases and sale of services, remittances and pensions, grants to foreign countries, investment in other countries, and foreign investment in the country in question.

13. An **exchange rate** is the number of units of one currency that it takes to buy a unit of another currency; that is, it is the price of one currency in terms of another.

14. A reduction in the price of the dollar in terms of marks has the effect of reducing the import supply of German goods in the United States, resulting in an increase in the dollar price paid and a decrease in the mark price received for German imports. The opposite occurred when the dollar appreciated in value relative to the German mark and other currencies in the early to mid-1980s.

15. A reduction in the price of the dollar in terms of marks has the effect of increasing the export demand for U.S. goods sold to Germany, resulting in an increase in the dollar price received and a decrease in the mark price paid for U.S. exports. Again the opposite occurred when the dollar appreciated in value relative to the German mark and other currencies.

16. The supply of dollars in the foreign exchange market is derived from the U.S. demand for imported goods, and the demand for dollars reflects the demand for goods exported by the United States.

17. The demand curve for dollars on the foreign exchange market is downward sloping, indicating that more dollars are demanded when the price of the dollar declines because of the increase in export demand for U.S. products.

18. The supply curve for dollars on the foreign exchange market will be upward sloping as long as the total dollar amount spent on imported goods in the United States declines with a decrease in the price of the dollar.

19. During the early part of the post–World War II period, exchange rates in most of the major trading nations were established by government decree.

20. **Devaluation** refers to a decision by a government to reduce the price of its currency relative to gold and other currencies. This action became necessary during prolonged periods of balance of payments deficits.

21. The official price of the dollar was maintained above its equilibrium price for a number of years by the purchase of U.S. dollars by foreign governments and the willingness of the United States to exchange gold for dollars at a fixed rate of exchange.

22. In countries where the dollar is undervalued, a black market in currency tends to emerge.

23. International monetary authorities have been reluctant to set exchange rates free from controls, ostensibly because of concern over a possible increase in exchange rate fluctuations in foreign exchange markets. Yet infrequent devaluations by countries after prolonged periods of balance of payments disequilbria also create instability.

24. Under a system of floating exchange rates a nation that is experiencing inflation will find its currency decreasing in value relative to other currencies. As a result the increase in domestic prices need not show up as higher prices in other countries that purchase the nation's products.

25. Gold long has been used as an international money to settle debts between nations. The U.S. dollar and the pound sterling also have served as reserve currencies.

26. In 1968 the IMF created special drawing rights (SDRs), sometimes called "paper gold," to ultimately replace gold as the main international money. So far the acceptance of SDRs has been less than enthusiastic, particularly after the price of gold was allowed to rise to its market equilibrium level, thereby eliminating the so-called world gold shortage.

QUESTIONS FOR THOUGHT AND DISCUSSION

1. What are the more obvious reasons for international trade to take place?

2. Consider the following production possibilities schedules for fish and potatoes (chips) for the United States and the United Kingdom:

Possibility	United States		United Kingdom	
	Fish	Chips	Fish	Chips
A	100	0	40	0
B	50	150	20	10
C	0	300	0	20

    a. Calculate the cost of chips in terms of fish given up in both countries.

    b. Calculate the cost of fish in terms of chips given up in both countries.

    c. Which country has a comparative advantage in fish? In chips?

3. What must be true of the trading price if trade is to take place between the two countries?

4. Assuming a trading price of one unit of chips for one unit of fish, show how consumers in both countries could have more of both fish and chips if each country specialized to a certain extent in the production of the good in which it had a comparative advantage and traded part of the increased output to the other country.

5. *a.* Who benefits from the trade discussed in question 3? How?

    b. Is anyone harmed by this trade? Explain.

6. *a.* What is the usual definition of a "favorable" balance of trade?

    b. In what sense is this situation "unfavorable"?

7. *a.* What happened to the supply of Volkswagens for U.S. consumers when the dollar decreased in value in terms of the mark? Explain.

    b. What happened to the dollar price paid and the mark price received for Volkswagens?

8. *a.* During the early to mid-1980s exports of U.S. agricultural product declined. Why?

    b. What happened to the mark price paid and the dollar price received for U.S. feed grains when the dollar appreciated in value?

9. *a.* Why are dollars demanded in foreign exchange markets?

    b. Why are dollars supplied in foreign exchange markets?

    c. Explain how exchange rates between dollars and foreign currencies are established in foreign exchange markets.

10. *a.* By what means did West Germany and Japan maintain the price of the U.S. dollar above the market equilibrium price during the 1960s and early 1970s? What were the consequences of such action?

    b. By what means did the United States maintain the price of gold below its market equilibrium price during the 1960s? What were the consequences of such action?

11. *a.* In the Soviet Union and other communist nations as well as in many less developed countries, U.S. tourists often are approached by locals with an offer to buy dollars at exchange rates higher (more favorable to U.S. citizens) than the official rates. What is this a symptom of?

    b. If countries that export goods to the United States experience inflation, then the United States also will experience inflation because these goods will cost more in terms of U.S. dollars. True or false? Explain.

12. *a.* During the 1960s and early 1970s there was a "shortage" of gold in the world. Why?

    b. At the current price of gold, what are you worth if you are worth your weight in gold?

CHAPTER 16

ECONOMIC GROWTH AND DEVELOPMENT

In this chapter, we will look briefly at the relatively recent phenomenon of economic growth. We say "recent" because from the standpoint of world history, several thousand years elapsed during which the economic well-being of most of the world's population remained at a relatively low level. Indeed, in the developed nations of the world the largest share of economic growth has taken place within the past two centuries.

At the outset it will be useful to define rather specifically what is meant by economic growth. We will define *economic growth* as a long-run sustained increase in the per capita real output of a society. Occasionally growth is defined in terms of the total output of a nation, but for our purposes, growth in the per capita context will be the most useful concept. For lack of a better measure, real output generally is gauged by one of the output measures discussed in Chapter 4 (GNP, NNP, etc.) adjusted by changes in the general price level. However, we should keep in mind the biases of these measures also discussed in Chapter 4.

GROWTH AND THE QUALITY OF LIFE

Until fairly recently, most people thought of economic growth as a desirable goal. In fact throughout a large part of the post–World War II period, nations seemed to have been engaged in a kind of contest to see who could grow the most rapidly. The contest was especially noticeable between the communist or centrally planned economies (mainly the Soviet Union, mainland China, and their satellites) and the nations that have more decentralized economic systems characterized by relatively free markets.

This is not to say that economic growth has now become totally undesirable. Most nations still rank economic growth as a high-priority goal. But in recent years, in the United States at least, a growing number of people have begun to question the wisdom of striving for a high rate of growth. They point to the growing amount of resource scarcities, pollution, congestion, and social instability as the consequences of growth. Some have even suggested that a more desirable goal should be a no-growth economy, implying that the United States is rich enough already.

Upon closer examination of their argument, it becomes apparent that the advocates of a no-growth economy really do not mean that at all. What they appear to be saying instead is that people now are consuming enough automobiles, appliances, luxuries of various types, but not enough of other things, such as clean air and water, a chance to see the blue sky once in a while, and the opportunity to enjoy more peace and serenity. In other words, the no-growth advocates really want growth in the output of such things as pollution control devices and parks—goods and services that improve the environment.

Perhaps a reason for some of the confusion about a no-growth economy is that many things that people once considered "free" goods, such as clean air and water, blue skies, green grass, and the sight of a bird, now are no longer free. In an industrialized society many of these items become economic goods in the sense that alternative goods and services must be given up to obtain them. For example, if we want clean air and water around industrial cities, some of the resources that formerly were devoted to the production of industrial products now must be devoted to the production of pollution control devices.

There may be a few people who would be willing to give up some of their present consumption to obtain more quality in their environment. Surely there are more people, however, who would prefer to retain their present level of consumption and obtain a higher quality of environment through the growth of the economy. Indeed, it seems reasonably safe to say that most people in the United States would prefer both more conventional goods and services and a higher-quality environment. This is particularly true of low-income people.

This point is more clearly seen by observing conditions in the poorer, or less developed, nations of the world. Not only do most people in these countries have substantially fewer conventional goods and services to consume than people in the United States and other developed nations, but they also live in a much more polluted environment. Thus, economic growth for most people of the world has meant an increase in both conventional goods and the quality of the environment as well as more leisure time to enjoy the environment. Of course, in some of the poorest nations economic growth still is a matter of life and death because of the necessity of increasing food production to avoid starvation. Much of the discussion in this chapter will center on the growth and development of the less developed nations of the world.

Perhaps the main point to be made here is that there is really no contradiction between economic growth and quality of life. Indeed it is the phenomenon of economic growth that has freed humans from a lifetime of struggle against famine, disease, and the elements, and allowed them to set their sights on a more comfortable, more enjoyable, and longer existence.

NEW TECHNOLOGY AND THE UNEXPECTED DIVIDEND

Ever since the publication of *Essay on the Principle of Population* in 1798 by Thomas Malthus, the Malthusian doctrine of ever-expanding population pressing against limited food supplies has been a major concern of people. Having the benefit of nearly 200 years of hindsight, we can now say that Malthus's dire predictions have not materialized, at least not for the United States and the more highly developed nations of the world. Indeed, instead of famine, the major agricultural problems of these nations have been overproduction and food surpluses. Why have these nations managed to escape the plague of long-run diminishing returns in the production of food? We know that their populations have grown considerably and that their total land areas have remained about the same or have even declined. For example, in 1950 the total land in farms in the United States (50 states) amounted to 1,162 million acres. By 1969 this figure had been reduced to 1,064 million acres. In 1972 the federal government paid farmers not to grow crops on 62.7 million acres of farmland.[1] During the 1970s much of this land was brought back into production because of the increase in agricultural exports to other countries.

It is interesting to note that the number of people engaged in the production of agricultural products also has declined substantially in the United States. At the end of World War II (1946), employment in agriculture totaled 8.3 million people. By 1984 farm employment had been reduced to 3.3 million people. These substantial reductions in both land and the number of farmers become even more impressive when we consider that the total U.S. population increased from 141 million people in 1946 to more than 236 million in 1984. Thus, we see that the United States, not only has a given land area supplied the food for a greatly increased population, but the amount of land used to produce food and the number of farm people have in fact declined. For the United States, at least, Malthus could not have been more wrong.

But we are still faced with the question of why Malthus was wrong. First, we should bear in mind that Malthus considered only two major resources in the production of food—land and labor. What he failed to consider was the host of new resources or inputs that have come on the scene since his time. Here we have in mind such things as new, improved varieties of crops like hybrid corn, better and cheaper sources of commercial fertilizer, new and improved pesticides and herbicides, and the tremendous increase in tractors and equipment of all kinds. In addition, and perhaps most important, people themselves have become a new and improved resource because of the increased skills they have acquired through research and education. These new synthetic resources,

---

[1] U.S. Department of Agriculture, *Agricultural Statistics,* 1972, pp. 506 and 637.

along with greater knowledge, have enabled mankind to greatly increase the production of food from a given land area.

Of course, we should not criticize Malthus too severely for failing to foresee the additional output that new technology has made possible. During his lifetime the primary inputs in the production of food were labor and land. Diminishing returns will indeed occur in any situation where there is the mere application of additional labor to a fixed amount of land. It is only the application of additional, complementary resources that makes labor and land more productive, thereby offsetting the phenomenon of diminishing returns. To be sure, the law of diminishing returns is still a useful concept in the study of microeconomics.

You may have recognized also that Malthus's pessimistic predictions about the future of mankind have been more nearly borne out in the underdeveloped nations of the world. In many of these nations food shortages and malnutrition have continued to be the major problems. Indeed, in some of these nations people are still perishing because of a lack of food. We will return to a more thorough discussion of the problem of achieving economic growth in the less developed nations later in this chapter.

TECHNOLOGICAL CHANGE

Our discussion thus far has centered mainly on the effects of new technology on the production of food, particularly in reference to the Malthusian doctrine of diminishing returns. We should be aware, however, that new technology has had pronounced effects on virtually every sector of the more highly developed nations. Indeed, the developed nations are characterized by the widespread use of new technology.

The utilization of new and improved resources to achieve a larger level of output in the economy has come to be known as *technological change*. For a long time economists have been aware of increased output that could not be explained by the increased use of conventional resources, such as land, labor, and traditional forms of capital. The additional or unexplained output was then attributed to the phenomenon of technological change. However, the more basic question still remains: What are the causes or sources of technological change? Using the phrase *technological change* as a label for the additional or unexplained output is really nothing more than giving a name to our ignorance.

In more recent years economists have begun to address themselves to the basic question of identifying the sources of technological change. There is still a great deal to be learned in this area, but at the present it is possible to at least make some general statements. At the most general level we can say that the basic source of new technology, or technological change, is new knowledge. By unlocking some of the secrets of the universe, humans have been able to create new inputs or resources that complement or replace traditional resources and increase the total output of goods and services. Hence, it has become possible to increase output without increasing the use of traditional resources. Thus, we observe an increase in output per unit of input because measures of total inputs tend not to reflect the improved quality of inputs or the completely new inputs that have come on the scene.

THE PRODUCTION AND DISTRIBUTION OF KNOWLEDGE

At this point it is legitimate to ask: What are the sources of new knowledge? The nations that have been most successful in acquiring new knowledge have done so through formal, structured research and development activities. Humans have learned a few things in their normal day-to-day activities, but the contributions of learning by doing have been relatively small compared with the contributions of scientists and engineers.

A very important step in the acquisition of new knowledge by a society is the transmission of this knowledge from research workers to the general public. Knowledge that exists only in the minds of scientists or perhaps in scientific journals is of little value to society until it is disseminated to the general public and put to widespread use.

The dissemination or "trickling down" of new knowledge is in most cases a complex process. New knowledge seems to first find its way into professional journals, then into textbooks, most likely at the upper levels of school first, and then gradually out into society as graduates begin to utilize it. For example, the concept of hybridization developed by Mendel was understood only by professional geneticists not too many years ago. Now it is found in undergraduate biology texts and is common knowledge to plant breeders. As knowledge becomes more widely known and accepted, it seems also to become simplified, so that what was initially understood only by a few scientists and teachers later becomes understandable to more and more of the general public, provided, of course, the knowledge proves useful to the public.

COSTS OF ECONOMIC GROWTH

First, we need to remind ourselves that two basic kinds of goods and services are produced in any society: (1) consumption goods and (2) investment goods. If a society insisted on producing only consumption goods and services—that is, if people did not save any of their income, there would be no resources available for investment goods. And, according to the preceding discussion, there would be no chance for economic growth to occur. The fact that most societies have chosen to devote a portion of their resources to the production of investment goods means that they have decided to forgo a certain amount of their present consumption in order to have more consumption goods in the future.

Thus, in one sense we can consider the cost of economic growth as the consumption goods and services we have to give up in order to undertake investment. As members of the present generation, we should be thankful that past generations decided to forgo part of their possible consumption goods in order to produce investment goods, or we would probably still be living in caves, cloaked in animal skins and sustaining ourselves on roots and raw meat.

The fact that a certain amount of present consumption must be given up in order to achieve economic growth presents a serious problem to the less developed nations. If the major part of a nation's resources is required to produce just the necessities of life—food, clothing, and shelter—there is not much chance to forgo consumption goods in order to invest. And if investment is small, the resulting economic growth will tend to be small. Since the end of World War II, many of the developed nations have attempted to provide investment goods, such as technical assistance (knowledge) and a small amount of machinery and other forms of nonhuman capital to their less developed neighbors, but progress has been slow.

In recent years there has been an increase in concern over what might be considered another cost of economic growth, namely the pollution, congestion, social unrest, and other problems that accompany an industrialized society. Part of the difficulty, which we alluded to at the beginning of this chapter, involves obtaining a meaningful measure of economic growth. If in fact the environment has deteriorated significantly over the years, then using GNP to gauge the economic well-being of society will result in an overstatement of economic growth. However, as mentioned, this does not mean that economic growth is undesirable. In order to obtain a more pleasing environment without giving up the consumption goods and services we now have, we must have continued economic growth.

CAPITAL AND GROWTH

Although economists still have a lot to learn about economic growth, it can at least be said that growth will not occur without an increase in the amount of resources or inputs per person; output cannot increase without more inputs. In order to increase per capita inputs there must first be investment. We continue to define investment as the production of new capital. Capital serves to augment labor, thereby increasing the productive capacity of the economy. All capital can be divided up into two broad categories: (1) nonhuman capital and (2) human capital. As the name implies, *nonhuman capital* consists of all the buildings, machines, tools, infrastructure, and so forth, that human beings utilize in the production of goods and services. *Human capital* is the knowledge and skills acquired by people which enable them to also increase their output. Human beings without skills and without tools are very unproductive creatures. Investment in the production of human capital can be further subdivided into two areas: (1) research and (2) education. *Research* is the process of producing new knowledge, whereas *education* distributes both new and formerly produced knowledge among the people. Part of human capital may be acquired through experience and self-teaching but most is acquired through organized research and teaching activities of professional scientists and teachers.

The importance of both human and nonhuman capital to economic growth can be seen more clearly by comparing measures of the per capita stocks of these two forms of capital between the developed and less developed countries. As shown in Table 16–1, per capita GNP is over 40 times greater in the five richest countries shown than in the five poorest. Notice also that the stock of nonhuman capital per person in the five developed countries averaged over 45 times that of the five less developed countries. Using years of schooling as a measure of the stock of human capital, the developed country figure is about 4 times the figure for the least developed countries. Although these are relatively rough measures of the two forms of capital, they do provide an indication of the magnitude of the difference in their stocks between the richest and poorest

TABLE 16-1   Relationship between per capita GNP and capital, 1975*

A. Selected developed countries	GNP (dollars per person)	Nonhuman capital (dollars per person)	Human capital (years of schooling per person)
United States	$5,188	$11,769	8.5
Canada	4,542	11,268	7.3
Sweden	4,423	12,578	6.2
Norway	3,457	11,210	6.3
Belgium	3,185	7,809	6.1
Average	4,159	10,926	6.9

B. Selected less developed countries	GNP (dollars per person)	Nonhuman capital (dollars per person)	Human capital (years of schooling per person)
Cameroon	$153	$386	2.5
Kenya	128	305	2.4
India	102	206	2.9
Upper Volta	63	110	.4
Niger	59	183	.3
Average	101	238	1.7

* Constant 1970 prices and 1970 exchange rates. Nonhuman capital was constructed by summing gross investment over the preceding 15 years. Years of schooling were obtained by estimating students enrolled by level of schooling. For the first level of schooling, enrollments were added over the preceding 50 years; the second level; over the preceding 45 years; the third level, over the preceding 40 years.
    Sources: GNP, investment, and population from World Bank, *World Tables*, 2d edition, 1980. Schooling data from Unesco, *Statistical Yearbook, 1963–74.*

nations.[2] It is interesting to note also that the poorest nations have further to go to catch up to the richest nations in nonhuman capital than in human capital.

INTERNATIONAL COMPARISONS

At this point it will be useful to compare the records of various nations in achieving economic growth. In Table 16–2 we present the 1970 and 1980 per capita GNPs for 14 representative countries, ranging from the most highly developed to the least developed. The average annual growth in per capita GNP in dollars per year for the intervening period also is shown.

There are two major points to be gleaned from Table 16–2. First, notice the extreme variation among countries in the per capita output of goods and services. The people fortunate enough to be born in the nations on the upper end of the scale enjoy 40 to 50 times the annual output of goods and services available to the people of the poorest nations.

The second point to note is the wide variation among countries in the annual growth of per capita GNP shown in the last column. Again in this case, the people living in the richest nations have been able to achieve much larger annual increases in per capita output than the inhabitants of the less developed countries. People living in the richest nations enjoyed close to a $100 annual

[2] For example, doubling the years of schooling probably does not double the stock of human capital.

TABLE 16–2 Estimates of average per capita gross national product in U.S. dollar equivalents, 14 selected countries*

Country	1970	1980	Average annual change, 1970–80
United States	$4,812	$5,456	$ 64
Canada	3,796	5,300	150
Sweden	4,103	4,992	89
West Germany	3,056	4,028	97
Japan	1,957	2,361	40
Austria	1,936	2,737	80
United Kingdom	2,233	2,686	45
Brazil	472	1,140	67
Mexico	657	591	−7
Philippines	224	258	3
Thailand	186	272	9
Pakistan	165	207	4
India	98	118	2
Haiti	73	104	3

* All figures are in constant 1970 dollars and constant 1970 exchange rates.
Source: World Bank, *World Tables*, 3d ed., 1983.

---

increase in per capita real GNP over the 1970–80 period, whereas the inhabitants of the poorest countries managed only two to three dollars per year growth. In order for the poor nations to catch up, they must achieve a larger average annual absolute growth than their richer neighbors. Considering their small base values of per capita GNP, this requires an extremely high percentage rate of growth—something most poor nations have not been able to achieve. In a relative sense, at least, it appears that the rich are getting richer and the poor are getting poorer, as far as nations are concerned.

GROWTH IN THE LESS DEVELOPED COUNTRIES

Because of the extremely low level of per capita output in the less developed countries (LDCs), together with their relatively small annual growth, the problem of achieving economic growth is both more critical and more perplexing than is the case in the richer nations. Of course, the general statements about the sources of new knowledge and the need to invest in activities that increase knowledge and education as well as the need for new forms of nonhuman capital to achieve economic growth apply to both the developed and less developed nations. However, because of the critical nature of the problem in the less developed nations, it will be useful to consider these in somewhat more detail.

First, we should bear in mind that the attainment of economic growth is a matter of life and death for many people in countries where the supply of food is extremely limited. Without food today, there is no tomorrow to enjoy the fruits of economic progress. It becomes apparent, then, that less developed nations are faced with a dilemma. The acquisition of new knowledge, increasing the level of education, and the production of new forms of nonhuman capital are long-run phenomena, taking perhaps several generations to bear significant results. Yet there is a critical short-run problem of staving off famine. An adequate food supply is necessary for people to be able to work and be reasonably productive.

To survive the difficult short-run future, most less developed nations have attempted to adapt the knowledge and technology of the developed nations to their situations. These efforts have been moderately successful. Certain knowledge (e.g., the concept of hybridization, the technology for harnessing power such as electricity, the internal combustion engine, jet propulsion, and the know-how for nitrogen fixation and chemical production) can be applied in any locality. On the other hand, certain technology, particularly that which is biological in nature such as new varieties of crops, must be developed in the area in which it is to be utilized. Varieties of hybrid corn that produce record yields in Iowa fare no better, and sometimes fare worse, than traditional varieties in Mexico and Argentina.

It is very important also to consider the profitability of new types of technology. It is a mistake to conclude that new inputs or resources that are profitable in the developed economies also will be profitable in the underdeveloped countries. A major consideration is differences in wage rates between nations. Laborsaving technology that is profitable in countries where labor is relatively scarce and wages are high can be unprofitable in countries where labor is abundant and wages low.

AGRICULTURAL DEVELOPMENT

Agriculture is by far the dominant industry in the less developed nations of the world. It is common to observe between two thirds and three fourths of the total population of the LDCs directly engaged in agriculture. In contrast, farmers constitute less than 5 percent of the population in the United States. As a general rule, the poorer the nation, the larger is the proportion of the population engaged in agriculture. This is not particularly surprising. The first order of business in staying alive is to obtain nourishment. Once food requirements are met and surpassed, some of the people engaged in food production can leave agriculture to produce such things as better housing, medical care, transportation, and the host of items that contribute to human comfort and enjoyment.[3]

This phenomenon of course has happened in the United States and the other more highly developed nations of the world. At the time of the American Revolution, the United States was as much an agricultural nation as most LDCs are today. But as the nation developed, a progressively smaller share of the population produced food and a progressively larger share produced other things.

It is apparent, therefore, that agricultural development is of major importance in the overall development of the LDCs. Unless their major industry can become more productive, there is little chance of releasing people from agriculture to produce more of the other amenities of life or to trade agricultural products for industrial products produced by other nations.

Unfortunately, there is no simple formula that a nation can follow to rap-

---

[3] An exception would be a nation that retains a relatively large agricultural sector but trades its excess agricultural commodities with other nations for industrial goods. Denmark and New Zealand are examples.

idly increase the productive capacity of its agriculture. The process is relatively slow and is likely to differ among countries. About all we can do here is to present some ideas that appear to have general application across various situations.[4]

The sources of economic growth presented in a previous section apply to agricultural development in particular as well as to overall economic growth and development. The key is making high-payoff investments, but the question is where these investments are to be found. From past experience, we can say with some confidence that they are not found in the production of more traditional inputs, such as bullocks or wooden plows. Although additions to these inputs provide some increase in food and fiber production, the increase will be relatively small.

The investments that give rise to new nontraditional inputs, particularly new varieties of crops, fertilizer, and irrigation facilities, appear to have paid off handsomely in the LDCs. Because plants can produce carbohydrates and protein more efficiently than animals, crops have been utilized much more as a direct source of food in the LDCs than in the developed nations. Unfortunately, because of differences in soil, day length, temperature, and so forth, it usually is not possible to relocate proven varieties of crops from one nation to another, or even from one locality to another. As a result investments first have to be made in research facilities that can develop new varieties suited for a particular area. The International Rice Research Institute in the Philippines and the Rockefeller corn and wheat programs in Mexico, headed by Dr. Norman Borlaug (a recent Nobel Prize winner for his efforts), have been particularly successful in this endeavor.

New varieties of crops with high-yield potentials usually cannot reach their potentials, and may not even achieve the yields of traditional varieties, without increased fertilization. Thus, investments are required in fertilizer production facilities, or imports of plant nutrients must be increased. In many parts of the world, irrigation water must be supplied in order for crops to approach their yield potential. North America and Europe are somewhat unique in that a large share of agricultural production can be carried on under conditions of natural rainfall. Many of the less developed nations do not have this advantage.

The application of fertilizer and water to improved varieties of crops may also require a change in production techniques. For example, increasing the fertility of the soil, as well as adding water, usually intensifies the weed problem. So farmers must become better managers and in a sense become a "new input" themselves. Greater use of agricultural chemicals, mainly herbicides and insecticides, also may be required to control weeds and insects. After all, more plant food and greater yields produce a more favorable environment for yield-reducing weeds, insects, and plant diseases. The timing of planting and harvesting also tends to become more critical with the higher yielding varieties.

The gradual shift from a subsistence type of agriculture (where farmers produce mainly for their own use) to a commercial agriculture (where a greater portion of the output is sold) requires additional transportation and marketing

---

[4] For additional reading on the problem of agricultural development, see T. W. Schultz, *Transforming Traditional Agriculture* (New Haven, Conn.: Yale University Press, 1964); A. W. Mosher, *Getting Agriculture Moving* (New York: Agricultural Development Council, 1966); and Y. Hayami and V. W. Ruttan, *Agricultural Development: An International Perspective* (Baltimore: The Johns Hopkins Press, 1971).

facilities. So additional investments generally are required in these areas. In the United States and many other developed nations of the world, farmers have formed cooperatives for the purpose of marketing their products. Farmers in LDCs also are turning in this direction. Certainly there is not much incentive for farmers to increase production by adopting new varieties and other new inputs unless they can be reasonably sure they can sell their added output for a profit. Although if there are profits to be made in buying from farmers and selling in urban markets, we can be quite sure that entrepreneurs will emerge to perform this service, provided the government allows this activity to take place.

It is quite common in LDCs for governments to restrict competition while giving monopoly power to government agencies both in the purchase of agricultural products and in the production and sale of inputs for agriculture, such as fertilizer and seeds. A common outcome of this situation is lower than market prices paid to farmers for their products, and higher than world prices charged for the inputs. This phenomenon is due in part to attempts by governments to obtain revenues from the profits of these purchases and sales. But it may also be due to inefficiency stemming from the monopoly position of the government agencies. In either case, farmers are poorly served; they receive low prices for their products and pay high prices for the inputs they purchase. Even when governments allow competition to prevail, the same outcome may result if taxes are levied on exports and imports. The general result of the disincentives faced by farmers is a retardation of agricultural development, and sometimes famine for the entire country. We will return to this issue in a later section.

INDUSTRIAL DEVELOPMENT

Although the LDCs by their nature are highly agricultural, the industrial or nonagricultural sector offers the greatest potential for growth. As implied in the previous section, the industrial sector must provide an increasing proportion of inputs utilized in the agricultural sector, such as machinery, tools, chemicals, fertilizers, and transportation facilities and equipment. One characteristic of a modern agricultural sector is that a large share of its inputs is produced off the farm. In other words, growth in the farm supply industries is an important determinant of growth in agriculture.

In addition to providing new, nontraditional inputs for agriculture, the industrial sector must provide many of the inputs for its own production of consumer goods. Industrial inputs, such as machinery, tools, buildings, and chemicals, are themselves the output of the industrial sector. Of course, as the economy grows, the industrial sector faces an ever-increasing demand for consumer goods of all types: housing, clothing, shoes, furniture, refrigerators, stoves, air conditioners, automobiles, radios, and television sets, to name a few.

Since industrial technology is not likely to be as location-specific as agricultural technology, it is somewhat easier for industrial firms in the LDCs to draw upon the technological base of the developed nations. However, a major difficulty of transferring industrial technology from the developed to the less developed nations stems from the wide difference between the two in wage rates relative to the price of capital. In the less developed nations wage rates tend to be low relative to the price of capital. The opposite is true in the developed nations. Because labor is relatively cheap in the LDCs, production should utilize more labor relative to capital in order to minimize costs. As a result the production processes of the developed nations cannot (or at least should not) be exactly reproduced in the LDCs if the LDCs wish to utilize their abundant supply of labor and minimize costs. The same, of course, holds true for agriculture as far as the substitution of machines for labor is concerned.

The kinds of products demanded and produced in the LDCs also differ from those of the developed nations. Instead of expensive two-ton automobiles designed to cruise at 70 miles per hour down a four- or six-lane expressway, they need motor bikes and relatively cheap, rugged cars that can maneuver down narrow, often unpaved roads. In general, their demand is mainly for relatively simple items that can be operated and repaired without a high degree of engineering skill.

By the same token, the manufacturing establishments themselves tend not to be large and highly sophisticated. Much of the manufacturing in the LDCs is carried out in relatively small establishments or machine shops, many employing no more than 5 to 10 people. Each establishment may produce a simple final product or a single component of a final product. Indeed, the phenomenon of subcontracting is quite common in the LDCs. Basically, it allows specialization of functions by employees without requiring the firms to be large. It is easy to underestimate the entrepreneurship of small businesspeople in the LDCs. If there are profits to be made, someone is usually there to take advantage of the situation.

Another problem of industrial development in the LDCs is the mobilization of sufficient funds to finance business firms. The most efficient way to draw together funds, at least large amounts, is by a stock market. Without a stock market, firms have to utilize borrowed funds to a large extent, which in turn places relatively low limits on firm size unless the owner already is wealthy.

The entrance of multinational firms into the LDCs provides another source of financing industrial development. Usually these firms provide the plant, equipment, and management while employing domestic labor and raw materials. This kind of arrangement can work to the benefit of both the firm and the LDC. The firm taps a relatively cheap source of labor, and possibly raw materials, in producing a product that can be sold for a profit in the LDC itself or can be shipped to another even more profitable market. The people of the LDC, on the other hand, gain some additional industrial output or the means to buy such output on the world market.

In recent years some LDCs have become more nationalistic, purposely making it more difficult for foreign firms to carry on business in their countries. In certain cases the firms' assets have been expropriated by their host country. Whether or not the charges of exploitation and the like levied against the firms involved are justified is a question we cannot answer here. It appears, however, that banishment of a foreign firm by a host LDC does not, in general, further the economic development of the country in question. The country obtains some physical assets, which in most cases it could have purchased in the world market, but loses the management skills provided by the firms. The latter input is usually the most difficult to come by in an LDC. When the risk of expropriation increases, other foreign firms may not wish to "touch the country with a 10-foot pole," or may insist on a higher rate of profit in order to write off their assets in a shorter period of time. Of course, if a host LDC gives up more than it receives from a foreign firm, it is not surprising that the firm will not be welcome. But there is no reason contractual arrangements cannot be worked out that can provide a mutual benefit to both the LDC and the foreign firm.

INFRASTRUCTURE: DEVELOPMENT AND FINANCE

In using the term *infrastructure* here, we have in mind a network of transportation and communication facilities, together with such public utilities as electricity, telephone, water supply, and waste disposal. Although the major cities in most LDCs (with the exception of the very poor districts) in general have modern and adequate infrastructures, the same usually is not true for the interior or rural regions. Such an imbalance of infrastructure contributes to the very uneven growth pattern in many LDCs. Their major cities become hardly distinguishable from New York, Chicago, or Los Angeles, while the interior lags a hundred years or more behind, not only in terms of per capita income but also in terms of public conveniences, such as paved roads, public transportation, electricity, telephones, radio and television, and waste and sewage disposal—services people take for granted in the large cities or in the developed nations. Understandably, this situation in turn contributes to increased migration from the backward areas to the cities, further aggravating the congestion and unemployment problems of the cities.

Of course, it is one thing to say that the interior needs roads, bridges, electric and telephone lines, and railroads; it is quite another thing to supply these facilities. Although their construction usually is in the hands of the government of the LDC, they still require the use of scarce resources. In order to buy these resources, either domestically or abroad, the government must acquire the money. The question is: Where and how?

Most LDCs have a small number of relatively rich (and influential) families that certainly could afford to pay more taxes to provide more government revenue. However, these families often have gotten to be rich because of special favors or tax advantages bestowed by past or present governments. And if the rich still enjoy considerable influence in the government, it is not difficult to understand why the government is reluctant to soak the rich.

Even if the government were to substantially increase the taxes paid by rich or high-income people, the total tax take may not increase substantially because the rich are relatively few in number. Certainly the added taxes would not meet the demand for infrastructure development. This leaves the poor (the vast majority of the people) and a small but growing middle class (if the nation is growing). Not even the most heartless of governments is anxious to tax the poor, which puts the major share of the tax burden on the middle class, usually the top-level civil service, management, and professional people in the large cities. But the ability to tax these people also is limited. For one thing, the income tax laws of most LDCs tend to have rather large loopholes. Also, the tradition of paying income taxes is not well established, so that tax evasion is a major problem. Moreover, an excessive rate of taxation dampens private incentive. Since these people are relatively mobile and usually can earn higher incomes in the developed nations, the LDCs certainly cannot afford to lose their services by taxing them out of the country. These people also are not likely to be very happy about paying a major part of the cost of infrastructure development in the interior. Certainly they are not likely to see much, if any, personal benefit from this public expenditure unless they are planning to migrate to the interior, which is most unlikely.

Because of the problems of taxing income, governments of LDCs have turned more to taxes on internationally traded commodities. Certainly these taxes are the easiest to collect. All the goods are funneled through one or at most a few ports of entry, so evasion is relatively difficult. It is not uncommon to observe taxes on certain imports equal to their world market prices, especially on so-called luxury items, such as automobiles and appliances. Because the higher-income people tend to buy these items, it is one way of taxing the rich. However, the low- and middle-income people are at the same time deprived of these commodities because their prices are driven up so high by the taxes.

Since exports also are easy to tax, they too provide a tempting source of government revenue. But because the LDCs are highly agricultural, exports are heavily weighted with these commodities. The major difficulty with export taxes is that they lower the price received by domestic producers of the items. As a consequence their profitability is reduced and output is less than it would otherwise be. In view of the importance of agricultural development in the LDCs, these taxes leave much to be desired.

As explained in Chapter 12, governments can of course spend more than they take in by tax revenues. Part of the deficit can be made up by selling government bonds and part by issuing new currency. In most LDCs the latter means of financing a deficit has been more popular than the former, and by now it is clear that large increases in the money supply result in high rates of inflation, which indeed is common in many LDCs. Of course, inflation also amounts to a tax on holders of money, so the government still is left with the two alternatives of taxing or borrowing.

Funds for infrastructure development also may be obtained by borrowing (or gifts) from governments of developed nations or international lending agencies such as the World Bank. Loans and interest must of course be paid eventually, but payment can be postponed until the government of the LDC is in a better position to raise the revenue, perhaps from a broader tax base.

EDUCATION: DEVELOPMENT AND FINANCE

Much of what we said about infrastructure development and finance applies also to education. People living in the major cities generally have access to at least average-quality public or private schooling, again with the possible exception of the very poor. In the rural areas, if schools even exist, the quantity and quality of schooling obtained by the people tend to be much lower than those in the major city or cities. In rural areas it is not uncommon to see only one third to one half of the children in school, with the number falling to 10 to 15 percent for young people of high school age. Nor is it uncommon to find two thirds to three quarters of the adult population illiterate in rural areas.

We should be careful, however, not to equate illiteracy with lack of intelligence. There is no reason to believe that the average level of innate intelligence (however measured) is lower for populations with a low level of schooling than it is for people living in the developed nations. Nor should we be so presumptuous as to believe that people with little or no schooling cannot learn. Granted the ability to read facilitates further learning, but learning also can take place by oral communication and observation. Experience has shown that illiterate farmers can and do adopt new inputs or techniques from their better-schooled neighbors, from farm supply firms, or from extension agents if the techniques or inputs are profitable. Similarly, new factory workers tend to grasp what they need to know after a few weeks on the job. This is not to downgrade the importance of education; we argue only that economic growth can take place without waiting several generations for the major portion of the population to become literate.

In the area of education the first order of business is to bring all children who are capable of learning up to the level where they can read and write with some facility; perhaps up to the equivalent of an eighth-grade education in the United States. This should enable them as adults to learn new things more easily and also make it possible for increasing numbers to obtain the equivalent of high school, college, or professional training.

Investment in human beings, like investment in infrastructure, requires scarce resources, namely teachers and school facilities. Someone has to pay for these resources. If they are to be provided by the government, the government must first acquire the necessary funds. We need not restate the problems discussed in the previous section in regard to obtaining tax revenue.

Assuming that some resources are allocated to education, it may be another matter to obtain teachers. Since relatively few people have advanced through the equivalent of the high school level, few are available as teachers. Those who have completed the necessary training are likely to prefer life in the major city rather than in the countryside. Thus, wages probably will have to be substantially higher in the interior in order to attract good teachers away from the advantages of the city. The opposite is usually the case.

Assuming that teachers and facilities can be provided, there has to be demand for the education. Parents with little or no schooling may not recognize the importance of educating their children beyond their level even if the education is free. The problem is that the education will not in general be free to the parents, because after the age of 9 or 10 children become economic assets to peasant farmers. If the children are in school, they cannot be contributing to the family income, which is likely to be extremely low as it is. The problem can be reduced somewhat by dismissing school during times of peak labor demand (such as planting and harvesting) and holding classes when the children are less in demand at home. To ensure anything near universal attendance, schooling probably has to be made mandatory up to a minimum level, such as the sixth or eighth year.

The cost of education increases as a greater proportion of young people go on to high school and college. In part this is due to more expensive (more highly trained) teachers and facilities. But even more important is the increase in forgone earnings (loss of output) that is incurred as young people attend school rather than enter the labor force. Although the absolute size of these earnings may be small relative to earnings forgone by comparable students in developed nations, they often make a substantial difference in the amount of food and clothing that the students and their families can enjoy. Consequently, the value of forgone earnings is likely to be even more important to young people in LDCs, particularly to students from rural areas, than to students in the developed nations.

In many developing nations, particularly the Latin American countries, a large proportion of college students hold full-time jobs during the day and attend classes in the evening. Although this practice reduces forgone earnings, it also reduces students' study time considerably and therefore reduces the quality of their education. Similarly, many college professors in these countries hold full-time positions in the government, the professions, or the business world, as well as teaching. Again, this limits the time teachers can spend in preparing for classes and in keeping up with new developments in their professions. The necessity for college professors to hold other jobs stems largely from the low salaries they receive relative to what they could earn in other occupations that require comparable training. Low salaries also deter capable people from entering the teaching profession, which in turn holds the quality of education below what it would otherwise be.

THE AGRICULTURAL ADJUSTMENT PROBLEM

In the event that the LDCs can overcome the problems we have been discussing and start down the road of sustained growth, there are some other problems that will be encountered because of that growth. A major one is the agricultural adjustment problem—the movement of a substantial share of the population out of agriculture into the industrial and service trades.

As the industrial sector of a nation begins to develop, wages of nonfarm people tend to increase relative to those of farm people. If at the same time, agriculture is able to increase its productivity, the supply of agricultural products is likely to increase relative to the demand causing the prices of farm products to decline. Both of the above factors cause nonfarm income to increase relative to farm income. This in turn provides an incentive for people to leave agriculture. As the agricultural population declines, the remaining land is left in the hands of fewer people, which increases their resources and helps them to increase their incomes along with the nonfarm population.[5]

The migration from agriculture usually begins with young people who have just completed their educations and are embarking on their careers. Young women go in greatest number, with the young men following close behind. Next in line are the small farmers who find their meager incomes becoming smaller relative to nonfarm wages. Of course, in order to leave agriculture, one must find a job in another occupation. This is where the problem begins.

Although the industrial sector is likely to be expanding in a growing economy, it may not be expanding fast enough to absorb the large influx of farm people. As a result unemployment grows in the cities. Shanty towns made of tin and cardboard inhabited by the poor, unemployed new arrivals from the countryside begin to spring up. It is unlikely that the already hard-pressed government can provide many public services such as waste disposal and health and education services. Because of the crowded and unsanitary conditions, disease and malnutrition are common. No doubt many wonder whether they should have left their former homes in the first place.

Some of the more fortunate and able-bodied migrants find jobs in factories and shops. Others find temporary employment, usually in the service trades. Selling newspapers, shining shoes, operating a taxi, and working as a maid or

---

[5] Yoav Kislev and Willis Peterson, "Prices, Technology and Farm Size," *Journal of Political Economy*, 90 (June 1982), pp. 578–95.

gardener are some of the common means of earning enough to stay alive while searching for more permanent employment.

In spite of low incomes in agriculture, some people choose to remain on their farms. Usually, these are the older farmers who are too young (or too poor) to retire but too old or unskilled to find employment in the cities. As a result they continue to work their small plots until they eventually pass from the scene.

What can be done to alleviate the agricultural adjustment problem? One big thing the government can do is to ensure freedom of entry into all occupations or training programs for all who have the necessary skills or capabilities. There is a natural tendency for unions representing the skilled trades to restrict entry into their respective trades. This is usually accomplished by regulating the number of people who can enter the training program—either apprenticeships or formal schooling. By so doing, unions limit the supply of labor and raise the wages of those lucky enough to be established members.

Powerful industrial unions also can make it more difficult for farm people to obtain work in the unskilled and semiskilled occupations. If these unions under threat of strike can obtain a union wage that is substantially above the free-market wage, employers will attempt to substitute machines for labor. Even if the established union members can retain their jobs, the newly arrived and inexperienced ex-farmers will have a more difficult time obtaining jobs at the comparatively high union wage.

A similar effect can be created by a government-imposed minimum wage if it is above what would prevail in a relatively free labor market. Here again, employers are motivated to substitute machines for labor. A high wage does not do a worker any good if the person cannot find a job at that wage.

Sometimes governments of LDCs have made the agricultural adjustment problem worse than it need be by subsidizing the purchase of agricultural machinery, particularly for large farmers. The subsidy often takes the form of providing low-interest credit for buying farm equipment. In this case, the large farmers are induced to substitute machines for labor. As you can see, a combination of a relatively high minimum (or union) wages together with subsidized farm machinery squeezes poor farm laborers or small farmers from two directions, leaving them unable to find employment in agriculture or in industry.

Governments could also take an active role in providing information to farmers on job vacancies in the cities. Many farm people probably migrate with the expectation of finding jobs that do not exist. If information were available on actual opportunities, or if farm workers could be hired before they migrate, the time spent living in slum conditions while looking or waiting for a permanent job could be eliminated or at least shortened for many.

The preceding discussion is not intended to convey the impression that a nation would be better off if farm people remained on farms. It is precisely the movement of people off the farms that provides the wherewithal for a nation to increase its output of goods and services. If a nation requires 70 to 80 percent of its people to produce food, it cannot produce much of anything else; hence, the country remains poor. The vast array of goods and services, such as housing, medical care, education, roads, transportation, and energy, that are produced by former farmers or descendants of farmers is what distinguishes rich from poor nations. This points up the key role that agriculture plays in overall economic development. Without agricultural development, there is not much chance for people to leave agriculture since food ranks number one on the list of essentials to stay alive.

THE POPULATION PROBLEM

Improvement in the economic well-being of the average person in a developing country depends on two factors: (1) growth in the total output of the economy and (2) growth in the population of the country. The per capita output of a nation can increase only if total output increases more rapidly than population. If population is growing at the same rate as total output, the economic well-being of the average person remains unchanged. Per capita output can be increased by a reduction in the population growth or by an increase in the rate of growth of total output.

An unfortunate characteristic of most less developed nations is that they exhibit a relatively high population growth. As more and more people press against the land area and other resources of these nations, the pessimistic predictions of Malthus are more nearly borne out. Hence, in recent years there has been an increased awareness of the need for the LDCs to practice some form of population control.

The extent of the population problem in the less developed nations is illustrated in Table 16–3. Notice that the average population growth rate of the

TABLE 16–3 Annual population growth rates, 14 selected countries, 1970–81

Developed	Percent	Less developed	Percent
Austria	0.1	Brazil	2.1
Canada	1.2	Colombia	1.9
West Germany	0.2	India	2.1
Japan	1.1	Kenya	4.0
Sweden	.3	Mexico	3.1
United Kingdom	0.1	Pakistan	3.0
United States	1.0	Zambia	3.1

Source: World Bank, *World Tables*, 3d ed., 1983.

group of representative developed nations shown in the left-hand column is less than one fourth of the average population growth rate of the selected group of less developed countries shown in the right-hand column.

Although we still have much to learn about population theory, a few factors seem to be important in determining or influencing population growth. Taking into account migration between countries, a nation's population growth depends both on its death rate and on its birth rate. If the birth rate is larger than the death rate, obviously population grows.

One of the important factors contributing to the spurt of population growth in the LDCs, particularly during the years following World War II, was the drop in infant mortality due to the availability of new drugs and better medical care. Families that had 8 to 10 babies with the expectation of 4 or 5 dying as infants found their family size increasing as fewer died than expected. Of course, a lower infant mortality need not lead to a preference for larger families. But during the time it took parents to become adjusted to the lower death rate among infants, population grew rapidly.

Assuming that families eventually return to a so-called equilibrium family size, it is likely that this size will still be substantially larger for the LDCs than for the developed nations. Why? There probably are a number of reasons, both economic and noneconomic. We still have much to learn about the factors determining family size. However it does appear that one important economic factor is the price (or cost) of rearing and educating a child.

The price, or total cost, of rearing a child depends on a number of items. Most obvious is the cost of food, clothing, and medical care. Education also is a major item that includes out-of-pocket costs (tuition, books, etc.) as well as forgone earnings. For poor rural families in LDCs, the forgone earnings to the family become important rather early in life. As mentioned earlier, a child going to school cannot be working in the fields. In fact, it is very likely that many children in LDCs turn out to be an economic asset to their parents rather than a cost. In contrast, children reared in cities, particularly in developed nations with child labor and minimum wage laws, do not have as many opportunities to contribute to the family income.

Another less obvious cost is the time spent by the mother in rearing the child. For a mother living on a farm in an LDC, this cost is not so important because she takes the child with her to work. But this time cost is quite important for a highly educated woman in developed nations. The reduced birth rate in the United States of late might be attributed to the increased educational levels and employment opportunities for women outside the home, thus raising the price of children.

At any rate, it appears that the price or cost of a child is least in the rural areas of the LDCs. And with a low price, we might expect that more will be demanded, which seems to be the case. The price of children in a nation tends to rise as a greater proportion of the children are reared in cities. So we might expect some tendency for the birth rate to fall in the LDCs as people migrate from rural areas.

Recent advances in birth control technology have made it easier for parents to voluntarily limit the size of their families. Of course, this is no guarantee that parents will want to do so, especially low-income parents in rural areas. Considering that such action may constitute a short-run economic loss to these parents, we have little basis for optimism. Also, children tend to be a major source of old-age assistance for parents in LDCs. If governments of the LDCs are determined to reduce population growth, they may have to institute policies that make children more expensive or less essential for survival of parents in their old age.

THE FOREIGN EXCHANGE PROBLEM

We argued that the key to economic growth in the LDCs is in the use of new, nontraditional inputs. However, in large part the knowledge and the facilities to produce these inputs do not exist in the LDCs. Thus, it is necessary for the LDCs to either purchase these inputs from the developed nations or import equipment and the technical know-how in order to produce them domestically. For most LDCs both lines of action generally are followed, but in either case, foreign currencies (or gold) are required to make such purchases. The needed foreign exchange is obtained mainly by selling to the developed nations.

What do the LDCs have to sell that the developed nations want to buy? A few of the more fortunate LDCs have petroleum, which is very much in demand in the developed nations and thus provides a good source of foreign exchange earnings. Other LDCs have rich mineral deposits, which are in high demand in the developed nations. But for the most part the LDCs are agricultural. One might expect the LDCs to have a comparative advantage in agriculture vis-à-vis the developed nations. However, because of the unproductive nature of agriculture in the LDCs, there is little surplus that can be exported. Some exceptions are the specialty crops such as coffee, sugar, tea, bananas, and citrus fruits. But in the case of livestock products and food and feed grains, the agricultural industries of the developed nations seem capable of satisfying their domestic demands and even producing surpluses.

Many LDCs therefore are caught in a situation where they are buying more from the developed nations than the developed nations are buying from them. The inevitable result is a drawing down of the international reserves of these countries. Hence, they must limit their imports of new inputs or facilities and live within their means. This in turn limits their ability to buy new inputs required for the development process.

In recent years some of the LDCs have been able to earn foreign exchange through the export of labor-intensive industrial products, such as clothing, shoes, radios, and electronic components. South Korea and Taiwan have been especially successful in this area. However, this requires some development of the industrial sector and a growing productivity of the agricultural sector in order to maintain food production with less labor. Of course, if the LDCs can buy some of their food and feed grains from the developed nations more cheaply than they can produce these products themselves, labor can (and should) be withdrawn from agriculture in order to increase the output of manufactured goods for export to the developed nations.

Thus, we observe a rather curious and unexpected phenomenon of the LDCs exporting manufactured products to the developed nations in return for agricultural products. However, this phenomenon is not so surprising if we keep in mind that the manufactured goods exported by the LDCs tend to be labor-intensive and that the food and feed grains are produced in the developed nations under capital-intensive techniques.

This is not to say that the developed nations will someday revert to an agricultural status, with the LDCs becoming industrial. It is not likely that even the very productive agriculture of the developed nations can make much of a dent in supplying the demand for food of the two thirds of the world's population that reside in the LDCs. In order for the people of the LDCs to enjoy some of the fruits of their growing industrial sectors, most will have to increase the productive capacity of their agricultural sectors as well. Otherwise their agricultural output will continue to decline as people are drawn into the industrial sector. As a result more and more food will have to be imported, most likely at increasing prices, which in turn have to be paid for by exports. In other words, a majority of their population will still be engaged in activities aimed at satisfying their demand for food.

INCOME REDISTRIBUTION

A common characteristic of virtually all LDCs is a relatively unequal distribution of income. We tend to observe the vast majority of people existing on a very low income and a relatively few people enjoying a lavish standard of living. In the main, these unfortunate situations have come about because of special favors or outright grants of land or property bestowed by past governments to a few privileged families or royalty.

In recent years governments of some LDCs have made progress toward redistributing income and wealth. In agriculture, land reform, whereby large holdings are split up into smaller plots and given or sold to landless peasants, has been a common device for redistributing wealth and income. It is also anticipated that an agriculture consisting of owner-operators will be more productive than one consisting of large holdings under absentee landlords. In the nonagricultural sector, increases in taxes on high incomes, the closing of tax loopholes, and higher excise taxes on luxury items have been used as redistributive devices.

Some nations have resorted to even more drastic means, such as the confiscation of property by the government. Usually this has come about in conjunction with a change in the political system, as in the Soviet Union, its satellites, and mainland China. Any reasonable person must abhor the wholesale slaughter of people that took place in communist regimes in order to establish their political systems. The loss of life as well as loss of virtually all personal freedoms represents an extremely high cost of income redistribution.

Although most of us desire peaceful and cooperative methods of income and wealth redistribution as opposed to violent and coercive means, its importance to economic growth should be emphasized. In a situation where a few are very rich and the masses are very poor, there is little incentive for those in power (the rich) to change the existing political-economic structure of the country. Those in power have much to lose and little to gain by change. As a result the very poor continue to live as they have done for centuries, while the rich, through income derived from property, are able to enjoy the fruits of economic progress of the developed nations.

Needless to say, this kind of situation tends to foster a great deal of resentment and hatred on the part of the masses toward the privileged few. Frequently the outcome of such an environment is violent revolution. Unfortunately, in the aftermath of such revolution the poor often find themselves suffering under just another kind of political and economic repression. In this case wealth and power may come from the "ownership" of positions in the military or the government rather than from ownership of physical property. It is not clear that the former is any more desirable than the latter. A landlord or property owner may have the power to influence a poor person's economic position but generally does not have the power or the incentive to imprison or execute a person on account of uncomplimentary things the person might say about his or her repressor.

ECONOMIC INCENTIVES AND GOVERNMENT POLICIES

One of the lessons that many have learned, and many more have yet to learn, about the people living in the LDCs is that they respond to economic incentives as much as people living in the developed nations. An explanation sometimes given for the existence of the LDCs is that their people lack the ambition or the motivation to better their lot and prefer instead the "simple life." The stereotyped native sleeping in the shade of a palm tree often is used to represent this attitude.

Yet the more we learn about the LDCs the more apparent it becomes that the vast majority of their people, whether rural or urban, do take advantage of opportunities to increase their incomes. Farmers readily adopt new higher-yielding varieties of crops, apply commercial fertilizer if it is profitable, and switch to crops that provide the greatest profits. By the same token, rural people migrate to cities in search of higher-paying occupations and urban workers sell their services to employers who pay the highest wages. People in the LDCs, as everywhere, attempt to spend their incomes on goods and services that provide the most for the money. Trite phrases such as "the Protestant ethic" or "the work ethic" no longer can be used to explain differences in income among nations.

The desire to increase one's income is, of course, the ultimate prerequisite for economic growth. Such a desire among the people of the LDCs provides a strong positive force for economic growth and development. At the same time, the desire for personal gain is often misdirected or controlled by various government policies.

Many, if not most, LDC governments have enacted "cheap food" policies whereby the prices of agricultural products have been held below world market levels. This has been accomplished by various methods, including the use of price controls on food, the imposition of special taxes on agricultural exports, and the creation of government marketing boards with monopoly privileges which allows them to pay farmers lower prices than would exist in free markets. It has been estimated that real prices received by farmers in the more highly developed nations average four to five times the real prices received by farmers in the poorest LDCs.[6] The result has been to dampen incentives of farmers to invest in output-increasing facilities and inputs and as a result retarded the development of agriculture, the major industry in most LDCs. In addition, "import substitution" policies, whereby governments of LDCs have placed high taxes or outright embargoes on imports from other countries, have deprived both agriculture and industry from modern inputs available in the developed nations. On the other hand, subsidized credit and minimum wage laws have led to a greater use of scarce capital and a reduction in demand for abundant labor—just the opposite of what is needed. Strict price controls and rationing also give rise to privately profitable but socially unproductive black-market activities.

Another common but economically destructive policy of many LDCs has been to overvalue their currencies relative to what they would bring in a free foreign exchange market. The effect of this policy has been to reduce the demand for their exports. Such policy again discriminates against agriculture which is the major source of exports for many LDCs. The imposition of high marginal tax rates by many LDCs represents another growth-dampening policy. As explained more thoroughly in Chapter 8, the existence of high marginal

---

[6] Willis L. Peterson, "International Farm Prices and the Social Cost of Cheap Food Policies," *American Journal of Agricultural Economics* 61, no. 1 (February 1979), pp. 12–21.

tax rates discourages saving and investment and may even drive talented and highly skilled people out of the country altogether.

In the centrally planned (communist) economies, the opportunity for personal gain is reduced even more, although the desire for such gain on the part of the average person is likely to be as great as in any decentralized economy. In short-run national emergencies such as wars, people may respond to slogans and production quotas without economic incentives. However, in the long run most people are not likely to perform up to their potential unless they can see that increased effort will better their own standard of living or that of their families. A realization of the importance of economic incentives has prompted the Soviet Union to institute more "material incentives" for workers in recent years, usually in the form of bonuses or prizes for increased production. Political leaders in the People's Republic of China have recognized the power of incentives and in recent years have allowed more private entrepreneurial activity to take place. Of course, as incomes increase there is an increasing demand for consumer goods. Unless these goods are available at reasonable prices, incentives may still be reduced. If there is not much to buy with one's income, why struggle to increase it?

ECONOMIC STABILITY

In the preceding discussion we argued that investment is the key to economic growth, particularly investment in people or facilities to produce new, nontraditional inputs for factory or farm. In a decentralized free-market economy, a person must be reasonably certain that a profitable return will be forthcoming before he or she is willing to invest. In an economically unstable society, the uncertainty associated with the future is increased.

One common source of uncertainty in the LDCs is inflation, especially fluctuating rates of inflation, and the controls that usually accompany it. Inflation creates uncertainty because prices do not all rise at the same rate and, more important, the rate at which they will rise is unknown. If one borrows money at a 20 percent rate of interest, a rate not uncommon in the LDCs, it makes a big difference whether the future rate of inflation is 10 percent or 30 percent. In the former case the real rate of interest is +10 percent, while in the latter it is −10 percent. If one could be sure the inflation rate would be 30 percent or higher, the chances would be good that the investment would be profitable. It does not take much skill to make money when borrowing at a negative real rate of interest. Of course, it is likely to be quite difficult to obtain a loan if other borrowers and lenders also expect the inflation rate to be much above the money rate of interest.

It is well to keep in mind that an inflation rate figure such as 30 percent is an average annual increase of all prices included in the price index. Certainly not all, or even any, prices have to rise by 30 percent.[7] Some prices may increase 40 to 50 percent, while others may rise only 10 to 20 percent. If the product to be produced is among the latter group and the inputs to be bought are among the former, the chances of making profits are diminished considerably. The imposition of government controls on prices also influences the profitability of

---

[7] You may have heard of the man who drowned while attempting to walk across a river that was on the average six inches deep.

investment. If the price of the product is controlled more tightly than the prices of the inputs, again profits are diminished.

If business is carried on in the international market, exchange rate fluctuations become important. If inflation is higher domestically than in countries where the product is sold, the local currency will probably become overvalued vis-à-vis other currencies and the product may become too expensive to compete in foreign markets. Of course, a substantial devaluation would have the effect of making the product less expensive to foreign buyers while increasing the price paid for imported inputs.

Thus, you can see that inflation and changes in government-controlled prices make it extremely difficult to predict conditions very far into the future. One never knows whether an investment will make a million or force the person into bankruptcy. For people who like to avoid risk of this nature and magnitude, it is often wisest to buy consumer durables such as automobiles and housing. The prices of these items tend to be fairly responsive during inflation. They can be especially attractive if purchased with borrowed funds that carry a money rate of interest that is less than the rate of inflation.

MAIN POINTS OF CHAPTER 16

1. From the standpoint of world history, economic growth is a relatively recent phenomenon, most of it occurring within the past two centuries.

2. There is really no contradiction between economic growth and the quality of life. Unless society is willing to reduce its present consumption of goods and services, the quality of the environment cannot be increased unless growth occurs.

3. Malthus's dire prediction for the future of mankind has not been borne out in the highly developed nations of the world because of new and improved inputs that have complemented labor and land to increase the human productive capacity.

4. The term **technological change** describes the phenomenon of increasing output per unit of input. It occurs because of quality improvements in traditional inputs or completely new inputs that have been adopted that are not fully reflected in the input measures.

5. The most important determinant of economic growth is high-payoff investment. For the developed nations this has proven to be investment in the production and distribution of knowledge together with investment in capital that utilizes new knowledge.

6. In order to have investment, people must be willing to save a portion of their income as opposed to spending it all on present consumption. This represents a major problem for people in the less developed countries (LDCs) because of their relatively small incomes.

7. Economic growth cannot take place without an increase in per capita resources or capital. The evidence suggests that LDCs lag farther behind the developed countries in nonhuman capital than in human capital.

8. Currently the annual per capita output of the richest nations in the world is 40 to 50 times greater than that of the poorest nations. Also, the annual growth in per capita output is much greater for the more highly developed nations, indicating that the poorer nations are falling farther and farther behind their more highly developed neighbors.

9. To a certain extent, LDCs have been able to utilize knowledge and technology from the developed countries, although not all knowledge can be successfully transferred between countries.

10. Agriculture is by far the dominant industry in the LDCs. Growth in agricultural productivity allows people to leave agriculture to produce additional goods and services that contribute to economic well-being.

11. Growth in agricultural productivity depends largely on the use of new, nontraditional inputs such as higher-yielding varieties of crops, fertilizer, irrigation water, herbicides, and insecticides. Each new input tends to be most productive if accompanied by other new inputs; that is, a complete package of new inputs works best.

12. Monopoly privileges given to government agencies in LDCs to purchase farm products and/or sell farm inputs commonly result in low prices received and high prices paid by farmers. The general result is a retardation of agricultural development and possibly even famine.

13. The industrial or nonagricultural sector offers the greatest potential for growth in the LDCs. Because industrial technology tends to be somewhat less location-specific than agricultural technology, it is somewhat easier to transfer industrial techniques from the developed nations to the LDCs. However, differences in input prices (labor versus capital costs) and differences in consumer demand between the developed nations and the LDCs generally require a modification of techniques that are transferred.

14. The rural or interior regions of the LDCs are most lacking in infrastructure (roads, bridges, railroads, communications, and electricity). However, scarce resources are required to build infrastructure. In order for the government to buy these resources, it must levy taxes on low-income people who are not accustomed to paying taxes. Taxes on exports and imports are relatively easy to collect, but they distort market prices in the economy and retard growth.

15. The illiteracy rate in the rural areas of many LDCs runs as high as two thirds to three fourths of the population. The cost of schooling includes not only teachers and facilities but also the forgone earnings (lost production) of children who are in school. The demand for education also may be lacking because of the low educational level of parents.

16. As economic development occurs farm incomes decline relative to nonfarm incomes. This serves as an incentive for people to leave agriculture and take employment in nonfarm occupations.

17. The agricultural adjustment problem can be eased by ensuring freedom of entry into all occupations for all who are or can become qualified. Subsidized credit for farm machinery intensifies the migration from agriculture, while high union wages and minimum wage laws make it more difficult for migrant farmers to find permanent employment in nonfarm occupations.

18. The LDCs tend to exhibit higher rates of population growth than the developed nations. A contributing factor is the relatively recent reduction in infant mortality due to better medical care. Also, children born and raised in rural areas tend to be less costly than children reared in cities. Indeed, many rural children are economic assets to their parents. Since most LDCs are highly rural in nature, the reduced cost of children provides an incentive for parents in those countries to have large families.

19. Imports of consumer or investment goods from the developed nations into the LDCs require foreign exchange, which can be earned by sales to the developed nations. Unfortunately, there may not always be a market in the developed nations for what the LDCs have to sell. A recent phenomenon in some developing nations is the production and export of labor-intensive manufactured goods.

20. Land reforms and progressive income taxes are two common methods of redistributing wealth and income in the LDCs. The violent confiscation of private property, which may occur when a new political regime takes power, is another means of redistributing wealth or income, although it is a rather costly means in terms of life and personal freedoms.

21. People living in the LDCs take advantage of opportunities to increase their standard of living as much as people in the developed nations. The desire to increase one's standard of living provides a strong motivating force for economic growth.

22. Governments of LDCs have enacted many economically and socially destructive policies and programs, including *(a)* cheap food policies, *(b)* import substitution poli-

cies, (c) subsidized credit, (d) minimum wage laws, (e) price controls, (f) overvalued currencies, and (g) high marginal tax rates. All have retarded economic growth and development.

23. High and fluctuating rates of inflation create uncertainty about future economic conditions and tend, therefore, to dampen investment. Under these conditions the best course of action for the individual may be to spend much of his or her income on consumer goods (especially durables) or foreign currencies in order to hedge against inflation.

QUESTIONS FOR THOUGHT AND DISCUSSION

1. Is economic growth inconsistent with a clean and healthful environment? Explain.

2. a. Why have Malthus's predictions not been borne out in the so-called developed nations?
   b. In which group of countries have Malthus's predictions come closest to being fulfilled? Why?

3. A large proportion of the world's poor people live within 20 degrees north and 20 degrees south of the equator. Do you think this is purely accidental, or could there be a reason for this phenomenon? Explain.

4. a. What is technological change?
   b. What is the basic source of new technology?
   c. What is the main source of new knowledge?

5. a. Why is investment required for economic growth to occur?
   b. What are the two main types of investment required for economic growth?
   c. In which area do LDCs lag the most?

6. If poor nations are not able to achieve higher percentage rates of growth than the rich nations, what will happen to the income gap between the two groups? Has this happened?

7. As a nation develops, the proportion of the population engaged in agricultural production invariably decreases.
   a. What causes this decrease in the number of farm people?
   b. Is this phenomenon desirable for a country or should every effort be made to keep people on farms? Explain.

8. Why is industrial development important for the development of agriculture?

9. A problem common to many LDCs is the exodus of people from rural areas into large cities, resulting in overcrowded slum areas and the host of problems that come with these conditions. What can LDC governments do to alleviate these problems?

10. It might be argued that children are less expensive for rural families in LDCs than anywhere in the world. Why?

11. Outline some of the policies adopted by governments of LDCs that possibly have retarded economic growth and development.

12. a. Inflation is a common problem in LDCs. Why?
   b. How does inflation affect development?

INDEX

This book has been set Quadex 202, in 10 and 9 point Times Roman, leaded 2 points. Part and chapter numbers are 12 point Avant Garde Gothic Bold. Part titles are 36 point, and chapter titles are 24 point Avant Garde Gothic Bold. The size of the type page is 31 by 52.5 picas.